REAL SOLDIERING

REAL SOLDIERING

The US Army in the

Aftermath of War, 1815–1980

Brian McAllister Linn

UNIVERSITY PRESS OF KANSAS

Published by the University Press of Kansas (Lawrence, Kansas 66045), which was organized by the Kansas Board of Regents and is operated and funded by Emporia State University, Fort Hays State University, Kansas State University, Pittsburg State University, the University of Kansas, and Wichita State University.

Library of Congress Cataloging-in-Publication Data

Names: Linn, Brian McAllister, author.
Title: Real soldiering : the US Army in the aftermath of war, 1815–1980 /
   Brian McAllister Linn.
Description: Lawrence, Kansas : University Press of Kansas, 2023. | Series:
   Modern war studies | Includes bibliographical references and index.
Identifiers: LCCN 2022042558 (print) | LCCN 2022042559 (ebook)
   ISBN 9780700634750 (cloth)
   ISBN 9780700634767 (ebook)
Subjects: LCSH: United States. Army—Military life. | United States.
   Amy—History. | Sociology, Military—United States. | BISAC: HISTORY /
   Military / United States | HISTORY / Military / Strategy
Classification: LCC UA25 .L634 2023 (print) | LCC UA25 (ebook) | DDC
   355/.033573–dc23/eng/20230206
LC record available at https://lccn.loc.gov/2022042558.
LC ebook record available at https://lccn.loc.gov/2022042559.

British Library Cataloguing-in-Publication Data is available.

Printed in the United States of America

10 9 8 7 6 5 4 3 2

The paper used in this publication is acid free and meets the minimum requirements of the American National Standard for Permanence of Paper for Printed Library Materials Z39.48-1992.

For Dinny

Contents

Preface: The Aftermath Army

On one occasion during the United States Army's long and painful recovery from the Vietnam War, Gen. Michael S. Davison sought to inspire his officers with an anecdote about a British sergeant. This career soldier, or "regular," was one of the first sent to France in 1939. After being rescued at Dunkirk, he campaigned in Africa and Italy, landed in Normandy, then fought across northwestern Europe and into Germany. With victory finally in sight, the sergeant turned to a fellow survivor from the old days and wearily declared: "I will be so glad when this bloody war is over and we can go back to real soldiering."[1]

Davison was a real soldier, one of the best of his generation, and a three-time veteran of the US Army in war's aftermath. Commissioned in 1939, he was a lieutenant colonel commanding an infantry battalion within five years. Over the next decades he witnessed drawdowns after World War II, the Korean War buildup, the 1950s' reductions in force, racial integration and conscription, and the army's experiments with atomic warfare. In the 1960s he was successively commandant of the United States Military Academy (USMA) and the Command and General Staff College (in Fort Leavenworth) and ended the decade directing III Field Force in Vietnam. As Commander-in-Chief, United States Army Europe, from 1971 to 1975, he inherited a post-Vietnam establishment so plagued by substance abuse, racial strife, poverty, and violence that it was common practice for officers to carry firearms when they inspected the enlisted barracks.

Davison understood real soldiering—those essential functions carried out by uniformed professionals in the aftermath of war to both maintain military capability and prepare for the future. In his experience, and in the historical experience of the US Army, real soldiering took place during periods of financial and manpower cuts, with little glory, an uncertain future, and few immediate rewards. He recognized that the army's fundamental postwar challenge was not securing higher budgets, writing a new doctrine, purchasing better equipment, or reshuffling the Pentagon's bureaucracy. Rather, what would determine whether the army successfully negotiated the aftermath of war would depend on those with "the will to soldier for peace in a peace-time army."[2]

Davison's anecdote and his recognition of future priorities address a question as pertinent in the twenty-first century as it was after Vietnam: What happens to standing armies after the war ends, the "for-the-duration" soldiers return to civilian life, and the battle flags are stowed away? For most, the dictum of Thomas Hardy's Spirit Sinister—"War makes rattling good history; but Peace is poor reading"—is all too applicable.[3] The images of peacetime garrisons and the "spit-shine syndrome"—glittering ceremonies and parades; gate guards in chromed helmets; soldiers on fatigue duty scrubbing pots and white-washing rocks—are all far removed from those of heroes closing with and destroying the enemy on the battlefield.[4] In the aftermath of war, public attention either ignores the US Army altogether or focuses on reports of waste and inefficiency, on punitive courts-martial, on chickenshit discipline, and on public gaffes by high-ranking officers. The service's image morphs from defenders of the nation to the employer of last resort. Blue-collar craftsmen dismiss soldiering as pretending to be busy and shirking hard labor. Combat veterans, once back in civilian life, dismiss their peacetime counterparts as playing at war, a stereotype still found in the comic strip *Beetle Bailey*.[5]

For those who have practiced the trade, peacetime soldiering connotes a host of very different and often contradictory definitions that no outsider can really understand. It entails extremes of comradeship and loneliness, hard work and slacking, modern weapons and centuries-old ritual, gratification and embarrassment. And for those who have worn the uniform of the US Army, soldiering also conveys both enormous respect for the institution and enormous frustration when it is not all it could be. The pride and paradoxes of American soldiering are encapsulated in the exchange between PFC Robert Lee Prewitt and 1st Sgt. Milton Warden in James Jones's classic book on the trade, *From Here to Eternity*:

> "I can soljer with any man" Prewitt repeated "and best him at it."
> "Okay," Warden said. "So what? Since when has being a good soljer had anything to do with the Army?"[6]

For most military historians, and for many civilians, the US Army's postwar decades were, to quote Col. William A. Ganoe, "The Army's Dark Ages"—individually and collectively dreary, demoralizing eras of budget and personnel reductions, crumbling facilities, obsolescent equipment, and perceived military impotence against rival Great Powers.[7] In this interpretation, only the officer corps' integrity and professionalism and the vision of a few great leaders preserved the service for a later renaissance. Ganoe's contemporary, Col. Oliver L. Spaulding, provided a more nuanced perspective on postwar service. Drawing a distinction between "military history"—or the history of warfare—and the history of the military, Spaulding reminded readers that, "while the Army is organized to fight, fighting occupies only a small part of the time of any particular unit. Often we shall find some peaceful incident having greater influence upon the Army than some active campaign."[8] But this insight was heeded neither by its author (whose book is almost entirely devoted to the army's wars) nor by his own service. Over a half-century later, Army Chief of Staff Gordon R. Sullivan was dismayed to hear officers deployed on peacekeeping missions complain that "this is not really important and I can hardly wait to get out of here so that I can get back to real soldiering."[9] They considered bloodless maneuvers in the California desert to be a legitimate warfighting task, but stopping endemic violence in Africa or the Balkans was not.

Real Soldiering employs Spaulding's second caveat: to assess the service "from the point of view of the Army at the time, not from that of the present date."[10] It questions the common tendency to conflate a *postwar* army with a *prewar* army, of interest chiefly for what it reveals about the individuals, weapons, doctrines, organizations, and so forth that proved decisive in later conflicts. This propensity for evaluating past military organizations by forthcoming conflicts—or *future-waritis*—invites anachronism. "No More Task Force Smiths" is a worthy slogan to encourage preparedness, but it is predicated on the audience's knowledge that an outnumbered, poorly trained scratch unit was thrown into combat against North Korean tanks in June 1950—a scenario everyone from Gen. Douglas MacArthur to Lt. Col. Charles B. Smith would have dismissed as ludicrous six months earlier. When to this slogan is added an unspoken lesson that from 1945 on the US Army's leaders should have been preparing the service for the imminent war with North Korea, the motto becomes a detriment to understanding both the past and present. The reality, as this book demonstrates, is that rarely has the postwar US Army had the luxury of focusing on a future war; its attention has been fully engaged in the here-and-now demands of maintaining the service's existence.[11]

Real Soldiering also challenges not only the prevalent tendency of applying dubious historical lessons to current military issues but also the underlying faith that the outcome of any war demonstrates how all problems confronting a prewar military contained a clear choice between the one, historically validated correct path and many false ones. From this preconception, it is a short intellectual leap to identify an apparently similar problem confronting today's policymakers—a similarly correct choice—and then to argue that reverse engineering a past solution will guarantee a future victory. Such context-driven lessons tend to mutate over time, as what appeared to be the ideal historical example to design the army for a quick war against the Soviet Union may contribute to that army's inability to conclusively defeat irregular opponents waging a campaign of attrition.

Real Soldiering also disputes the tendency to see each postwar decade as unique, in what might be termed "era exceptionalism." It is true that the aftermath of some wars presented the US Army with unique dilemmas—reconstruction, overseas empire administration, occupation, desegregation, conscription—as many superb histories attest. But it is also true that in part that, due to such superb histories, some eras have become invested in narratives that emphasize their distinctiveness at the expense of appreciating their commonalities with other postwar decades. For example, in most histories the immediate years after the Spanish–American War are dominated by the impact of Secretary of War Elihu Root. Similarly, the era after Vietnam is often confined to the transition to the all-volunteer force, the writing of doctrine, and the social tensions exacerbated by race, drugs, and indiscipline. Thus, "era exceptionalism" often means that the similarities between the army's past or future postwar experiences—that is, the common challenges and responses—are overlooked or dismissed outright.[12]

 *army goes in circles*

Real Soldiering also differs from many previous histories of the postwar US Army by shifting the focus from Washington-centric institutional history to the troops in the field forces who have inherited the unglamorous cleanup of the mess left by war. It draws from official documents but also personal diaries, letters, memoirs, oral histories, officers' student papers, and other anecdotal sources. It emphasizes a central (but too often ignored) truth in American military history: the rarified perspective at higher headquarters can be vastly different from that of the field. In advice that too few of his successors have followed, the editor of the *Army and Navy Journal* reminded incoming Secretary of War Root in 1899 not to make the mistake of his predecessors and ignore the fact that "the officers a Secretary meets in Washington are not the Army."[13]

Much of this disconnect between the top-down perspective of

Washington and the bottom-up perspective of the field results from two factors that govern how the US Army collects information, analyzes it, incorporates it, and turns it into history. The first is that for at least fifty years the army's historical programs have been largely absorbed by its Training and Doctrine Command (TRADOC). And much like the topics of race and gender have come to preoccupy the humanities, so TRADOC's own institutional priorities of doctrine, training, force structure, and materiel have emerged as the dominant themes in army histories. One unforeseen and unrecognized consequence is that the random elements that complicate the study of doctrine, training, force structure, and materiel tend to be dismissed. And among these random elements, the most random of all are the individuals—especially the enlisted and lower-grade officers—who have worn, and now wear, army uniforms.[14]

A second factor contributing to the persistent disconnect between senior supervisors and those attempting to carry out their directives is common to other armed forces and, with slight changes in terminology, to all large bureaucratic organizations (including my own university). The army's key institutional priority is to demonstrate its ability to fulfill its missions, usually defined as readiness, and to demonstrate that doctrine, force structure, leadership, and equipment are all performing as they should. In the field, this encourages officers reporting back to their superiors to believe that they must minimize difficulties and demonstrate success, if for no other reason than career security. As their "can do" analysis passes through successive headquarters, it is further massaged, purged of the discordant or what is deemed the irrelevant, until by the time it arrives at the highest levels of the army headquarters in Washington and is read by the appropriate authorities (and by historians) a tidy, coherent, convincing, and instructive interpretation is wrapped around a discordant, fragmented, and somewhat chaotic reality. This pristine interpretation is then further distilled and endorsed by the service's historical agencies, which in turn provide the foundational basis upon which later authors, both military and civilian, will base their own versions of army history. At its worst, and at the risk of oversimplification, the end product is a condensed and familiar narrative in which the same generals, the same events, the same topics, and the same lessons appear and reappear. It is, to appropriate an analogy popular among American soldiers, the historical equivalent of a self-licking ice cream cone.

The Washington-centric, institutional, streamlined, and doctrine-driven version of postwar military history tends to tidy away many of the inconvenient truths of America's aftermath armies: disciplinary infractions, failed inspections, resignations, poor retention rates, squalid housing, maintenance failures, and other tedious and unglamorous details. It downplays the lessons unlearned, the money squandered on defective equipment, the toxic commanders, and the training exercises that proved, eventually, that the mismatch between materiel, doctrine, leadership, and troops could not be reconciled. It is a version of soldiering, but not one that many in the rank and file—who lived through the experience, served under such-and-such a commander, were stationed in such-and-such a unit—would recognize. The isolated, frustrated captain trying to chivvy his recalcitrant, poorly equipped, quarter-strength company into some semblance of soldiering may have quite another, and perhaps more realistic, assessment of the actual state of the service than do his superiors in Washington (or, for that matter, historians).

Real Soldiering's central argument is that in the decade following every major conflict since the War of 1812, the United States Army has undergone a long, painful, and remarkably consistent recovery process as it struggles to build a new model force to replace the "Old Army" that entered that conflict. During this decade-long process, two constants stand out. The first is seen in two roughly five-year sequences after each war wherein the postwar army wrestled with many of the same dilemmas. In the first postwar half-decade, institutional reforms seek to apply the lessons of the recent war by restructuring the aftermath army's personnel, doctrine, organization, and mission to reposition the service within the current national defense policy. In the second postwar half-decade, the consequences of these reforms, along with those from the inevitable congressional cutbacks, are manifested. The focus shifts from Washington policymakers to the field as changing missions, personnel shortages, insufficient training, insupportable force structure, deteriorating facilities, obsolete equipment, and other related problems present the service with assorted dilemmas. During this second phase, Washington and local commanders must frantically thimblerig an increasingly unbalanced skeleton or hollow army. It is, in many respects, a variation of the traditional shell-and-pea con that the comedian W. C. Fields referred to as "the Old Army Game."[15]

In order to provide an appreciation of the complexity of each postwar decade while identifying their similarities, *Real Soldiering* is organized in five topical chapters. Chapter 1 summarizes the Old Army of the nineteenth century. It identifies the precedents manifested in the creation of the first new model army in the decade after the end of the War of 1812 that were repeated after the Mexican–American War and the Civil War. Later chapters explore the new model armies in the postwar decades after the imperial wars of 1898–1902, World War I, World War II and Korea, and the Vietnam War.

In researching and writing *Real Soldiering*, I made three editorial decisions. First, I focus on soldiering in the field forces in the aftermath of war, particularly on lower-level officers and the enlisted ranks. Second, I conclude each chapter roughly a decade after each war's end, before the participants—and historians—recognized either the correct lessons of the previous war or the nature of the next one. Third, I end my chapter treatment with the decade after the Vietnam War because of the absence of sufficient declassified, accessible archival sources. In the conclusion, I provide a brief analysis of the post–Desert Storm and post–Afghanistan/Iraq War armies to conform to the historic precedents of the US Army.[16]

Real Soldiering is based on four decades of scholarly research on the US Army, but much of its analysis has been shaped by my own experiences as an observer, teacher, and colleague to soldiers. Much of the book is a deliberate challenge to the often triumphalist narratives perpetrated by many both in and out of the service. Less directly, the book also contests the exclusionary top-down, bottom-up, outsider-insider models put forth by students of peacetime military innovation. Rather, its implicit argument is that no tidy cause-effect model can explain the historical complexity of postwar changes and consistencies. Finally, it challenges *future-waritis*—the prevailing tendency by both scholars and soldiers to evaluate postwar armies solely on their effectiveness in the next conflict. In my view, it does neither historians, nor analysts, nor military personnel much good to attempt to resolve the inevitable postwar dilemmas by reengineering solutions based on faux-mythical narratives of the German Blitzkrieg or Desert Storm. Those in uniform in war's aftermath are better served by an understanding that they are participants in a decade-long process of rebirth and revival similar to those that their army has undergone since the War of 1812. Perhaps they can take heart from the sober advice given by Creighton W. Abrams to Arthur S. Collins in the hard times after the Korean War:

> You'll have reason to quit every day. You just don't see any point in going on, or how you're going to get things done . . . but we know

the soldier and we know the conditions of the battlefield, so no matter what they do, or how tough they make it, our job is to hang in there, day in and day out, so that when that soldier has to fight, he can be as well-equipped and as well-prepared as we can make him. And that's why we hang on.[17]

Acknowledgments

As always when making acknowledgments, I know that I will probably omit many more deserving individuals than I thank. However, the only alternative is not thanking anyone. Thus it is only fair to start with thanking Joyce Harrison, Bill Allison, and the staff at the University Press of Kansas who got this through in record time.

Real Soldiering is the product of decades of interest in the peacetime US Army, and its intellectual roots draw from diverse influences. First and foremost was my four-decade relationship with the history and the individuals (both living and past) of the US Army. From the outset, army officers (many of them friends) told me that I had an obligation to them to write history, not mythology. The idea for a book on the peacetime US Army began during a 1999–2000 visiting professorship at the US Army War College as I absorbed student and faculty tales of garrison life. Since then, I've had the opportunity to engage with later generations of US Army officers in seminars with Bill Pierce, Doug Douds, and the Advanced Strategic Arts Program and Dean Nowowiejski and the Art of War Scholars. In writing this book, I have relied on the knowledge and friendship of many soldiers, both serving and retired, and some sadly passed on. The list is very long and extends from Spec 5s to generals, but three demand special recognition. I have known Paul H. Herbert since we were both graduate students, and since then I have relied on him not only for his military expertise but also for his thoughtful, dispassionate, and practical guidance in negotiating army history. If there is any one source to my interest in the peacetime US Army, it is Paul. Jim Willbanks took me under his avuncular wing many years ago and has since been a fount of information, wisdom, and often pungent insight into the army he served in. J. P. Clark is a more recent scholar-friend, but he has been an invaluable guide to army history, culture, and reform. All three received dozens of emails, phone calls, and draft chapters along with demands they drop everything and get back to me immediately. All always came through with patience, good humor, and suggestions for how to make the book better. Henry G. Gole deserves credit for the title and for always being a source of anecdotes and observations on the service he loves. Among the many other scholar-soldiers who have provided advice and support would be Andrew J. Bacevich, Fred Borch, Janet Borch, Charles Bowery, John Sloan Brown, Conrad C. Crane, Greg Daddis, Robert T. Davis II, William Donnelly, Shawn Faulkner, Joe Fischer, Antulio J. Echevarria, David A. Fastabend, David Fitzpatrick, Jeffrey French, Gian Gentile, Roger Goodell, Robert Griffith, John Hall, Thomas E. Hanson, Richard C. Hall, Rick Herrera, Charles Jacoby, David Johnson, Doug Johnson, Paul Jussel, R. Matthew Lee, Michael Lynch, Pete Mansoor, Gregg Martin, Jeff McCausland, H. R. McMaster, Edward G. Miller, Harley Mooney, Matt Morton, Hal Nelson, Raymond T. Odierno, Mark Pernell, James Powell, Michael Perry, Ray Porter, Gordon Rudd, Kyle Ryman, David Shugart, Don Snider, Theodore Stroup, Gordon Sullivan, Michael M. Toler, Richard G. Trefry, Walter Ulmer, Gerhard Weinberg, and Zen Ed Werkheiser. I should also note that many of these individuals I know as couples, and their spouses have often provided a different perspective on the joys of life in the US Army, among them Kelly Clark, Heidi Hall, Nancy Herbert, Debbie Jussel, Julie Morton, Maggie Martin, Lisa Vanarian, Kathleen Trotter, and many more. As I look forward to a diminution if not cessation in research, these individuals and the hundreds of others I have met either in person or through their writings have made me aware of what a great privilege it has been to spend my professional career being what one academic sneeringly termed "just an army historian."

I would next like to thank the academic community of military historians. I would be remiss if I did not single out among many individuals Allan R. Millett and the late Edward "Mac" Coffman who encouraged me never to forget that military history without soldiers is both incomplete and uninteresting. I hope readers will detect some of Allan's superlative research and analytical skills and some of Mac's humorous voice in the writing. If Alan and Mac shaped my early interests, then Samuel J. Watson carried them into the present. Emily Andrew and David Silbey were in on the project from the beginning, and their support and encouragement sustained it through completion. Among my comrades in the military history field, I owe much to Beth Bailey, Jennifer Keene, Mark E. Grotelueschen, Rich Muller, Michael Neiberg, Ingo Trauschweizer, Susannah Ural, and Kara Vuic. The staff at the US Army Center of Military History and the US Army Heritage and Education Center have been generous in opening up their archives and their expertise, as the citations show. I also thank the archivists who digitized so much of the sources in the Combined Arms Research

Library, the Maneuver Center of Excellence Library, and the Defense Technical Information Center. Special thanks to Bill Donnelly, Mike Lynch, and Shane P. Reilly, who obtained crucial documents to save me from my own poor notetaking. From very early on, Britt McCarley and the historians at Training and Doctrine Command welcomed me to their organization's impressive archives. Much of the earlier research was done quite unknowing of its later use at the National Archives, where archivists such as Tim Nenninger, Richard Boylan, and Richard Peuser were essential in providing access to records and negotiating the classification system. I've also gained great insight, advice, and support from C. C. Felker and my colleagues in the Society for Military History and from Robyn Rodriguez, Randy Papadopolous, the US Commission on Military History, and its parent organization, the International Commission on Military History. I also want to thank Eliot Cohen, Tom Keaney, Tom Mahnken, Peter Feaver, and the other participants of the SAIS Basin Harbor Workshop who provided me with an appreciation of the complexities of current national security issues.

This work has been something of an international effort that has benefited from discussions with military historians from several nations. I have long relied on scholars of the British Army such as Hew Strachan, Ed Spiers, and Brian Bond to help me understand the American version. The organization for the book came together during a US–UK Fulbright Fellowship at the University of Birmingham, where participating in the War Studies Seminar introduced me to the next generation of stars such as Daniel Whittingham and Aimée Fox. I also thank Peter Wilson for a very informative and inspirational chat in his quarters at Oxford. Two Canadian army scholars, Doug Delaney and Ian Hope, gave me a comparative perspective; Ian was kind enough to read and make extensive comments on one chapter. The writing of the book was interrupted by the opportunity to be part of a multinational project on the wars of decolonization under the direction of Thijs Brocades Zaalberg and Bart Luttikhuis. Hosted at the National Institute of Advanced Study in Amsterdam, I spent months both on the project and discussing the book with fellow project members Pierre Asselin, Huw Bennett, Roel Frakking, Martin Thomas, and my co-author, Azarja Harmany, as well as Piet Kamphuis and Jan Hoffenaar of the Netherlands Institute for Military Studies. To my surprise, it turned out that much of my research and writing for the Netherlands project had direct application for this book.

My research and writing would not have been possible without considerable financial and collegial support. Much of the book was researched and written during a fellowship from the National Endowment for the Humanities, which has asked me to include a caveat: any views, findings, conclusions, or recommendations expressed in this publication do not necessarily reflect those of the National Endowment for the Humanities. I was singularly fortunate to have financial support from my institution in the form of a faculty development leave, a Glasscock Center for Humanities fellowship, and the collegiality and insights of my former department head and good friend, David Vaught, as well as R. J. Q Adams, Terry Anderson, Jonathan Brunstedt, Joseph G. Dawson, Olga Dror and Keith Taylor, Lorien Foote, Adam Seipp, and others. John Schuessler and Jasen Castillo at Texas A&M's Albritton Center for Grand Strategy gave me a useful international affairs perspective and are exemplars of multidisciplinary scholarship. My graduate students, current and former, turned out to be an invaluable resource. Three US marines (and one spouse)—Brian Donlon, Chris Hemler, and Michael F. (and Sue) Morris—went out of their way to assist, even if I was writing about a rival service. Some of my other graduate student advisees have been mentioned in other lists, but Jonathan Carroll, Kendall Cosley, Cameron McCoy, Ross Phillips, Troy Sacquety, Paul Springer, and Nathaniel Weber all deserve thanks.

Last but by no means least are all the civilian friends who rallied around and listened to me go off on long lectures about the US Army. I need to thank my friends in Hawaii. Tom Dye and Dore Minatodani deserve special mahalo for adopting me during a bad time and being there for the far more frequent good times. Roger and Merle I have known since "hanabata days" and Andie Gill since high school, but all remind me of what I missed by moving off the islands. Jan Kramer and Scott Petty were always up for some wine. Rocking Rob Citino (backed by Roberta) has enlightened me on history, music, and life despite the fact that our psychic link sometimes scares both of us. Cousins Gary and Harriet Tuckman hosted us several times in the Colorado mountains when it all got too much. Cousin Peter McNab provided much wisdom and humor, often at his own expense. In Texas, thanks to Ken and Kathi Appelt, Rose Eder, and the people who have kept the places open that make life in BSC enjoyable, such as the Bryan Aquatic Center, Karen Langston at SPECs, and Carney's. When I got tired of writing, the Rolling Stones, George Thorogood, Joan Jett, Commander Cody, Jack Vance, and many others were always there to pick me up.

Last but first is my wife, editor, life companion, and fellow scout, Dinny.

1

The Nineteenth-Century
Aftermath Army

"The ax, pick, saw and trowel has become more the implement of the American soldier than the cannon, musket, or sword," while among officers "a good overseer, or negro driver, is better qualified for our service than one who has received a first rate military education."[1] Thus did Lt. Col. Zachary Taylor sum up the state of the nation's military forces barely ten years after the end of the War of 1812. Taylor could speak with some authority. Since taking command, his 8th Infantry Regiment had spent eighteen months building a hundred-mile stretch of government road connecting Columbia, Tennessee, to Madisonville, Louisiana. During that time military training was so neglected that soldiers had forgotten such basic drill orders as "right face" or "left face," never mind how to maneuver or fire their weapons as a disciplined unit. The regiment was marching to its permanent station at Bay St. Louis, Mississippi, when Taylor's department commander appropriated two of his six companies and all his skilled craftsmen to labor in Baton Rouge. Soon after, Taylor was ordered to send two more companies. Adding insult to injury, these soldiers were not commanded by their own officers but by the officer supervising the project. The consequences, Taylor warned, were ominous: Enlisted men lacked rudimentary martial skills; undermanned companies functioned as construction crews; regiments were broken up and scattered across hundreds of miles; officers turned into foremen; colonels became labor agents. The heady days of defending the nation against the British invaders were over, and Taylor and his troops were receiving a hard lesson in what real soldiering would entail in the postwar United States Army (or "Regular Army").

Taylor was a not untypical representative of the post–War of 1812 Regular Army officer corps. As a plantation owner himself, Taylor possessed firsthand knowledge of overseers and chattel labor. His Kentucky family connections, and not his indifferent education, had

1

secured his appointment as a first lieutenant in 1808. He distinguished himself in the war against Britain but was so insulted by his postwar demotion that he left the service, albeit briefly. Taylor was a charismatic if eccentric commander whose paternalism was balanced by such informal disciplinary methods as "wooling"—seizing an offending ranker and vigorously shaking his head. He would cement his reputation as an inspirational combat commander in the 1832 Black Hawk War and later against Mexico. But his fighting days were few and far between. For most of his four decades in uniform he served on the frontier, where he fulfilled a variety of less martial roles: construction supervisor, administrator, policeman, peacekeeper, and whatever else his political supervisors demanded. "Taylor was not an officer to trouble the administration much with his demands," an admiring Ulysses S. Grant recalled; he would do "the best he could with the means at hand without parading his grievance before the public."[2] It was only when his authority was undermined by placing his troops under an inferior in rank, and not even a combat officer, that Taylor felt moved to protest. In both his subordination to national necessity and his insistence on maintaining his caste's status, Taylor was typical of the senior commanders who would supervise the US Army's first transition from wartime to peacetime.[3]

The Regular Army, at least in terms of a national, professional, standing force, took shape in the decade after the War of 1812.[4] Congress created the Continental Army in 1776 to secure independence, but it was never intended to be permanent. When on 2 June 1784 Congress demobilized the last Continental units and left only a handful of depot guards, it severed all direct connection with today's force. Having overthrown what they viewed as Great Britain's attempt to impose a military tyranny, Americans were adamantly opposed to the domestic threat posed by a standing army. Henceforth the republic's defense would rest on the citizen-soldiers of the states' militias, summoned into federal service only for three specified emergencies. Yet Congress, having, in the colorful phrase of one service historian, "flung aside" the last national armed force, was left with the problem of multiple threats to national security that could not be resolved by the individual states.[5] The most pressing of these was the Northwest Territory where the British refused to hand over their trading posts and fortresses and encouraged Indian tribes to resist any expansion by their former adversaries. No sooner had it terminated the Continental Army establishment than Congress reluctantly authorized the creation of the 1st American Regiment. Poorly trained, inadequately armed and supplied, and plagued by desertion, the federal military contribution did little to pacify the frontier.

With the ratification of the United States Constitution in 1789, Congress assumed the responsibility to raise and support armies, and it took tentative steps to found a federal military establishment. It was soon apparent the states were unwilling or unable to furnish either effective or sufficient militia for extended campaigns on the frontier. Bowing to exigency, Congress incorporated the 1st American Regiment into federal service, established the War Department to administer military affairs, and made the secretary of war a cabinet post. Such reactive policies were insufficient. In 1791 the tiny standing army lost over half its personnel campaigning against Native Americans. Congress reluctantly authorized new regiments and provided sufficient time and resources to train them. In 1794 the reconstituted regulars and contingents of citizen-soldiers defeated an Indian confederation, pushing the frontier across territory including the current state of Ohio. That same year, recognizing how deteriorating relations with Great Britain raised the threat of naval raids against Atlantic port cities, Congress began planning a system of fortifications and established an elite corps of artillerists and engineers. In both cases, the political leadership required the army to be ready to defend against an immediate threat and to initiate projects for a more complete future defense. In practice, these often proved contradictory, forcing commanders to choose between drilling their troops or construction. And as was to be the case in the future, while officers might prefer the immediate rewards of short-term training, their missions required them to devote much of their time to the long-term objectives of national defense.[6]

In common with other federal departments, the army became embroiled in the toxic partisanship between Federalists and Republicans at the turn of the nineteenth century. The regulars policed the frontier, but the Federalists authorized a new military establishment to deter invasion and, more ominously, to provide internal security. The election of Thomas Jefferson and the Republicans in 1800 brought to power a president and a party with a strong anti–standing army ideology. Jefferson recognized that the question was not whether the United States required a standing army but rather how to make that force politically reliable, affordable, and of service to the nation. He purged partisan Federalists, reduced the officer corps from 248 to 172, and cut authorized force strength to slightly over 3,000. In 1802 he reversed his party's previous opposition and founded the United States Military Academy at West Point. Jefferson's decision to place the school under the recently created Corps of Engineers reflected his own and his party's view that the Regular Army's mission was to provide technical expertise the militia lacked. But he also expanded the army's missions, pushing it farther geographically into the western frontier. During his presidency officers such as Zebulon Pike, Merriweather Lewis, and William Clark explored the territory of the Louisiana Purchase, negotiated with Spanish representatives regarding the border with Texas, supervised internal improvements, assisted settlers and merchants, and performed numerous other federal duties only tangentially related to preparing for war.[7]

In the three decades between 1784 and 1812 the nation created a weak and unsteady framework of a peacetime standing army, one often teetering on extinction. The secretary of war remained a political appointee of low privilege and often lower talents. The War Department's small staff was seldom able to provide administrative or logistical support to forces in the field. Its ineffectiveness, as well as the incompetence and corruption of contractors and commanders, was illustrated tragically in 1809 when within six months over 800 of the 2,000 troops assigned to New Orleans died of disease and neglect. The senior leadership, made up of rapidly aging Revolutionary War veterans, was undistinguished. Some were invalids, some were incompetent, and the most senior, James Wilkinson, was both corrupt and a likely traitor. West Point suffered from birthing pains: its status remained uncertain, it was riven by clashes among faculty, superintendents, and the Corps of Engineers, and many cadets were unprepared for the curriculum. With the exception of engineers and artillerists, most officers viewed their army service as temporary, more a prerequisite of gentlemanly status than a career. Like William Henry Harrison, such officers often combined military, commercial, and political activities, with little concern about possible conflicts of interest. Taken as a group they were undereducated, quarrelsome, insubordinate, tyrannical, often truant, and quick to resign and return as it suited their interests. After almost two decades, the Regular Army remained a haphazard, disorganized force that many citizens viewed as an expedient to be abolished as soon as possible.[8]

As relations with Great Britain deteriorated in late 1811, Congress authorized the US Army to be increased from 8,000 to 25,000. But it voted only a third of the funds that President James Madison requested. It followed a similar pattern when war was declared on 18 June 1812, increasing the regulars to 35,000 but failing to secure sufficient pay. Six months after war's outbreak the army numbered only

15,000, many poorly trained, badly armed, and wretchedly led. Even these numbers were largely guesswork, since by this time the War Department had descended into administrative chaos, incapable of coordinating, supplying, or directing military operations.

Although the War of 1812 was hailed as a "second war of independence," in practice the Americans fought four uncoordinated regional conflicts. In the Northwest Territory in October 1813 a predominantly citizen-soldier force under Harrison killed the Indigenous leader Tecumseh and broke his confederation at the Battle of the Thames. In the Southeast, another citizen-soldier army under Andrew Jackson waged its own conflict against a Creek tribal confederation, defeating it in March 1814. Jackson then marched his troops to New Orleans, arriving in time to repel a British attack in January 1815.

The nation's military efforts in the theaters of war along the Niagara and St. Lawrence Rivers and on the Atlantic Coast were less successful. Disorganized and ineptly commanded, American military forces failed in multiple efforts to capture and hold Canadian territory. A defining moment in the army's self-identity occurred at the Battle of Chippawa (or Chippewa) on 5 July 1814 when Jacob Brown's and Winfield Scott's well-drilled battalions stood toe to toe against British veterans, trading volleys and prompting an admiring (or shocked) opponent to proclaim "Those are Regulars, by God." On the Atlantic Coast, however, disaster loomed. British fleets blocked the Chesapeake in 1813 and raided coastal towns. The following year an amphibious expedition burned the capital of Washington, though the more important port of Baltimore was saved by its harbor fortifications, later immortalized by Francis Scott Key in "The Star-Spangled Banner." With neither side able to progress beyond a stalemate, antiwar sentiment growing, and economies on both sides of the Atlantic teetering, the Treaty of Ghent restored the status quo antebellum in December 1814. News of the treaty's signing and of Jackson's victory at New Orleans arrived simultaneously, convincing many Americans they had won the war.[9]

In the immediate aftermath of the War of 1812 the US Army underwent the first of what would become a familiar pattern of transition from wartime to peacetime force. This process would take roughly a decade and consist of two parts. In the first half-decade Washington's civilian and military leaders would attempt to assimilate the last war's lessons. There would be extensive changes in administration, doctrine, mission, force structure, and personnel policies. In the second half-decade many of these reforms would be delayed, if not utterly frustrated, by conditions affecting the field forces: inadequate resources, personnel shortages, internal tensions, new missions, and other competing and irreconcilable priorities. By 1825 the Regular Army had transitioned from postwar to peacetime, assuming the character it would retain, with slight changes until the next war. At its simplest, if a hypothetical officer in 1815 were allowed a preview of 1820, he would be stunned at the administrative, doctrinal, personnel, organizational, social, and other changes. In contrast, that same officer looking at 1820 from the vantage of 1830 or even 1840 would readily identify the similarities, particularly the familiar dilemmas, of the force he served in.

As the ninth anniversary of the nation's second war with Great Britain approached, President James Monroe declared its enduring lesson was that "in the wars of other Powers, we can rely only on force for the protection of our neutral rights."[10] But in contrast to the Jeffersonian's long championing of the militia, Monroe emphasized the importance of the standing establishment. A few years earlier Secretary of War John C. Calhoun declared that henceforth the nation's primary military policy was "to obtain a regular force, adequate to the emergencies for the country, properly organized and prepared for actual service. It is thus only, that we can be in the condition to meet the first shocks of hostilities with unyielding firmness, and to press on an enemy, while our resources are yet unexhausted."[11] By 1831 this judgment was entrenched; as one secretary of war clarified, in the next war citizen-soldiers would be a "valuable auxiliary," but "a regular force [would be] indispensable to the vigorous prosecution of any permanent military operations, offensive or defensive."[12] Congress approved these sentiments, as least initially. In 1815 it demobilized the wartime army from 33,500 to 10,000, still a considerable increase from its peak of 7,000 in the prewar decade. And in a further acknowledgement of the war's lessons, it allocated unprecedented sums to the Corps of Engineers for the construction of coastal defenses.

As they would in later aftermath narratives, postwar regular officers interpreted the War of 1812 as professional vindication. Politicians and an indifferent public had dismissed sound military advice and then, after provoking the war, had turned to the militia and appointed politicians-turned-amateur generals. The inevitable result had been "a succession of disasters, unexampled in history." Despite having an overwhelming superiority in resources and personnel, the United States was unable to conquer the "petty province" of Canada and had itself been "invaded and defeated at all points."[13] Later, officer-historians cemented this interpretation: the Regular Army had preserved the nation, whereas citizen-soldiers had contributed little but "mutinies, cowardly retreats and insubordination."[14] This self-promoting cause-and-effect myth, like later postwar allegories, discounted the US Army's own operational failings and the bickering among career officers that had all but paralyzed some campaigns. More seriously, the myth ignored the standing army's underrepresentation in the decisive frontier campaigns. There were barely a hundred regulars at the Battle of the Thames, and volunteers outnumbered US Army personnel by over four-to-one at the Battle of New Orleans. Rather than incorporate these frontier campaigns into the war's narrative, the service exalted the 1814 battles with British regular soldiers in the Niagara Campaign. This nostalgia was as much personal as institutional, since among those who remained in uniform a majority served in that theater. In later years those stationed on the northern border would toast their British counterparts, receiving in return the compliments and recognition from their martial peers.[15]

The war had revealed the title of War Department as a misnomer. Even before the outbreak of hostilities its clerks were overwhelmed by paperwork, its staff agencies ineffective, and its secretary reportedly wandering the streets seeking contractors to supply the army with hats. It had seldom managed to coordinate operations, communicate with commanders, or provide supplies and troops, and regional commanders routinely disregarded department directives with impunity. Perhaps even more shocking to penny-pinching politicians, the department's outstanding accounts totaled nearly half the federal budget. Indicative of the War Department's administrative breakdown is that, according to its records, some 500,000 soldiers were mobilized—and over 180,000 veterans or their families would claim a military pension—while the armies numbered in the thousands. In a particularly humiliating example, at the Battle of Bladensburg, fought just outside Washington on 24 August 1814, the Americans could assemble less than 7,000 troops, most of them militia. Incompetently commanded, they were quickly routed by a numerically inferior British force, which then entered and burned the capital.

The aftermath of the war brought the gradual establishment of a staff, by which contemporaries meant a rational, stable, and skilled bureaucracy. Secretary of War Calhoun, who took office in 1817, was determined that the War Department be not only efficient but also cheap. He recognized that the secretary, as a civilian cabinet official with probably no military experience, required expert advice on the multitude of army activities. He centralized the administrative and technical bureaus such as the adjutant general, quartermaster general, surgeon general, commissary general, inspector general, and so forth. The Adjutant General's Office, which collected, collated, and distributed the service's correspondence, served as the coordinating agency between the bureaus, the secretary, and the commanders in the field. Such coordination became much easier after the 1821 *General Regulations for the Army* provided precise directions—including the thirteen distinct registers and the dimensions of the boxes—for filing the correct forms. To the confusion of later historians, the collected bureaus were referred to as the "General Staff," but this organization bore little similarity to the Prussian organization of the same name that would so inspire later army reformers. The Prussian General Staff planned and coordinated its army for war; the American version was a bureaucratic agency for managing the force.[16]

Calhoun took great pains to ensure his new administrative organization drew from the army's best and brightest. Typical of his selections was Quartermaster General Thomas Sidney Jesup, who had proven his command and administrative skills in the War of 1812. Relying more on quality than quantity, the secretary kept the bureaus' permanent personnel at a minimum. The uniformed contingent of Jesup's department consisted of himself and one deputy in Washington and fifteen assistant quartermasters assigned to posts or districts—a paltry number to supply an army of over 8,000 spread from Florida to Minnesota.[17] The Inspector General's Office under Brig. Gen. John E. Wool was even smaller, its chief in Washington and two peripatetic inspectors reporting on the army's far-flung posts and units. The bureau chiefs' long tenures—Wool would hold office until 1840, Jesup until 1860—made them fixtures in the Washington political scene. Congressional limitations on staff officer slots encouraged them to appropriate regimental officers as temporary assistants. Between 1820 and 1830 one out of every five regular officers was seconded to a staff bureau or the Corps of Engineers at least once. Whether supplying the garrisons or testing cannons, staff duty required educated, efficient middle managers more than charismatic warriors.[18]

The cumulative result of bureau assignments was to enhance the officer corps' managerial and technical abilities. Indeed, in having to administer and supply garrisons hundreds of miles from their location, in establishing and supervising factories, in experimenting with and assimilating new technologies, in supervising its labor and middle management, and in many other tasks, the War Department bureaucrats would develop executive skills that preceded those often credited to big business. The result was increased occupational specialization, shared experience, and group identity among the officer corps—what might be viewed as the emergence of a distinct professional character. But this process occurred unevenly, for West Pointers' college education—an attainment of which perhaps 1 percent of the adult male population could boast—provided graduates with administrative expertise that their seniors' service with troops did not. Whether intended or not, Calhoun's reforms encouraged a bureaucratic caste within the service with greater access to privileged assignments than their comrades on garrison duty. And the secondment of line officers to staff assignments, often without their superiors' acquiescence, provided further grounds for feuding over authority, precedence, and responsibility. The consequences of bureau privileges, as well as the tensions of line-staff relations, were perhaps best demonstrated when post commander Braxton Bragg pressed charges against himself in his role as acting quartermaster.[19]

The army's combat forces, or "the line," underwent a rockier transition to peacetime service than the bureaus. The War Department, in the words of one outraged officer-historian, "diabolically jumbled" the infantry, breaking up and consolidating regiments that had distinguished themselves in the recent war and reorganizing them into one rifle and eight infantry regiments.[20] Thus the 25th Infantry Regiment, the heroes of Chippawa, were amalgamated with the 11th, 27th, 29th, and 37th Regiments to form the 6th Infantry Regiment, while the troops from the 6th Infantry were folded into the reconstituted 2nd Infantry. In 1821 a second wave of consolidations, reductions in force, and redeployments further splintered the tenuous ties that had contributed to regimental spirit and unit pride. Whether intended or not, the result was an irrevocable physical and spiritual break with the standing army that had existed prior to the War of 1812. Postwar officers soon developed new loyalties to regiment, combat arm, and patron, often aided by shared wartime service on the Niagara front, and these new loyalties, and the internal divisions they engendered, would underlie much of the culture of the line officer corps until the Civil War.

The collective wisdom of the bureau chiefs on the General Staff could provide the civilian head of the War Department with information on particular military functions such as supply, materiel, and administration. But Calhoun recognized that the secretary also required advice on issues that transcended bureau prerogatives. He expanded his predecessors' practice of convening a board of officers to study a particular problem. The most important of these was the Fortification Board, which until the Civil War operated as the service's primary strategic planning agency. Other boards wrote the infantry regulations that stipulated fighting formations and drill, selected those officers to be retained in the 1815 and 1821 drawdowns, and determined the caliber and equipment of the artillery.[21]

From their Washington offices near the White House, bureau chiefs could advise on their specialties and the boards on specific problems, but what was missing was an officer or agency to inform the secretary on the status of the infantry and artillery regiments. Calhoun attempted to fill this vacancy by appointing the army's senior line officer, Maj. Gen. Jacob Brown, as the commanding general. That title (and its alternative, general of the army), were immediate misnomers, for Congress refused to give the holder command authority over the bureaus, boards, or forces in the field.[22] Brown accepted his role as purely advisory and gave good service until he died in 1828. But his successor, Alexander Macomb, immediately attempted to issue orders to the bureau chiefs. They resisted with all the skill of entrenched officeholders and found allies in the secretary and in Congress. The struggle between the commanding general and the bureau chiefs was sometimes paralleled in line-staff rivalry outside Washington and would plague intra-army relations for the rest of the nineteenth century.[23]

The postwar decision to organize the field forces by geographical rather than tactical priorities accelerated the service's tendency toward discrete, almost tribal identities. There was no line organization higher than the regiment. Officers were divided not only by membership in the line or staff establishments but also by region, branch, and regiment. The harbor defense forces, almost entirely heavy artillery, remained along the Atlantic while the mobile forces of infantry, and later cavalry and field artillery, remained on the frontier. The line-staff, organizational, and regional rivalries were amplified by persistent clashes between Washington and the field over strategy, resources, force structure, and many other issues.

The potential for conflicts between theater commanders and higher-ups in Washington were manifested, perhaps not surprisingly, in the person of Andrew Jackson, commanding the Southern Division. In 1818 Jackson launched an unauthorized invasion of Spanish Florida and resisted leaving without guarantees from Washington that many of his conquests would be retained. He also protested when bureau chiefs transferred personnel out of his division. When Calhoun supported the chiefs, Jackson responded with intemperate and insubordinate rebukes that escalated to the president, who sided with the War Department. The quarrel revealed much about the postwar army. On one level it was an important civil-military dispute that resolved whether the civilian secretary outranked a general officer. On another level it became a conflict over whether Washington or local commanders were best qualified to determine policy. And on a third level, it manifested into an intraservice struggle between field officers and the War Department bureaucracy that highlighted the potential problems of Calhoun's administrative reforms.[24]

The reforms in the first half-decade of the aftermath the War of 1812 left a mixed legacy. As with later efforts to transform the service, they were primarily administrative and thus their impact was more apparent in Washington than with the field forces. By 1825 the secretary of war could call on a corps of expert bureaucrats, and they in turn managed the administration, supply, transport, and equipage of the service efficiently. Their expertise was facilitated by the reformation of the US Military Academy, which soon produced graduates with sufficient managerial and technical expertise to remedy the logistical and administrative chaos that had plagued the prewar service. But the creation of a powerful War Department bureaucracy produced new tensions and dilemmas, exacerbating tensions between administrators and field officers that would persist throughout the nineteenth century. Regional commanders complained they were undermined by staff personnel of lower rank and limited field experience who were responsible only to their bureau chiefs in Washington. Line officers became embittered that colleagues who secured, often through their patrons, a transfer to a bureau obtained preferential treatment, better living conditions, and higher pay. This friction between Washington-based specialists and line officers who prided themselves on their common sense and combat experience was one of the most divisive legacies of the postwar decade. pentagon vs field

The primary missions of the postwar army, and in most respects the nineteenth-century army, were defined by President James Monroe in his 1817 inaugural speech: to "garrison and preserve our fortifications" and "meet the first invasions of a foreign foe."[25] The Fortification Board embraced this dual mission with enthusiasm. In 1821 it unveiled the nation's first all-inclusive defense plan, later known as the "3rd System." Drawing on recent events, the Fortification Board envisioned a British maritime attack seizing a major coastal city as a base, landing a powerful expeditionary force, and then moving inland to ravage the countryside, devastate urban centers, and perhaps instigate a slave revolt.[26] To stop this existential threat, the 3rd System incorporated a navy to harass enemy shipping, fortifications to deter a sudden raid to seize a port, and a militia able and ready to mobilize in the event of invasion. The board gave little attention to the navy's role or to the border with Canada; its primary interest was on building a chain of masonry fortifications with enough cannons to destroy a hostile fleet. But it did tie coastal defense to national defense by recommending an inland communication network that would connect the interior to the littoral states. This would allow personnel and supplies to be moved more rapidly, thereby facilitating frontier campaigns and avoiding the logistical problems of the War of 1812. Equally important, it secured support for the 3rd System from landbound states, though at the cost of making the construction of harbor forts competitive with internal improvements.

The Fortification Board program represented an extraordinary commitment of military and financial resources. Its estimated costs were impressive: $18 million—triple the entire national debt—to build over fifty forts. But the board argued such an expense was negligible compared to the cost of a large standing army or, even worse, the occupation of even one city by an invader. In the next decade Congress appropriated nearly half that amount for a chain of fixed defenses running from the Canadian border down to Florida. The 3rd System became the Corps of Engineers' great project; the officers sent to design, construct, and command these fortifications represented the Corps' current and future elite. Within a decade of war's end, West Point's curriculum had been molded to prepare its top graduates, inevitably either engineers or artillerists, to immediately contribute their expertise. But they also created what would emerge as an all-too-common dilemma in the postwar army. The coastal defense system may have been the strongest aspect of the defense plan in its planning and construction phases, with the Corps of Engineers providing the former and the federal funding to local contractors the latter. However, in the reduced circumstances of the Regular Army, the fortifications proved impossible to either equip or garrison. Indeed, even the Fortification Board's initial estimate of 5,000 soldiers to operate the forts' artillery would have required 80 percent of the standing army.[27]

The postwar army's other mission—stabilizing the expanding frontier in the West—evolved as the federal government increasingly made regulars its primary agent of expansion. In May 1815, three months after the formal end of the hostilities with Great Britain, the War

Department instructed department commanders to extend posts into areas previously dominated by European traders. Soon troops were moving up the Mississippi River, building forts from Chicago to St. Louis. Calhoun accelerated this westward push dramatically, proposing to extend the military frontier 1,600 miles to the headwaters of the Minnesota and Missouri Rivers. Although Calhoun's successors slowed the expansion, by 1828 there were over seventy military stations scattered along the various frontier areas. The posts and their garrisons were intended to serve a variety of purposes, most more economic and diplomatic than martial. Writing to Calhoun in 1823, Brig. Gen. Edmund P. Gaines, commanding the Western Department, argued that the army's commercial role had strategic benefits because it brought Native Americans within the government's sphere and thereby pacified the frontier more effectively than warfare would. To Gaines, "trade forms the rein and curb by which the turbulent and towering spirit of these lords of the forest can alone be governed."[28]

As Gaines recognized, the expansion of the frontier, the protection of settlers and traders, and the construction of forts invariably brought the Regular Army into contact with the Native Americans who lived there. The army also played a significant role in mediating intertribal conflict, as when it built Fort Smith to keep peace between Cherokee and Osage warriors. Except for skirmishes with the Seminoles in Florida, the decade after the War of 1812 saw no major confrontations between soldiers and Native American tribes. Indeed, one of the few large campaigns, the misnamed Arikara War of 1823, reveals the extent of the army's duties as the federal government's peacekeeper. After fur traders claimed they were attacked by hostile tribes in present-day South Dakota, Col. Henry Leavenworth, commanding the garrison at Council Bluffs, set out with 220 infantry and two cannons. He was joined by dozens of frontier volunteers and several hundred Sioux, the ancestral enemies of the Arikara, for a combined total of 800. A seven week march that covered 640 miles brought Leavenworth's force to the site of the attack, where another Sioux contingent joined them. Leavenworth's infantry entered the village, then pulled back. But with the Sioux attack imminent, the Arikara leaders waffled on returning the traders' goods. The accompanying Indian agent advocated violent retribution. Leavenworth chose instead to declare victory, provided the means for the Arikara to escape, and trekked back.

The Arikara campaign was characteristic of the frontier army's role in the decade after the war. Leavenworth's small expedition marched long distances, endured great physical hardship, but engaged in limited combat. The campaign was also characteristic as both Regular–Indian and intratribal conflict. Perhaps most characteristic of the army's frontier mission, the expedition received vitriolic abuse from traders, the press, and politicians—and probably the Sioux—for failing to destroy the Arikara. By taking on the burden of dispute resolution between whites and Native Americans, and among the tribes themselves, Leavenworth and other military frontier ambassadors established a more rational, and undoubtedly less bloody, solution.[29]

Perhaps the greatest change in the decade after the War of 1812 was the federal government's reliance on the Regular Army rather than civilian militias or volunteers. But it was a reliance based on technical and administrative capacity, not necessarily on combat forces. Militias and volunteers were often called into federal service against Native Americans.[30] Regular officers' martial duties were often secondary to their assignments as surveyors, canal- and road-builders, contractors, governors, scientists, diplomats, police, or any other function the government required. In contrast to the individualism and disobedience exhibited by prewar officers, the postwar officer corps obeyed government directives. Although many expressed revulsion at some white settlers' violence and the injustice of Indian removal, officers carried out their orders. They were equally compliant when required to remove settlers, to stop filibustering (unauthorized) expeditions, or to resolve other white-generated challenges to the general order. Gaines, a dutiful participant in Jackson's Florida incursion, would prove equally resolute in restraining American incursions into Texas. Scott, initially sympathetic with insurgents seeking to overthrow British rule in Canada, negotiated a settlement that ensured the international boundary. Perhaps the best indicator of the bipartisan acceptance of the army's role as federal peacemaker is Jackson's evolution from quasi-filibusterer in 1818 to threatening to unleash the regulars on South Carolina during the Nullification Crisis of 1832.[31]

Regular officers agreed that a primary lesson of the war with Great Britain was the lack of any coherent tactical doctrine or service-wide training. During the conflict some officers followed one set of manuals and others followed another, adding further confusion to the battlefield. Immediately after the end of hostilities, a War Department board headed by Winfield Scott established a common infantry system that remained in place until after the Mexican–American War. Heavily influenced by Napoleonic practices, the 1815 *Infantry Tactics* outlined the precise drills for marching, maneuver, and fire on the European battlefield. But the postwar army's ability to put Scott's tactics into practice was constrained by its small size and the dispersal of its many garrisons, especially after the troop reductions of 1821. Drills designed to move a hundred soldiers into the firing line had little practical utility for garrisons that might have a quarter that number. And the postwar tactical reforms applied only to the infantry: there were no similar manuals for cavalry or artillery, much less a doctrine to have all maneuver together. The four understrength artillery regiments, scattered in coastal forts from Maine to New Orleans and along the Canadian border, had even more difficulties, being desperately short not only of men but also of cannons. Indeed, postwar officers had more opportunity to practice infantry and artillery tactics as cadets at the Military Academy than as officers in the field.[32]

As the postwar army became further dispersed across the frontiers and increasingly occupied in public works projects, its preparedness for war became of increasing concern to senior leaders. In an effort to revive the moribund artillery, Calhoun in 1824 concentrated eleven companies and established a school of practice. Artillerymen could train with a variety of ordnance at Fort Monroe, and the officers received special education in advanced gunnery. Two years later an infantry school was established to provide large (or at least larger) unit training and to serve as a ready deployment force. But by the early 1830s such schools fell victim to financial cutbacks, increasing violence on the western frontier, the Canada–Maine border dispute, and the construction and repair of harbor fortifications. Thereafter the army possessed not a single facility with enough troops for its officers to practice waging war against a Western European opponent.[33]

The War of 1812 had virtually destroyed the prewar officer corps. Totaling less than 300, some of whom had fought in the Revolutionary War, those in uniform at war's beginning were a tiny percentage of the almost 3,500 officers at war's end. In 1812 the average general was fifty-five; three years later he was almost twenty years younger. The aftermath of the War of 1812 established precedents for future efforts to create a postwar military officer corps.[34] One was that those who remained in the postwar force would be selected internally rather than through the political favoritism that had shaped the prewar corps. The 1815 legislation authorizing the peacetime establishment mandated a drastic reduction from 3,500 to 674, still a sizeable increase from the prewar officer corps. In a major break with past practice, a board of officers picked those to be kept in the Regular Army and those to be "deranged." Officers were now assigned a number (termed a "file") upon commissioning and could advance within their regiment (infantry or artillery) or bureau (staff and technical) only as fast as those in front were promoted, retired, or died. By legislating promotion by seniority, and making no provision for retirement, the legislation created a third condition for later aftermath armies: a perpetual postwar "hump," or cluster, of officers—in 1815 some 80 percent of the remaining force—with roughly equivalent rank and commissioning date. And in common with its successors, the post-1815 hump would creep glacially, blocking advancement not only for its members but also all who entered the army afterward. At the outbreak of the Civil War, of the nineteen regimental colonels, eleven were veterans of the War of 1812 and another four had entered shortly afterward.[35]

The seniority system was egalitarian in its assumption that officers of the same grade were equivalent in ability. The standard to assess individual competence, character, and abilities was experience, for which the measure was time in grade. Proponents claimed that seniority was the sole defense against the vagaries of politics and partisanship and that it fostered unit cohesion, loyalty, and esprit because, at least in theory, it removed all motive for individual competition. The most junior officer could recognize that, however low his status now, he was guaranteed eventual rise to higher rank if he remained in uniform. Moreover, it was a fair exchange: in return for discomfort, isolation, and restricted advancement, an officer could be assured of lifetime employment. Its detractors charged that seniority stifled individual initiative, guaranteed advancement to mediocre men and "deadwood," and ensured that only the aged and infirm would command. The perennial disagreement was exacerbated by generational differences. Veterans of the War of 1812 believed they had demonstrated their competence in the hard test of war. Their juniors—postwar graduates of the US Military Academy—held that officership required professional skills obtainable only through the specialized education that they had received.

The post-1815 officer corps provided a warning for later aftermath armies: many wartime heroes made wretched peacetime officers. Within five years over half had resigned their commissions; another 15 percent would be terminated. During this period one in five officers was absent from duty, and those on post were prone to insobriety, inefficiency, insubordination, and violence. There is ample documentation to support Samuel J. Watson's dismal conclusion that "between 1815 and 1821 the Army was probably more disorderly than in any period of similar length. . . . The Army's officers were the prime contributors to the discord."[36] Such indiscipline among the officer corps invalidated many initiatives undertaken by the War Department's reformed bureaucracy and could sometimes result in administrative and logistic breakdowns reminiscent of the war years.

The practice of brevet rank—an honorary advancement as a reward for gallantry or enhanced responsibilities—was a further source of friction. Then and later, there was incessant bickering over when officers were entitled to brevet rank, with the accompanying pay, allowances, and prestige when assigned responsibilities commiserate with the higher rank. Although two such egotists as Scott and Gaines were inevitable rivals, their brevet statuses played a significant role in their extended feud.

In what would become a recurrent pattern, in the second half of the postwar decade the service tried to resolve multiple dilemmas, many the result of the first half-decade's reforms. One of the most significant was the drastic reduction of the postwar establishment. In 1821, with the possibility of war with Britain or Spain diminished, the frontiers stabilizing, and the nation in economic recession, Congress announced it intended to cut the Regular Army from 10,000 to 6,000. And as another part of the recurring pattern, it did so without modifying or reducing the service's peacetime responsibilities.

The reduction in force contributed to a debate over both the organization and the missions of the peacetime military establishment. Secretary of War Calhoun believed the most efficient force structure should allow the Regular Army to both "perpetuate military skill and experience" and provide an immediate combat force for any emergency.[37] His "expansible army" plan therefore contained a disproportionately large officer corps, retaining the existing tactical units but manning them at a fraction of their enlisted wartime strength. Upon mobilization for war, these skeleton companies could be filled with enlistees and the force doubled without adding a single officer. Calhoun may have been influenced by how rapidly experienced officers had drilled recruits during the war. Indeed, most of the vaunted regulars Scott had led at Chippawa had only a few months of realistic training. Opponents questioned whether such skeletonized units could perform their missions as well as the need for so many officers. Although never formally acknowledged, the expansible army became the peacetime norm in practice. Enlisted strength was cut almost in half, but the officer corps was reduced by only 20 percent (from 712 in December 1820 to 512 a year later). With three officers for each forty-soldier infantry company, and four officers per artillery company, tactical units would have sufficient commanders when increased to war strength. And in peacetime the surplus of officers allowed the army to serve the nation in a variety of administrative, engineering, diplomatic, political, and other tasks.[38]

With five years to assess postwar requirements, the selection board that supervised the 1821 reduction placed minimal emphasis on past battlefield gallantry and much more on proven or potential excellence for the current and future establishment. Perhaps as a result, its primary criteria for retention was graduation from the United States Military Academy, with engineering and administrative skills crucial to the real soldiering of the postwar era. The proportion of West Pointers after the 1821 drawdown almost doubled, and the War Department ensured this would continue by awarding them a virtual monopoly on peacetime commissions. Although between 1803 and 1860 almost half of those who entered West Point dropped out, the thirty to fifty who graduated often exceeded the regular establishment's annual allotment. To retain the excess in uniform, the War Department, with congressional support, assigned them brevet second lieutenancies with full pay. Sometimes these surplus "sous-officers" remained in uniform for several years before finally being commissioned, but in the meantime they served as effective and honest federal agents. With such demand for their services, the proportion of Military Academy graduates in the officer corps climbed from 14 percent in 1815, to 30 percent in 1821, to 64 percent by 1830, and to 76 percent in 1860.[39]

The postwar corps was divided by generation and by experience. What J. P. Clark identified as "the foundational generation of the American military profession" established the norms of managerial and tactical expertise within the officer corps.[40] They had usually distinguished themselves in the War of 1812 and emerged at the height of the rank structure. Among them were General Staff managers such as Thomas Jesup, who imposed systematic, methodical bureaucratic procedures on all who served as quartermasters. Another was Brig. Gen. Joseph G. Totten, an 1805 West Point graduate who co-authored the Fortification Board's initial reports. As Chief of Engineers from 1838 to 1863, Totten ensured the continuance of the 3rd System. His priorities in turn shaped the Military Academy's curriculum, which under Sylvanus Thayer and Dennis Hart Mahan helped propagate what Ian Hope terms "the scientific way of warfare" throughout the service.[41] Winfield Scott, commissioned in 1808 and the hero at Chippewa, was another. As commander of the Eastern Division and the author of the service's infantry drill and general regulations, Scott played a crucial role in ensuring that the postwar army was organized to engage a European opponent. A commander whose own career personified martial genius, Scott nonetheless mentored Academy-educated scientific officers. He also did much to encourage common standards among his officers, whether it was reading, drilling, or treating soldiers humanely.[42] Both Scott and his great rival, Gaines, developed extensive patronage networks that ensured favorable assignments and faster promotion for many who would distinguish themselves in Mexico and later in the Civil War.[43]

The Military Academy's postwar emergence as both a premier engineering school and the incubator of officer culture owed much to Thayer's tenure as superintendent between 1817 and 1833. Thayer established its scientific/engineering curriculum, essential to developing the expertise to construct and command the nation's primary strategic enterprise: the 3rd System of coastal fortifications. The top students entered the Corps of Engineers and often devoted their careers to these very projects. Close behind engineers in status and skills were those assigned to artillery regiments. These officers acquired not only the mathematical skills to calculate trajectory and effect against fast-moving warships but also the ability to supervise arsenals and to design and cast cannons. Both engineers and artillery were heavily represented on the Fortification Board and various internal improvement projects, which from 1818 to 1838 employed over a quarter of West Point's graduates on permanent or detached duties.

Even those officers who did not join the elite engineers and artillery benefited from the curriculum, since the conduct of war itself depended on the mathematics needed for logistics, march distances, construction, and combat. Cadets began their first year learning infantry squad and cannon crew tactics and by their senior year were participating in battalion maneuvers. During summer they practiced designing and building field fortifications, marching, camp assembly, and field craft. By the time they were commissioned, they were skilled bureaucrats with the managerial skills to work in one of the bureaus, oversee a field headquarters, plan a campaign, and inspect troops for drill, health, and morale. Although a West Pointer after graduation might become a lowly brevet second lieutenant with a handful of soldiers, he had the education and training to organize, train, administer, and direct a volunteer or militia force many times that size. Whether in or out of uniform, his specialized capabilities equipped him for service to the nation. It was no coincidence that many West Point graduates became successful businessmen.[44]

The military component of the West Point education during this period should not be exaggerated. Future skills in the administration, training, and deployment of military forces during war were valued, but so too was readiness to deal with the peacetime establishment's logistical, administrative, communication, and other managerial problems. In recognition that West Pointers constituted the sole source of formal engineering education in the United States, the General Survey Act of 1824 allowed officers to be assigned to either civil or military projects. Within four years officers were supervising almost fifty public projects and twenty surveys. In the 1830s their civic duties were expanded to escorting trading parties along the Santa Fe Trail, a role they had prepared for while serving as acting commissaries and quartermasters.[45]

The composition of the enlisted force, unlike the officer corps, changed little in the decade after the War of 1812. Americans celebrated their state militias and native-born volunteers as the true defenders of republican ideals. Images of militia cavalry killing Tecumseh and ballads of the "half horse, half alligator" riflemen at the Battle of New Orleans remained popular for decades.[46] No such respect was accorded to the regular enlisted man, who was usually portrayed as part of a faceless column following a resplendent officer. In peacetime even this positive image disappeared, replaced by one of lazy, violent, drunken, profane brutes who had swapped their rights as citizens for five dollars each month. As would be true until the mid-twentieth century, the peacetime army was the nation's employer of last resort.

The enlisted force was drawn overwhelmingly from the Northeast, from unskilled workers, and the foreign-born. They joined an army whose enlisted pay had ossified since 1802 and whose highest-paid members, the eleven sergeant majors, received only nine dollars. In the 1820s, despite restrictions on enlistment, immigrants comprised at least a quarter of the enlisted force; in later years it was over two-thirds. With good reason Dale R. Steinhauer's study of the pre–Civil War enlisted force subtitled one chapter "The Foreignization of the Regular Army."[47] Often illiterate—one 1820s sample revealed 40 percent could not sign their names—and sometimes barely conversant in English, such men had little prospects for decent jobs. Indicative of their low esteem, civilians adopted the term "sojer" as a reference for shirking hard work.

The decade after the war demonstrated another truth of peacetime service that would continue throughout the nineteenth century: the army was as much a federal construction agency as it was a combat force. Rankers provided the labor for fortifications and frontier posts, transported supplies, dug wells and canals, and performed any other work the service required. The first task of a company of perhaps one or two officers and forty enlisted when they arrived at their designated station would often be to build barracks and officers quarters, kitchens and ovens, workshops, storehouses, hospitals, and blockhouses. In larger posts they often constructed sawmills, quarries, grain mills, carpentry and blacksmith sheds, and so on. Soldiers were even required to grow their own food, a lifesaving chore after scurvy or delayed supplies threatened some garrisons. In 1822 the 6th Infantry Regiment maintained almost 400 acres of corn and dozens of acres devoted to potatoes, beans, and other crops as well as 382 cattle and 600 hogs. One observer complimented the regiment's health and high morale but noted that the troops bragged more about their gardens than they did about their military expertise.[48]

The postwar decade also engraved a clear caste line between officers and enlisted men. The line was rigorously enforced, as evidenced by the number of courts-martial in the early 1820s for commissioned personnel who drank, gamed, danced, or otherwise fraternized with their inferiors. Although many West Pointers came from families of modest means, they were often criticized for their condescending attitude toward enlisted personnel. Regardless of their background, postwar officers were determined to assert both their identity and their prerogatives as gentlemen, and this required that subordinates be truly subordinate, rendering, as the formula went, prompt and cheerful service to orders. Officers did no manual labor; they supervised their workforces. They took full advantage of all the privileges of rank: soldiers cut their wood, painted their houses, tended their gardens, served as their valets, butlers, and waiters, and performed any other chore required. To officers, enlisted men served their officers and the regiment but had no higher loyalty. Yet when the Civil War broke out, hundreds of these officers would place loyalty to their states above the nation they had sworn to serve; in contrast, almost no enlisted men joined the Confederacy.[49]

Given that enlisted men served so often as manual laborers, it is perhaps not surprising that individual officers interpreted their role, in Taylor's words, more as a "good overseer[] or negro driver" than as leaders. Some commanders, including Taylor, took a paternal interest in their troops' welfare, but they seem to have been few and far between. Officers had come to view military justice as a mechanism to impose absolute subordination during the war, when immediate adherence was essential to tactical proficiency. They continued to demand such compliance in its aftermath, sometimes elevating the forms of discipline over their functions. Between 1823 and 1825 the army annually court-martialed nearly one soldier in four. The most common general courts-martial sentence between 1826 and 1832 was some form of bodily restraint—an iron collar or ball and chain—and nearly 20 percent were expelled (or "drummed out") of the service.[50]

Officers also inflicted such inventive and extralegal punishments as branding, mutilation, hanging by the thumbs, carrying a rock or heavy log for hours, straddling a sharp wooden beam (the punishment horse), and binding in a stress position with a rag forced into the mouth (bucking-and-gagging). Making matters worse for enlisted men, officers inflicted these tortures as much for perceived insults as for military failures. In a not untypical incident, in 1822 a court-martial found a lieutenant guilty of illegally flogging his soldiers but acquitted him because he alleged his victims had been insolent. This instance is unusual not for its injustice but rather because the officer was tried at all.[51] There is little reason to doubt Samuel Watson's conclusion that "although few enlisted men were killed, their routine subjugation to casual blows and elaborate punishments meant that they, rather than Native Americans, suffered the most frequent violence at the army's hands."[52]

Not surprisingly, enlisted personnel fled the service in droves. Between 1815 and 1821 one in five soldiers deserted; between 1821 and 1845 it was often one in four. In what would characterize the officer corps up to the present, most officers denied either individual or corporate responsibility for this mass repudiation of their leadership. There was nothing wrong with the command climate of the US Army that could not be fixed by a better class of enlisted men. Officers blamed everything from the recruiting service to the individualistic, undisciplined, and unpatriotic spirit of American society. And while the War Department may have sympathized, the exigencies of service and restricted budgets meant recruiters had to take what was available. Congress acceded to minor reforms in 1833 when it restored flogging, though restricting punishment to fifty lashes and only for desertion; raised soldiers' pay by the princely sum of one dollar (but held a portion back until the completion of the second year); and briefly cut the enlistment period from five years to three. None of these reforms lowered desertion or improved quality, and neither would similar efforts in the future.[53]

The inability to retain soldiers past one enlistment, and often not even that long, stymied the creation of the core of career noncommissioned officers (noncoms). Each line company was authorized four sergeants and four corporals, bossed by the first sergeant. Like privates, noncoms were increasingly foreign-born, and also like privates the majority of corporals and sergeants were in their first enlistment. In many cases their chief requirement was a good set of fists. There was little incentive to take the responsibilities and hatred that rank imposed: the first sergeant was paid only three dollars a month more than the lowest private. In some cases, a private who possessed a vocational skill that entitled him to extra compensation might have to accept a salary reduction if advanced to corporal.[54]

The transformation of the military establishment in the ten years following the War of 1812 was so complete and so long-lasting that in many respects it is not 1784 but 1815 that marks the creation of the peacetime Regular Army. This postwar decade also witnessed the first of many cycles of recovery and established precedents later postwar armies would follow. The first five years brought extensive reforms in War Department administration, force structure, tactics, and officer procurement. By the end of that period the War Department, helmed by Secretary of War Calhoun, had instituted a more efficient administrative bureaucracy and confirmed the peacetime army's authorized missions of frontier constabulary, harbor defense, and conventional (or Western) warfare. In practice, Calhoun expanded these missions to include diplomacy, internal security, governance, and others of immediate importance to the federal government. These recognized duties and the more flexible ones would remain in place until the end of the century. Senior commanders such as Scott, Gaines, Jesup, and others established standards of competence and conduct that shaped the cultural identity of the officer corps. The postwar US Military Academy became the school for officers, imbuing its graduates with the martial and engineering skills required for most civil or military contingencies. The Fortification Board outlined the nation's first coherent national security strategy, one that that would be largely adhered to for a hundred years.

The cycle of recovery also created other, less desirable trends that would also characterize later postwar armies. After the burst of reforms, the succeeding five years forced the service to address a number of dilemmas, more than a few caused by these very reforms. Scattered across hundreds of miles, line officers and enlisted men now identified themselves by their combat arm, company, or regiment, but not necessarily as part of a coherent army preparing for war. The enmity between Washington-based bureaus and regional commanders created constant turbulence. There was a persistent generational divide between those commissioned before 1815 and their postwar juniors, almost always West Pointers. The former took pride in their wartime service, experience, and common sense, while the latter viewed many of their superiors as overaged, uneducated, and unprofessional. An even sharper divide, tantamount to a caste system, arose between officers and enlisted personnel, with officers maintaining their authority more by punitive discipline and a rigged judicial system than inspirational leadership.

To some historians the decade after the war with Mexico (1846–1848) is important only for what it reveals of the personalities, ideologies, and incidents that would emerge as crucial during the Civil War (1861–1865). Without this foreknowledge, there appears so little of interest that one eminent historian of the US Army devoted fully half his treatment to the petty and indecisive feud between Secretary of War Jefferson Davis and Commanding General Winfield Scott.[55] For both the service and its civilian superiors, the war vindicated the reform program put into place after the War of 1812, and thus the dominant trend was toward conservatism and minimal change. After the war the administrative system bequeathed by Calhoun remained intact, as did the service's missions of harbor defense and frontier constabulary. The officer corps returned to making West Point the gateway to commissions. And the enlisted ranks continued to be drawn from the marginal, immigrants, and the unskilled.

At the start of hostilities with Mexico the Regular Army included 734 officers and 7,885 rankers, of which 1,500 were with Zachary Taylor's Army of Occupation. Over the course of the war the regulars were augmented by 1,016 officers and 35,000 soldiers to a total strength of 42,587, but many of these were never sufficiently trained to take the field. The war brought great glory, making Scott an international star, and also demonstrated the skill with which West Pointers executed their scientific way of war. It was also a comparatively bloodless war for the US Army. Only 585 regulars were killed in action and another 425 died of wounds; 4,899 died of disease and other causes. In a rather damning commentary on professional leadership, ten times more soldiers deserted than died in battle. The army's infantry tactics and training methods proved valuable; in particular, West Pointers were able to step in and provide instruction to War of 1812 veterans unfamiliar with anything above company drill.[56]

Regular officers, with some justification, concluded that the war's primary lesson was to validate their professional expertise and superiority over citizen-soldiers.[57] President James K. Polk's effort to undercut those senior commanders he deemed political threats, such as Scott and Taylor, was a direct attack on the service's independence and integrity. His appointment of favorites, such as his former law partner, to high rank infuriated those passed over, especially when most of his appointees proved grossly incompetent. The citizen-soldier volunteers were accorded a less blanket condemnation. Regulars applauded their fighting spirit and morale while deploring their ill discipline, sanitation practices, poor training, and penchant for atrocities against the Mexican population. The controversial war did not bring officers closer to their fellow countrymen, who they viewed somewhat contradictorily as simultaneously overly quick to go to war and insufficiently supportive once war was declared.[58]

As after the War of 1812, the end of fighting brought an immediate and far-reaching drawdown. Within a few months after ratification of the peace treaty in March 1848, Polk announced he intended to reduce the army to its prewar strength of 10,000. The president did not explain how a force overly stretched before the war would now also occupy and police over a million square miles of newly acquired territory. And in what may have been a not-so-subtle rebuke, the Adjutant General's report noted that the service already had a shortfall of almost 5,000. The disconnect between personnel and mission was soon apparent as the army moved into territory defended by such premier warriors as the Apache, Comanche, and Sioux tribes. In what would be an exception, after holding the service to under 11,000 in the first five postwar years, Congress increased it to almost 18,000 in the succeeding five. That this was a specific response to the Western frontier was apparent in both force structure and the personnel assignments. Between 1821 and 1833 the line-force structure had been four artillery and seven infantry regiments. By 1855 there were five mounted regiments, but infantry regiments had increased by only three (and artillery not at all). Similarly, in the five years after the War of 1812, 75 percent of the standing army was stationed near the Atlantic Coast, while in the decade after the Mexican–American War it was under 10 percent. These changes in priorities, force structure, and personnel were already well underway, but they accelerated dramatically in the postwar decade.[59]

The War Department had been the center of military reform in the first five years following the War of 1812. But the decade after the war with Mexico witnessed only minor administrative changes, in large measure due to personality clashes. The thorny issue of authority among the staff bureaus, secretary of war, and commanding general sparked a vitriolic battle between the latter two. Scott moved to New York, and he and Davis bombarded each other with insults. The squabble was unfortunate, since both saw the War Department bureaus as a common enemy. Having perfected their managerial and technical expertise in a narrow field of specialization, these officers displayed little understanding of the realities of field service. In a not untypical example, in 1851 a department commander confronting an Indian war with barely 350 soldiers received an angry letter from the Quartermaster General threatening to withhold all funding because of improper paperwork.[60] The bureau chiefs found an ally in Congress, itself always suspicious of military centralization and comfortable with the bureaus' ability to deliver information, contracts, and local improvements. The conflict in the War Department produced much turmoil but little tangible change in the system bequeathed following the Calhoun era.

The Mexican–American War and contemporary European conflicts did spark one significant innovation: adapting the army's three-decades-old tactics to new advances in firepower. The development of the rifled musket extended the lethality of the battlefield and made Napoleonic tactics such as massed columns suicidal. Davis authorized a board of officers under Lt. Col. William J. Hardee that borrowed, as had Scott, from French manuals. But whereas Scott's tactics had been based on Napoleon, the 1855 *Rifle and Light Infantry Tactics* envisioned agile, mobile infantry rushing through the enemy's volleys and closing with the bayonet. As with Scott's tactics, the small size of the postwar army and its distribution into company-size garrisons permitted little opportunity to test Hardee's methods in the battlefield environment for which they were intended.[61]

The aftermath army continued the twin missions following the War of 1812—coastal defense and frontier constabulary—but the disconnect between the two grew exponentially. In its officer education, doctrine, tactics, and regulations, the Regular Army retained its post–War of 1812 focus on European-style conventional war. The Military Academy's elite still entered the Corps of Engineers and the artillery regiments, the Fortification Board remained in session, and the 3rd System remained the nation's strategic plan. In actuality the grand design was crumbling even more rapidly than its cherished masonry casemates.

The 1821 estimate of fifty forts and $18 million expanded in a few decades to 126 forts and $31 million. Yet five years after the end of the Mexican–American War, less than half the forts were completed. An even smaller proportion of the authorized artillery was mounted, and much of it was obsolete or broken. Compounding the danger, most forts were manned by caretaker detachments of a few dozen men who spent their time on repairs. Many soldiers had received little or no instruction on how to fire their (usually obsolete) cannons if enemy warships ever appeared. Despite this obvious dysfunction, the 3rd System's advocates insisted it was the only viable means of national defense. Their answer to any criticism was more funding, more forts, more guns, and more personnel.[62]

Although dramatically changed by the acquisition of new territory, the army's frontier duties after the Mexican–American War remained unchanged from the Calhoun era. Officers still served as diplomats, peacemakers, surveyors, road-builders, contractors, and in myriad other functions. A year before the war there were barely a dozen forts on the frontier; a decade later there were fifty spread across 2 million square miles, most of them inaccessible except by animal transport. Only two of these posts held more than 500 soldiers, the majority less than half that many. Scott acerbically noted in 1849 that the Regular Army could hardly be termed a "peace establishment" when 80 percent of it was "under threats of hostilities, in a state of constant activity or alert on our Indian borders."[63]

Despite the commitment to frontier constabulary duties, postwar doctrine remained predicated on "modern" or Western European warfare. Two works published in the immediate aftermath are indicative of this. Henry W. Halleck's opus *Elements of Military Science* (1846) outlined the best practices of European armies and warned of relying on ignorant political leaders and "disorganized and frantic masses" of untrained soldiers.[64] West Point professor Dennis Hart Mahan's book *Advanced-Guard* (1847) shared Halleck's admiration for European military practices but provided guidance for company commanders on detached duty. Among line officers there was a consensus that heroic leadership, experience, and mentoring by seniors was sufficient for the frontier. In many respects such ad hoc methods were all that was possible given the wide variations from area to area. Officers stationed for multiyear tours in the Southwest might develop tactics effective against border brigands and Navajo warriors that would have been disastrous against the Comanche or Mormon insurgents. But perhaps the greatest inhibitor to doctrinal coherence was the postwar army's success in keeping both Native American and settler violence at an acceptable level, at least by contemporary standards. With some reason, military intellectuals preferred to envision a large-scale conventional war against a hypothetical European opponent rather than the frontier irregulars that engaged their service.[65]

The Mexican–American War had little direct impact on the officer corps. The war confirmed the cherished lesson of the War of 1812: any regular officer was better than his civilian counterparts, especially political appointees. Certainly West Pointers, who represented three-quarters of the officer corps, provided a level of administrative and tactical competence that had been sorely lacking in 1812. But almost all graduates served at the lower field or company grade under seniors who were often relics of a bygone era. Among many contenders, the Adjutant General noted one officer commissioned almost a half-century earlier, another who had been convalescing for a decade, and a third who "cannot walk or ride[] and has not performed a day's duty for seven years."[66] If anything, the senior leadership when the Civil War broke out was even older and rustier. In the decade prior to that war, whether in coastal fortifications or on the border, officers were usually confined to humdrum details: supervising a few dozen soldiers, dealing with excessive paperwork, and spending a great deal of time socializing, hunting, and drinking. Even more than after the War of 1812, the bureaus pulled officers out of line units at a prodigious rate. Two years after peace with Mexico almost a third of the officer corps were on staff assignments.[67]

The enlisted force, with the possible exception of the frontier cavalry, also reflected the decisions made after the War of 1812. Recruited from urban centers in the Northeast, it was made up largely of the unskilled, immigrants, and those whose employment prospects were even less than the army's offer of three meals, a shared bunk, and a payday debauch. A foreign observer was so struck by the contrast between the appearance of American citizens and the "sluggish and impassive physiognomy" of the rankers that he deduced they were "infected with some moral infirmity, which renders them unfit for a useful and laborious life." Fortunately, "the greater part of these troops live entirely beyond American society."[68] The inability to retain soldiers past their first enlistment, coupled with desertion rates that often topped 20 percent, resulted in a perpetually new, untrained force with few experienced noncoms. One regiment lost over half its 500 recruits within a year.[69]

Some progressive-minded reformers wanted to overturn the post-1815 recruitment process and revolutionize the officer–enlisted relationship. New technology, new tactics, and new methods of training required intelligent, motivated troops. As one reformer declaimed: "Let us have no more mechanical, wooden-headed soldiers, fit food for powder, but let the mentality, the manhood of rank and file to be roused and trained, so that if soldiers are to continue as machines, they shall be rational, conscious instruments of precision."[70] Such idealism was lost on colleagues, who wanted little more from their rankers than obedience, drilling, and manual labor.

Within US Army mythology the decade after the Civil War became *the* postwar era—the one later generations harkened to in times of isolation, public indifference, and penury. It was mythologized as the service's "Dark Ages," a prolonged twilight of the "Old Army" out of which emerged the professionalizing renaissance in the 1880s.[71] Later scholarship largely demolished many of these myths, demonstrating how the Regular Army was neither isolated nor apolitical. And despite the unprecedented size and scope of the Civil War, the aftermath army was not radically different than the organization that existed before the conflict. Despite the apparent changes in the service in terms of size and the challenges of the frontier and Reconstruction, in most respects the army's cycle of post–Civil War recovery paralleled that after the War of 1812.

In the context of the Civil War, the first and most manifest similarity to previous aftermath armies was the immediate and drastic drawdown of personnel. Within a year after the 1865 Confederate surrender at Appomattox, the Union Army had shrunk from 1 million to 80,000. For over a year the status of the peacetime establishment remained in limbo; thousands of volunteers were kept in involuntary service in the former Confederacy, on the Mexico border, or in the West. The cycle of a large increase in the immediate postwar era followed by steep cuts shortly afterward reemerged. In 1866 the Act to Fix and Increase the Military Peace Establishment authorized forty-five infantry (four composed of invalids), five artillery, and ten cavalry regiments. Together with the bureau personnel, this represented a potential standing army of 55,000, or almost three times the prewar army, confirming the pattern of postwar armies larger than their predecessors. One significant change was the addition of four regiments of Black soldiers, but this was less due to any effort to uplift them than an unwilling recognition of the high rate of desertion—approaching 20 percent—in the white units.[72] As was also the pattern, congressional delays and budget-paring, a lack of recruits, and desertion kept actual strength under 40,000. Regiments, commanders, and troops were broken up, reorganized, and shifted around with little regard for morale or efficiency. Five years after war's end there were almost 200 posts, of which barely half had garrisons of more than a hundred soldiers. In July 1870, following what was already a common pattern, Congress ordered further reductions to 30,000 enlisted men and cut officer strength by 13 percent. As in later wars, the US Army emerged believing it been the nation's savior, only to find in the aftermath that in many ways it was one of the war's losers.[73]

The Civil War, as with previous wars, had been fought with a mixture of regulars and volunteers. But whereas the Mexican–American War had been decided predominantly by regulars, the Civil War was almost entirely a citizen-soldier conflict. Congress increased the regular establishment by only nine infantry, one cavalry, and one artillery regiments—perhaps 3 percent of the US Army's total strength—and these were segregated in a few brigades in the Army of the Potomac. Union soldiers, particularly those who served in the western theater, might never have seen a regular unit. Although the regular regiments performed well in the war's early years, by war's end some companies consisted of only a dozen or so soldiers. Small wonder that many volunteers dismissed the standing army's contribution to the Union victory. It is also small wonder that they segregated themselves— patriots, responsible members of the community, citizens—from the lower-class roughs that made up the career rank and file.[74]

As in previous wars, relations between volunteer and regular officers were often fraught. At the request of state political leaders many career officers were transferred to command volunteer regiments. Some proved exceptional: both Emory Upton and George A. Custer rose from lieutenants to brevet major generals. But the gap between them and their troops could approach a chasm: Custer was never forgiven after he executed a citizen-soldier for a minor infraction. Regulars routinely denigrated volunteer officers and selected West Pointers for choice assignments. And while the career officers had cause to damn inept politicians-turned-generals, their outrage when outsiders questioned the competence of one of their own, particularly George B. McClellan, reflected more caste allegiance than professional military judgment. The leadership of Ulysses S. Grant and William T. Sherman, both of whom reentered the army due to their political connections, dispelled some of this sentiment, but enough rancor lingered after the war to weaken the service's popular appeal.[75]

The service's reputation among civilians was tarnished further by the demobilization of over a million troops. The War Department had done little to prepare, and the result was a catalogue of "delays, waste, individual injustices, mass confusion, and the penalties of improvisation."[76] Unfortunately, all these failings—and many more—would be inflicted on the veterans of subsequent wars, leaving a legacy of bitterness that would greatly hamper postwar army efforts to gain popular support. In part because of their uneasy relationship with citizen-soldiers, career officers also failed to build a powerful veterans lobby. The Grand Army of the Republic was a political force for decades, but regulars were a conspicuous minority. Pensions, a nonissue to professionals, dominated volunteer veterans' concerns. Veterans were routinely elected to high public office, but the long list of governors, congressmen, senators, and even presidents that extended into the twentieth century included few regulars.

Upton and his colleagues might extol the Regular Army's contribution in print, but others, such as John A. Logan, hailed the citizen-soldier and assailed the Military Academy as a breeder of aristocrats. Even issues that both regulars and the veterans lobby agreed on, such as military instruction in colleges, floundered because regulars and volunteers took opposite positions on who should be in charge.[77] The contentious relations between volunteers and career officers was a major weakness in the postwar era. Generals such as Grant, Sherman, and Philip Sheridan were treated as national treasures, but their popularity did not translate into political or financial support for the standing army. The service faced unremitting criticism from Democrats, and military appropriations were a constant battle even after the end of Reconstruction.

The Civil War reinforced the primary lesson that the regulars had derived from their earlier wars: they were the unrecognized architects of the nation's victory. On the battlefield it had been the professionals who, despite the meddling of political appointees, had imposed discipline and order on the nation's armies. But for most postwar officers the lessons of the recent war were intensely personnel, almost to the exclusion of everything else. Who deserved credit for captured cannons? Which regiment had held the line or fled in panic? Who had been first to carry the flag into the enemy trenches? These and other burning questions were fought over in newspapers, magazines, and books. As more and more veterans published their memoirs, those who felt their honor slighted were compelled to respond, often precipitating a new round of accusations and denials. Both individually and cumulatively the postwar battle of the books not only damaged the army's reputation with the public; it contributed to the toxic internal politics of the service. It would take nearly two decades after Appomattox before the service would have sufficient distance to begin an impartial, scholarly analysis of campaigns and commanders.[78]

Unable to agree on the war's strategic lessons, the army had almost as much trouble agreeing on the smaller ones. The 1867 infantry tactics were the inspiration of Upton, who posthumously would be lauded as perhaps the postwar Regular Army's most influential thinker. Whereas prewar tactics had been little more than plagiarized French manuals, Upton intended to create a distinctly American way of fighting. Perhaps revealing his own experience with cautious, micromanaging commanders, his tactics decentralized authority, placing far more emphasis on junior officers' initiative. Conservatives argued they were too decentralized and too unwieldy, perhaps a reflection of the Civil War veterans' experience of fighting in lines they could observe and control. Progressives argued they were not decentralized enough and failed to acknowledge the increased firepower of breechloading rifles. But Upton's primary error—one repeated by later tactical manuals— was his assumption that the officers and soldiers who executed his system would be well-trained, tightly disciplined regulars in complete, war-strength units.[79]

The decade after the Civil War saw the army return to its historic peacetime missions of coastal defense, internal peacekeeping, and frontier campaigns against Native Americans. And as with previous eras, the postwar commitments were far greater than those before the conflict. Sheridan missed the triumphal victory march in Washington because he and 52,000 soldiers were deploying to Texas as a show of force against the French-supported monarchy in Mexico. In the West the US Army, which had all but ceded military operations to locally raised volunteers, faced Native American resistance from Texas to the Dakotas. In the former Confederacy, the victorious Union troops waited, their objectives being the topic of increasingly vitriolic debate between the president and Congress. Almost forgotten, the masonry casemates of the 3rd System had failed against modern artillery, and the coastal defense community was desperately seeking a new solution.

The most controversial and unpopular new mission was Reconstruction. As Union armies moved into the Confederacy they had assumed governing powers, and at war's end they inherited a broken society.

Civilian resistance, both passive and violent, was the most obvious problem, but so was the destruction of transportation, agriculture, and industry. In many areas public order had broken down and brigands, deserters, and local political-military chiefs were in control. Congress, both to circumvent President Andrew Johnson and for lack of options, placed the army in charge of Reconstruction in 1867. But Congress never provided sufficient resources, particularly in personnel, to give the great experiment a real chance of success. Occupation duties in the South involved up to 40 percent of regular personnel, still less than 20,000 soldiers scattered in 134 posts to control 8 million Southerners. Compounding the problem, dozens of officers were detached from their units to serve in the Freedman's Bureau, to assist state governments, or to rebuild infrastructure. By 1870 much of the military effort was turned toward protecting Blacks from white terrorists. Although increasing numbers of troops were withdrawn for frontier duty, occupation duties still tied up one soldier in six as late as 1876.

Most senior commanders disliked occupation duty intensely and viewed it as an ill-conceived, poorly managed civilian initiative best avoided. An army historian summarized Reconstruction in barely a page as "the most distasteful employment which ever falls to the lot of military men—interference in civil affairs."[80] Yet the very year the last troops were withdrawn, they were deployed in another, quelling the Great Strike of 1877. Instead of pursuing Ku Klux Klan terrorists and protecting Black citizens, the regulars would spend many of the next twenty years putting down strikers, a duty that further embittered working-class Americans against the standing army, especially its officers.[81]

The Regular Army returned to the Western frontier in 1866 to find affairs both different and similar. The regulars, including the newly formed Black regiments, were drawn into traditional peacekeeping duties that involved finding and suppressing Indians, recalcitrant Confederates, and brigands smuggling guns, horses, and liquor.[82] Although portrayed later with much romance in western novels and movies, these post–Civil War conflicts were regarded by contemporary officers as a temporary aberration. They did provide a few officers with both reputation and promotion, but they entailed extraordinary physical hardship, isolation, and danger. In the nearly 1,000 engagements between soldiers and Native Americans, most between 1865 and 1898, the US Army lost only 919 killed in action—over a quarter of them in 1876 at the Battle of the Little Big Horn. Such large-scale engagements were rare and wars seldom won by glorious cavalry charges; rather success was achieved by maintaining troops in the field in all seasons, destroying shelters and livestock, and rounding up the starving. And as in the past, these wars often pitted Native Americans against tribal opponents. Few people then or now realize that the Battle of the Little Big Horn was fought on Crow tribal land, that the Crow leaders had petitioned for US Army help to evict encroaching tribes, and that the Crows who participated in the battle were with the US Army.[83]

One significant casualty of the Civil War had been the 3rd System of harbor fortifications. Not only had the vulnerability of its sacrosanct masonry casemate forts been exposed; the Corps of Engineers had lost its decades-long institutional preeminence to field generals such as Grant and Sherman. Immediately after the war's conclusion Congress authorized a series of joint army–navy boards to study the nation's vulnerability to maritime attack, but none of their suggestions were adopted. In contrast to its prewar largesse, Congress devoted little attention or funding to harbor protection. The five regiments of artillery were scattered in small detachments, caretaking decaying forts armed with obsolete cast-iron cannons that were as dangerous to their ill-trained crews as to any enemy. Not until the late 1880s would artillerists design a defensive system and guns with the potential to defeat modern warships.[84]

In many respects the post–Civil War decade replicated the patterns of earlier aftermath forces. The surrender of Confederate forces was followed by an immediate reduction in officers so chaotic that the exact personnel numbers are still unknown. After taking eighteen months to decide, Congress in 1866 established a Regular Army officer corps of 2,835, a threefold increase from the prewar corps. The size of this postwar "hump" was astounding: of 3,598 officers commissioned between 1865 and 1898 over 40 percent (1,530) entered between 1865 and 1867, and of these 1,360 came from the volunteer ranks, almost all of whom entered as company-grade lieutenants and captains. Military Academy graduates, who had made up three-quarters of the prewar officer corps, would soon resume their monopoly on new commissions. But with West Point producing only a few dozen second lieutenants each year, only in the 1890s did its graduates approach equality with the hump generation. Although this change in officer backgrounds was shocking to contemporaries, particularly West Pointers, in fact the composition of the post–Civil War officer corps strongly resembled that after the War of 1812. And as with the officer corps following the War of 1812, many were insubordinate to superiors, tyrannical to subordinates, and quarrelsome with peers.[85]

The Civil War also disrupted, if only temporarily, the cherished seniority system. Sheridan entered the Civil War as a junior captain of thirty; he emerged at thirty-four as a major general. He served in this rank for the next thirty-four years while his classmates waited years to make captain. Such rapid promotions for favored individuals came at the cost of much resentment from other regulars, many with exceptional war records, who reverted to their prewar ranks. Even more embittering than obvious line-cutting was a widely held belief (not entirely mistaken) that the postwar service was riddled with careerism, mentor–client networks, and politicking. One of the most successful intriguers was Arthur MacArthur. A seventeen-year-old lieutenant in 1862, MacArthur two years later was the US Army's youngest volunteer lieutenant colonel. Commissioned a captain in the infantry in 1866, MacArthur's stuffy personality masked a flair for scheming, insubordination, and manipulating the system that ultimately secured his transfer to the Adjutant General's bureau. When the war with Spain broke out, MacArthur's connections secured his promotion to brigadier general, where he outranked his former infantry comrades despite not having been in troop command for a decade.[86]

One frontier officer described his brother officers as "an aristocracy of merit, intellect, honor, integrity, and loyalty," and Samuel P. Huntington solidified this image in an influential study arguing that this aristocracy, isolated from the corrupting influences of Gilded Age society and politics, became a profession.[87] Historians have since undercut much of this narrative. Far from isolated, officers traveled and read extensively, were immersed in social and business activities, and cultivated political favors. The thirst for respectability and social recognition was probably even stronger in the former volunteers, since West Pointers were members of the elite simply by having a college education. The rigid caste line was immediately enforced, with officers and enlisted having virtually no interaction except through noncommissioned officer intermediaries. With the 1871 troop reductions, an infantry company's three officers might have to supervise perhaps forty soldiers in their daily drill and work details. With such minimal responsibilities, staving off boredom was a significant challenge. Social life on the post often compensated with "hops" (dances) and dinners, singing and dramatic events, hunting, reading novels, and other activities. For some that was not enough, and they succumbed to depression, gambling, alcohol, and absenteeism.

This generation of the officer corps was also similar to the post–War of 1812 officer corps in its propensity for feuds, cliques, and personality clashes. Officers might claim to belong to a band of brothers, but fratri-cide was common. Sheridan pursued those who had incurred his wrath for decades after the Civil War, one victim saved only when his former commander became president. With limited opportunities for fame and promotion, frontier officers eagerly competed for assignments and were furious if they lost. Nelson A. Miles, firmly in the Sherman/ Sheridan camp, was notorious for his intrigues against rival frontier commanders such as Ranald S. Mackenzie. Both were such competent and charismatic leaders that their regiments—Miles's 5th Infantry and Mackenzie's 4th Cavalry—were seen as extensions of themselves. In contrast, the infighting in Custer's 7th Cavalry Regiment was a signifi-cant contributor to the disaster at Little Big Horn. Although he was referring to political interference, Upton's comment that "there is no peace for the army except in time of war" applied equally to the social relations of the officer corps.[88]

Upton's own tenure as commandant of cadets at the Military Acad-emy (1870–1875) found no peace even there. The institution, convinced that it had produced the winning generals and deeply embittered by those who had fought for the Confederacy, remained committed to an outdated curriculum that emphasized mathematics, rote learning, and rigid subordination. In a major shift from the priorities of the post–War of 1812 establishment, Congress in 1866 removed the school from the Corps of Engineers and placed it under direct command of the secretary of war. If this was intended as reform, it failed: in 1869 West Point's Board of Visitors delivered a scathing commentary on the low quality of the applicants and the school's academic decline.[89] One graduate described his instructors as aloof, uninterested in either their subjects or their students, and mediocre: "The cadets generally disliked them, lampooned them in private, and gave them credit for nothing."[90] Typical of its aging faculty was Dennis Hart Mahan, who, when one veteran pointed out the army had long abandoned his cher-ished Napoleonic tactics, shouted: "I don't care what you did or what you saw during the Civil War, you stick to the text!"[91] With stultifying ritual passing as teaching, it is small wonder that the cadets took mat-ters into their own hands, and "deviling" (hazing) and rioting seemed to have been as much a part of their education as the classroom.

To some, the Military Academy's small size and limited curricu-lum, together with the influx of hundreds of volunteer officers lacking formal military schooling, required a revision of the school system. Some, impressed by the recent success of Prussia, wanted to adopt its progressive system of officer education, culminating in a war college for strategists. But senior officers were far more concerned with company officers who lacked basic training in their administrative and tactical responsibilities. The reestablishment of the Artillery School at Fort Monroe in 1866 typified the course of postwar education. Although Upton sought to broaden officers' perspectives with lectures on strategy, military operations, and command, the majority of the curriculum was practical. Officers learned to improve their gunnery in conformance with regulations, not to think of new ways to mass and direct firepower. A similar remedial school for infantry and cavalry junior officers was founded in 1881 at Fort Leavenworth. Because of its later importance as a center of intellectual thought, it is tempting to see this as a major step on the path to the alleged renaissance of the 1880s. But for most of its first decade this School of Application would be referred to as a "kindergarten" where regiments dumped their most unproductive officers.[92]

For enlisted personnel the decade after the Civil War marked a return to the status quo antebellum—and not in a good way. Neither Congress, nor the public, nor the army were much concerned with improving the soldier's lot. In 1867, for example, the War Department mandated that each post establish a school to teach the troopers basic literacy. But the Quartermaster's Bureau skirted this by declaring it would not authorize construction on any post deemed temporary, a qualification that included nearly every frontier garrison. Even had these schools been built, it is likely they would have remained empty, since most officers were vociferous in declaring that learning only ruined men for soldiering. Although some Civil War veterans liked military life enough to reenlist, the postwar force, like the prewar force, was soon composed of the unemployed, immigrants, and others who lacked alternatives. The army provided them with minimal housing, badly prepared food, indifferent medical care, exhaustive workloads, and thirteen dollars each month.[93]

The combination of insufficient resources and too many missions stretched the enlisted ranks almost to breaking. Military training was minimal beyond basic formations, many of them ceremonial. The soldiers, almost entirely drawn from urban centers, were taught how to march and salute at the recruit depot and then shipped to their regiments. For most of the decade they wore Civil War surplus uniforms that were often poorly made and ill-suited for their duties. The army shoes were notorious for falling apart—but not before they had crippled their wearers. Many soldiers, at least initially, were equipped with war-surplus weapons inferior to those of their opponents. It would not be until 1872 that the army decided on the postwar weapons—the breechloading Springfield rifle and carbine—that were rugged, accurate, and effective. Even when they received modern rifles, soldiers seldom trained for war with them and almost never practiced marksmanship. The cavalry, supposedly the frontier's elite, were restricted to forty rounds for practice per year and often lacked the funding for even this minimal qualification. Horsemanship was equally ignored. When the supposedly crack 7th Cavalry Regiment embarked on the fateful campaign against the Sioux, some troopers had not been in uniform long enough to manage their horses or weapons.[94]

The officer corps' life of leisure was built on having access to a large supply of menial labor, so much so that Col. William B. Hazen suggested soldiers be recruited by the "simple common-sense rules which every good business man applies when he employs a servant."[95] And by the officer corps' inverted logic, their very freedom from physical work confirmed their superior status. John Bourke was something of an exception when he pitied "the poor wretch who enlisted under the vague notion that his admiring country needed to quell hostile Indians, suddenly finds himself a brevet architect, carrying a hod and doing odd jobs."[96] Bourke was correct about a soldier's incessant work details to maintain posts that were poorly constructed and exposed to horrific weather. Congressional parsimony, along with general supply chain difficulties, meant there was seldom recourse to any but military laborers. Adding insult to injury, soldiers were often detailed for nonmilitary assignments such as building roads or public buildings.[97] They also tended the officers' gardens, groomed the horses, built and moved furniture, served as babysitters, and performed myriad other unsoldierly and unpaid menial duties.

As with the post–War of 1812 army, soldiers in the decade after the Civil War protested their servitude. And as before, all overt or perceived resistance was punished swiftly and ruthlessly. Courts-martial ran constantly, and in some years the equivalent of half the enlisted ranks were put on trial—and inevitably found guilty. For minor infractions soldiers might have to march for hours in full kit with their rucksack loaded with fifty pounds of rocks, or stand on a barrel exposed to the elements, or be put on night guard for weeks. Prisoners were shackled to a heavy iron ball, a process so painful that the comrades claimed they could hear the screams miles away.

Many rankers didn't fight the system; they simply deserted. They took the attitude that an enlistment was a contract, and if the army violated the terms of labor and living conditions they were justified in seeking another employer. In 1867 over 17 percent tried to escape, a figure that remained relatively consistent until 1872 before declining to 7 percent. The response of the officer corps could be ferocious: Custer opened fire on fugitives, killing one and denying medical treatment to the wounded. He was tried and suspended, but the court concluded his actions were not criminal. Since repression failed, the army declared an amnesty for deserters in 1873, but this had little effect on retention. Indeed, none of the army's solutions prevented soldiers from fleeing; only economic downturns, as occurred in the 1890s, kept troops in uniform.[98]

Imagine a young lieutenant standing duty a decade after the Civil War visited by the ghosts of two other postwar predecessors, one a decade past the War of 1812 and the other a decade after the Mexican–American War. The spectral visitors might have been impressed at the growth of military personnel—25,500 officers and rankers—compared to 6,000 in 1825 and 17,600 in 1848. The ghosts would be both amazed and proud at the extent of territory their service now covered, and they would be appalled that the nation's sectional divisions had escalated to civil war. But very soon after commenting on changes in uniforms, drills, and equipment, these officers would soon find the similarities of their experiences outweighing their differences. With few explanations they would all recognize the composition of the postwar army: the West Point junior officers; the war-relic "hump" blocking advancement above them; the tough but often semicompetent sergeants; and the transitory immigrants and urban unskilled labor in the enlisted ranks. All would share their frustration with the War Department, the constant demands to fill out—in some cases nearly identical—forms and requisitions, and Washington's habit of disapproving them for the most trivial reasons. They would complain of the glacial promotion system but take some comfort that seniority would guarantee them at least a captain's epaulets by the time they reached fifty. They might trade stories of West Point and be either amused or appalled at how little the curriculum—and with only slight exaggeration the faculty—had altered. All could swap stories of assignments as engineers, negotiators, surveyors, construction supervisors, lawyers, and in myriad other roles tangentially related to preparing for war. They would have similar memories of the isolation and deprivation of frontier duty, of skeleton tactical units, of constant labor details to maintain their one-company post, of camaraderie and social events. Were they at a decaying coastal fortification, the oldest ghost might nod and comment how "that roof leaked when we built it," a second that it had leaked back when he served, and the other that it still did. As his two ghostly friends left, the lieutenant would probably shake his head and ponder at the eternal certainties of postwar soldiering in the US Army.

Postscript to the Imperial Wars

From the vantage of almost half a century, William Lassiter reflected on the peacetime army he had joined in the 1890s. A young man "devoid of any particular object or aim in life," he had no ambition to be a soldier, but the free education at the United States Military Academy inspired him to accept his congressman's appointment. His initiation to West Point "was very much like being hurled suddenly from a group of very loving and admiring relations and friends into a den of lions." His mathematical ability secured him a commission as second lieutenant in the artillery, a combat arm that should have been busy transforming itself for the recently approved massive coastal defense program. But it remained in "suspended animation" under aging Civil War veterans, "the great majority of who still lived in that period." The "light" field artillery batteries' annual live-fire training "consisted in putting a cloth target on one hill and the guns on another hill, 1200 or 1500 yards away, firing a shot, getting a report as to where it hit and then firing another shot, and so on. No thought of tactics, no thought of what the enemy might be doing while you were thus engaged." Those assigned to the "heavy" harbor defense artillery "kept their antiquated guns well painted," practiced putting them on and taking them off carriages endlessly, but fired them only once a year. His own battery was housed in a crumbling stone fort originally built as a refuge from a potential slave revolt; its entire armament was an ancient 12-pounder cannon restricted to firing salutes. Not surprisingly, when in April 1898 the nation went to war with Spain, "confusion reigned supreme" throughout the army, "and in the midst of that confusion our battery was soon to find itself."[1]

When Lassiter and his comrades later referred to the "Old Army," they were being both literal and figurative. Its senior ranks, almost all field grades, and many captains were Civil War veterans. Like the turn-of-the-century middle class to which it belonged, the officer corps' culture and professional identity were in flux. Despite the efforts of later analysts, officers at the turn of the century could not be typecast easily as reformers or reactionaries, intellectuals or warriors, Indian fighters or modern warfare advocates. Perhaps the most contentious issue was whether the army could create leaders by schooling rather than by experience. Whatever their vision of the army's future, far too many found their duties limited to the routines of drill, administration, supervising fatigue (work) details, and social events. The enlisted force was far more static and had much in common with the one a decade after the War of 1812. Budget conscious during peacetime, Congress for two decades had capped its strength at 25,000. Although pay remained unchanged throughout the 1890s—a first-enlistment private earned $13 a month—the lot of many rankers improved. The army closed some of its more desolate posts, built better quarters, created programs for athletics and education, improved medical treatment, issued better clothing and equipment, allowed the sale of beer in post canteens, and otherwise improved the soldiers' lives. Their tailored uniforms, snappy close-order drill, and physical hardiness made for an impressive parade-ground display. Many, both civilians and military, would confuse such martial spectacle with effectiveness in war.[2]

The comfortable routines of post–Civil War Old Army were shattered when President William McKinley reluctantly asked Congress to declare war against Spain on 25 April 1898, initiating over four years of conflict. The crusade to free Cuba ultimately sent soldiers to locales as far as China, transforming a small home defense force into the military arm of a global power. These military adventures and their ensuing controversies—the legacy of a permanent empire—combined with a Progressive Era search for efficiency, provoked what one historian termed "a transition that amounted almost to a revolution within the United States Army."[3] Looking back from a perspective informed by future conflicts, historians and defense analysts assumed a direct cause-and-effect relationship in which the postwar decade "provided the foundation for American victory in two world wars."[4]

McKinley's military opportunism soon laid bare the limitations of both the War Department and the Regular Army. His 4 May decision to send an expedition to the Philippines, and soon demanding the immediate commencement of land operations in Cuba, required shipping most of the mobile units in the Regular Army overseas. Fired up by patriotism and a burning desire to prove themselves the worthy descendants of Civil War heroes, 125,000 volunteers enlisted to fight Spain within six weeks. They poured into hastily organized and soon pestilential training facilities: almost nine times as many soldiers would die of disease as enemy bullets between May and December 1898. Although a presidential commission and subsequent historical scholarship would attest to the War Department's rapid adaptation and improvement, its reputation was so damaged that even conservatives demanded its reform. As this fiasco was unfolding, the Regular Army line regiments, still at peacetime strength, were frantically trying to fill their depleted ranks. From the V Corps' concentration at the inadequate port of Tampa to the return of its fevered survivors, the Cuban expedition continuously teetered on disaster.[5]

For decades ambitious, talented officers trapped by the post–Civil War "hump" in line regiments had transferred to the administrative and technical bureaus where pay, promotion, and postings were far better. When war loomed, the politically connected, such as Arthur MacArthur, pulled strings for assignments in combat commands, superseding long-serving regimental officers while at the same time stripping the bureaus of their top management. "Among the acts of army officers" one victim of such careerism declared, "perhaps none were considered by the army to be more reprehensible than this."[6] His peers clearly agreed, awarding his essay a silver medal.

The imperial wars soon revealed that, while the superannuated Old Army officers were individually heroic, collectively they lacked rudimentary competence in large-unit logistics, planning, coordinating infantry and artillery, deploying their forces on the battlefield, and other skills befitting their rank. One rehearsed his battalion in the manual of arms while exposed to withering enemy fire; another fell leading a bayonet charge; a colonel died waving a flag to rally his troops; and a major general was shot down as he strolled along the firing line dressed in a bright yellow raincoat. During the charge up San Juan Heights, John Bigelow observed that the troops "advanced without any command that I know of, and the men commenced firing of their own accord." When Bigelow suggested a senior officer exert some control, that officer "replied to the effect that we could not halt them, and that they might as well keep a-going."[7]

The VIII Corps' expedition to the Philippines went far more smoothly, at least initially, and it occupied Manila on 13 August. But like many of America's quick victory campaigns, it proved easier to conquer than occupy. Emilio Aguinaldo, the self-proclaimed president of the Philippine Republic, held together an uneasy military alliance in the Manila region. McKinley believed that his "benevolent assimilation" policies would win over the Filipinos. The hopes of both men were thwarted on 4 February 1899 when a violent encounter between two patrols touched off a series of battles that secured American control of Manila and inflicted catastrophic casualties on Aguinaldo's army. Over the summer of 1899 the army recruited to fill up the hollowed ranks of its regular units and, more significantly, raised 35,000 United States Volunteers. Breaking with seniority, these volunteer regiments were commanded by some of the Regular Army's best younger officers who were carefully selected by Adj. Gen. Henry C. Corbin, McKinley's de facto chief of staff. When the American offensive resumed in the fall it quickly smashed the remaining nationalist forces, drove Aguinaldo into mountain exile, and occupied most of the archipelago's municipalities. But law and order did not necessarily follow occupation: in roughly half the provinces a vicious, internecine struggle for local control pitted nationalists, sectarians, bandits, and other irregulars against Americans and their ever-increasing Filipino auxiliaries. Although most provinces were declared pacified by mid-1901, resistance continued in a handful of areas for another year. On 4 July 1902 President Theodore Roosevelt officially proclaimed the "insurrection" in the Philippines over and instructed the army to support the new colonial government.[8]

The Regular Army drew conflicting lessons from the imperial wars of 1898–1902. The familiar unpreparedness narrative was automatic: the nation went to war with "no army, no supplies" and had, as in the past, reacted with "plenty of hasty legislation, prodigal appropriations of money, abundant egotism, and Yankee confidence in our ability to thrash anything or anybody. None nor all of these could furnish the three or four good infantry corps we needed so badly."[9] Matthew Forney Steele's 1910 textbook *American Campaigns* decried the "chaos and confusion" of the mobilization against Spain but concluded that "the whole blame rests upon the military policy of our Government."[10] Very soon after the Philippine War's termination, discussion on the guerrilla war and its lessons had evaporated. Perhaps that war's most immediate legacy was the career officers who had commanded the volunteers and who recognized the possibilities of rapidly mobilizing and training citizen-soldiers for war.[11]

The five years after the declaration of war against Spain witnessed the most extensive administrative reforms since the aftermath of the War of 1812. When Elihu Root became secretary of war in August 1899 his agency was in a state of siege. Rumors of Spanish fleets descending on the Atlantic Coast had spurred demands to complete the new coast defense system. Public outrage over the War Department's alleged mismanagement and callousness during the war with Spain was still at a fever pitch. The military government in Cuba had accomplished much in the way of law and order, roads, and schools. Another source of optimism was the Philippines, where commanders would soon report the complete destruction of Aguinaldo's army. However, as later American armies would discover, battlefield victory—even the collapse of the opposition government and flight of its political leader—did not mark the end of the war but rather the beginning of a new and far more difficult phase. McKinley had appointed Root to repair the problems within the War Department and the army exposed by the war against Spain. The new secretary would have to adjust his policies constantly to meet the demands of the Philippines and the new American empire.

Although he lacked military experience, Root's expertise in corporate law and political infighting, combined with his Progressive Era instincts, made him a natural ally of army reformers primed for sweeping postwar changes. He quickly identified and empowered a cadre of officers, most notably William Harding Carter, who provided Root, the lawyer-turned-secretary, with practical guidance on force structure, mission, education, and so forth. Yet impressive as their vaunted accomplishments are, Carter and his fellow military crusaders wanted an army unburdened by what they saw as the cardinal failings in the old one, the pre-1898 army they had served in as juniors. Their agenda was influenced by the Progressive Era, but its intellectual foundations were predicated on the past, so much so that their "bible" was Emory Upton's *The Military Policy of the United States*, an 1881 manuscript that they convinced Root to publish. Given their background, it is not surprising that in the immediate aftermath of 1898 the reformers' agenda was directed at decades-old concerns such as coast defense, increasing personnel, a general staff, officer education, reforming the War Department administration, and establishing a federal reserve force to support the Regular Army in time of war. But having accomplished the majority of these goals within five years of the war with Spain, the reformers faced many new problems emerging in part from empire-building and in part from consequences of their own reforms. The army they envisioned in 1899 was not the one they had by 1912. They were, in J. P. Clark's insightful description, "old soldiers in a new army."[12]

Root's first report to Congress in November 1899 outlined the scope of his ambitions. He declared that the nation's historic military policy had created a force "very sufficient for police duty against Indians" but lacking "effective organization and training" for its "real object . . . to provide for war."[13] He did not have to remind Congress that this police force had proved barely sufficient to defeat a decrepit imperial power, and then only with much confusion and near-criminal administrative blundering. But he did remind them that in barely eighteen months the army must shrink to its prewar strength of 28,000, far too few to man the coast defenses or maintain order in the newly acquired overseas territories. He proposed reorganizing the service on fundamental principles: (1) The purpose of the Regular Army was to prepare for a major war with a Great Power; and (2) in any major conflict, the Regular Army would provide leadership for a much larger citizen-soldier wartime army. To implement the first principle, officers required peacetime education and career assignments that prepared them for wartime duties. The field forces must be increased and provided with modern weapons and realistic training, especially in large-scale maneuvers that would replicate combat conditions. Despite the opposition of many regulars, Root recognized that his second principle required accepting the notion that the National Guard was the Constitution's "regulated militia."

In his almost five-year tenure, Root laid the administrative foundation for implementing these two principles. The February 1901 Army Reorganization Act increased the authorized postwar military establishment from 1898's 28,000 to a maximum of 100,000. And although Congress did not fund the full amount, it still approved a standing army of 3,253 officers and 76,000 enlisted, tripling the prewar number. In 1903 the Militia Act established the National Guard as the nation's primary reserve force and authorized the distribution of weapons, funded monthly practice and summer training, provided regular advisers, and left open the possibility of service overseas. That same year, Congress reorganized the War Department's bureaucracy to provide a permanent advisory and planning agency—the General Staff—to the secretary of war. Root reinvigorated the coastal defense program, though some of his initiatives, such as combining the coast and field artillery, proved failures. However, despite his injunction that the purpose of the Regular Army was to prepare for war, Root was a corporate administrator, not a strategist. Although he increased the size of the army, in terms of force structure the service was still configured in its nineteenth-century role of border constabulary and harbor defense. The secretary's legacy was a bigger, more efficient, and more modern army, though not one with a clear vision of where, when, or how it would be committed to war. Perhaps most curious, neither Root nor his military supporters gave sufficient thought to how the modernization of the army might be affected by the new military commitments thousands of miles away. The empire, which was perhaps the greatest single justification for the post-1898 reforms, would often prove their captor.

Even at their birth, the secretary of war's reforms were hailed as a renaissance, stamped as the time when the old army gave way to the new. The era is still held up as the model for successful institutional reform for subsequent recovering armies encountering what appear to be similar postwar problems. In part this was because Root and his military coterie were adept at public relations, promoting their goals by cultivating editors, writing articles, and giving numerous speeches. There was some meat on the bones. Within the War Department there were monumental changes: the replacement of the commanding general with a chief of staff to advise the Secretary of War on the state of the service, a staff to advise the new chief, and a war college to educate strategic leaders. Yet it is important not to confuse, as too many have, legislation with results.

One of Root's most anticipated postwar reforms, the General Staff, endured a tumultuous first decade of existence. The first three Chiefs of Staff were complacent Civil War veterans, but even active chiefs such as J. Franklin Bell (1906–1910) and Leonard Wood (1910–1914) often failed to provide clear and consistent direction. The General Staff's composition proved both unwieldy and ineffective, it had to be entirely reorganized within a decade. The 1st Division was charged with studying doctrine and training for the combat arms, mobilization, and organization. The Military Information Division dealt with foreign armed forces and maps of possible areas of conflict. The third element, the Army War College, had responsibility for war plans, joint operations, coastal defense, and the rather vague subject of "technical questions." Few General Staff members arrived prepared for high-level strategic planning, and one officer commented that the primary qualification for appointment, rather than merit, was being a general's aide or, in the case of Douglas MacArthur, a general's son. And in a damning summation of the much-praised postwar educational system, George C. Marshall recalled that, although the army had three schools to qualify officers for General Staff duty, at the outbreak of World War I almost half currently on duty had not graduated from a single one.[14]

It is no surprise that the General Staff was a lightning rod for criticism given the vagueness of its authority, its diverse responsibilities, its inability to create a rational selection process, and the animosity of conservatives. Both internal and external critics charged that staff officers, instead of following Root's directives "to investigate and report upon all questions affecting the efficiency of the Army and state of preparation," frittered away their time on trivial subjects.[15] Evidence of such ephemera was provided by Johnson Hagood's challenge to Chief of Staff Wood to read a hundred staff papers at random and determine how many were useful. Wood could not find a single one. Wood probably needed little convincing; before he took office he was convinced "the General Staff is working on projects which in no way pertain to it and seems to be steadily losing ground in the War Department."[16]

Paradoxically, many of the General Staff's failings owed their origin to Secretary Root and internal disagreements within the reform movement. Unwilling to risk losing the position in a confrontation with Congress, he failed to clearly define the responsibilities of Chief of Staff and the heads of the administrative, technical, and supply bureaus. And the bureaus, having administered the army for over a century, used their extensive political connections to resist the authority of the Chief of Staff. In 1912 this exploded into a fratricidal contest between Wood and Adj. Gen. Fred C. Ainsworth. Ainsworth was forced to retire, but Congress retaliated by cutting the General Staff from forty-five to thirty-six officers. Although this was part of an effort to weaken Wood, Congress correctly saw the General Staff as an entrenched clique. In a revealing comment on who still held the reins of power, Eli Helmick, arriving at the Inspector General Department after Ainsworth's departure, recalled that the "Chief of Staff gave as much attention to petty details as to matters of real importance. To do business with him meant delay. The new Adjutant General, on the other hand, possessed a keen active mind, and any matter presented to him received prompt attention. Hence, the mass of the business went through the office of the Adjutant General."[17]

The Root-era changes were equally vexing outside the capital. Congress's February 1901 postwar increase in authorized manpower lasted less than two years. In October 1902 the army was ordered to reduce itself to the minimum allowed by law; by October 1903 it numbered only 3,681 officers and 55,500 enlisted, of whom almost 20 percent were overseas. So hollow were the stateside units that, in 1906, deploying a necessary 5,000-man expedition to Cuba "practically cleaned up all the available armed forces of the republic within the United States."[18] Neither was building an organized reserve for the Regular Army showing much progress. Its membership hovered between 105,000 and 120,000 in the decade after the Militia Act, and many soldiers and political leaders publicly questioned whether the Constitution allowed the militia to be deployed outside the nation's borders.[19]

The new imperial commitments in the Pacific were one of the primary drivers behind Root's reforms, but here again the secretary left an ambivalent legacy. For the decade after Roosevelt had declared peace in the Philippines, American and Filipino forces still battled Muslim tribes, religious sectarians, bandits, self-proclaimed revolutionaries, and other violent opposition. But if suppressing indigenous resistance was a return to nineteenth-century missions, protecting an empire thousands of miles from the metropole was radically new. In 1902 army planners had concluded the Philippines required 10,000 to 12,000 American soldiers, supported by between 5,000 and 10,000 Philippine Scouts for internal security. Drawing on the lesson of the last war, American planners feared a rival European imperial squadron would replicate the surprise naval attack on Manila that had served as McKinley's pretext to claim the entire archipelago. Drawing on the lessons of over a century of harbor defense, army engineers began construction of a network of fortifications on the islands at the mouth of Manila Bay. But five years later, Japanese-American relations had reached crisis levels. An Army War College exercise estimated that it would take less than a month for a Japanese invading force to defeat the garrison and occupy the capital. This dismal outlook darkened even further when an inspired officer demonstrated that the Manila Bay fortifications, however strong they were against a seaborne attack, could be quickly reduced by land-based artillery. The navy's response would be repeated for the next three decades: the army must defend Manila Bay to allow the navy access to an Asian fleet base—but the battle fleet could not be committed to relieve the garrison at Manila Bay, and in any circumstance would not arrive in Asian waters for two or three months. The army declined to force the issue, and in this both services collaborated, concealing the strategic impasse from the civilian superiors who might resolve them.[20]

The Philippines were only part of the army's postwar external defense priorities. The newly acquired protectorates of Hawaii and the Panama Canal also competed for scarce resources. As in the Philippines, as the strategic situation changed between 1900 and 1912, so did army estimates of how many troops were required. A 1903 a survey projected that 2,000 soldiers could protect Honolulu and Pearl Harbor; a decade later the Hawaiian garrison was over 7,000 and would almost double within four years. As the Pacific sucked up military personnel, so the Caribbean pulled them east. Theodore Roosevelt might boast he had taken Panama, but it was the army that had to garrison its harbor defenses and keep order. Between 1902 and 1912, imperial duties annually required between a quarter and a third of the army's personnel. Army strategists came to recognize that, whereas acquiring an empire took barely four years, the consequences presented a dilemma that defied resolution for decades.

At the same time it faced new overseas commitments, the army assumed new responsibilities for continental defense. Reports of phantom Spanish fleets and the ensuing public hysteria in 1898 had revived the moribund harbor defense program. In 1905 the nation paid privates $14 per month, but in the next decade it would spend over $140 million on construction and ordnance for fortifications. A single 12-inch gun cost $60,000 to manufacture and an almost equal amount to mount, and the cost of each shell was $440. Yet if Congress rushed to line the pockets of builders and steel manufactures, it was far less generous in allocating the manpower necessary to maintain them. The Coast Artillery Corps was so short of personnel, particularly technical specialists, that most harbor defenses were held by skeleton maintenance crews. And although the nation's harbors might bristle with guns, the land forces remained scattered and disorganized. In 1910 Chief of Staff Wood opined that any opponent who wished to capture an American port would disembark nearby and capture its fortifications from the rear long before the Regular Army and National Guard could mobilize.[21]

Root's declaration that the American army's purpose was to prepare for war was embraced by most officers, albeit with little consensus on either the nature of the next conflict or how to prepare for it. Given the vagueness of the threat, not surprisingly the new agencies he created focused more on organization than on strategy. Faced with a specific crisis, such as a war with Japan in 1907, the General Staff's Army War College Division quickly identified the most likely enemy actions and provided a realistic, if pessimistic, military response. But much of the War College's planning function was subsumed in its teaching responsibilities. Its strategic assessments were based on assigned worst-case scenarios so that, while confirming regular officers' conviction that the nation was dangerously unprepared, they often verged on the fantastic.[22]

In 1899 Root declared that the US Army's primary peacetime duty was to prepare for war, and by 1903, at least outwardly, he had apparently created the force structure, training facilities, and administrative staff to fulfill this mission. But the ensuring decade would reveal the army's dilemma in implementing Root's charge. One of the primary problems was what war to prepare for. Throughout the following decade military intellectuals spun apocalyptic visions of racial conflict, foreign invasion, and violent struggle between labor and capital. In a not untypical example, a 1908 article by Lt. Hugh S. Johnson pictured 200,000 Germans seizing New York and the Japanese overrunning the West Coast.[23] Alarmism aside, the nation's security situation had changed radically. The acquisition of the Philippines, Hawaii, and other territories had thrust the United States into global rivalries unforeseen by the Monroe Doctrine. The worst-case scenario was an Anglo-Japanese alliance that would threaten the nation on both coasts and require mobilizing a citizen-soldier army in the millions. The most likely eventuality was a Caribbean intervention or a border clash with Mexico, both of which would necessitate the immediate dispatch of small, mobile well-trained expeditionary forces. Further roiling the debate was the military impact of new technologies ranging from the machine gun to quick-firing artillery, developments that some feared rendered worthless the weapons issued only a few years ago. But one Civil War veteran (and former Chief of Staff) was skeptical: "I believe damned little of this aeroplane business. I don't believe aeroplanes are ever going to win a war. And I hold the same opinion of automobiles."[24]

The army's uncertainty about the nature of future war was reflected its tactical reforms for how it would fight. Aside from a brief postwar outpouring of articles on guerrilla warfare and jungle tactics, the Philippine experience was all but forgotten. Instead, like their European counterparts, military intellectuals studied the German Wars of Unification and the Russo-Japanese War for insights into what they termed "modern warfare." The 1905 *Field Service Regulations* (*FSR 1905*) emphasized that troops must maneuver in open order; flanking or enveloping attacks were preferable to frontal ones; and infantry-artillery coordination was crucial. The doctrine marked a victory for progressives in stressing that the "individual intelligence and courage" of soldiers must be encouraged so that they would be able to seek cover, aim accurately, and fight dispersed without the close supervision of their officers.[25] But *FRS 1905* was conservative in its appreciation of weaponry. It adapted to repeating long-range rifles, but it regulated the machine gun to an auxiliary weapon and stressed artillery's mobility rather than its lethality. More seriously, although *FRS 1905* accepted Root's argument that "the real object of having an Army is to provide for war," it assumed that the nation could quickly mobilize, train, and deploy millions of soldiers to implement its tactics.[26]

If the intellectual foundations of army tactics were flawed, their implementation in the postwar decade was equally problematic. In the immediate aftermath of the war, the service staged its first-ever peacetime maneuvers. In 1902 tactical exercises at Fort Riley brought together infantry, cavalry, and field artillery. A 1904 exercise concentrated over 25,000 troops in Virginia, the largest military force assembled since the Civil War. Supporters claimed these exercises were a great improvement over the small-unit parade-ground drill of prewar training and the sham battles and dress balls that had served for the militia. Officers gained valuable experience as commanders, instructors, and umpires, and guardsmen benefited not only from instruction in field craft and marksmanship but also from maneuvering as both small and large combat formations.[27]

As with other postwar reforms, both the realism and the scale of maneuvers diminished as martial enthusiasm waned and cost-cutting took precedence. In 1905 Congress stopped funding the exercises; when they resumed the next year they were on a much smaller scale and scattered across seven locations. In order to soothe National Guard sensitivities, maneuvers were retitled "camps of instruction," and umpires gave way to instructors. But as supportive regulars acknowledged, however great the commitment of its personnel, the guardsmens' obsolete equipment, high turnover, and inability to train beyond the company level made it impossible for its units to prepare for complex tactical problems. Indeed, even within the regulars there were problems integrating the combat arms, with further problems incorporating new communication technologies. The joint army–navy exercises to test the nation's land defense were even more fraught in part because both sides placed more emphasis on winning than cooperating. Military observers routinely complained that warships gallantly steamed along the seaboard basking in the admiration of the press and public, blithely ignoring the coastal batteries. Another hindrance to realism was a concealed political agenda. Chief of Staff Wood, for example, believed maneuvers were "the best way to impress upon the people the necessity for action . . . [by] demonstrat[ing] the facility with which an invading force can land and deliver successful attacks upon our seaboard cities."[28] Thus, Regular Army officers who viewed preparedness as a national emergency or who disliked the National Guard might also have been overly critical of any maneuver's positive results.

A final postwar mission hearkened back to Reconstruction: internal security. Army officers had no faith in the loyalty of the conquered Filipinos or the acquired Hawaiians. The "official" insurgents might have all surrendered by 1902, but the following decade witnessed endemic brigandage, regional and religious outbreaks, and the long pacification of "Moroland," the army-controlled, Muslim-majority southern Philippines. The army created indigenous military forces in the Philippines and Puerto Rico and a small National Guard in Hawaii but remained distrustful of their inhabitants. Manila's Military Information Division, particularly its Secret Service Section, kept itself and much of the army leadership in a perpetual panic by its self-generated rumors of Japanese agents suborning Filipino politicians, landing weapons, training secret armies, and otherwise preparing for the inevitable invasion. In Hawaii the presence of a majority Japanese-born population, many with military training, created similar foreboding. Arriving almost simultaneously with Oahu's permanent military garrison, intelligence personnel were charged with tracking the activities of putative spies, monitoring Japanese vessels, and infiltrating labor associations. Their methods and prejudices migrated back from the Pacific, encouraging a potentially dangerous military interest in internal security. Such racist alarmism all but ensured that the army would not look to indigenous populations to remedy its crippling overseas manpower deficiencies with local defense forces.[29]

One of the most urgent priorities of the postwar reforms had been making the officer corps an improvement over that of the Old Army. The compulsory schooling, more rigorous educational and physical standards, and examinations for promotion were examples of this effort to raise individual and collective quality. Where the army differed from similar efforts in civilian professions was its massive influx of new arrivals. The Old Army officer corps was literally shattered by combat, disease, mental strain, and age. Between 1890 and 1897 an average of thirty-five officers annually left the service due to death, disease, disability, or retirement; in 1901 alone over 600 died or were discharged, 238 for medical reasons. That year the commanding general in the Philippines reported a third of his officers were absent from their units, many because they were "breaking down."[30] This breakdown hit Civil War veterans the hardest, but many of the recent wars' most outstanding young combat commanders also were forced out of the service.

The Old Army officer corps was replaced by one very different than its predecessor. Four years after the end of the war with Spain, 1,818 of the army's 3,598 officers—and virtually all of the combat arms lieutenants (1,542)—held their commissions for less than four years. Only 276 of them were West Pointers. Two-thirds of the new entries were veterans of the war with Spain or the Philippine campaigns. The rest, such as George C. Marshall, entered through competitive examinations that were, as one successful applicant recalled, "trivial in scope but in thoroughness they were alarming."[31] This influx embittered many Old Army survivors who had patiently marked time under prewar seniority and felt insulted by what they construed as "the slight estimation in which observation and experience are now held."[32] They believed that the "Crime of 1901" had inundated their band of brothers with parvenus lacking military skills and military decorum. Such caste snobbery obscured a far more significant problem that emerged in the second half of the decade. As Wood noted in 1906, the real crime was commissioning men based on wartime valor rather than the education, the administrative and specialist skills, and the leadership needed for the peacetime force.[33]

In the immediate postwar period, the army's top priority was to professionalize and homogenize these new officers. Some of this was done informally by seniors, and some on the drill field, but the Root-era reformers placed their faith in military education. In 1901 the War Department consolidated the scattered service schools into a progressively demanding, competitive, merit-based system. All commissioned personnel would have to pass a basic curriculum on tactics, administration, and other practical subjects during the winter garrison schools. Line officers would then attend troop schools for instruction in company duties, materiel, and tactics. Those in the newly organized Artillery Corps would learn the technical intricacies of both field and harbor gunnery, mines, weapons technology, and so forth. Every year roughly fifty officers would be selected for the Infantry and Cavalry School at Fort Leavenworth. There they would be taught not only tactics and command but also the necessary professional skills of law, administration, and logistics. The top scorers would attend a second-year course at the Staff College to develop administrative and management skills for modern warfare. An elect of about a dozen would continue to the War College, where they would learn and apply planning for mobilization, operations, logistics, and strategy, thereby preventing the confusion and disorganization of 1898. The school system offered one of the few ways for officers to escape the ironclad law of seniority and rise on merit rather than rank. Marshall, for example, attended Leavenworth as a lieutenant and the War College as a junior captain.[34]

In theory this progressive education system ensured a professional officer corps at all levels of command. But implementing these reforms required the army to resolve a dilemma that many American academic institutions still wrestle with: Should its school system create an elite cadre, or provide sufficient schooling for the majority? The influx of hundreds of newly commissioned officers clearly required the latter. Had there been any doubt, the dismal classroom performance of many of these officers would have ended the discussion. Half the introductory class at Fort Leavenworth failed at least one entry-level exam, and those who remained endured what one historian identified as "a relatively advanced curriculum . . . thrust upon a student body littered with the army's most junior officers."[35]

As was true in past and subsequent postwar educational initiatives, the results were mixed. Busy with day-to-day problems, the General Staff provided insufficient coordination and supervision. Although education was supposed to be progressive, the curriculums were often repetitious or omitted essential subjects. A combination of lack of funding, bureaucratic lethargy, and insufficient personnel delayed the opening of the Field Artillery School until 1911, ensuring that many of its members sent to other schools lacked sufficient competence in their own specialty. A similar lack of supervision by the Infantry over its Musketry School ensured that students learned how to win shooting competitions but not how to mass firepower on the battlefield. The school's sole expert on machine guns was an enthusiastic junior lieutenant, and upon the reassignment of this "youthful crank" the school terminated all experiments with such "complicated engines."[36] Despite the problems that emerged in the years after Root's departure, his educational initiatives did succeed in two essential missions: By the outbreak of World War I they had provided a basic education to the new generation of postwar officers, and they created a small but competent cadre of command and staff officers to direct the war's mobilization, training, deployment, and operations.

Both the augmentation and the background of the postwar officer corps put the Military Academy on notice that its decades-long monopoly on commissions into the Regular Army was threatened. The challenge of competition with officers educated in civilian institutions pushed the school to change. During his 1898–1906 tenure at West Point, Superintendent Albert Mills introduced more militarily relevant subjects and reformed teaching methods; retention increased from 50 to 70 percent. But the longstanding predicament of reconciling West Point's twin missions—instilling both military character and providing an academic education—remained. The school's facilities were inadequate, a failing that became increasingly apparent in comparison to contemporary colleges. Successive cadets and administrators complained of incompetent, unqualified instructors—many tenured for decades—who relentlessly opposed any change to a pedagogy they believed had won the Civil War.[37]

More disturbing was the criticism that the school was failing to instill martial character and skills. One observer noted that few cadets, although they could shoulder their rifles with precision, met the minimum marksmanship standard. The validity of such criticism was manifested in a number of hazing scandals, public outrage, and congressional investigations that would culminate in a concerted effort to abolish the Academy. Smart cadets rapidly learned not to draw attention to themselves, to keep their mouths shut, and to conform. John C. H. "Court House" Lee, who graduated in 1909, described the secret of his success as not seeking academic merit but to "work at any chore that seemed to please the upper classmen."[38] Among such chores were inscribing dance cards, which earned promotion to corporal, and running an efficient kitchen, which secured him a sergeant's stripes. During World War II, Court House Lee's ability to cater to his superiors, self-indulgence, and rigorous enforcement of "chicken" discipline would make him among the GIs' most hated generals.

Whatever its academic and martial merits or demerits, the primary shortcoming of West Point was simply not providing enough officers for the new army. With a congressional allocation of 492 in 1902—and annual vacancy rates ranging from 10 to 25 percent and attrition rates of between 30 and 50 percent per class—the school annually graduated barely a hundred. Even with the 1910 allocation increased to 629, West Point was too small: in 1912, with 529 vacancies for incoming second lieutenant, West Pointers could fill only 177. With some reluctance, the service increased its efforts to commission college graduates.[39]

Almost as important as educating the postwar officers was socializing them. As it had been for almost a century, the primary fount of army traditions in line units was the regiment. In service lore this was a military family, with the colonel as patriarch, majors as uncles, and captains and lieutenants as older brothers—and their respective wives acting in similar roles. On a large post, all dined in the regimental mess or post club, in what one admirer termed "the social equality of gentlemen" held to strict rules limiting most conversation to sport, social events, and prestige.[40] Although its supporters lauded its role instilling pride and loyalty, regimental culture hampered the army's drive for professional identity. John McAuley Palmer recalled "how narrowly partisan were our loyalties in those days before World War I. We looked first to our regiment and then to our branch. We tended to think of ourselves as 15th Infantry or 6th Cavalry rather than as officers of the U.S. Army."[41] A darker view was provided by one anonymous correspondent: "It was consistent with being an officer and a gentleman to organize petty garrison rows, get drunk in the club, cultivate the old colonel's young wife, and beat up a Filipino—or water-cure him. It was not consistent therewith to steal from the company fund, appear drunk on parade, cultivate the sergeant's wife, or lay hands on a private."[42]

The problem of the postwar officer corps' quality paled beside the crisis of quantity, prompting one journal to headline a 1909 article "An Army without Officers."[43] In 1905 nearly one of every four officers in the line regiments was missing due to poor health, leave, or detached service. By 1909 it was two of every five, a figure that would not have been out of place in the post–War of 1812 or post–Civil War officer corps. Most of those absent—over 80 percent in some years—were lieutenants and captains.[44] Overseas commitments and the rigid rules of seniority made an already bad situation worse. In the first decade after peace had been declared in the Philippines, officers rotated with their regiments for overseas assignments. The costs, both financial and emotional, of having to pack, travel thousands of miles on uncomfortable and overcrowded transports, take up new quarters—and then repeat the process a few years or months later—traumatized individuals and families until the army stabilized overseas tours of duty in 1912.[45]

One of the service's most important postwar priorities was to attract and retain a sufficient number of high-quality officers for Root's new model army. But by many standards conditions for junior officers in the postwar army were as bad or worse than those endured by their Old Army predecessors. In the 1890s an optimistic second lieutenant could take a morbid satisfaction that within a few years the forced retirement of the hump of Civil War veterans in the senior captain to colonel levels would break open the floodgates. But the imperial wars created a new hump of lieutenants and captains and added a new layer of senior field officers. By 1910 their average age—fifty-two for majors and fifty-seven for lieutenant colonels—approximated that of the Old Army.[46] Behind them the hump marked time. One lieutenant noted that in 1901 he stood 2,333 on the Infantry branch's promotion list; eight years later he had advanced to 2,245.[47] By mid-decade a newly commissioned second lieutenant could count on spending five to seven years at that grade at a salary of $1,400, $600 less than a police lieutenant's in New York City. From this he would be expected to cover his mess bill, equipment, and the many uniforms required for various seasons and duties, as well as most of his biannual moving expenses.

If promoted to first lieutenant he could expect another ten to fifteen years at that grade, with but a $100 increase in salary for only the first five years. Not until he was in his mid-forties would he enjoy a captain's salary of $2,500, and he would not wear a colonel's eagles until shortly before retiring at sixty-four. In what was to become a common postwar phenomena, many resigned. Between 1902 and 1912 they left at sometimes four to five times the rate of the decade before, while vacancies at West Point reached unprecedented levels. In 1907, out of the authorized 1,006 second lieutenant slots 381 were vacant.[48]

The postimperial war army underwent a similarly difficult transition in embracing twentieth-century Progressive Era concepts of professionalism. Nineteenth-century officers had believed that leaders were born, not made. The ability to command was inherent in an individual's character and often revealed itself only on the battlefield. But at Leavenworth students were taught that responsible command or "safe leadership" derived from acquired knowledge of military art and science.[49] Their education provided the basis for regular officers to claim that they—and they alone—possessed the professional expertise necessary to lead the nation in war.

In practice, many Old Army survivors proved less than willing to accept their subordinates' professional qualifications. Junior officers complained of oversupervision and "fussiness": assuming "a multitude of responsibilities for minor details" and issuing "a multitude of petty orders of a harassing description and enforcing trivial regulations."[50] During the 1907 maneuvers an inspector found colonels who were supposed to be directing brigades attempting to control individual artillery batteries. Hunter Liggett noted that under such commanders their subordinates "were given no opportunity of exercising their initiative or of accustoming themselves to responsibility [and] became chronic buck passers as they grew older."[51]

Those who remained in the service had mixed experiences. In the first five years after being commissioned in 1903, Douglas MacArthur had a short tour in the Philippines, much of it in Manila, as well as an extended Far East junket with his family, a stint as Theodore Roosevelt's aide, and a comfortable stateside assignment close to his family. But despite rapid promotion to first lieutenant, he performed his military duties in such a lackadaisical manner that he twice received unsatisfactory evaluations. Had he been held to the standards of most junior officers and not those of a general's son, the Root reforms might well have put him before a board for dismissal. Only when he arrived to command an engineer company at Fort Leavenworth in 1908 did

MacArthur begin to demonstrate the promise he had shown as a top cadet at West Point. Within two years he had left troop duties and obtained an unmerited appointment to the General Staff. Other political connections secured him a brigadier generalship when the nation entered World War I. With no little irony, MacArthur's biographer titled this chapter "Important Friendships."[52]

George C. Marshall, commissioned in 1902, was immediately assigned tough infantry duty in the Philippines, slogging through mud and jungle to track down insurgents and bandits, weathering a cholera epidemic, and guarding the hard cases in the military prison. He was then sent to isolated Fort Reno, Oklahoma, and exposed to both the small-post emphasis on spit and polish and the rigors of mapping hundreds of miles of Texas desert in heat that sometimes topped 130 degrees. In 1907 he received his first significant career break when he was assigned to the Leavenworth course, graduating first in his class and being automatically selected for the next year's Staff College course. The difference between Marshall's hard field service and MacArthur's privileged posts illustrates both the vast variations in officers' careers and the variations in what constituted professionalism in the Root-era army.[53]

President Roosevelt was deeply involved in shaping the postwar corps, so much so that one satirical poem concluded "on all sides, deep yearning prayers arise. That you the army cease to Rooseveltize."[54] He brought to this task a number of prejudices shaped by his brief experience in the Spanish–American War and his progressive, elitist perspective. A man who personalized almost any issue, he took a special interest in "weeding out officers who were inefficient—professionally, physically, temperamentally, or through 'dry-rot'"—and promoting those he viewed as intelligent, active professionals.[55] One of his first initiatives was for combat arms officers to accompany their troops on marches, rides, field exercises, and encampments; any incapable of doing so were put on report. When this failed to spur enough officers to embrace the strenuous life, he ordered each officer tested twice a year, either by riding thirty miles a day for three days or hiking fifty miles in three days or twenty hours. One officer, commissioned in 1888, remarked that for the first time in his experience "we now have some colonels who have head and tail up and can mount a horse without standing on a wash tub."[56]

Roosevelt was equally determined to impose rigorous standards for professional competence. But the service's inability to retain sufficient junior officers, and the reluctance of promotion boards to terminate the careers of officers who had otherwise served faithfully, frustrated this initiative. In 1905 only eleven of the 346 officers failed the promotion exams for professional or ethical causes.[57] The results of such leniency, at least to reformers, was catastrophic: one major general fulminated that "officers utterly incompetent for the commands they exercise have clearly demonstrated their inefficiency, yet under existing regulations and interpretations thereof it has been found impossible to get rid of these officers."[58] More than a decade after Root's initial reform, his successor wanted to impose new standards to accelerate "getting rid of deadwood."[59] He had no more success than Root.

Even more polarizing than the removal of deadwood was the promotion of political favorites. This antipathy was so widespread that, when Roosevelt warned officers to stop politicking for advancement, the *Army and Navy Journal* noted tartly that he was the nation's worst offender.[60] In the new army, one officer complained, the one left out was "the poor devil without friends in Washington or who is not a good boot-licker."[61] William H. Carter ridiculed such charges. Root's reforms had banished the "widespread opinion that influence is more potent than trained talent and fitness" in advancing to the army's top ranks.[62] Yet Carter himself owed his general's stars to his cultivation of Root. And while few would dispute the promotion of J. Franklin Bell to general, what had John F. Weston done of any merit beyond assisting Roosevelt in Cuba? A civilian in 1898, Frederick Funston had captured Aguinaldo. But did that qualify him as a Regular Army brigadier general? What of Tasker H. Bliss, elevated from major to brigadier general for his work as a customs administrator but whose total troop time in his quarter-century career was barely three years? And was Capt. John J. Pershing's service as a colonial administrator sufficient to elevate him over 257 other captains, 364 majors, 131 lieutenant colonels, and 110 colonels to the rank of brigadier general? Or was it Pershing's marriage to the daughter of the Republican chairman of the Senate Military Affairs Committee?[63]

The most controversial of Roosevelt's appointees was his close friend Leonard Wood. Brilliant, charismatic, courageous, athletic, and a self-righteous opportunist, Wood entered the army in 1884 as a contract surgeon and never overcame a tendency to view both the service and its members as recalcitrant patients. Whereas most post–Civil War officers received a mediocre and terminal education at West Point and then marked time in routine garrison duty, Wood graduated from Harvard's medical school, won a Medal of Honor without hearing a shot fired in anger, read widely in military subjects, and became physician and confidant to President McKinley and other powerful Republicans. In 1898 Wood and Roosevelt parlayed their connections into command of the 1st Volunteer Cavalry Regiment, then pulled further strings to ensure their Rough Riders preferential treatment. Arriving in Cuba, Wood was promoted to acting brigadier general in the volunteers, but his martial reputation suffered when he became separated from his brigade—and perhaps lost—during the attack on San Juan Heights.

Wood's effectiveness as a colonial administrator in Cuba and ruthless elimination of rivals led to his unprecedented advancement from medical captain to a Regular Army brigadier general in 1901. Two years later, over fevered congressional and military opposition, Roosevelt pushed through Wood's promotion to major general; by the end of the decade he was Army Chief of Staff. Like the attitudes toward Roosevelt, Wood was either admired or despised; no one was neutral. Occasionally the depth of this animosity bubbled to the surface, most notably when a court-martial acquitted a captain against whom Wood had brought charges. The *Army and Navy Journal* concluded that, irrespective of the merits of the case, the verdict was "an expression of the belief of the members of the court that favoritism prevails to an improper extent in the conduct of our military affairs."[64] Certainly it was an indication that much of the factionalism and politicking of the late nineteenth-century Old Army was very much alive in the first decade of the new modern army of the twentieth.

The problematic reformation of the postwar officer corps had important implications for its relations both with the peacetime enlisted ranks and the citizen-soldier wartime army. Many Regular Army officers had a low opinion of citizen soldiers. They had no patience with the popular belief that every Americans was a natural warrior, a crack marksman, and an indomitable fighter. They brooded at the decline of the "Anglo-Saxon stock" and worried they would have to go to war with immigrants, illiterates, and perhaps even anarchists.[65] In their view, all soldiers, peacetime or wartime, must render "prompt, unquestioning and accurate obedience" and could be controlled only by fear of punishment.[66] Such attitudes were by no means restricted to Old Army traditionalists. Lt. Hugh M. Kelly typified a patronizing, paternalistic view held by some junior officers: "Soldiers are a peculiar breed. They are more nearly like children in certain characteristics than any other class of men. They are so used to be taken care of by their officers that they look to the latter for everything."[67] How Kelly and his fellow officers would have gained such psychological insight is difficult to determine. Between officers and rankers, "the Chinese Wall of rank is an impassible barrier," observed one veteran, and the soldier "is treated by his officers as though contact were contamination"[68] To another, "the attitude of the Southerner toward the Negro seems the only perfect comparison with the officer's attitude toward the soldier."[69]

The enlisted ranks of the recovering army were as tumultuous as that of the officer corps. Prior to the Spanish–American War the service required but 8,000 enlistments a year, and many of these had been filled by career soldiers signing up for another tour. By the time Roosevelt declared the Philippine War over, these old soldiers, and most of the wartime veterans, were long gone. In June 1902 there were 79,000 enlisted men in the army; a year later there were 64,600. But during this period almost 30,000 trained soldiers left the service due to all causes: 837 died; 13,276 upon expiration of their service; a significant number, 9,791, discharged due to courts-martial or disability; and over 5,000 deserted. As for the rookies who replaced these veterans, one chief of staff mordantly observed, "evidently the minimums of the standards for admission to the army had been closely observed, if not trespassed on."[70]

Compounding the problem was that in the postwar decade reenlistments plummeted. The vacancies most alarming were in the infantry (20 percent), since it bore the greatest burden of overseas service, and in the coast artillery (50 percent), since it was the first land-based line of continental defense. One infantry captain reported that his regiment's companies had but a single officer, a fraction of noncoms, and only 10 percent of troops adequately trained. Another regiment with an authorized strength of 1,200 could field barely 400 for a public ceremony, including a company that paraded with one officer and thirteen privates.[71] Although the infantry was the hit the hardest, the other combat arms were little better. In 1904 the 7th Cavalry Regiment maintained an average strength of 800, about 200 short of its peacetime authorization. But over the course of the year 131 privates and forty-seven noncommissioned officers finished their enlistments, another eighty-five troopers deserted, and 200 others were transferred, while only twenty-six privates and five noncommissioned officers reenlisted. When the regiment embarked for Manila almost two-thirds of its enlisted personnel were rookies. Ten years later the army's reenlistment rate was only 5,000, or roughly one out of every four.[72]

The four Black regiments were conspicuous exceptions to the army's retention problem, yet neither Root nor Roosevelt saw them as vital in the postwar force. Although two volunteer regiments had been among those raised for the Philippines, the postwar expansion of the Regular Army included no new Black regiments. This omission was not due to any failings of the troops. In contrast to the rest of the postwar army, Black soldiers seldom deserted and were known for their discipline, sobriety, and courage. Yet, if anything, over the course of the decade their position deteriorated. In 1906 a confused, violent outbreak involving Black soldiers in Brownsville, Texas, demonstrated that racism was not confined to American society at large. Lacking evidence—no soldier was found out of quarters and no rifles were missing—army investigators determined the soldiers' silence must be a conspiracy. The army ultimately dishonorably discharged 167 of them, and with much sanctimony Roosevelt upheld the decision. It would be sixty years before this miscarriage was reversed, by which time only two members were alive.[73]

The aftermath army's nadir may have been 1907, when the service barely enlisted 13,000 soldiers and was understrength by 19,000. Chief of Staff J. Franklin Bell compared his force with that of a decade earlier. In 1898 the army had been composed of experienced soldiers isolated from civilian society, tribally connected to their regiments, bossed by long-service sergeants, and led by officers with decades of company experience. Now it was winnowed by high turnover, its recruits were of poor quality, its officers were often absent or inexperienced, and its tactical units were skeletonized. Throughout the entire service there was profound demoralization, so that privates and generals agreed "conditions are growing steadily worse."[74]

Bell's solution was not to return to the army of 1898. In a 1906 lecture at Fort Leavenworth, he regaled officers with tales of that force's unrealistic training and lack of preparation for war. Today's officers should not blindly follow the routines of the past simply because they were told to by some "hide-bound military iconoclast who had not given cordial reception to a new idea in thirty years."[75] The general insisted that Old Army discipline intended to create "unreasoning automatons" and "servile submission" were no longer acceptable; "large businesses learned this long ago," he said, "and subordinates not gifted with intelligence, interest, and enterprise are promptly gotten rid of."[76] Bell had commanded a volunteer regiment in the Philippines, and the experience had convinced him that "the highest standard of individual intelligence which any army has ever reached is exemplified in the soldiers of the nation."[77] By implication, it was the army's and its officer corps' task to establish a command climate in which Americans wanted to serve.

The rebuilding of the enlisted ranks in the immediate postwar years was slowed by the absence of experienced and competent noncommissioned officers. Company commanders complained that the corporals' and junior sergeants' pay was so low, and their duties so onerous, that few intelligent or motivated privates sought to wear stripes—and few cared if they lost them. A further disincentive was the lack of job security. Until they reached the highest grade, sergeants retained their rank entirely at the discretion of their company commander. This lack of permanent tenure meant that when discharged they had to reenlist as privates and, unless signed back into their original company, lost not only their rank but also pay and privileges. Meanwhile, the outside world beckoned. A random study of sergeants discharged from line units found that most were making five to ten times more working as police, firemen, telegraph operators, shop foremen, or, most insulting of all, by enlisting in the National Guard. Given the miserable housing, restrictions on marriage, constant deployments overseas, caste-bound commanders, and rookie soldiers, it is not surprising many potential career soldiers shed their uniforms.[78]

Compounding the rebuilding of a noncommissioned cadre was the rapidly increasing importance of complex technology in the waging of modern war. For a century the US Army could get by with a few highly skilled enlisted specialists in the technical bureaus and a larger number of journeymen tradesmen such as blacksmiths, carpenters, masons, and farriers to build and maintain the posts. With this veneer of occupational skills, the army could fill the majority of its combat units with unskilled laborers. Although this came at some cost to small-unit efficiency, since a private often made more extra pay as a carpenter or farrier than as a corporal, it was sustainable. But with the arrival of more complex weapons systems, particularly the expensive and sophisticated artillery system for the coastal fortifications, the service required a new type of soldier, what one termed "the mechanical specialist."[79] Not only would the postwar army have to train those who operated the tools of modern war; it would have to ensure they remained in uniform.

As both military and civilian observers realized, the primary obstacle to retaining enlisted men, and thus stabilizing its career noncom cadre, was low pay. A 1907 General Staff study found that a private's monthly wages were less than a semiskilled worker received in a week. With postwar stinginess threatening the basic missions, Congress in 1908 passed legislation aimed at retaining the most skilled and experienced by classifying enlisted personnel into nine categories, with the top six being noncommissioned officers of various grades and skills. The pay structure was unbalanced: The most skilled technicians were paid more than line-unit sergeants, but the latter would receive bonuses for longevity, qualifications, and some overseas tours. In the new model army, the enlisted ranks' top grade included chief musicians, master electricians, and engineers and received $75 a month, followed by descending grades of sergeants, which bottomed out at $30 a month. Below them were corporals, blacksmiths, and tradesmen at $21 a month, privates first class at $16, and privates at $15. Retention was encouraged by a generous $3 a month bonus for each successive three-year reenlistment up to the seventh. At least initially, the pay increase was a success, prompting a reenlistment rate of 75 percent in 1909, dropping the desertion rate, and allowing the service to suspend recruiting for several months.[80]

As Root and other reformers hailed the creation of a modern army preparing for war, enlisted personnel still toiled as underpaid laborers much as their Old Army predecessors had. Brig. Gen. Frederick Funston observed that wannabe warriors soon found that, "from the standpoint of their post commanders, the most important part of their training consists of cutting brush and weeds."[81] Another officer confessed that an enlisted man devoted his time to "locate and build his posts, clean and beautify them, make gardens, streets, roads, walks and drives, transport supplies, and be carpenter, saddler, plumber, blacksmith, engineer, teamster, and what-not, to do all which means the neglect and outcrowding, often entirely, of that which is essentially and properly the work of soldiers, military preparation for war."[82] In a scathing 1912 editorial titled "Why We Have No Army," Wood claimed that on many posts half the daily chores were "unnecessary and useless from a military point of view" and that the nation had created less a military force than a contingent of "gardeners and watchmen."[83] In an effort to explain why so much soldiering was poorly paid labor, a War Department recruitment pamphlet rationalized that since a "military station is like any other community" it was just public service to maintain buildings, move goods and supplies, and perform other such tasks.[84] Soldiers were not impressed. With the nation suffering from an acute skilled labor shortage, every enlisted man knew that a better-paying job waited just outside his post.

The most embarrassing indication of postwar demoralization—what one journalist termed "the shame of our Army"—was skyrocketing desertion.[85] In the year prior to the war with Spain the desertion rate was less than 2 percent. Five years later it stood at over 10 percent and would not decline to under 5 percent until the end of the decade. In 1906 the army enlisted 15,486 recruits, and 3,190—or one in five—deserted within three years. The following year the equivalent of eight regiments of soldiers deserted.[86] This epidemic had its statistical anomalies. Educated, skilled recruits were four times more likely to flee, an ominous trend for a service that was becoming increasingly reliant on technical ability. Most enlisted men took off during the summer. Black units had a quarter of the desertions of white units. The field artillery, with the onerous and dangerous task of hauling heavy guns back and forth for training, always had a significantly higher rate than the infantry.[87]

There was disagreement over desertion's causes and cures. One survey of almost 300 field officers and noncoms found near-universal consensus that the primary reason was low pay.[88] But close behind was the conviction that postwar recruiters had placed a "careless, worthless lot of young men" in uniform.[89] This may have been true, but surely the shock of the harshness of soldiering and unfilled expectations contributed to the fact that three-quarters of desertions occurred in the first year of enlistment. This view was shared by many civilians who endorsed one journalist's portrayal of the typical soldier as an illiterate drunkard "brought up in a gutter" who "took on" (enlisted) to avoid starvation and jail.[90] Reflecting the anxieties of an increasingly urbanized, industrialized, and progressive nation, Sgt. Henry B. Sullivan opined that the underlying cause of desertion was "the early education of our recruit had been feminine, and feminism explains the marked and ingrained lawlessness, inefficiency, and instability of purpose, which characterizes so many of the recruits presented to the recruiting officer."[91]

The army's response to the rise in postwar desertion blended coercion and conciliation. In 1907 it mandated recruiters to do more investigation into each potential soldier's suitability and, under some circumstances, try to convince an individual to quit before induction. A year later it took a different tack and adopted the Bertillon system to deal with deserters, taking photographs and fingerprints of all soldiers, later distributing thousands of wanted circulars, increasing the reward for capture fivefold, and imposing a sentence of three years at hard labor upon conviction. But the failure of harsh penalties to stem desertion convinced Chief of Staff Wood that "the present method of handling these young men [is] fundamentally wrong, contrary to modern penology, and to the application of just and humane principles, and . . .

it is doing infinite harm to those brought under its influence."[92] In Wood's view, the army had moral responsibility to reclaim these lost soldiers, restore their self-respect, and make them productive citizens. Instead of confinement to primitive guardhouses, first-time deserters were segregated from criminals and placed in special companies that emphasized both citizenship and military skills, given vocational training and schooling, and then returned to duty. Wood's progressive methods increased retention rates, lowered dishonorable discharges, and improved morale to sustainable, if not acceptable, levels.[93]

Only slightly behind desertion as a source of demoralization among the enlisted was substance abuse, which one chaplain warned "had made of many hopeless mental, moral, and physical wrecks."[94] A 1903 report to the American Pharmaceutical Association claimed that many soldiers had become addicted in the Philippines but provided little evidence. It is probable some soldiers took opium either for recreation or to treat dysentery and could do so legally for several years. But officers did not view drugs as a problem. Indeed, most of the hysteria may owe more to the association's efforts to pass restrictive legislation—and secure for itself a monopoly on narcotic distribution—than any concern for enlisted personnel.[95]

If narcotic abuse was a nonissue, alcohol was a primary cause of disciplinary and health problems. Post and unit records are filled with incidents of fighting, insubordination, and other offenses caused by drunkenness. Many officers blamed a craven Congress, which on 2 February 1901 kowtowed to the prohibitionist lobby and banned the 1890s permission for post canteens to sell beer and wine. The temperance advocates, almost entirely civilian, claimed they were protecting the young and innocent from demon drink and debauchery. Their opponents, largely military, drew an immediate cause and effect between prohibition and an epidemic of intoxication, particularly in the Philippines during and after combat operations. They argued that the canteen had provided a healthy, safe environment, what one veteran described as the only place a soldier "can buy a glass of beer and forget he is a slave."[96] Having won the battle of the post canteen, prohibitionists marched off to impose their agenda on the nation, leaving the army to suffer the consequences. Soon every military post was surrounded by saloons where, according to the *North American Review*, soldiers were "drugged with vile liquors, they come under the spell of evil women, and the natural results follow."[97] One survey of officers and senior noncoms listed "the lack of canteen and resultant trouble in dives surrounding the post" among the top three causes for desertion.[98]

A study of 3,363 courts-martial dealing with the most serious military offenses found that 1,193 were alcohol-related.[99]

Alcohol abuse was an especially controversial issue in the Philippines. *Vino*, a potent spirit made of distilled palm sap, could be bought for a few cents outside any post. Its effects were immediate and usually dangerous, as it was often contaminated by methanol and other toxins. Commanders tried to ban *vino*, arresting bootleggers and putting saloons off-limits, but the civil government, whose hypocrisy matched stateside prohibitionists, overturned these decisions while piously decrying soldiers' public drunkenness. As Brig. Gen. Charles A. Woodruff explained, the "exiles" stationed in the Philippines had few options other than alcohol: bereft of "innocent, wholesome, decent recreation," the only places that provided "open doors and welcome" were "vino joints, gambling houses, [and] brothels."[100]

Woodruff's comments regarding soldiers, saloons, and brothels acknowledged a third pernicious postwar problem: a sexually transmitted disease rate that sometimes tripled that of the prewar force.[101] Recognizing both the public relations and health implications, Root in 1902 issued a general order warning that "venereal disease is almost sure to follow licentious living."[102] Such exhortations had so little effect that a decade later another secretary of war conceded that sexually transmitted disease "continues to be the reproach of the American Army."[103] From 1904 to 1911 the army's venereal disease rate only once slipped under 17 percent. In 1905 sexually transmitted diseases accounted for a sixth of all hospital admissions, a fifth of all medical discharges, and over a quarter of all soldiers unfit for duty at any time. Moreover, in this pre-antibiotic era, infected soldiers spent months in painful and debilitating treatment before they recovered. The War Department tried to curb venereal disease through exhortation by presidents and generals, graphic lectures, forfeiture of wages and rank, incarceration, courts-martial, and appeals to moral reform societies. None had any effect. Brothels flourished in most overseas territories, and stateside civic authorities turned a blind eye to establishments catering to soldiers.

Ultimately the army was forced to take a different tack. Perhaps reflecting Progressive Era medical opinion, army officers argued that abstinence might endanger the mental and physical health of sexually active men. Without public fanfare, in some locales, near red-light districts, commanders established dispensaries to administer an immediately effective, if excruciating, injected prophylactic. A soldier who could produce a "pro-shop" receipt and later developed an infection was held innocent, but the infected soldier who had no receipt was fined, reduced in rank, and lost all pay while under treatment. With the exception of the Manila garrisons, the army's improved medical procedures and its pragmatic, if somewhat amoral, approach to prostitution contributed to lowering venereal disease by half in 1913.[104]

Some officers believed the army's postwar personnel problems, in both quantity and quality, demanded radical solutions. They wanted a new army for a new century. At the heart of the debate was whether the army should return to its traditional emphasis on bringing the small peacetime establishment to maximum efficiency or instead serve as a training cadre for a mass citizen-soldier wartime force. To replace an army of lifetime privates sequestered in remote camps, the reformers wanted a short-service force whose graduates would return to civilian life with an education, a trade, and the character needed to be productive citizens. The service's reputation would soar as the public witnessed firsthand the benefits of military service. In the event of war, the nation could summon hundreds of thousands of trained soldiers who could, in turn, train the millions needed to achieve victory. In the years immediately before the American intervention in World War I, an alliance of military and civilian reformers would embrace this vision of the army as a laboratory, able to instill both martial and moral values and thereby improve not only its military efficiency but also the nation.[105]

Reformers might envision the army as the school of the nation, but in the postwar service education outside the technical branches was haphazard and dependent on command interest. Some larger posts offered classes for soldiers in the fundamentals of literacy and mathematics, but attendance was voluntary, restricted to off-duty hours, and required the permission of superiors, many of whom equated schooling with goldbricking. The service did better with vocational schools, teaching low-level practical skills such as cooking, clerking, and the construction needed to maintain posts. But for the most part, officers viewed their commitment to their soldiers' improvement as limited to teaching snappy drill, cleanliness, and obedience. It would take Congress, in the form of the National Defense Act of 1916, to compel the army to provide education and technical training to all enlisted men.[106]

Mirroring some twenty-first-century universities, the army had better success with athletics than education. Roosevelt was a physical fitness advocate, as was Wood, and they and other military progressives were determined to turn the American soldier into an "all-around man" and "human fighting machine."[107] West Point graduates exported not only its pioneering physical fitness program but also a more scientific approach to coaching baseball, football, boxing, and other competitive sports. Under pressure from powerful advocates inside and outside the service, and recognizing the seriousness of the morale and retention problems, the War Department began to construct firing ranges and gymnasiums on most posts; imposed a strenuous morning exercise program emphasizing endurance, strength, and agility; and ordered at least one day a week be given to sports.[108] The comparative youth of the aftermath army meant that officers as well as enlisted men were sports enthusiasts; as one advocate proclaimed, "a confident baseball player will be a confident soldier."[109] Cavalry regiments often formed demonstration teams that thrilled audiences with death-defying equestrian displays. Army field days became a fixture at many civilian fairs and expositions, with soldiers competing in recognized sports such as track and field and also in distinctly martial arts such as precision drill and bayonet fighting. The penultimate event in military athletics was the Army–Navy football game, and Roosevelt's attendance at this spectacle began a presidential tradition continuing to this day.[110]

Athletics aside, some officers saw signs of public disrespect everywhere, from state laws against soldiers voting to hotel doormen wearing generals' uniforms. Many were embittered by the role of correspondents, or the so-called yellow press, in initiating the war with Spain and exposing war crimes in the Philippines. To those who held to Old Army traditions, the only way to preserve the army's honor was complete segregation from the corrupting influence of commercialism, politics, and the press. But most officers recognized that, in an age of increasing literacy and public entertainment, the service could no longer isolate itself. Some sought to capitalize on the residue of war fever by publishing factual and fictional accounts of military operations in the tropics. But recounting wartime heroics attracted neither peacetime popular support nor the type of enlistments the new methods of warfare required. Throughout the postwar decade there was increasing discussion in the service's journals on how to mold public opinion.[111] Progressives argued the army had to market itself to its customers, just like any modern big business. But what was the message? Should it be, as one officer explained in 1902, that service life taught "manhood, straight, without squirming, dodging, whining, or playing baby"?[112] Should it be adventure and romance, an image highlighted in army-sponsored exhibitions, one of which drew over a million spectators in 1910?[113]

Instead of manliness or warrior skills, the institutional army increasingly emphasized the peacetime benefits of service life. Beginning in 1904 a series of War Department recruiting pamphlets extolled job security, steady pay, free housing and medical treatment, and savings programs that could bestow hundreds of dollars upon discharge. It promised that ambitious and skilled soldiers could leave the service not only with money but also certificates in a variety of trades that would guarantee quick and profitable civilian employment. And in a marked shift from its traditional distrust of the public, the pamphlet invited citizens to visit the local post, speak with the commanding officer, and see for themselves the good life soldiers were leading. Despite its efforts, the trade of soldiering remained a disreputable one in the eyes of most Americans. Of the 120,000 men seeking to enlist over a twelve-month period, only twenty-one stated they did so at the urging of friends or relations.[114]

A decade after Roosevelt's 1902 declaration of the end of hostilities in the Philippines, the Regular Army was still recovering from the imperial wars. Despite the declared intention of Secretary Root and his fellow reformers, few believed the army had the human or financial resources to prepare for war. At best the Root agenda was incomplete. In 1901 Congress had authorized a regular peacetime establishment of 90,000, and in 1912 the army was down only 8 percent below this at 83,000. But that increase represented an 8 percent growth since 1909 and a 50 percent increase since 1907.[115] Not only had the reformers failed to achieve the quantity of troops they believed the nation required; their efforts to also raise quality were at best mixed. The branch schools were educating company leaders; Leavenworth and the Army War College were graduating a small but highly skilled elite of staff officers. But the General Staff had not met its supporters' expectations, and many officers and political leaders viewed it as dysfunctional. In 1911 Chief of Staff Wood imposed a complete reorganization of its divisions and their responsibilities. He also designated four staff officers—among them William Lassiter and John McAuley Palmer—to draw up a clear statement of the nation's military policy and the army's role. Their *Report on the Organization of the Land Forces of the United States* was an impressive study and would influence military policy before, during, and after World War I.[116] But the fact that it had to be written at all was testimony to both the intellectual and practical limitations of the reforms under Root.

Some postwar officers believed the mission to create a modern army capable of waging Great Power warfare was a sacrifice to imperial defense. Each year the service had to commit 20 percent of its limited personnel to the new empire: 11,000 in the Philippines, 1,200 in China, 4,000 in Hawaii, 800 in the Canal Zone, another 2,000 in transit.[117] Those remaining in the continental United States were so skeletonized that in 1911 the secretary of war complained "we have scattered our Army over the country as if it were merely groups of local constabulary instead of a national organization," with the result that the army's ability to defend the nation against a "first-class power" were severely compromised.[118] That year the deployment of 13,000 soldiers for possible commitment to Mexico required three months and stripped virtually every line unit in the United States. And this commitment did not go away: a year later almost 7,000 regulars were still on border duty.[119] Unable to reconcile continental and overseas commitments, the War Department sacrificed the latter. Beginning with the Philippines garrisons in 1912, it halved the number of overseas regiments but increased their personnel to war strength. This allowed for a more stable rotation policy, but its initial result was that within two years the number of American troops in the Philippines had declined by almost a quarter. It is small wonder that officers remained pessimistic about their nation's preparations for defense or that war scenarios often featured successful attacks by Japanese or European opponents.[120]

The National Guard had been a crucial component of Root's plan for a mass citizen-soldier wartime army, and in 1908 Congress confirmed it could serve in both internal and external operations. But in 1912 it was in decline, with its numbers at a ten-year low of 112,000 and annually suffering a 40 percent turnover in its enlisted force. That year, with War Department support, the United States Attorney General ruled that the National Guard's federal responsibilities were limited to within the nation's borders. To replace the National Guard and provide for overseas service, Wood advocated creating a new federal reserve force, insisting that the army would need only six months to train its soldiers. Thus provoked, the National Guard retaliated both in the press and in Congress, and the fight over its overseas commitments would drag on for another four years. It was, in retrospect, an entirely unnecessary conflict that further confirmed the guard's view that the Regular Army was determined to create its own reserves and relegate the guard to acting as state police.[121]

Conditions in the field army remained unsettled. The officer corps was still less stable and perhaps less content than it had been before the war. As had occurred after the wars in the nineteenth century, absenteeism remained a chronic problem. In 1912 one in five officers was missing from his command; the actual figure was probably much higher, since many officers were still on the company rolls but serving on battalion or regimental staffs. There was little indication this problem would resolve itself and many indications it would not, with a third of the army's second lieutenancies vacant. Frustrated by the army's persistent inability to put officers in the field, Congress mandated that no combat arms captain or lieutenant could be assigned to detached duty unless he had spent two of the last six years with his regiment.[122]

Looking back from a perspective informed by World War I and subsequent military reform movements, scholars and soldiers have proclaimed the decade after the imperial wars as the foundations of the modern, professional US Army. They have downplayed—or simply ignored—the unpleasant truth that contemporary officers were unaware of these imminent conflicts. The tension between preparing for war, sustaining the empire, and maintaining a grossly insufficient force had brought Root's new model army to a near crisis. Most regulars were too busy dealing with the aftermath of the last war—personnel turbulence, demoralization, absenteeism, intermittent tactical training, deployments, and other such problems—to envision an army of four million fighting "the war to end all wars." Indeed, less than two years before the United States entered World War I, William Lassiter's diary described a typical day of real soldiering: "Not very much in the way of training now. Same old business . . . a little work in the morning. Golf, polo, tennis, riding in the hills in the afternoon. The Club at sunset. Dinner in the evening." Contrasting this "lazy man's paradise" with the titanic struggle that was tearing apart Europe, Lassiter concluded that "our Army hasn't begun to grasp the idea of preparing to work together as a whole in real serious business."[123]

3

The Aftermath Army in the Decade after World War I

Returning from service with the American Expeditionary Forces (AEF) following World War I, Maj. Gen. William Lassiter was dismayed at what he termed "the open or latent hostility toward the Regular Army." The aftermath of that war was indeed a bad time to be a professional officer. Veterans, particularly the emergency officers commissioned for the duration, castigated the Regular Army officers for their West Point cliquishness, disdain for citizen-soldiers, and rigid discipline. Politicians targeted the service to appease such diverse constituencies as isolationists, pacifists, states' rights proponents, and budget-cutters. The press, freed from wartime censorship, got busy exposing duplicitous allies, military inefficiency, and other scandals. In conversations with civilians, Lassiter found their understanding of the war restricted to the exploits of heroic sergeants. They were openly bored by his efforts to explain the enormity of the conflict, the complexity of military operations, and the army's success in recruiting, training, and sending millions of soldiers overseas. As for his homecoming, he concluded, "I can't say that [it] was a very rosy experience."[1]

Having lived through the martial enthusiasm of 1898, Lassiter had little patience with boomeranging popular sentiment: "Our people ought to realize that if they insist on having wars they must have professionals to lead them." When the war began in April 1917, his Field Artillery branch had only 275 officers and 5,253 rankers with more than one year's service. At war's end it had 22,393 officers and 440,000 soldiers.[2] Lassiter had gone to France as a major commanding a four-gun artillery battery and ended the war as a major general commanding some 28,000 soldiers in the National Guard's 32nd Infantry Division. Now, two years after first shipping off to Europe, Lassiter could see little future in wearing the uniform on behalf of such an ungrateful, ignorant nation. Only the opportunity to command a vocational training program in Kentucky persuaded him to stay. He soon found a calling helping soldiers learn not only mechanical trades but also scientific farming, and "when wearied of military problems, I would seek rest and peace among the cows and the chickens."[3] Deliberately turning his back on a career path to Chief of Staff, Lassiter soon became the army's fireman, shifted from one key command assignment to the next. In the process he would become one of the most astute observers of an era that may have represented the army's most difficult postwar recovery.

The interwar era (between the two world wars) generated extensive and controversial literature. To some, the period not only set the stage for World War II but also witnessed what is sometimes referred to as a "revolution in military affairs," with particular implications for current military policy. Important as this historical discussion is, it has often treated the force that existed between 1919 and 1929 not as a *postwar* army but as a *prewar* army. Almost inevitably, historians concentrate on individuals, doctrines, organizations, and weapons that proved decisive in the future conflict. But the choices, the prophets, and the mistakes so apparent in hindsight were far from clear to those serving in the ten years after World War I. From their perspective, the army was facing an existential crisis. Far from being ready for modern warfare, one officer commented that barely half a decade after the Armistice the force was "in about the same state as regards the effective strength of units as we were before the Spanish War."[4]

When Lassiter returned to the United States, the wartime army, in the words of one witness, "was fading away like a snowbank before an April shower."[5] At the declaration of war the total ground forces in the United States numbered under 300,000. By the Armistice on 11 November 1918 there were almost 4 million, half either overseas or in transit. The unexpected end of hostilities threw into reverse the immense federal apparatus for funneling troops into uniform. One authority declared that, if the government during the mobilization for war resembled an asylum for the insane, during the demobilization the inmates were running amok.[6] While President Woodrow Wilson alternately bloviated, dithered, or sulked, the War Department drifted. With typical fecklessness, Congress on 21 November mandated that, within four months, all citizen-soldiers drafted for the "emergency," as the war was now termed, must be discharged. It compounded its mistake by failing to authorize new enlistments; even those who wanted to continue in service could not remain. Within a year the veterans were gone and most soldiers were first-enlistment rookies. By 1921 the Regular Army had shrunk to 228,000, and four years later it stood at 134,000, where it would remain for the rest of the 1920s.[7] In the

immediate postwar administrative upheaval, rapid drawdown, and replacement of veterans with rookies, the post–World War I force was
treading a familiar path.

In July 1917 an American officer speaking for the first contingent of
14,000 soldiers recently arrived in France grandiloquently proclaimed
to enthusiastic Parisians: "Lafayette, we are here!" But it was another
ten months before the Americans could commit 4,000 doughboys into
battle. When the United States declared war in April 1917 the entire
Regular Army numbered only 121,000, and that was almost a 25 percent
increase since 1914. Yet at the September 1918 initiation of the Meuse–
Argonne Offensive, the US First Army alone mustered 600,000 soldiers. The War Department was now fully mobilized: in the fall of
1918 it conscripted tens of thousands of young men monthly, provided
them rudimentary training, organized them by occupation, and sent
them overseas. Lassiter concluded that the long wait was over: "The
AEF was just beginning to hit its stride. If, as everybody had expected
the war had gone on into 1919, we would have had the most formidable
army in Europe."[8] The immense and ultimately successful effort did
not obscure the war's most essential teaching: the nation could no longer afford to isolate itself from a predatory international order with a
token peacetime regular establishment. It must, as army officers had
been urging for decades, create not only a sufficiently large active force
to deter aggression and respond to emergencies but also an organized
reserve that could be mobilized for a million-man wartime force.

The Armistice halted the fighting. But was the war over? Or simply on hold? The AEF's commanding general, John J. Pershing, urged
continuing the offensive until Germany unconditionally surrendered.
Unless Germans witnessed Allied troops on their soil they would not
accept their armies' defeat, as the entrenched "stabbed in the back"
myth soon proved. But the Allies' political and military leaders could
not agree on whether to continue offensive action, and President
Wilson viewed the very suggestion as insubordinate. The AEF commander, his prescient advice spurned, turned his attention to sending
the Third Army to hold bridges on the Rhine River per one of the
Armistice's conditions. Just over the horizon was the possibility of
American soldiers having to rescue Europe from revolution. Germany
was in chaos: during the Armistice negotiations its delegates had requested Allied weapons to suppress insurgents. Wilson's muddled diplomacy had already sent 15,000 doughboys to Russia; clashes between
them and revolutionary forces were escalating.

Pershing was justifiably concerned about a resumption of hostilities—and perhaps even more worried that his doughboys would immediately turn to drinking, fighting, and fornicating. He recognized that maintaining the stern, righteous, all-American image created by the press and his staff—what some termed his "clique"—at AEF General Headquarters (GHQ) was critical. Beyond these immediate concerns, questions over the postwar army and the AEF's potential as a future trained peacetime reserve loomed. Far from the mud and danger of the trenches, ensconced in a comfortable chateau at Chaumont, Pershing and GHQ made a serious miscalculation: the AEF, they declared, faced a "critical situation" that could be remedied only by rigorous military exercises and rigid enforcement of all regulations, from morning roll calls to buttoned top collars.[9]

If what many combat officers dismissed as the "Chaumont Gang" believed they could impose compliance by either decree or punitive discipline, they were soon disabused. At a conference in Paris the participants, almost all war-commissioned (or emergency) officers cited a litany of grievances at West Pointers, the Regular Army, the promotion and decoration process, and especially GHQ bureaucrats, who they viewed as out of touch, interfering, careless with troops lives, and combat-averse.[10] Chaumont's strictures were resisted even more fiercely within the ranks. Doughboys believed that the last months had demonstrated their courage and martial skills. They had, in their parlance, "made the Kaiser dance," and they were in no mood to slog through the mud on long training marches, engage in exhausting combat exercises, and tolerate rear-echelon inspectors. Throughout the AEF there was a collective breakdown in authority, a sometimes cheerful, sometimes violent refusal to comply with orders, and an outbreak of "French leave" as tens of thousands went AWOL. There was an alarming rise in brawling, civil-military discord, and venereal disease. Perhaps most serious, the doughboys flooded the newspapers, as well as their families and political representatives, with complaints.[11]

Commanders in earlier wars had often inadvertently antagonized their troops, but Pershing was unique in learning just how angry his soldiers were. After extensive polling, the AEF's Morale branch reported that if GHQ did not act quickly to moderate training and reduce punishments, it would alienate millions of potential voters, with disastrous consequences for the postwar army. Overriding the spit-and-polish conservatives on his staff, Pershing abruptly switched tack. He curtailed the military exercises and authorized an extensive program of social reform including athletics, entertainment, travel, education, and other morale-building activities. Pershing's change of heart may have been prompted by common sense or by possible presidential ambitions, but much of the goodwill he and the army might have gained soon evaporated during the dehumanizing, demoralizing, and humiliating demobilization process. Suddenly and arbitrarily pulled out of their units, separated from their buddies, and then shipped in crowded and verminous railcars to desolate French ports, the doughboys marched into muddy fields under the hostile eyes of military police, feeling more like prisoners than victorious soldiers. Often they lived in decrepit tents and were used as common laborers while they waited, sometimes for months, for their transports to arrive. The misery was compounded by the horrors of the Spanish influenza epidemic, which killed thousands at the disembarking posts and millions across the globe, rekindling memories of the army's pestilential camps during the war with Spain two decades earlier.[12]

Demobilization also revealed a growing class—or, more accurately, caste—antagonism that spread from the top of the AEF on down. The son of a Missouri postman, Pershing was a self-made man who retained, in Lassiter's words "a certain crudity about him. Years of rubbing against the world had produced a polish, but the polish was not very deep."[13] Perhaps some sensitivity to his own roots encouraged the general's determination to subordinate doughboys and exalt the gentlemen status of officers. The general made caste distinction a daily reminder by ordering AEF officers to wear the Sam Browne belt, a sartorial relic for holding an officer's sword. That swords were inadequate as a means of self-defense, impediments for movement in the trenches, and a clear identifier—as was the belt itself—of officer status for enemy snipers was of far less importance than a snappy appearance. The term "Sam Browne" soon came to mean what "chickenshit" would to a later generation of warriors, and with the Armistice, those wearing the belt often were treated with open disrespect—or worse. On some transports, troops insisted that their officers throw the belts overboard; sometimes they held mock funerals and ceremoniously buried them at sea.[14]

Given the rigid emphasis on spit-and-polish protocol, antipathy for officers' privileges, and the collective humiliations of demobilization, many doughboys brought home an abiding resentment of the Regular Army, encapsulated in a short story about two AEF veterans. Barely disembarked stateside, they were confronted by a newly commissioned lieutenant who lectured them that "your overseas discipline may have been sloppy and lax, but now you're here you'll find out what it means to be a soldier!" One protagonist's final words—"Good Old Army! Good Old War! I wouldn't have missed it for ten thousand dollars, but I wouldn't reenlist for ten million!"—held ominous consequences for the postwar force.[15]

World War I left a largely inimical relationship between the Regular Army establishment and the National Guard, the heirs (at least in their view) of the wartime volunteers and militia of the previous century. With the declaration of war, Wilson called the National Guard into federal service; with a rush of volunteers, it mustered some 377,000 by the end of summer. But from the beginning, the War Department seemed to go out of its way to denigrate them as second-class soldiers. The AEF's four-regiment, two-brigade tactical organization required reconfiguring the three-regiment Guard divisions. In the process many proud militia units, some predating the Regular Army, were sacrificed, their soldiers scattered and their identities obliterated. Guard officers were summarily replaced by Regular Army officers, often at the very instant they were about to lead their troops into battle. Twice as many Guard officers as regulars served, but at war's end only twenty-five of the army's 403 generals were guardsmen. The War Department demobilized guardsmen as individuals, not units, thereby denying many a victory parade in their home states. The bitterness engendered by such treatment—at best insensitive and often contemptuous—long poisoned relations between regulars and national guardsmen. Three decades later, Guard veteran Harry S. Truman would still retain his war-induced suspicion and dislike of career officers—with momentous consequences for the next postwar army.[16]

The Regular Army also failed to build a strong veterans lobby among the millions of citizen-soldier doughboys. Both Wilson and Pershing supported the YMCA initiative Comrades in Service. But AEF veterans, many of whom believed the "damned Y" guilty of gouging, rejected Comrades in Service as a thinly disguised political lobby. Acting on their own authority, Theodore Roosevelt Jr. and a committee of emergency officers established the American Legion. This was so emphatically a citizen-soldier organization that only with difficulty could its founders block a motion to deny membership to regulars. The American Legion's spirit was captured in Roosevelt's 1919 memoir, *Average Americans*, which celebrated those who had fought for their country but satirized the professional soldiers' conservatism, lack of education, and passion for red tape. Throughout the 1920s the American Legion remained militantly anticommunist and championed "Americanism," patriotism, comradeship, benefits, and a strong national defense. But it was, above all, a veterans' interest group and had little concern for those soldiering in the peacetime force.[17]

As had occurred after earlier conflicts, military and political policy-makers emerged from the war determined to rectify what they viewed as the most serious failings. Also as had occurred earlier, there was consensus on the most pressing issues: the disorganization and lethargy of the General Staff; the lack of a mobilization base of organized reserves—especially officers—for expansion during war; developing new doctrine; assimilating new technologies, particularly the airplane; and so on. But very quickly, as John Gary Clifford recognized: "Army reorganization became caught up in the whirlpool of confusion and prejudice that seemed to characterize all public questions in 1919 and 1920."[18]

Given its alienation from both the Guard and many veterans, the Regular Army's ambitions for a large postwar establishment may have been doomed from the start. But its own leadership delivered the death-blow by failing to agree on a common agenda. The Washington-based War Department and its General Staff and Pershing and the GHQ in Chaumont interpreted the lessons of the recent conflict from their respective experiences—and with little sympathy for the others' problems. The War Department's great challenge had been to mobilize the nation's manpower, industrial potential, and public support to raise, train, equip, and deploy millions of soldiers. Its General Staff plan for a new model postwar force sought to prevent similar chaos in the next great conflict. It called for a peace establishment of a 500,000-man Regular Army, an equally large citizen-soldier reserve, and the organizational structure for immediate wartime service. The GHQ plan was more narrowly focused on creating an AEF equivalent in which the War Department, the General Staff, and, indeed, the nation itself would unhesitatingly meet the demands of the field commander.

These legitimate disagreements over postwar force structure were exacerbated by personal animosities and factionalism that would have done credit to the Old Army. Chief of Staff Peyton C. March was tactless and impatient. Pershing, no mean intriguer himself, was convinced March had not adequately supported him in France and now was actively engaged in relegating him to the sidelines. Thus, when the War Department asked Pershing to support its plan, he sent Col. John McAuley Palmer as his agent. On the face of it, Palmer was a logical choice. He was politically connected, had served on the prewar

General Staff, and was instrumental in drawing up both the 1912 *Report on the Organization of the Land Forces of the United States* and the 1916 National Defense Act. But Palmer, as even his sympathetic biographer conceded, also had an almost infinite "capacity for self-delusion when appraising the reaction of others to the views he put forward."[19] Lassiter, who knew and liked Palmer, recognized that his friend's "visionary impractical obsession as to a citizen army" made him a natural opponent of a large peacetime establishment.[20] Palmer's opposition to the General Staff plan so delighted the Senate subcommittee that they tasked him with helping draft legislation for the postwar force. The politicians acclaimed his exalted vision of a citizen-soldier short-service peacetime establishment but declined to legislate the budget, laws, or force structure that would have made it possible.

In offering two alternative plans, the generals tempted a Congress that, like the country as a whole, was eager to move on from war with an excellent excuse to ignore both. But a further complication was added in the person of Leonard Wood, who hated both Pershing and March for denying him a combat command in France. As the senior line general and the front-runner for the Republican presidential nomination in 1920, Wood was, in Walter Lippman's astute assessment, "a successful agitator with a following."[21] He quickly rallied his allies in the Military Training Camps Association and together they concocted an American military policy based on compulsory martial education for young American males, or Universal Military Training (UMT).

What finally emerged from Washington's tumultuous and toxic dealmaking was the National Defense Act of 4 June 1920. It authorized a peacetime standing army of approximately 300,000 and two citizen-soldier reserves: a 435,000-man National Guard, and an organized federal reserve of officers and enlisted men. Responding to a long-voiced complaint, it created chiefs of the respective combat branches, though it did not create an overall chief to ensure they worked together.[22] The defense act also created a war mobilization framework of nine corps as well as both active and reserve divisions, brigades, and so forth. In theory it would take only a few months for the nation to call to arms over 2 million trained, equipped, and organized soldiers. The Regular Army retained its century-old missions of continental defense and providing a readily deployable emergency force and its post-1898 mandate to protect the overseas possessions.

The most revolutionary aspect of the 1920 act was that it made training a citizen-soldier reserve the Regular Army's primary responsibility. It assumed (correctly) that the nation's next conflict would require a citizen-soldier army of millions and officers in the hundreds of thousands. From this, two consequences followed. The first was that the standing army's primary mission was to serve as the core of the wartime Army of the United States composed of the Regular Army, National Guard and Organized Reserves, and Selective Service conscripts. All other peacetime priorities—overseas defense, readiness, modernization—were secondary to ensuring the capacity to mobilize quickly. In the first years after the act's passage, the mantra of the citizen-soldier army was drummed into the regular officer corps. Speaking to the War College in 1923, Chief of Staff Pershing's aide, Lt. Col. George C. Marshall, prophesized that "if we fail in the development of a citizen army we will be impotent in the first year of war."[23] A year later, the *Infantry Journal* declared that professional officers must "think only of the American citizen who is to be a soldier in that Army and to prepare him in time of peace for his duties in war."[24] Some historians have seen this as a near-revolutionary shift: instead of its century-long mission of maintaining a small force in being for immediate deployment, the nation made the foundation of American defense policy the creation of a large citizen-soldier army. This may be correct when seen from a perspective informed by World War II and the 1950s draftee army, but few 1920s officers who endured the immediate consequences of this alleged revolution would have agreed.[25]

After the bruising fight for its acceptance, many officers were optimistic about the 1920 Defense Act. One army historian later termed it "the most comprehensive and suitable legislation ever made for the military service of the United States."[26] But a journalist, wiser to the ways of politicians, presciently observed that, should Congress fail to authorize the necessary personnel, equipment, and facilities, all that was left of the 1920 act was "a fine skeleton of an army."[27] He shared this insight with a War College audience in May 1922. A month later Congress reduced the Regular Army's authorized personnel to a 137,000-man cadaver—and not a particularly fine one.

The 1920 act also failed to resolve two significant issues that would continue to roil the postwar force. It did not resolve the thorny issue of institutional administration, particularly the responsibilities and powers of the General Staff. During the war, March had ruthlessly centralized power in the staff and crushed bureau opposition. But in the war's aftermath the bureaus asserted their traditional prerogatives in matters managerial and materiel. The branch chiefs proved equally zealous in defending their perceived bailiwick. Unless the Chief of

Staff was willing to step in and devote prestige and power to overriding bureau and branch obstructionism, the General Staff was often stymied. A second problem seemed endemic to the General Staff. When Pershing became Army Chief of Staff in 1920 it had already undergone two major and numerous minor reorganizations since its founding in 1903. Pershing undertook a third one along the lines of his AEF GHQ. Functions were concentrated in G-1 (personnel), G-2 (intelligence), G-3 (operations and training), G-4 (logistics), and the War Plans Division, whose duties included strategy and policy. But throughout the postwar period chiefs complained, as they had before the war, that the General Staff remained compartmentalized, slow, and too narrowly focused on a particular "G." When Douglas MacArthur became chief in 1930 he reorganized the General Staff once again, and his successors would find it necessary to make further modifications.[28]

If the General Staff's performance was essentially an inside Washington concern, that was not true of army aviation. Considering that aviation had been a tiny section of the Signal Corps when the war began, the 1920 act marked a giant step forward. Drawing on the AEF's experience, the Army Air Service became a separate combat branch with primary missions to provide aerial observation, bombardment, protection, and other support for ground forces. Such a subordinate role was anathema to enthusiasts such as William "Billy" Mitchell, who wanted what he termed an "air force" with the independent strategic mission of directly attacking enemy industries and cities. As with many advocates of military reform, Mitchell's agenda was a mix of idealism and ambition. As the most prominent and, in his view, sole authority on military aviation, he saw himself as the only choice to head this organization. When his erratic and insubordinate behavior rendered him toxic to civilian and military superiors, Mitchell's attacks on the "brass" escalated, and his visions became more and more apocalyptic. By 1923 he was convinced that war was imminent, the nation was in peril, and the United States was now responsible for "maintaining not only the political supremacy but also the very existence of the white race."[29] His constant drumbeat of criticism, combined with his flair for publicity, meant the army would have to defend, reform, and defend again its relationship with aviation.

While Washington concerned itself with postwar administrative matters, many in the field forces were experiencing the truth of Col. Sherman Miles's reminder in 1921 that "the aftermath of the last war has been almost as involved as the war itself. We were in the war a little over a year and a half, and we have so far spent rather more than two and a half years trying to clear ourselves of the wreckage."[30] Recent work by Dean A. Nowowiejski has shown that the success of the 1918–1923 American occupation of the Rhineland was in large measure due to the diplomatic skills of its commanders, particularly Maj. Gen. Henry T. Allen, and the friendliness and sympathy of the doughboys.[31] Allen restored discipline, improved training, and shipped troublemakers out while charming the population and maintaining American prestige in his dealings with the French and the British. A progressive, Allen implemented a number of social reform initiatives to allow soldiers ample opportunities for education, learning a trade, entertainment, and travel. Returnees often stated they would rather have stayed in Prohibition-free Germany. But they soon found the nation's attitudes much changed since Wilson's idealistic vision of America remaking the world. At their welcoming reception, the keynote speaker expressed his happiness that "the last strand of the rope of our military connection with the Old World and its affairs had been severed."[32]

The troops who had just returned from Russia might have heartily agreed. In one of Wilson's more misbegotten initiatives, he had overruled March, Pershing, and the General Staff and sent an infantry regiment under British command to Archangel in late 1918. Their mission ostensibly was to protect supplies, but they rapidly became involved in skirmishing with the Bolsheviks. Cut off, demoralized, and outnumbered, they were withdrawn in early 1920. Another occupation force in Siberia, ostensibly protecting the withdrawal of a Czech contingent, was soon trapped in a vicious regional civil war, with few positive results. Indeed, one officer concluded it was likely "we will be hated until the day they die by the Russian people for encouraging the traditional enemies of Russia to throttle the masses."[33] The Russian interventions confirmed the army's dislike of what a later generation would denigrate as "mission creep." From a perspective informed by a decade's distance, one officer summed up the army's view of Wilson's naïve intervention: "It was utterly puerile to suggest that any military force, however small, could go uninvited into a country in the throes of revolution and not become entangled in its 'internal affairs.'"[34]

The same officer might have noted that in the aftermath of war the Regular Army was also deeply involved in the internal affairs of its own country. Once committed to war, the Wilson administration mobilized the entire nation in a great crusade to crush Germany—and any domestic dissent as well. During this process, as its director, Marlborough Churchill, admitted, the Military Information Division (MID) became "a sort of military secret police" hunting down radicals, pacifists, union members, and other perceived internal threats.[35] In the immediate aftermath, MID played an active role in the Red Scare, reporting as many as 3.7 million potential insurgents and outlining such alarmist scenarios as a cadre of dedicated radicals linking with discontented workers, seizing control of transportation, cutting off food to the cities, inducing famine, and then taking control of the government. In May 1920, Secretary of War Newton D. Baker tasked the Chief of Staff to develop a national emergency plan to avert insurrection, which became "War Plan White." The early plans were, in the words of two US Army historians, "more like preparations to fight a second civil war than those developed merely to restore law and order."[36] By fall 1920, the director of the War Plans Division, Maj. Gen. William G. Haan, under the advice of the Army's Judge Advocate General, instructed staffers that the White War Plan must conform to prewar legislation restricting the deployment of troops. Although still replete with the dangers posed by Blacks, radicals, Japanese, and other perceived threats, by 1923 War Plan White, now downgraded to an "emergency plan," had become what one critic termed a "fairly modern and thorough set of instructions" for dealing with internal disturbances.[37]

Ultimately, it took a series of events—revelations of MID interference, Churchill's replacement, MID's subordination to the General Staff's G-2 Division, the deconstruction of its wartime network of informants, and Pershing's insistence in separating military and police duties—to detach the US Army from domestic surveillance. Most career officers, deeply committed to staying above the muck of politics, shared the sentiments of Brig. Gen. Francis H. French: "Spying and secret reporting upon officers, enlisted men and other persons connected with the service are not proper functions of our Army in peace time."[38] Another officer confessed his "dislike to see my profession made a cat's-paw in the endless rows of capital and labor, the big rascals and the little rascals."[39]

What did arouse regular officers' interest was their service's portrayal in popular culture. Later historians made much of the postwar literature of disillusionment from authors such as John Dos Passos, F. Scott Fitzgerald, and Ernest Hemingway, perhaps because of being required to read their books as undergraduates. But in the decade after the war, tales of military heroics outsold works by jaded intellectuals moping in Paris coffeehouses. Americans devoured movies, novels, comics, and pulp magazines that portrayed doughboys killing scores of Germans, pilots battling the Hun in knightly aerial combat, and former soldiers thwarting mad scientists, fighting in exotic locales, and bringing vigilante justice to crime-ridden American cities. Today's readers would be surprised to learn it was not an expat esthete who aroused outrage in the officer corps but AEF veteran Lawrence Stalling's play *What Price Glory?* And their complaint was that it was too realistic in its portrayal of "Pershing's Crusaders" cursing, drinking, consorting with prostitutes, and, most disturbing of all, failing to respect the caste line between officers and enlisted ranks.[40]

The army's determination to rapidly shed its immediate postwar missions of foreign intervention and internal security reflected far more urgent defense concerns. The war had only exacerbated this ongoing strategic conundrum. Japan retained several formerly German island chains, and the Washington Naval Treaties of 1920–1921, particularly the Five-Power agreement limiting naval power, halted further fortifications in the Philippines. These postwar changes reignited the two-decades-old dispute between those who viewed the Philippines as a base for projecting power into Asia and those wanting to abandon the archipelago and establish an Alaska–Hawaii–Panama barrier to guard the continental United States.

The immediate postwar plans against Japan (codenamed War Plan Orange) were dominated by the first group, envisioning the navy's battle fleet and 50,000 soldiers—roughly equivalent to all the mobile combat forces in the metropole—embarking for the Philippines within two weeks of mobilization. By 1924 the General Staff recognized it could not maintain the 1920 defense act's mandate for a domestic mobilization base and still protect overseas territories. Bowing to reality, the army's 1928 War Plan Orange called for the immediate reinforcement of Hawaii, but the army delayed any expedition to the occupied Philippines by months from when planners estimated they would be in Japanese hands. In a better indication of military priorities, throughout the 1920s the Philippine garrison rarely topped 12,000—with seldom more than 5,000 Americans—less than a third what the 1920 National Defense Act had authorized. Hawaii's garrison remained under 15,000, or less than half its authorization, but it still remained the only large tactical organization in the postwar army with some semblance of preparedness for war.[41]

As the AEF demobilized, the Regular Army analyzed the recent conflict and pondered its implications for the postwar force. Military boards and committees, the General Staff, the military schools, and individuals quickly generated thousands of pages of analysis. But from the beginning, the lessons to be learned were intended to shape postwar military policy as much as future battlefields. An early staff study concluded that American soldiers were unprepared and their battle-field success came against "weak German divisions weary with four years of war."[42] Such a pessimistic interpretation contradicted the war-time narrative, propagated through both civilian and military propa-ganda agencies, of the AEF and its doughboys being America's finest. Soon GHQ perpetrated a very different, and far more self-serving, myth that all but ignored American dependence on Allied shipping, equipment, transport, supplies, and training. In this myth the Allies had been confined to trench warfare—attritional, stagnant, defensive, indecisive—that had resulted in little but "a series of failures or minor successes utterly out of proportion to the losses sustained."[43] The war was won only after the AEF, employing uniquely American "open war-fare," had smashed through the toughest enemy positions and forced Germany to capitulate.[44]

In the war's immediate aftermath, the army's interpretation of its tactical lessons was disseminated with impressive speed. Haan's 1920 "Positive System of Coast Defense" transposed the intricate defense-in-depth methods of trench warfare—interlocking fields of fire, strongpoints, lightly defended delaying lines, mobile reserves, chemi-cal warfare—to the protection of the nation's coasts. These beach de-fense concepts had immediate relevance for Panama, Hawaii, and the Philippines, and their precepts were tested and largely validated in a series of army and joint army–navy exercises throughout the decade.[45]

The impact of emerging war technology such as tanks, aviation, artillery, and gas generated extensive and controversial debate, with some insisting that "in a mechanical age we must be prepared for me-chanical warfare."[46] Others, most notably in the cavalry, insisted that traditional martial virtues would triumph and that, "as for tanks, their invention has no effect whatsoever on the future of cavalry."[47] Still oth-ers warned of the danger of placing the nation's future on the belief, still prevalent in some army circles today, that "if we gather together enough mechanical means and become highly skilled in their use we can face any foe, confidant in our ability to crush him into the ground or blast him from the face of the earth."[48]

The culmination of the AEF's lessons on the Western Front were assimilated in the 1923 *Field Service Manual* (*FSR 1923*). The army's primary source of doctrine for over a decade, it recognized both the size and complexity of modern warfare, incorporating much higher levels of command and organization than previously. Although it re-tained the army's traditional emphasis on the primacy of the infantry, the new doctrine stressed that the smooth integration of all combat elements, or "combined arms"—infantry, artillery, cavalry, aviation, tanks, and so on—was essential for operational success. In his extensive study of *FSR 1923*, the historian William O. Odom concluded that it not only "correctly interpreted the war's lessons" but also provided "a first-rate operations manual that fully addressed modern combat at that time."[49] The ideals and the tactics of combined arms were inculcated by the faculty at the elite Command and General Staff College by instructors, many of them AEF veterans.[50]

Although often ignored by advocates, military doctrine differs from its religious equivalent in that there are no divine authors, and often no institutional consequences for ignoring it. *FSR 1923*'s ideal of combined arms warfare was honored more in the breach than the observance. Interbranch feuding continued throughout the decade. The Air Service (later the Air Corps) and Coast Artillery Corps contested for control of the antiaircraft mission. Infantry and Cavalry branches each claimed primacy in mechanized warfare, though some officers in both branches were not sure they even needed tanks. Many cavalrymen questioned the need for any doctrinal change, since the trench warfare of Western Front was clearly an anomaly. They found inspiration in the horse charges that had occurred on the Eastern Front and in the Middle East as well as in such counterfactual assertions as "the only reason the German army was not annihilated in November 1918, was that the cavalry . . . never got its chance to follow up a breakthrough."[51]

A further problem with *FSR 1923*: even as it was being written, too few posts had the personnel or materiel to train for combined arms warfare at a large scale. With the exception of the aviation units and the overseas and Mexico border garrisons, any war training that occurred took such traditional forms as testing the coast artillery, small-unit drill, marksmanship, marching, and fieldcraft. As in the previous postwar armies, soldiers spent far more time as laborers than as warriors, a problem compounded by the deterioration of many posts and insufficient personnel. With funding for modernization virtually nonexistent, troops practiced for war on battered and antiquated vehicles that were prone to malfunctioning, difficult to find parts for, and often dangerous. Even commanders who had the energy and patience to insist on training programs had to be satisfied with the small-unit, branch-specific exercises that had characterized the prewar force.

Officially the Regular Army stationed nine infantry divisions stateside, but only three were considered active; the others were caretaker units charged with maintaining administrative records, facilities, and equipment in case of mobilization. As commander of the 2nd Infantry

Division in Texas, Maj. Gen. John L. Hines tried to stage realistic exercises incorporating tanks and airplanes and what would now be termed "mission command," giving latitude to subordinates on how they chose to fulfill their tasks. But by the mid-1920s active divisions were themselves skeletonized to the point of ineffectiveness. The 1st Infantry Division had a peacetime authorization of 10,400—its AEF strength had been 28,000—but barely two-thirds were on its rosters, and many of them were on detached duty. It is unlikely any of the division's regiments, scattered across two states in a number of small posts, had more than a battalion-size exercise during the decade. Over the decade, a combination of austerity, tradition, and comfort led to the few large exercises being more choreographed and less realistic. By 1930, the commander of VIII Corps complained that "troops are to be seen operating at maneuvers much as they would have operated years ago before aviation, concentrated fire power, and motor driven vehicles were introduced."[52]

As with the Washington administrative reforms, once the initial burst of war-influenced tactical initiatives were finalized, new developments were rare. To their credit, the branch and staff schools and the military journals encouraged officers to explore the possibilities of future warfare involving tanks, motorized troops, airplanes, and other weapons that would prove so important in the next conflict.[53] In one promising experiment in 1928, Chief of Staff Charles P. Summerall authorized the Experimental Mechanized Force to test both materiel and tactics. Unfortunately, the former's obsolescence—most tanks were of wartime vintage—hampered the effective testing of the latter. The experiment ended when MacArthur, who termed tanks "expensive toys," disbanded the force based on economy and branch parochialism.[54]

By far the most important postwar exercises were the joint army–navy tests of the Panama and Hawaii defenses. These almost invariably involved a sea-based aerial attack met by the defender's airplanes, then a shelling of the coast fortifications and an amphibious landing. Service competition ensured these were taken very seriously: they could be lethal for careers. Lassiter had to relieve Palmer, after that general so mishandled his brigade that the "enemy" quickly overran it, and then broke down under the stress of relieving an incompetent subordinate.[55] The maneuvers inevitably generated acrimonious debate over who had won or lost. A typical interservice imbroglio occurred during the 1925 joint exercises in Hawaii. The navy claimed that putting ashore 1,500 marines aboard a hodgepodge of small boats was the equivalent of landing 42,000, waving aside protests that the defender's artillery had obliterated the invaders on the beaches. A more ominous debate emerged over who controlled Hawaii's aviation. The attacking navy forces, with copious numbers of imaginary—termed "constructive"—aircraft, were able to seize control of the air, aided by a complete refusal of the Pearl Harbor naval commander to cooperate in mutual air defense.[56]

Despite the best efforts of officers, the exercises often revealed a certain farcical component, as if officers occasionally recognized their skeletonized peacetime units could only play at war. At the Panama maneuvers of 1924, navy "spies" broke into army offices, and pilots retaliated by bombing the fleet with fruits and vegetables. Bored by the annual retreat-to-Manila scenario, the Philippine Division's commander declared the enemy fleet had been sunk and ordered a triumphal counterattack. In Texas, Lassiter observed a cavalry brigade "careening over the open plains of this desert-like country waving their antiquated sabers and yelling at the top of their lungs. Stirring to the senses in peacetime, but murder in war. . . . Shades of General Custer!"[57]

The Regular Army's training for war was constrained by the 1920 defense act's commitment to a citizen-soldier reserve. The War Department initially envisioned half of the regular combat branch officers annually assigned to assist the Organized Reserves. This projection was probably too low. In 1925 one writer claimed that 5,000 of the 6,000 officers and 45,000 of the 60,000 enlisted men in the combat arms spent their summers "in mad scrambles through crammed schedules in the citizen camps."[58] Reserves training was not only monotonous but also uncomfortable, since the camps were usually decaying wartime posts requiring extensive annual maintenance before they were habitable. Soldiers usually lived in decrepit war-surplus tents, ate badly prepared food, and shuffled their charges through classrooms, rifle ranges, and drill fields—with an occasional patriotic speech, variety show, or sporting event. The training was supposed to be progressive—from individual to company to battalion, and so forth—culminating in a combined Regular-Guard combat exercise. But the high turnover of personnel in postwar Guard units meant that most training remained at the basic level and that the culminating exercise was as much a parade as a chance to practice battle tactics. By 1923 the War Plans Division concluded reserve training did little to prepare citizen-soldiers for future wars and crippled the Regular establishment's own preparations.[59]

In common with predecessors, the postwar army's officer corps endured years of turmoil. By the Armistice, the prewar Regular officer corps of 3,885 had been "swallowed up and practically disappeared," representing less than 2 percent of the 184,434 wartime officers.[60] The war also led to a temporary suspension of promotion by seniority in favor of temporary promotions in the amalgamated National Army of Regulars, the guardsmen, and draftee units. With peacetime, the establishment shrank almost as quickly as it had expanded. On 30 July 1919 there were 70,000 active-duty officers and a year later 15,523, with the numbers diminishing at 2,000 a month. The 1920 act seemed to halt this downsizing by establishing a Regular Army officer corps of up to 18,000. In theory this would provide not only sufficient leaders for the active forces but also a surplus to train reserves and maintain facilities. In keeping with the goal of rapid mobilization in the event of war, the act mandated a top-heavy peacetime rank structure: there were almost as many majors as there were second lieutenants.[61]

The individual trauma occasioned by this cycle of reductions and buildups was tremendous. Some officers prospered. MacArthur was a major when the war began and a brigadier general at its end. March's patronage made him superintendent of the Military Academy, allowing him to keep his general's stars: it took over a decade for many in his year group to regain theirs. Lassiter was demoted from major general to his prewar rank of colonel, then advanced to brigadier general in 1920 and major general four years later. Dwight D. Eisenhower, a 1915 graduate of West Point, began the war as a first lieutenant and remained stateside throughout its duration. He was promoted or demoted an average of once a year until confirmed as a major in 1924; he then waited a dozen years to advance to lieutenant colonel.[62]

The 1920 act not only slowed promotion; it drastically altered the century-old career path. In the prewar force, line officers had been promoted by seniority first within their regiment and later within their branch. The 1920 act placed all line officers, and those below captain in the technical and administrative branches, on a single promotion list. Supporters argued that "the day of the specialist officer on the battle-field has passed"; modern war required generalists with a broad understanding of the complexities of command, logistics, tactics, and related military skills.[63] For both individuals and some branches, the impact of the single-list system was immediate and often devastating. John C. Arrowsmith was on the verge of promotion to captain in the Corps of Engineers when the single list came out. He stayed a lieutenant for fourteen years.[64] Ambitious branch officers transferred as opportunities for command declined, so that by 1928, of the 1,467 Regular Army officers in the Field Artillery, 457 were assigned to duties outside their branch.[65] A more serious implication of the new equivalence was raised by those in the technical branches. Did decades spent riding horses or bossing around an infantry company provide the expertise of an ordnance officer in designing cannons or that of a quartermaster in negotiating contracts?

The single list only compounded a greater problem: the giant "hump" of company-grade officers created by the 1920 act's authorization of a regular officer corps to 18,000. This produced over 15,000 qualified applicants, three-quarters of whom were within ten years of each other in age and half within five years. Most had been commissioned to fill the war's immediate demand for thousands of small-unit combat leaders, waiving any requirement for the education expected in a peacetime military career. Faced with this deluge of virtually identical candidates, the selection boards concocted a simple solution—but one with momentous consequences. They ranked the almost 6,000 successful candidates by age and date of commission (year group), creating a block of lieutenants and captains beginning with file number 2,754 and ending at 8,138. All were commissioned within twenty months of each other, and they soon represented nearly 60 percent of the officer corps. Because the 1920 legislation had swollen the ranks of field-grade officers (majors and colonels) to almost 40 percent of the officer corps, and since many were in their thirties, their prospects for promotion from company rank were grim indeed. One study concluded that, if even half those lieutenants and captains commissioned between 1919 and 1921 remained in uniform their full thirty years, it would not be until 1953 that the senior member reached the top of the colonel's list, while the most junior member would be a thousand files from its bottom.[66] The historian Peter Schifferle aptly compared the postwar hump to "a pig in a python" sluggishly working its way through the promotion system.[67]

Both the postwar hump and the single list struck hardest at the pilot officers in the Air Service. Mitchell's grandiose claims for the value of air power might stir their emotions, but like Mitchell, aviators had careerist reasons to support an independent air force. Their extra months of flight training delayed commissioning dates, placing them several files below peers entering the other combat arms. Adding to their frustration, nonflying officers transferred to take senior Air Service positions, including branch chief. In 1920 Congress mandated 10 percent of these careerists had to qualify as pilots within a year or transfer back out. The congressional remedy soon proved to have unforeseen consequences. Most aviators were lieutenants and

captains in their twenties. They were expert flyers but lacked the seniority for promotion to upper-management field-grade positions in
the peacetime force. The result was that in contrast to the rest of
the army—which had far more field-grade officers than places to put
them—in 1924 the Air Service could fill only four of its twenty-five
colonel and half of its captain slots internally. Worse, it had 539 lieutenants in its authorized 393 slots. This plethora of lieutenants—all
within a hundred files of each other—caused a minor panic when the
General Staff recognized that in thirty years they would dominate the
colonels' ranks. It ordered a War College study, which after actuarial
calculations concluded there was little chance of this happening. Each
year 4 percent of the pilots died and another 8 percent resigned, so less
than 190 would still be in uniform in a decade. The danger was not that
pilots would eventually take control of the army's ranks but that there
would be too few in the event of war.[68]

Relief for aviation officers arrived with the Army Air Corps Act of
1926. This not only expanded the branch's duties beyond assisting the
land forces; it authorized a five-year buildup from 900 to 1,514 officers,
of which 90 percent in each grade had to be pilots. This increase had
to be taken from the Regular Army authorization, resulting in even
slower promotion in the other branches. Further boosting pilots' morale was the change in title from an "air service," which existed to support the land forces, to an "air force" with an independent mission to
attack the enemy far beyond the battlefield. The Army Air Corps Act
did not resolve iniquities in rank. In 1929 the Cavalry and Air Corps
had slightly over 1,000 officers, but the Cavalry had 68 colonels, 98
lieutenant colonels, and 183 majors: the respective numbers in the Air
Corps were three, 16, and 99. Yet if the Air Corps was "rank light,"
it was clearly the choice of the future. Not only did it have twice the
lieutenants of the Cavalry, but 214 nonbranch officers were serving
with it, whereas almost 40 percent of Cavalry officers were assigned
to other branches.[69]

Along with assimilating and retaining good officers came the
equally vexing task of expelling the bad ones. As commander of the
2nd Infantry Division in 1921–1922, Hines complained he had to relieve
every one of his aged and incompetent regimental commanders; since
there were no worthy colonels to replace them, he had turned over one
regiment to a major.[70] Congress was equally concerned about shedding
deadwood, and in June 1922, as part of the reduction of the force, it
shrank the officer corps from 16,000 to 12,000. Secretary of War John
M. Weeks announced his intention "to apply the principles of modern

industrial efficiency to the administration of our officer body."[71] Many of the older officers retired, 800 accepted a cut in grade, and 1,000 were involuntarily discharged.

In the postwar period, army officers were "separated" under a process established by the 1920 act that supposedly identified the best and removed the worst. A superior rated each active-duty officer, with a follow-up assessment by his branch's personnel department. For those who received unsatisfactory ratings (Class B) a review panel determined whether they would be discharged. Although the process succeeded in whittling the officer corps down to its authorized strength by 1923, it did little thereafter. A presidential executive order required each separation appeal to go before the War Department, essentially taking it out of the army's hands and turning it over to the secretary. Relegated to advisory rather than executive status and convinced, perhaps correctly, that any appeal would be overturned by political superiors, the Class B boards seldom rated an officer unfit. One study of the 1920s found that on average only forty-eight of the army's roughly 14,000 officers earned Class B status, and of these only fourteen were eliminated.[72] Beyond its failure to remove the substandard personnel, the officer evaluation process was inconsistent. It was biased by branch: engineer officers were four times more likely to receive the top score than infantry officers. It was even more biased by rank: one in five colonels was rated as superior but barely one in fifteen majors, one in a hundred captains, and not a single second lieutenant.[73]

As had occurred in the aftermath of previous wars, the senior leadership emerged scarred by faction. The animosity between March and Pershing led to consequences persisting almost two decades, breaking out refreshed whenever they and their supporters engaged in a battle of the books. Lassiter, who knew both, believed they excelled in their wartime roles but were failures in peacetime. Pershing was "a man who ruled by fear rather than devotion, but he ruled," while March was "vindictive to the last degree."[74] When Pershing became Chief of Staff in 1921 he expelled most of March's supporters. He and his successor, Hines, initiated five years of dominance through what one hostile officer termed "a closed corporation" of former GHQ officers.[75] During that time the careers of officers who had been protégés of March, such as MacArthur, were reputed to have suffered (though in that individual's case army gossip held it was competition over a mistress). Chief of Staff Summerall (1926–1930), one of the AEF's self-defined "fighting element," struck back at the "GHQ gang." On taking office he demanded of one of them: "How soon can you get

out of Washington?" That officer's flip reply—"Not before lunch"—
resulted in exile to Panama.[76] Whether true or not, many in the army
were convinced that during MacArthur's tenure (1930–1935) he stalled
the advancement of those too closely identified with Pershing, such as
George C. Marshall.[77]

Bemoaning the "politically surcharged ether around the capital,"
Deputy Chief of Staff James G. Harbord warned his successor in 1921
that he had "inherited a good deal of mess" and that "the hostility
of Congress is extreme."[78] Neither the political atmosphere nor the
animosity diminished in the decade after the war. Successive chiefs
of staff spoke out against cuts in budgets, manpower, and equipment,
though only MacArthur claimed to have vomited on the White House
steps.[79] Given civil-military relations in Washington in the 1920s, the
army's leaders may have accomplished all they could. But individually
they were a mixed lot. Pershing enjoyed the prerequisites as Chief of
Staff but was frequently absent and completed very little. Hines tried
to improve overseas defense, in part by cutting back on the army's
commitment to citizen-soldier training. Summerall shifted the army's
priorities toward preparedness, developing realistic war plans in the
Pacific and encouraging aviation, tanks, and motorization. But his
ruthlessness alienated many. MacArthur's supporters hailed him for
reinvigorating the force and restoring morale. His detractors pointed
to the damage he inflicted on the service's reputation over the Bonus
Army, his evisceration of the experimental armor force, his opposition to aviation, and his lack of tangible support for Pacific defense.[80]
Despite their efforts, both individually and collectively, the postwar
army's senior leadership could never overcome the political and citizen
apathy to providing for the common defense.

World War I had revealed the enormous gulf between the tiny
minority of officers who had attended the staff and war colleges and
their colleagues. Many who spent their careers in regimental assignments marked time while these graduates, some not even in the combat
arms, leapfrogged them. The postwar army continued this emphasis
on educating its elite, further enhanced by the 1920 defense act's mandate that the service would train, administer, and command millions
of citizen-soldiers. Congress, which cut most military funding to the
bone, was far more generous in budgeting construction of school facilities and paying for instructors and students. The military educational
institutions provided a rare opportunity, at least for the motivated, to
escape the drudgery of garrison life and enjoy the intellectual stimula-
tion, comradeship, and shared perspectives and techniques. They also

served as evaluation boards that analyzed and tested materiel, wrote doctrine, and worked on projects directed by their branch chiefs. They became so associated with the service's professional credentials that one officer remarked that "it is almost rank heresy to criticize our schools."[81]

Although West Point remained the postwar army's primary source of career officers, it emerged from the war with its reputation under a cloud—an ominous precursor for what it would endure in later postwar decades. As would be the case in the future, the Military Academy believed it had fostered the leadership that had guided the army to victory, from Pershing and March on down. Its complacency contributed to public criticism, much of it from veterans, that ran the gamut from pusillanimity to price. That there were only thirty-two graduates among the AEF's battle deaths, and the resignation of almost a hundred cadets shortly after the Armistice gave credence to charges that the school was a hideout for combat-averse sons of the elite. Even more serious was the question of whether West Point had outlived its use to the nation. Despite graduating four classes in two years, the Military Academy produced barely 700 officers eligible for wartime service. In that same time the army's officer schools generated almost 200,000, most within ninety days. Postwar critics, including some within the service, noted its facilities, curriculum, and instruction were decades behind those in the top civilian schools it purported to equal. Few of its faculty had academic qualifications other than having attended the school. Two typical examples, later outstanding combat commanders, were J. Lawton Collins, who was appointed a chemistry instructor solely on his grades as a cadet, and Matthew B. Ridgway, who spent his days "bluffing and blundering" as he tried to teach French, a language he had not studied since his first year.[82] With an annual cost for a senior cadet ten times that of one at a public university's Reserve Officers' Training Corps (ROTC) program, skeptics wondered why taxpayers needed "a school for snobs at $20,000 a snob?"[83]

MacArthur's arrival in late 1919 gave West Point a superintendent with a triple mandate: restore its standing with the public, reform the school's curriculum for twentieth-century military priorities, and prepare its graduates for duties commanding citizen-soldiers. Against much opposition from the faculty and alumni, he expanded its courses in humanities and cut those in mathematics and drawing. He also revised the cadets' summer encampment, a ritual that included indoctrinating (or hazing) incoming freshmen (Beast Barracks), military pageants, family visits, dances, and much socializing. Under MacArthur, cadets now actually soldiered, spending summers at military posts learning modern weapons and tactics. His sponsorship of the football team whose season culminated in the Army–Navy game—what one journalist termed "the greatest show on earth"—was a public relations triumph.[84] MacArthur made some progress in restoring West Point's academic standing, military relevance, and image. But neither he nor his successors could overcome the innate conservatism of a school that believed its curriculum had been vindicated in every war since 1812.

Established in 1916, ROTC had collapsed during the war, replaced by the Officer Training Camps that provided a three-month crash course for combat leaders. The 1920 National Defense Act's emphasis on building up a mass reserve army made ROTC's recovery a top War Department priority. In contrast to much of the army, it thrived in the war's aftermath. In 1921 it produced 1,100 reserve second lieutenants (many of whom had wartime service); 90,000 cadets took summer training. Two years later there were ROTC contingents at 178 colleges, and the number of reserve commissions tripled. After ten years the program had graduated an average of 6,000, almost all of whom accepted Organized Reserves commissions. These impressive figures reflect the close connections ROTC officers formed with school administrators and the normalization of an armed forces presence on campus. Indeed, some military and civilian authorities hailed ROTC for countering the "godless philosophy" and "scholastic liberalism" of college campuses.[85] George H. Decker, who graduated in 1924, recalled: "It was just part of life in the college. We had a choice; you could take ROTC or you could take gym." Decker was very impressed by a general who assured the cadets there would always be wars: "I thought, 'Well, if there are always are going to be more wars maybe the Army is a good place to be to find them.'"[86] Thus inspired, he passed the competitive exam for a Regular commission and would retire four decades later as Army Chief of Staff.

Once commissioned, a postwar officer's professional instruction began when he entered his unit's troop or garrison school. In the morning he might supervise drill or check the company paperwork; in the afternoon he would attend classes, complete reading assignments, and write papers. The troop school curriculum was not easy, and the final written and oral examinations took days. At any time, his instructors might give additional assignments, such as mapping, completing the tactical exercises in the *Infantry Journal*, or tackling the War Department's forty-four-book professional reading list.[87] The next step was the equivalent of a company command course. There an officer alternated between classrooms, demonstrations, and field exercises, at all times rigorously graded by an expert faculty. These company-level schools ensured that all lieutenants and captains became fully conversant in tactics, weapons, maintenance, and administration. They also separated the good from the great. Some commanders went far beyond the required curriculum. Between 1927 and 1932, during Marshall's tenure at the Infantry School, he hosted a weekly seminar in which officers discussed books, military affairs, and the issues of the day. Perhaps not coincidentally, in those five years 150 future World War II generals were students and a fifty others were instructors.[88]

For many of those commissioned during the war, professional education essentially stopped at branch school. They remained lieutenants and captains, toiling away in the hope seniority would eventually bring promotion. But for the particularly ambitious, intelligent, and lucky there were further opportunities. Each year some 200 carefully screened officers arrived at the Command and General Staff School at Fort Leavenworth to begin an exhausting intellectual regimen on large-unit (division and corps) operations, doctrine, and logistics. By the late 1920s Leavenworth was recognized as career-enhancing: those who graduated near the top were almost certain to eventually be promoted to colonel.

In addition to identifying and educating the army's future commanders, Leavenworth inculcated a shared perspective on military problems and techniques to resolve them. Many complained about its intellectual rigidity and insistence that students provide the "school solution" to all problems rather than think of their own answers. But when graduates later worked together on staff problems—sometimes from offices as distant as Washington and Manila—Leavenworth's common language facilitated prompt and practical resolutions. The best of the best, at least intellectually, went on to the War College in Washington. There the curriculum was more theoretical and innovative, and the seventy-odd students were often seconded to the General Staff to work on war plans or other significant topics. The Leavenworth/War College elite provided most of the top commanders in World War II, and in the aftermath of that war they credited the school system with preparing them for higher rank.[89]

Although the postwar army provided a better education and more varied duties compared to the prewar army, it offered less opportunity to serve with troops. Thanks to the rank-heavy structure imposed by the 1920 defense act, there were simply not enough field commands. Those who could not direct troops or attend a service school marked time in the occupational limbo termed "branch duty." They might be assigned to the skeleton of a skeleton division or corps and fill out forms assessing mobilization capabilities, advise the National Guard, teach military science for ROTC, head a recruitment station, or be seconded as adjutants, inspectors, construction supervisors, or a variety of other tasks. Not surprisingly, any occasion in which officers might get a chance to practice their profession attracted attention. One major witnessed a tactical exercise in which those observing—including two generals and three colonels—far outnumbered the handful of enlisted men. At a Hawaiian Division maneuver an inspired lieutenant faked an emergency mule-shoeing to attract the reviewing general's attention. Such antics should obscure neither the seriousness with which most officers took the larger mission nor their commendable efforts to keep their forces ready.[90]

In an effort to provide a modicum of experience, the War Department shifted officers in and out, and it was not untypical for a unit to experience 100 percent turnover within two years. Despite these measures, by the end of the 1920s there were many lieutenants who had never commanded a platoon, captains who had never commanded a company, and lieutenant colonels who had never commanded a battalion. Eisenhower served as the model. Graduating from the Military Academy in 1915, he missed overseas service with the AEF. In its aftermath he served on the American Battlefield Monuments Commission, the General Staff, and with MacArthur's abortive effort to create a Filipino army.[91] The military careers of those who would follow Eisenhower as Army Chief of Staff in the 1950s—Omar Bradley, J. Lawton Collins, Matthew B. Ridgway, Maxwell B. Taylor, and Lyman L. Lemnitzer—had much in common with that of their mentor. All were students and instructors at West Point, graduated from staff and war colleges, and had extensive administrative experience. But their most common characteristic was that, together with Eisenhower, their combined years of peacetime troop command between the two wars totaled somewhere around two dozen.

A more immediate problem was the abysmal living conditions of most company officers. A second lieutenant's annual salary remained the same as in 1908. Responsible commanders found it necessary to hold classes on budgeting, to keep a wary eye on gambling at the club, and to counsel subordinates in financial trouble. If pay was bad, housing was usually worse. As a major's wife in Panama in 1922, Mamie Eisenhower slept on an army cot in a decrepit, decades-old shack infested with bedbugs, cockroaches, and other vermin; its tin roof leaked during the frequent rains. Captains taking courses at Fort Benning's

Infantry School lived in collapsing wooden barracks with leaking roofs, rotten flooring, inoperable doors and windows, and perpetually balky plumbing. They were lucky compared to those living in tents or the lieutenant assigned to a cabin so decrepit that it had been abandoned by its sharecropper-tenant. At both the cavalry and field artillery schools, the quarters were such tinderboxes that the student-officers were constantly distracted by fears their families would be incinerated while they were at class.[92]

As in the postimperial army, those commissioned in World War I served under senior officers viewing themselves as the guardians and inculcators of Regular Army custom and tradition. A 1920 editorial in the *Infantry Journal* typified their condescending attitude: "Without reflecting in any way upon the great mass of our officers of the future, it must be admitted that they are not in any proper sense trained for the duties and responsibilities they will be called upon to exercise and bear."[93] To some denizens of the prewar army, this meant snappy drill, spit and polish, shiny brass work, sharp uniforms, unquestioning obedience to regulations, and other "eyewash." Barely two years after the trenches, the Chief of Cavalry interrupted his War College lecture to fulminate about a newly commissioned upstart allowing his troops to wear nonregulation hatbands.[94] Old Army relics took great pleasure in "knocking a youngster's ears down" if he presumed to challenge hoary traditions.[95] As a junior lieutenant, Herbert B. Powell recalled "loud and severe bawling outs, called 'crawlings' . . . you would stand at attention while your company commander or somebody else would bawl you out in every way you could think of in a loud voice."[96] For junior officers who were combat veterans, such hectoring from seniors who had enjoyed "good wars" stateside or in the rear must have been intolerable.

The combination of stagnant promotion, a booming economy, and the discomforts and frustration of service life led to a familiar crisis in the postwar army. Behind the postwar "hump" came the "valley" of unfilled junior officer slots. Each year between 1921 and 1927 the service suffered a 20 percent deficit in its quota of new second lieutenants. In 1922, there were only 1,420 applicants for the 2,500 vacancies, and just 242 qualified. Only because Congress cut 1,500 slots did the army avoid a catastrophic shortfall. The problem of too few junior officers coming in was compounded by too many getting out. Of the West Point classes of 1921 to 1925 almost one in five graduates were no longer in service by 1928. Between 1924 and 1926 armywide resignations increased by a third, and among second lieutenants they doubled. To make matters worse, a disproportionate number of those who left were from the branches that required the most training and education.[97]

For those officers who remained in the service and who had a supplemental income to participate fully, peacetime soldiering was a pleasant and not particularly stressful occupation. Seniority guaranteed eventual promotion, pay, and allowances; if insufficient for lieutenants, they were usually adequate for captains and above, and noncommissioned officers did most of the drudge work. On a large post, such as Hawaii's Schofield Barracks, officers enjoyed entertainment that far exceeded that available in neighboring towns, including movie theaters, a boxing stadium, an officers club, and numerous other venues. During his tour, Omar Bradley rarely worked past noon, played golf five afternoons each week, and spent a great deal of time at the beaches.[98]

The postwar officer corps was even more enthusiastic about sports than its prewar predecessor. This was displayed most conspicuously at West Point when MacArthur ordered his tribute to the "fields of friendly strife" motto chiseled over the gymnasium.[99] The strife was not always friendly, for both personal and unit antagonisms found an outlet on the playing fields. The rivalry extended into the mess; as Decker recalled, "commanding officers were rated on the success or failure of their athletic teams."[100] One conspicuous example was Eisenhower, whose reputation as a coach secured him some plum assignments—but led his superiors to block his transfer to better ones.[101]

The ultimate game for officers was polo. The War Department was so convinced the sport taught warrior skills that it paid horse owners a bonus and provided stables, feed, and, in some cases, a permanent detail of enlisted personnel. Military journals reported on the post and branch teams, and the *Field Artillery Journal* published an eleven-page listing of officers' polo handicaps.[102] Hines was passionate about the sport, and his efforts to build up his divisional team by transferring in top players prompted a none-too-subtle warning from his superiors.[103] But a decade later commanders were following his example. Responding to a request from VI Corps for a certain Captain Wilkinson, Chief of Cavalry Guy V. Henry cautioned: "As far as we know he seems little interested in anything other than polo and horses. If you desire him for polo, of course he is an outstanding officer but if you desire him for all around service, his record hardly indicates that he is outstanding."[104] Wilkinson was soon on his way to VI Corps.

Garrison social life may have provided some respite from the stagnation of most careers. A 1930 War Department study on promotion found that the war generation commissioned between April 1917 and

November 1918 represented roughly half the officer corps. Of this 5,000-odd cadre, 1,500 were still lieutenants, some of whom would not be promoted to major for another twenty years. It concluded that the army could anticipate another two decades of stagnation, followed by "violent turnover" as this group reached retirement age.[105] In the meantime, the officer corps grew elderly while marking time. In 1935 the average age of lieutenants was thirty-four (one was fifty-seven) and only 430 of the 3,450 captains were under forty.[106] Internal surveys disclosed widespread demoralization marked by anxiety over pay and living conditions, as well as resentment at the humdrum and boring routine of garrison duty. A 1930 survey of 1,330 officers from second lieutenant to colonel revealed over half to be in debt; a quarter could not afford to send their children to college; and many had wives seeking employment to stretch the family budget. It confirmed other studies indicating that without access to private income no young man could afford to be an officer. Only with the onset of the Great Depression did officers begin to enjoy the relative benefits of a guaranteed (if still paltry) salary. Indeed, it is likely that the nation's economic catastrophe may have been the primary reason there was a sufficient pool of highly qualified officers to serve in World War II.[107]

If the interwar period was difficult for officers, it was miserable for most enlisted personnel. Because of the turmoil surrounding the reconstitution of the Regular Army in the months after World War I, the service lost many of those who might have wanted to remain in uniform. Recruiters might do their best to pitch the service slogan "The Army Builds Men," but the reality was far different. Uniforms, food, and housing continued to deteriorate as Congress insisted that wartime stocks be used up before it would fund their replacement. One Hawaii-based officer estimated that 90 percent of construction and maintenance was performed by enlisted personnel, with another estimating that at any time 15 percent of each unit's troops were on work details. The consequence of the "heavy burden of fatigue" borne by soldiers, the Chief of Field Artillery explained, was that "the men being thus overworked become disgusted" and left the service as soon as their enlistments expired.[108]

In many respects the service never recovered from the chaos of demobilization, as turmoil in the ranks continued throughout the decade of the 1920s. The transition from a small, professional peacetime volunteer force to the predominantly draftee wartime army had been wrenching enough. But the transition back was worse. Convinced that conscription was more democratic and the war would continue to mid-1919, Congress stopped voluntary recruitment for the Regular Army. When the Armistice came, Congress ordered the army to discharge the roughly 3.5 million for-the-duration (or emergency) soldiers brought in through Selective Service by April 1919. In belated recognition of the consequences of this hasty action, Congress then ordered the army to recruit 125,000 replacements. Hopes that most would be experienced troopers who could quickly be sent to the field were soon dispelled. Recruiters sadly reported that veterans were almost unanimous: "I am through with the Army."[109]

Congress made the service's personnel problems worse by mandating one-third of all new enlistments be for one year rather than the normal three. This may have been a well-intentioned stopgap initiative to provide vocational skills, education, pay, and housing for the tens of thousands of returning soldiers flooding the job market. But it saddled the service with a substantial bloc in uniform for only a few months. The reductions of 1921 further diminished the trained reservoir by forcing the premature discharge of 54,000 soldiers. The following year Congress funded only 118,000 enlisted personnel—or barely a third of that authorized by the 1920 defense act—and this remained relatively constant the rest of the decade.[110] Despite the hopes of reformers, the postwar army proved unable to change the fundamental attitude that soldiering represented "a profession for the officer but for the enlisted man it [is] a temporary job."[111] A survey of 236 recruits found that only forty-five enlisted to pursue the trade: the Inspector General categorized the rest as "young men; their minds immature; they come into the service often on account of their habits or for other reasons. Often they have not been able to find satisfactory occupation in civil life. Many times they are disappointed in their belief that the Army is an easy place, without much work."[112]

Black soldiers represented one group that was marginalized in the aftermath of the war. The army overlooked their combat contribution—most notably the excellent record of those serving with the French. The postwar legislation that increased the army's size did not increase the four existing Black regiments; neither did the War Department support any expansion. Both the war and its aftermath witnessed horrific violence against Blacks, especially veterans. Racist fears of arming them played a major role in the defeat of UMT, despite army officers' claims that "military training will make of the colored man a far better citizen, one more amenable to discipline, and will secure in southern communities the very best part of the colored population for the preservation of law and order."[113]

Officers' attitudes toward Black soldiers should be interpreted within the context of the resurgent racism that occurred in much of 1920s America. Reflecting such sentiments, one 1921 War College paper opined that "the negro makes an excellent soldier when thoroughly trained and led by carefully selected white officers" but "has little or no initiative, lacks a sense of responsibility and is very generally untruthful."[114] Fearing mass protests and violence, the service excluded Black regiments in the old Confederacy from its mobilization plans. Col. A. J. Dougherty, who commanded the 25th Infantry, commended his regiment's excellent discipline and morale and took great pride that his sports teams consistently bettered their white opponents.[115] But Dougherty's regiment, like other Black units, was largely invisible. During the postwar, Black soldiers were stationed either in isolated posts on the border, assigned to maintaining West Point's facilities, or scattered in service detachments.

Perhaps reflecting field officers' prejudices, in the immediate postwar era there was some support for confining noncommissioned officer status to those with leadership duties in combat units. Technical and administrative specialists would remain privates but draw higher pay based on their rating. But then, as now, the belief that only warriors were wanted soon gave way to the reality that, even more than after the war with Spain, the army desperately needed skilled laborers. Those who had an occupation that they could offer on the civilian market would remain only if they received comparable pay and benefits. Pershing and GHQ might claim the AEF had won the war with rifle- and bayonet-wielding doughboys practicing "open warfare," but the postwar army valued clerks and mechanics more than combatants. At the end of the war almost a quarter of the army had been in the Field Artillery branch, which could (with some justification) claim coequality with the infantry in winning the war. But by the mid-1920s the chairbound paper-shufflers of the Quartermaster Corps had more privates with specialist ratings despite being half the size.[116] And within a decade of the war's end the Air Corps' 10,860 enlisted personnel included 176 first-class master sergeants, 917 third-class staff sergeants, and 660 privates in the top-three specialist classes. The comparable numbers for the Field Artillery, which had 4,000 more soldiers, were 78, 189, and 73.[117]

The 1920 defense act reflected the army's real, as opposed to ideal, personnel requirements and continued the 1908 pay act's efforts to make skilled tradesmen and proven foremen choose soldiering as a career. It consolidated the almost fifty leadership and technical ratings that had emerged from the war into five noncommissioned and two private grades. At the top were master sergeant equivalents (.6 percent) who earned $74 a month; the first sergeants who bossed line companies (1.8 percent) made $53, and the rest of the sergeants (11.5 percent) received $45. At the bottom of the noncom grades were corporals (9.5 percent) who were paid $37 each month. These wages were lower than civilian equivalents, but they were supplemented with allowances, rations, housing, longevity and skill bonuses, and other perks. But the chevroned elite were a minority. The defense act mandated 75 percent of the force be privates, and half of these were the lowest grade ("buck" privates) who were paid $21 per month. Of these the army did not expect or demand much, for as one officer only half-jokingly avowed, "any man who can dodge a Section 8 [mental unfitness] board can be made into a fair soldier."[118] To encourage at least some to take on necessary occupations, there were bonuses for those who learned vocational skills such as cooking or who qualified in martial skills such as marksmanship.

In theory, the 1920 act created a personnel structure that retained skilled laborers and troop leaders while annually training thousands of short-service privates who, upon completion of their enlistments, would go into the reserves. But the drastic personnel reductions of 1921 and 1922 sabotaged these plans, compressing noncommissioned and specialist grades and creating many surplus soldiers. In response, the army froze enlisted promotions, then reduced many by one grade, and then involuntarily separated thousands from the service. Even with these drastic steps, there remained a "hump" in the top noncommissioned grades that blocked promotion all down the line. Very soon it was exceptional for any soldier of less than three enlistments—a decade's service—to rise to corporal. As in the prewar army, the vast majority of soldiers remained privates, some for the entirety of their military careers. In the combat arms, enlisted grade was attached to the unit; a noncom who transferred risked his stripes. The first sergeant (or "top kick") ruled his company (or "outfit"): his three chevrons and two "rockers" showing he had reached the top of the five enlisted grades. Like Milton Warden in *From Here to Eternity*, these men were masters of company regulations ("the Book"), administration, drill, tradition, and deportment.[119] They served as intermediaries between privates and the exalted commissioned ranks, preserving the forms and subordination of the caste system. As one officer recalled, the sergeants made him and his peers look good, and if a soldier stepped out of line these enforcers did not hesitate to "beat the hell out of him."[120] Another had less favorable memories of "a sizeable residue of muddle-headed non-commissioned veterans . . . treading water in the manpower pool since the Great War" and "more hoodlums were wearing chevrons" than most officers acknowledged.[121]

As had occurred after the war with Spain, high turnover in the lower enlisted ranks drained the potential pool of noncoms. Of the 77,696 enlistments in fiscal year 1924, less than a quarter (17,555) were reenlistments, less than a fifth (14,432) were prior service, and three-fifths (45,709) were first enlistments. Some branches were viewed as either more permanent or more temporary than others. The small, elite staff and technical bureaus had reenlistment rates approaching 60 percent, but the combat arms were perennially filled with recruits. In 1924, a not untypical year, only 1,516 out of 7,884 enlistments in the Field Artillery branch and 895 of the 6,621 in the Cavalry branch had prior service. The personnel turbulence continued throughout the decade. Between 1928 and 1930 enlisted personnel averaged 125,000, and each year separations for all causes were almost half that. The impact on readiness was explained by the commanding general of the Hawaiian Department, who complained that in fiscal year 1926 his command of 14,000 had suffered a turnover rate of almost two-fifths of the officers and half the enlisted personnel, with the result that "constant shifting and reassignment is necessary within the command with consequent disrupting effects on training."[122]

Not only did the postwar army fail to convince soldiers to reenlist; a large number never completed their first enlistments. In 1925 this category totaled 21,428 out of an enlisted force of 121,788. Perhaps most discouraging, 10,053 of these soldiers disliked military service so intensely that they paid the equivalent of nine months' wages to buy themselves out of further service. A 1928 study concluded that if every soldier served out his enlistment the army would cut its recruitment needs by over a third.[123]

In truth, there was little to recommend postwar soldiering. A long-service regular sarcastically noted that, whereas prior to World War I it was common to refer to a soldier disgracing his uniform, in the postwar army "the uniform is disgracing the soldier."[124] Responding to appeals from domestic industries, Congress forbade the purchase of acceptable khaki cloth until the army used up its wartime purchases. In 1925 the War Department's warehouses still held 3 million pairs of breeches and 2.5 million blouses—not to mention equivalent stores of underwear and socks—so it might take decades for soldiers to be issued modern clothing.[125] The shoddy olive-drab fabric tore easily, soon lost its shape, and was so badly dyed that no two enlisted men possessed the same shade. The troops had their own resolution—a subtle one-finger salute to their government's mistreatment of them. An unspoken rule of acceptance into an "outfit" was the purchase of a tailored cotton khaki uniform and cobbler-made shoes, leggings, cravats, insignia, and campaign hat.[126]

The enlisted personnel's living conditions were as appalling as their clothing. The service tried to concentrate forces into a handful of large camps to allow for combined arms warfare. Congress refused, as local merchants were too dependent on the profits made by gouging soldiers. This condemned the service to maintain, and soldiers to reside in, decaying coast artillery forts, frontier posts, or hastily built wartime camps. The latter were particularly awful. Most lacked functioning heating or toilets, and with broken doors, cracked windows, and leaking roofs, they were infested with insects and rodents and constantly at risk of catching fire. Even officers committed to realistic training found they first had to make inordinate efforts simply to sustain their existence. When Maj. Orlando Ward took command of the 76th Field Artillery Regiment at Fort D. A. Russell, Wyoming, he was upset to find that most of his troopers were assigned to housekeeping duties. With great effort he managed to bring back most to the regiment, but then he had to reassign many to build a nursery, grow seedlings, and plant 30,000 trees and shrubs as a windbreak to keep his troops fed and the post habitable.[127]

One 1928 War Department survey found that troops lived on an unremitting regime of bread, coffee, potatoes, and tough, stringy beef cooked as "hash, meat balls, stews and similar unpalatable and innutritious dishes."[128] Throughout the decade troops often dined on "forced issues" of food that had been canned during the last war. Officers and men employed a variety of methods to vary this monotonous diet. Some commanders created company gardens and sent enlisted men and officers to the Cooks and Bakers Schools. But even trained and dedicated chefs could do little with twenty-year-old stoves, warped utensils, broken cutlery, and smashed pots and pans. In some posts conditions were so bad that cooks had to purchase their own knives and soldiers paid for their own flatware and plates.[129]

If, as one War College paper argued, "desertion is the barometer of the morale of a command," then the postwar army was a demoralized force.[130] In 1919 the desertion rate was .2 percent, by 1921 it was 4.6 percent, and from 1926 to the end of the decade it was over 7 percent. Desertions and AWOLs accounted for three out of every five general courts-martial between 1923 and 1926. In a telling comment on how much the army's reputation had deteriorated, less than 33 percent of its deserters were apprehended in contrast to the US Navy's 75 percent.[131] As after the imperial wars, there were great statistical variations. Black soldiers' desertion rate was a fraction of their white comrades'. Between 1920 and 1925 the rate for Coast Artillery Corps was half that of the Cavalry and the Field Artillery, both of which had desertion rates that sometimes topped 10 percent. As might be expected, many officers blamed high desertion rates on American society, their soldiers, and other factors outside their own control. But one 1930 study concluded that the commander was responsible in a third of the cases.[132]

For many officers the answer to desertion, and all other perceived threats to discipline, was punitive justice. Between 1919 and 1925 the instances of general, special, and summary courts-martial increased by almost 10 percent, and the army annually tried the equivalent of a quarter of its enlisted personnel. Statistically, it appears that military justice was arbitrary and biased, especially against enlisted personnel. There was little uniformity: in one year the 1st Infantry Division had four times more general courts-martial than the Hawaiian Division despite having a quarter of its manpower. In 1925 courts-martial acquitted in less than 300 of 5,475 cases. Of those tried, sixty (or .5 percent) were Regular officers, of which twenty-four (40 percent) were convicted and eight were dismissed from the service. In contrast, the army tried 4.6 percent of its enlisted strength and convicted 98 percent; courts recommended confinement in all cases and dishonorable discharge in 77 percent of cases.[133]

Harsh sanctions were indicative of unhappy soldiers, and even the most hard-boiled officer recognized the importance of improving morale. For most commanders, this took the form of practical measures such as finding competent mess sergeants and cooks, improving the mess halls, increasing educational and technical classes, awarding passes for exceptional performance, and allowing troops permission to wear cravats, special caps, insignia, or other variations to their uniforms. On the windswept prairies of Wyoming, Orlando Ward staged spectacular reviews with bands playing, cannons polished, and troopers performing intricate mounted drills. Dougherty recruited a top-level band, held dances and parades, and on the 25th Infantry's organization day scheduled a parade and a reading of the regiment's history. He also sponsored an enlisted review that, he noted with some pride, included some devastating impersonations of officers.[134] However, not all efforts to raise morale were successful. The commander of the Hawaiian Department instituted competitions in military and administrative skills, such as the best-looking barracks, best-dressed unit, fastest transport, or tidiest bookkeeping. When Chief of Staff Hines visited, he found officers and enlisted personnel furious at what they viewed as rebranded fatigue duties and even angrier that their company funds were appropriated to pay for post beautification. He ordered the competitions stopped.[135]

In a lecture at the Army War College, the General Staff officer who directed personnel reminded the audience that "recreational athletics offer perhaps the best channel for the relief of the repressions inherent in the military service."[136] Indeed, sports was one of the great passions of the postwar force. Some units maintained a stable of semiprofessional sportsmen, often wearing corporal's stripes, who did no fatigue duty and spent their "soldiering" years competing against rivals for trophies and prestige. It was not unknown within the "jockstrap army" for commanders to contact friends to ensure that a soldier-athlete arrived at his new posting with stripes intact and a place on the team. Military tournaments were enormously popular with military and public audiences. The Hawaiian Department commander ordered boxing "fostered and encouraged throughout this command" as "an invigorating and healthful sport, tending to cultivate in the participant certain qualities of mind and body that are essential in the efficient soldier."[137] With such support, it is not surprising that Schofield Barracks boxing matches, housed in the post's own stadium, often drew 7,500 spectators and became a permanent feature of that command's culture, much like *From Here to Eternity* depicts.[138]

When it came to off-duty activities, the postwar army had a mature (if amoral) view that since respectable women would not date enlisted men—and they could not marry—the men would have to either shack up with a girlfriend or visit brothels. As with hangovers, as long as a private had a pass and could soldier the next day, the service did not care how he spent his nights. Venereal disease was less a moral issue than a health issue: the treatment incapacitated soldiers for several months. The sexually transmitted rates varied widely: In China almost 20 percent of the troops were infected; in Hawaii the rate was less than 3 percent, with the armywide average about 6 percent. Some commanders favored punitive measures. When he commanded the Panama garrison, Maj. Gen. Fox Conner directed that any infected soldier would be court-martialed and assigned the maximum sentence: the disease rates showed negligible change, making Conner even more unpopular with his soldiers. Hawaii's low rate can be explained by its regulated brothels, open to medical and military inspection, and to the free-access clinics providing prophylactics just outside Honolulu's red light district. If a soldier underwent the painful injection treatment and later was found to be infected, he was not charged.[139]

Alcohol remained the favored recreational stimulant for officers and men. The Philippines became a preferred posting because it did not fall under Prohibition. However, in the United States the law was widely ignored. Soldiers made "swipes" from fruit juice or bought bootleg liquor, sometimes selling their uniforms to obtain cash. Indicative of the service's lax attitude were the few alcohol-related court-martial convictions; in one fiscal year there were barely a hundred. The military grapevine alerted drinkers to teetotalers, and some pranksters delighted in confounding them. Bradford Chynoweth was a repeat offender, once ostentatiously sipping mouthwash from a flask in hopes his temperance-advocate commander would arrest him.[140]

The prevalence of recreational drugs is difficult to determine. The service had no medical tests for drug use, so charges were limited to soldiers caught in the act. General court-martial records show an increase in narcotics usage in the first five years after the war, peaking at 107 in fiscal year 1923. But this was an anomaly and may have been the result of a zealous investigator or the purging of a drug ring. In the years immediately before and after, the use and possession of narcotics only accounted for twenty-nine and fifty-one courts-martial respectively, and after 1927 they never reached double digits.[141] However, the court-martial records may not provide the full picture. Marijuana was technically illegal, but soldiers along the Mexico border and in Panama were usually left alone unless their behavior caused problems. The army's tolerant outlook is illustrated in the well-known anecdote about the bridge near the main post in Panama where small groups of smokers would gather. One day a new colonel heard an officer referring to "Marijuana Bridge," lost his temper, and ordered that no one ever use that term again. The troops complied, referring to it thereafter as "that bridge that used to be called Marijuana Bridge."[142]

In 1920 the service took as its recruiting slogan—"Education, Vocation and Americanization"—as testimony to its intention to attract motivated enlistees and to serve as an agency of social reform.[143] Indicative of the service's commitment, recruiting posters encouraged young men to "Join the University in Khaki" and learn a trade.[144] Congress allocated $2 million for education and technical training in 1919, and a further $3.5 million the next year. War Department General Orders No. 109 (1919) allowed all soldiers except illiterates to enroll in classes up to three hours a day (and more if their commanders agreed).[145] Very quickly the enlisted education system expanded to seventeen separate vocations ranging from agriculture to textiles, offered 107 courses, employed almost 3,500 military and civilian instructors, and taught over 100,000 soldiers every day. At Camp Upton's Recruit Educational Center the army concentrated 1,800 illiterates from forty-five nationalities who were given curriculum that emphasized literacy, vocational trades, and "manhood and Americanism."[146]

The service's education program was initially a triumph, greatly enhancing its reputation among the public. One enthusiast contrasted the prewar force "recruited from the drifters and toughs of the big cities, from the down-and-outers, from the hapless and aimless and the adventurers," with its successor, the "soberest, busiest army that ever was. . . . It is perhaps the greatest public school for adults in the world."[147] Yet it was also expensive, time-consuming, a drain on personnel, and completely dependent on annual appropriations by Congress. Even those who advocated "selling the Army to the people" were worried the result was "an army of schoolboys."[148] As Congress cut back, so did the army, first ending the Recruit Education Centers and then the education stipend. Within five years of the war's end the army's education experiment had all but ceased, thereby demoralizing those who had enlisted on the promise of schools and jobs and contributing to its own retention problems.

Education was but one way that the army, in the words of one officer, sought to "guide the thoughts of their men to correct channels"; because once so guided, "the minds of the men are readily controlled and they become better soldiers and better citizens."[149] This was not only a military goal. Civilian enthusiasts argued that service would "combat the destructive seditions and invasions of vicious ideas and crooked thinking" among rankers who "come from and return to the very stratum of society in which Red unrest breeds and where it is most secure."[150] To some officers, such propaganda was hypocritical and counterproductive. "Uplifters" had seized control of the army during the war and since then continued their "fantastic efforts to make recruits into salesmen, into electricians, into accountants, into Christians, into anything under Heaven except soldiers." What were the results of this moral indoctrination? "The desertion rate go[es] up; marksmanship, discipline, and reenlistments go down; and an army produced that could be routed by about three-fourths its strength of pre-war men." The American people needed to stop and recognize an essential truth: "An army exists to kill men, when ordered, in the nation's quarrel, irrespective of its justice. . . . If we want an army, we should recognize it for what it is. We should not tell lies about it being a school for citizenship or manual training, nor clutter up its drill-grounds with disciples of these irrelevant arts."[151]

A decade after the November 1918 Armistice, the army was buckling under the missions outlined in the 1920 National Defense Act and being starved by congressional budget cuts. With obligations that would have challenged the 300,000 called for in the defense act, in actuality it numbered a little more than 12,000 officers and 124,000 enlisted personnel, of which 30,000 were overseas. Save for a few demonstration units at the schools, most companies, batteries, and troops were at their minimal peacetime strength of seventy, with many absent on detached duty or otherwise unavailable for training. Only the garrison in Hawaii approached a sufficiency of troops and materiel to practice the large-scale, combined arms warfare required by army doctrine. But even there, most training, such as it was, ended at noon, leaving the rest of the day to sports or fatigue duties. The problem of an army without officers was never resolved. Less than four years after the Armistice, the Chief of Field Artillery complained his branch had but 60 percent of its authorized officers, and the Chief of the Air Service confessed "we are really in a rather desperate situation," as his branch was short 600 of the 1,500 instructors they required.[152] At decade's end roughly one of every three officers in the Infantry, Cavalry, Field Artillery, and Coast Artillery were detailed to duties outside their branches.[153]

The creation of a trained reserve for rapid wartime mobilization that underlay much of the National Defense Act's mission was equally illusory. Although ROTC thrived on campuses, only 15 percent of ROTC graduates could attend the army's schools or participate in the field exercises to qualify for promotion. Frustrated by the lack of advancement after commissioning, by the end of the decade over 2,000 more were leaving the Reserve Officer Corps than were entering, and there was a shortfall of 37,000 officers in the mobilization plan. In both the Organized Reserves and the National Guard, the high turnover of officers and enlisted men meant that annual summer training rarely progressed above small unit-level tactics, marching, and fieldcraft. Any professional enthusiasm for building up a citizen-soldier force had long dissipated. Dwight D. Eisenhower's 1928 War College paper concluded that neither the Organized Reserves nor the National Guard could be relied on in the event of a sudden emergency. Returning to a decades-old theme, he advocated creating a reserve force that was entirely under Regular Army control. A contemporary War College survey, reflecting careerist priorities, found that "a strong feeling in the Regular Army that a detail with the National Guard is a waste of time for any ambitious officer."[154]

Further confounding the hopes of the 1920 act, the decade's end revealed the enlisted ranks were, much like their predecessors, a small cadre of career rankers augmented by yearly influxes of recruits. Half the soldiers remained privates and included "a fair share of street sweepings and military vegetables."[155] As Congress progressively cut benefits such as foreign service pay and double retirement pay for overseas service, and reduced the clothing, ration, and marksmanship allowances, soldiers simply chose to leave. In 1929 alone an army of 117,000 enlisted personnel lost 50,000, including roughly 10,000 deserters and 2,000 by expulsion.[156] The previous year the service court-martialed an average of one out of every five soldiers. This figure is all the more stunning since, as one officer recalled, "the iron hand of discipline" was generally imposed "crudely, perhaps, but usually effectively" by noncommissioned "motivators."[157]

A decade after he returned to his unsympathetic and uncaring homeland, Lassiter reflected on a decade of lessons. He had served in three postwar armies: the Civil War legacy force, the postimperial army of the early 1900s, and the hollow army after World War I. His own career had prospered, first with the War Plans Division and then as chairman of the board whose report, in the words of the historian David E. Johnson, "completely changed the framework of the discourse on American aviation policy."[158] He had remained his own person, avoiding Washington politics in order to command troops and resolve strategic problems. In Panama he had helped direct the army–navy maneuvers, and in the Philippines he had authored a comprehensive plan of defense against a Japanese landing that integrated aviation, land defenses, and a sizable Filipino force. As commanding general in Hawaii, in 1931 Lassiter predicted "the most probable form of hostile attack on Oahu in the early stages of a Pacific war would be a sea-air raid intended to destroy or damage naval installations here."[159] He speculated on the future: "What sort of war is the next one going to be? Great rapidity of movement will characterize its first phases. Airplanes in the skies, motorized units on the ground. The strain of those first weeks will be tremendous. Woe to the nation that lets an aggressor get the jump on it."[160] But in 1929 Lassiter commanded VIII Corps, watching warily as across the US southern border Mexico threatened to again descend into civil war. He was determined to keep the peacetime army at peace, dismissing all demands from his political and military superiors that he take a more confrontational role:

> We are totally unfitted to take over the governance of 15 million alien people. We do not need more land than we have now. . . . We should strictly abandon the idea, unfortunately held by President Wilson, that it is up to us to instruct them, to lead them into better ways. We should appreciate that our own way of life is far from producing ideal results, that the average Mexican community may perhaps be happier, certainly a more restful community than ours, and that hence we should drop all pretense of superiority over them. As for revolutions, they may find that revolutions add to the zest of life. So, let them alone. Be friendly. Live and let live."[161]

The Aftermath Army of World War II and Korea

A week before the ninth anniversary of the ending of World War II, the *Saturday Evening Post* published a shocking interview with Lt. Gen. James M. Gavin. The "paratrooper in the Pentagon" was a renaissance man—war hero, author, athlete, painter—and the intellectual founder of the new model atomic-capable army. But less than a decade after he had led his division into Germany, and with the armistice in Korea only months old, Gavin declared that these once-victorious organizations, weapons, and doctrines were irrelevant. In the near future, war would be waged by airborne assaults, nuclear strikes, and "scores, perhaps hundreds, of widely separated battle groups. . . . Each cell will be a self-sufficient fighting force. Into it will be integrated infantry, light, fast-moving armor, and artillery that can call for, control or deliver atomic missiles."[1] In this chaotic, fast-moving, lethal nuclear environment, American soldiers would require all the martial fortitude they had displayed at Normandy and Pork Chop Hill. But Gavin was pessimistic his service would rise to the challenge: "In the American Army that pride and spirit has been almost destroyed . . . the career soldier of today is gripped by a sickness of spirit, by a sense of hopelessness and frustration."[2]

Gavin's grim appraisal was shared by many colleagues who witnessed the breakup of the army that triumphed in World War II. At war's end it numbered 8,270,000; five years later it was 590,000, with more cuts expected. The rapid, haphazard drawdown that followed that war prompted Chief of Staff George C. Marshall to characterize it more as a disintegration than a demobilization.[3] Barely had the hostilities ended before antimilitary agitation broke out: GI protest marches that occasionally turned violent, citizen delegations, political denunciations, a flood of embarrassing media reports on black-marketing, physical abuse, fraternizing, and venereal disease, and a general breakdown of morale, discipline, and military effectiveness.[4]

At least initially, the first five years following World War II followed the familiar historical pattern of every postwar decade since the War of 1812—but on a much greater scale. There was the flight from the colors: between June 1945 and June 1947 the US Army (less its air forces) shrank from almost 6 million to 684,000 personnel. There was a new spate of administrative reforms from Washington that promised to fix the problems of the past and set the army on the right course for the future. There was a concerted effort to extract the doctrinal, organizational, and materiel lessons of the last conflict and apply them to preparing for the next. As in earlier eras, many of these reforms were delayed or stillborn for lack of budgets and personnel. There was the familiar shock of recognition that, instead of victory lessening the army's commitments, its postwar missions had increased. Yet despite the emergence of the Cold War and the globalization of American foreign policy, in many respects the postwar resembled its predecessors. Indeed, five years after the war's end, many believed the service would return to its historic existence: a small, isolated, dispersed professional force tidying up the remains of the last conflict before returning to peacetime garrisoning.

The outbreak of the Korean War interrupted this pattern and set the army on a radically different course. Service personnel almost tripled to 1.5 million by mid-1953, most of them draftees or draft-motivated volunteers who would provide the majority of enlisted personnel for the next two decades. But with the July 1953 armistice, the interrupted postwar reel unspooled with a vengeance. In five years, the army shed 600,000 soldiers and suffered through equally harsh cutbacks in budgets, equipment, and resources. The service was simultaneously engulfed by social upheaval prompted by racial desegregation, peacetime conscription, character development initiatives, public relations, new methods of officer acquisition, and other imperatives. By 1958 it had signed on to Gavin's vision of a new model army, restructuring its doctrine, equipment, training, and organization to wage tactical atomic war against the Soviet Union.[5]

The military analyst Carl Builder concluded that World War II left the US Army with a "split personality," a contradictory self-image of past and future missions—the nation's military "handyman" with "sweet memories of the Army that liberated France and swept victoriously into Germany."[6] Today, the World War II legacy lives on in everything from curriculum to clothing. Yet this idealized, and in many ways sanitized, image of the war did not emerge immediately. In his summation of the war to Congress in October 1945, Chief of

Staff Marshall focused less on the final triumphs than the catastrophic defeats at the beginning. Reiterating the familiar army unpreparedness narrative, he emphasized Axis mistakes and the stubbornness of the Allies who held the line while the nation's small professional force prepared the legions of citizen-soldiers for battle. The great lesson, as after all previous wars, was that the nation must finally commit itself to a peacetime establishment of trained, organized armed forces that could be rapidly mobilized to defend the nation. But Marshall's second lesson was even more ominous: "The formless rubble of Berlin and the cities of Japan" revealed that in future war "the cities of New York, Pittsburgh, Detroit, Chicago, or San Francisco may be subject to annihilation from other continents in a matter of hours."[7] Perhaps unknowingly, its chief of staff had highlighted the army's great postwar dilemma: explaining to the public, politicians, and its own soldiers why the nation required a great land-based establishment if the next war would be fought and won in a few days by scientists, airplanes, and atomic bombs.

The army's process of learning lessons from World War II was extensive and varied. As after the previous world war, military analysts generated hundreds of studies, observer reports, boards, and other materials providing immediate recommendations for adapting tactics, materiel, personnel, and practices. In 1946 it began publishing what would ultimately be a seventy-eight-volume history of the war that included detailed studies of operations, strategy, personnel procurement, and training, the technical and support services, the Women's Army Corps (WAC), and the atomic bomb. Until the Vietnam War intervened, officers from lieutenant to colonel advancing through the school system refought the great campaigns and prepared for one against the Soviets, perhaps on the same battlefields. Army historians interviewed hundreds of German generals for over 2,000 special studies, in the process providing far too credulous confirmation for their self-exculpating denial of Wehrmacht involvement in Nazi war crimes. However, there was no absolute consensus on the war's lessons. And as in previous conflicts, there was extensive and continued debate between the various combat arms. The armor and airborne communities quickly conceived radically different visions of future war, one based on mechanized columns smashing enemy armies, the other of airplanes transporting entire armies deep into the enemy rear. But with few exceptions the service concluded that its prewar concepts of warfare, doctrine, and leadership had been validated once again.[8]

Within a decade, the army's narrative of the war against the Axis powers had morphed into that of the previous world war. It began with the familiar introduction that the nation, despite the army's warnings, had once again been unprepared and had taken far too long to mobilize. But once ground forces were committed, the great citizen-solider army, led by regular professionals, had mastered the complex structure of modern conflict—combat formations, combined arms, firepower, mobility, leadership—in a later-day version of "open warfare." The service's attachment to this narrative was so strong that by the mid-1950s army leaders felt compelled to warn their fellow veterans: "We must avoid thinking in World War II terms. We all have a tendency to look back—to lean on our own experiences. We can no longer afford to do so; what is past is history. In all probability we shall never fight such a war again."[9]

The institutional assimilation of the war's lessons was both influenced and complicated by the speedy publication of generals' memoirs. As with their Civil War and World War I predecessors, these were useful to establish credentials, assign credit, and settle scores. Douglas MacArthur launched his claim to have masterminded Japan's defeat a year before it occurred. This public relations coup was so successful that even today, with his reputation for military genius much diminished, it is commonplace to slap MacArthur's name on the title of any book dealing with US Army operations in the Pacific.[10] But almost from the beginning, military biography was dominated by the European Theater of Operations (ETO). It included not only Dwight D. Eisenhower's impressive *Crusade in Europe* but also books by the "GI's general," Omar Bradley, "Old Blood and Guts" George S. Patton, and the supremely competent Lucian K. Truscott. Moreover, not only was the ETO fought in areas that most Americans could find on a map; its armored breakthroughs, airborne assaults, and massive firepower-and-maneuver campaigns corresponded to the army's vision of future war against the Soviet Union.[11]

Among the citizenry, including most veterans, memoirs by veterans such as Audie Murphy, Charles D. Macdonald, and others solidified the GI image established by Bill Mauldin and Ernie Pyle. With honesty, humor, and brutal candor they drove home the lesson that service at the front was ruled by dirt, discomfort, and death, and far away from Regular Army custom, caste, and chickenshit. The GIs' attitude was encapsulated in a Mauldin cartoon portraying a scruffy, combat-worn infantryman saying to his comrade: "I wanna long rest after th' war. Mebbe I'll do a hitch with th' regulars."[12] In similar fashion, the heroes of movies such as *Battleground, Breakthrough* and *Go for Broke* were the in-it-for-the-duration enlisted ranks and junior officers.[13] Whether real or fictive, the veterans' brotherhood of war was a khaki-collared subculture that excluded almost everyone not at the front and any brass higher than captain. Career soldiers were often stereotyped as rigid, bigoted, and toxic, as typified by *A Bell for Adano*'s General Marvin or *The Teahouse of the August Moon*'s Colonel Wainwright Purdy. That the public recognized both characters as slightly fictionalized portrayals of real Regular Army officers made them even more devastating.[14]

Despite this outpouring of institutional and individual literature, neither the public nor their political leaders accepted what the army took as the war's primary lesson: the need for a large peacetime establishment. Instead, from President Harry S Truman on down they shared the air force's conviction that the atomic bomb and aviation would serve to defend the nation. As the Cold War escalated, the now independent United States Air Force's dominance increased while the army's shrank. War plans called for large-scale ground operations *after* the nation had secured its borders and its atomic bombs had destroyed Soviet military power. This secondary wartime role and the end of postwar occupation duties made the army an ideal target for further cuts. By spring 1948 it was clear that army manpower was in crisis, both qualitatively and quantitatively. The active enlisted ranks stood at 486,000, of which shocking numbers—in some cases almost half— scored in the lowest mental category. With the nation's economy booming, jobs plentiful, and the draft ended, one officer recalled that "we were taking the dregs of society in."[15]

The unanticipated war in Korea, and the rapid series of tactical misfortunes that followed, revealed just how far the service's combat effectiveness had slipped since 1945. "During the early weeks of the campaign," the Eighth Army in Korea's analysis concluded, American soldiers were "trained by combat and taught by disaster."[16] The vaunted American technological superiority proved largely mythical: over the course of the war the cause of six out of every ten tank casualties was mechanical, only one in ten to hostile forces. The retreat to Pusan and the long attritional struggle over the summer were partially redeemed by the triumph at Inchon. But the decision to push northward resulted in Chinese intervention, a chaotic retreat, and MacArthur's dire warning of imminent evacuation. Fortunately, a combination of enemy exhaustion, the recovery of the UN allied forces, and the generalship of Lt. Gen. Matthew B. Ridgway managed to hold position and then drive back the communist forces and stabilize the front. President Harry S Truman's decision to sack MacArthur and Ridgway's conclusion that further advances of the front would have little strategic value helped clear the way for negotiations. These would drag on until an armistice in mid-1953, by which time battles such as Heartbreak Ridge would become symbolic for sacrifice, hardship, and frustration.[17]

Interviewed thirty years after hostilities ended, Gen. James Hilliard Polk summarized the conflict's impact on his service: "When we came out of Korea we were tired of war."[18] If World War II left the army with a nostalgic vision of armored columns, paratroop drops, and massed artillery barrages pulverizing a worthy enemy, Korea's legacy was one of frustration and disillusionment. This is not to say the service did not use the war to convey its message. In his first report after the beginning of hostilities, the secretary of the army declared that "the war in Korea unquestionably had already affirmed in the eyes of the world the imperative necessity for the ground soldier in war."[19] But beyond this, the conflict brought little but exasperation and a commitment to avoid any further such wars on the periphery. The fate of Task Force Smith, a poorly equipped scratch force wiped out in a few hours in the first days of the war, provided yet another example of national unpreparedness. Rather than leveling a critique of the army's senior leaders who had failed to effectively train or, all too often, lead their troops, many in the service blamed a decadent civilian society, "momism," teenagers, politicians, and other social ills.[20]

Another lesson that many officers assimilated: the evils of political interference in the areas in which they claimed unique professional expertise. MacArthur fulminated there was no substitute for victory, but in Washington military and political leaders were determined to confine the war to the Korean Peninsula. A more immediate source of frustration was Washington-induced meddling in active combat operations, which led to some senior commanders micromanaging company-level patrols. There was a consensus that Korea's mountainous peninsula denied the army's employing its superior mobility, compelling a trench-bound slugfest. But perhaps the greatest lesson the army drew from the war was the need to modernize materiel to offset the communists' willingness to accept disproportionate casualties. Ridgway later acknowledged that by mid-1951 the war had become a brutal struggle for attrition in which "it was the massed firepower of the American soldier which balanced the weight of massed manpower of the enemy's 'human sea' attacks."[21] Public and political aversion to American deaths in a stalemated conflict made it clear that in future conflicts the army would need to win quickly. This, in turn, meant it needed a doctrine of rapid, decisive land operations as well as the weapons that could inflict far more death and destruction at far less cost to itself.

As had occurred in the aftermath of previous wars, in the half-decade following World War II several administrative reforms addressed problems revealed in the conflict and attempted to create a peacetime establishment sufficient for the nation's war needs. The National Security Act of 1947 and its 1949 revisions replaced the War Department with the Department of the Army, uniting it with the other services under the Department of Defense. A secretary of the army replaced the secretary of war. The Army Chief of Staff became a member of the Joint Chiefs of Staff, whose chairman became the secretary of defense's primary military adviser. The armed forces were to share a common legal doctrine: the Uniform Code of Military Justice. Responding to the threat of global communism and Russian aggression, the United States adopted a policy of deterrence and containment, backed by the threat of all-out nuclear warfare. As with most reorganizations, the process was long, messy, and controversial, and it spawned consequences that few anticipated.

The US Army was more the recipient than initiator of many of these momentous changes. It lost the battle for defense establishment reorganization to the navy; outsiders took over key administrative positions. Civil-military relations were often toxic. Secretary of Defense Louis A. Johnson proved an enthusiastic disciple of Truman's military budget–cutting and alienated his military subordinates. President Dwight D. Eisenhower's appointee at Defense, Charles Wilson, was described by one army chief of staff as "the most uninformed man, and the most determined to remain so, that has ever been Secretary."[22] Relations within the Department of the Army were sometimes little better. Agencies, divisions, bureaus, and other administrative organizations were created, abolished, split off, and reconfigured with bewildering speed. The promotion and transfer of many veterans of comparatively junior age over former superiors who had spent the war chairbound added an element of personal tension.[23]

A nearly radical reform, the Officer Personnel Act of 1947 (OPA-47), had consequences far beyond what its creators intended. Recognizing the large peacetime force needed for Cold War missions, it tried to forestall a perennial problem: the aged, the infirm, and the deadwood would block promotion of the meritorious. It replaced historic promotion by lineal seniority with—at least in spirit—"up-or-out" merit. To counteract seniority's slow but predictable escalator to rank, OPA-47 established a career track with clear gates to advancement. Promotion would be rapid in the early grades, with a second lieutenant pinning on lieutenant bars after three years, a captain's after seven, and a major's oak leaves at fourteen. Once promoted to major in the Regular Army, an officer had tenure of rank until his twenty-first year of service. Most would retire then, reaping what boosters termed the "million-dollar package" of pension, health care, and other benefits. An ever-shrinking elite—perhaps a third—would advance to lieutenant colonel. All but the few raised to general would retire at thirty years, with even more generous pensions. In this system, to ensure that only the best advanced, a lieutenant was on probationary status for three years, and promotion to subsequent grades was competitive, with each year's candidates evaluated by selection boards. Those turned back twice were to be dropped from active duty. In theory, OPA-47 provided the nation two great benefits: It outlined a fair and stable and rewarding path to advancement by dedicated career military professionals; and it furthered the army's mobilization plans by ensuring the Organized Reserves contained a second tier of experienced commanders, specialists, and managers who could be called back to the colors in the event of war.[24]

By mid-1944 Marshall had concluded that the service could not return to the model for enlisted recruitment based on the small, all-volunteer establishment created in the aftermath of the War of 1812. In looking for an alternative, the Chief of Staff revived his friend John McAuley Palmer's model of a small peacetime Regular cadre whose primary mission would be to organize, train, and lead a large citizen-soldier force provided by Universal Military Training (UMT). Reflecting the Progressive ideals of the early 1900s, Palmer's plan would have young men serving perhaps six months on active duty—assimilating not only martial discipline but also citizenship, morality, physical fitness, vocational skills, and education—then spending several years as citizen-soldiers periodically training in Organized Reserves formations to be made available in the event of war. UMT offered a solution to the nation's historic problem of raising trained and organized forces in war, but it arrived just when the atomic bomb appeared to make such armies obsolete.

Universal Military Training became a cornerstone of the army's postwar personnel policy, consuming inordinate amounts of time, publicity, resources, and budgets. Much of the manpower planning in 1947 and 1948 focused on locations and schedules for basic training divisions ballooning from four to twenty-three with UMT. To sell the plan, the service cultivated a large network of civilian sympathizers, including

President Truman, and unleashed an extensive public relations campaign. The concept of a citizen-soldier force was quickly polished: the new model army would be progressive, patriotic, and prepared. As after World War I, advertising portrayed the UMT-based postwar army as an agency of military and social transformation: teaching martial and manual skills, bestowing physical and moral development, and providing for the common defense and a more perfect union. Among the many marketing experiments was a model camp to display UMT's benefits. Over 600 young men underwent a program that stressed "decent human relations" between trainees and trainers, physical fitness, education, vocational training, and character guidance.[25]

The goal of a large, well-trained reserve force for a future great war conflicted with the service's immediate peace obligations. That these could be met only by continuing Selective Service was soon demonstrated. In June 1946 the War Department announced plans to recruit a million soldiers within a year, or 30,000 a month. After six months, it reached barely two-thirds of that quota, and Regular Army reenlistments barely topped 20,000. In June 1948, after fourteen months of self-evident proof that the all-volunteer force was both a quantitative and qualitative failure, Congress grudgingly approved the revival of Selective Service. But it did so only as an emergency measure to encourage enlistments, not as a permanent solution to filling the ranks. By that time it was clear to everyone except perhaps Palmer that UMT, with its sustained commitment of a large army in the future, was not going to make it through Congress.[26]

Congress did the army a favor by tabling UMT and returning to conscription. Had it passed, the Regular Army's failure to develop the reserve organizations for UMT graduates would have been exposed. Regular Army–National Guard amity had been a casualty of the war, with many guardsmen furious at the regulars' arrogance in replacing their officers and the callous leadership displayed at the Rapido River and elsewhere. Their antagonism was reciprocated by career soldiers who believed that "the National Guard had been a disaster when we mobilized it and hadn't worked very well after it was mobilized."[27] If Regular–Guard relations were fraught, the service's efforts to build a large, ready-to-mobilize federal reserve force approached farce. The Selective Service Act of 1940, under which the great majority of enlisted personnel had entered the service, would have allowed the army to transfer all those discharged from active duty into the reserves. In part because they assumed the imminent passage of UMT would provide sufficient new trainees, the army failed to exercise this option.

The result was immediate: a few months after the war ended there were only 113,000 members of the Enlisted Reserve Corps, and almost none had been assigned to a specific organization. Overlooking this inconvenient truth, army mobilization plans stipulated a trained UMT-generated force seven times that size.[28]

On 28 April 1948 Maj. Gen. Edward F. Witsell submitted an alarming study to the Army Staff. At the current rate of discharges and enlistments, in two months the service would be 41,000 understrength, 190,000 short by November, and by next April would require 395,000 soldiers, or almost a 90 percent augmentation. Witsell identified only three solutions: Call the reserves to active duty; reimpose the draft; or lift the 10 percent quota on African Americans.[29] The first option was politically and militarily impossible. Not only were most veteran reservists now integrated in civilian society; they were "organized" more in name than in reality.[30] Witsell's second alternative was only slightly more palatable, but with UMT frozen, conscription was the fastest means to push young men into uniform. The Selective Service Act of 1948 and its 1951 revisions were landmark shifts in military personnel policy. Conscription became an essential element of peacetime deterrence rather than immediate preparation for an imminent war or the temporary consolidation of a recent one. Almost as important, the amended Selective Service Act's holistic view of America's long-range strategic interests allowed many young men to fulfill its expanded definition of "national service" as students, husbands, and fathers and in draft-exempt occupations. The effect of this legislation was to transform the character of the enlisted ranks: In 1949 only 8 percent of the force were conscripts; within five years it was 60 percent.[31]

Less than three months after Witsell's report, Truman's Executive Order 9981 ending segregation in the armed forces implemented the third of his solutions. If the Selective Service Act of 1948 was a radical change in the acquisition of the army's peacetime soldiers, the racial integration of the armed forces was an equally radical social change. Initially the order's effect was miniscule: the army continued to impose a 10 percent quota and to segregate assignments to schools, units, and specialties. But this obstruction crumbled when the Selective Service Agency declared it would no longer make race a qualification for induction. The Korean War accelerated this trend as officers, desperate to fill depleted units, assigned arriving soldiers to units without regard to race. Ridgway supported this colorblind policy, with the result that almost two-thirds of his infantry companies were integrated by mid-1951. In Europe, desegregation was slower but ultimately was forced by equally practical needs. With time to prepare, United States Army Europe (USAREUR) drew up a plan to swap soldiers by "packets" while simultaneously abolishing the "colored" unit designation. To the surprise of doomsayers, the soldiers accepted integration without protest. Although de facto segregation lingered, enforced in part by education, the army moved forward at a pace that stunned outsiders and, as one historian recognized, "propelled [it] into the vanguard of campaigns for equal opportunity for more than a decade."[32]

Of less immediate but equal future social significance was the Women's Armed Services Integration Act of 1948 and the assimilation of the Women's Army Corps into the Regular establishment. Although over 400 noncombat jobs were open to them, most were assigned to administrative or clerical duties. As their first director boasted, WAC policy from the beginning was "quality, not quantity."[33] They provided educated, skilled, disciplined, and motivated personnel to a postwar army desperate for such talent. Indeed, the Army's main problem in the 1950s was that WAC standards were so high that the force seldom rose above 7,500.

By 1950 the era of great administrative restructuring had passed. The institutional reforms, though transformational, still had much in common with the historic pattern of postwar change dating back to 1815. As in the previous eras, they were often mandated by outside authorities, occurred within roughly half a decade, and left the service, however ultimately strengthened, in temporary disarray. Also as with the antecedents, the post–World War II transformation was Washington-centric. The service's traditional organization had been totally overhauled. It could no longer claim the singular distinction of being the War Department; it was now a member—and not even the most important—in the joint-service Department of Defense. Its officer corps and enlisted systems had been drastically altered. The former was now predicated on the assumption that officership was a career, not a calling, and established clear guidelines for promotion, tenure, and removal. The peacetime army was no longer all-volunteer but instead a mix of Selective Service conscripts, draft-induced volunteers, and career soldiers. After three social revolutions, the army was now racially integrated, included women soldiers, and imposed discipline not through the caprice of commanders but under the Uniform Code of Military Justice.

In common with previous eras of transformation, the Washington-directed change was not immediately apparent outside the Beltway. In the immediate aftermath of World War II, conditions within the field forces closely resembled that of their postwar predecessors. As after every war, the service's personnel fell far below its needs. In February 1948 it could muster only 552,000 of its authorized strength of 667,000, and estimates predicted a 165,000-man shortfall. As before, the service resorted to its long-established shell game of designating many units "active" with few active soldiers. Instead of a wartime strength of 19,000, each infantry division was given an arbitrary peacetime strength of 12,500 and stripped of a third of its infantry and artillery battalions. Even these numbers were more fantasy than real, as constant personnel turmoil—one division had a 500 percent turnover within four years—and detached duty in administration, school, transport, and so forth took many soldiers from their units. Some stateside regiments had to combine all their personnel to train a single battalion. In Japan, Eighth Army's commander confessed his forces had "disintegrated"; all the veterans had left and "we are building a new army around badly depleted units" made up of recently arrived and barely trained recruits.[34]

A 1948 board on service morale found widespread uncertainty: soldiers were "groping for guidance as to the mission of the Army and its objectives," in part because "so much has been written as to how any future war will be won with rockets and air power that the necessity for an Army needs to be explained and emphasized."[35] This uncertainly was particularly unsettling, because in many respects the army's role had never been as well-defined as it was in the aftermath of World War II. The National Security Act of 1947 emphasized the first of the service's "general functions" as the "prompt and sustained combat incident to military operations in major land areas."[36] But it was vague on such key details as where these forces would come from—conscripts, reserves, volunteers—as well as their organizations and likely areas of deployment.

Whatever their source and future composition, it was obvious to all—including the Soviets—that army forces in the field were incapable of implementing this grandiose vision. In the five years after the end of the war, the service's already inadequate budget was plundered to support the Marshall Plan, occupation duties, and other projects unrelated to its core missions. Much of the materiel leftover from the war quickly deteriorated, and much was shipped overseas to Greece, China, and other new allies in the Cold War. By 1948 the service estimated it needed $6 billion just to equip its existing divisions: of the 15,526 tanks in inventory, only 1,762 were considered sufficiently functional for issue to field forces. But most of the $5 billion spent on procurement between 1948 and 1950—roughly one-third of its budget—went to relief agencies, barely one-eighth to new equipment. In the half-decade after the end of World War II the army was overwhelmed with so many immediate duties—and with so few resources to perform them—that training for combat was rarely a possibility.[37]

A primary distraction from the long-term mission of preparing for war were the overseas commitments, particularly occupation duties in Europe and Asia. In the first year of peace, roughly one of every two soldiers was either stationed or in transit outside the continental United States. Personnel turbulence never ceased, and to this was added the problem that many of those sent overseas were barely trained, in the lowest mental categories, socially maladjusted, and often had discipline problems. Military government required the army to balance a number of long-range submissions—democratization, education, encouraging US economic and political interests, anticommunism—with clear and present crises such as the Berlin Airlift or the nationwide railroad strike in Japan.[38] In Germany the sole combat division, the 1st Infantry, was often at half-strength, its troops scattered across the American zone.[39] In early 1948 the commander of Eighth Army in Japan reported that less than half his 47,000 soldiers were even assigned to combat units, much less actually in them. He confided that "if I had to get into a fight tomorrow about my only defense would be to rise up out of a thicket and wave a night shirt while yelling 'Wah! Wah!'"[40] It would not be until four years after the defeat of Japan that army inspectors could confirm that Eighth Army's four divisions—none at more than two-thirds strength and equally deficient in materiel and logistical support—had initiated company and battalion training. Nine months later, many of these units would be thrown into combat in Korea.[41]

The Korean War prompted a massive buildup of ground forces and a shift in their strategic focus. Not only did the size of the ground forces triple between 1950 and 1953, from 593,000 to 1,534,000; their deployment changed as well. Over half of these soldiers served overseas—a massive foreign commitment that would last until the end of the Cold War. Between July 1950 and July 1953, forces in the Far East increased from 92,158 (485 in Korea) to 354,660 (276,581 in Korea). In the same period, ground forces in Europe swelled from 81,000 to 236,000. United States Army Europe and its combatant commands—V Corps and VII Corps—soon became the top-priority destination for the best equipment, training, combat units, and personnel. By 1955 popular articles hailed them as "the world's newest army," armed with a nuclear-backed "revolution in weapons." Should the Soviets dare come across the border, their commander warned, "we are now able to make an act of aggression a very costly venture."[42]

Perhaps because the post–World War II reforms were so comprehensive, the administrative changes in the five years following the Korean War can be characterized more accurately as corrections or amendments. The overseas commands shifted from occupation to preparing for war as guardians of the nation's global Cold War commitments. In the United States, Army Field Forces inherited the wartime responsibilities of organizing and training its fighting and support forces for both domestic and overseas assignments, identifying and developing materiel, and administering stateside units. In 1955 Army Field Forces was replaced by Continental Army Command (CONARC), supposedly to streamline administration and increase control over United States–based forces. From its inception, CONARC was a dumping ground for any mission that could not be pushed overseas. Its responsibilities ranged from maintaining installations to integrating active and reserve training, administering schools, supervising the combat arms, coordinating the staff and administrative services, and writing doctrine for atomic and conventional war. Its diverse responsibilities only increased. In 1957 CONARC took control of such miscellaneous missions as army aviation and domestic intelligence. A year later, its chief was not only the "manager as well as commander" of the programs governing troops, installations, materiel, reserves, and research and development; he also supervised 328,000 soldiers in the six stateside armies and the elite airborne rapid deployment units (Strategic Army Forces). Together with the combatant commands in Europe and the Pacific, CONARC marked a vast shift from the prewar army's largely passive missions of stateside and overseas defense to the Cold War objective of immediately projecting military power across the globe.[43]

The Korean War and the Eisenhower administration's commitment to strategic nuclear deterrence—often simplified as "massive retaliation"—catalyzed a very different army-centric approach to Cold War strategy and atomic war. After the bombing of Hiroshima and Nagasaki, an influential coterie of army intellectuals argued that a national strategy based on targeting enemy cities and populations with atomic weapons was misguided both strategically and ethically. Such views were manifest by 1947, when Army Deputy Chief of Staff J. Lawton Collins warned against confusing destructive capacity with strategic results: "With the present temporary tactical advantage of the atomic bomb, there is little doubt that a relatively small professional mobile force could bring about world chaos. But that would be an aggravation, not a solution, to the problem of permanent peace."[44] Encouraged by James M. Gavin's 1947 book *Airborne Warfare*, service theorists envisioned a new model army that would rely on surprise, mobility, dispersion, and smaller, more precise atomic weapons directed at specific military targets.[45]

The bloody stalemate in Korea reinforced the attraction of such rapid, decisive warfare. If, as that war showed, "enemy combatant manpower is the real tactical hurdle," then "the Atomic Bomb is a weapon which can produce mass battle casualties."[46] To counter a defense policy based on massive retaliation, military spokesmen articulated a rationale for the role of large, forward-deployed ground forces. They rejected claims that a small tripwire deterrent was enough to demonstrate American resolve to unleash its strategic bombers. Soon—if not already—the American nuclear threat would be checked, and the Soviet Union's Red Army—recognizing that no president would accept the destruction of New York to protect Munich—could sweep into Western Europe from its positions inside the Iron Curtain. Without conventional forces to deter or halt such an onslaught, the United States faced three unacceptable choices: Honor the NATO alliance and launch (and accept) a strategic nuclear attack; stem the Red Army's advance with atomic weapons, in the process destroying its NATO allies; or acquiesce to the Red Army's conquest of Western Europe and the loss of the Cold War.

In place of this grim menu, theorists on limited atomic warfare advanced a positive plan for victory. Rather than accept mutual annihilation, American and Russian policymakers would find a rational alternative, agreeing to limit atomics to low-kiloton weapons and restrict targets to enemy military forces. With the war now deescalated to a conventional conflict, the question became how to stop the Warsaw Pact's overwhelming advantages in manpower and materiel. Fortunately, the answer had already been supplied by Gavin and his acolytes: a new model army of wide-ranging, dispersed forces, maneuvering to avoid the Red Army steamroller, quickly striking its rear and flanks with small-yield, precisely targeted atomic weapons, concentrating to suppress resistance, and then dispersing to begin the process anew. Increasingly, army intellectuals emphasized that theirs was the truly scientific version of atomic war: unlike the holocaust guaranteed by multimegaton thermonuclear bombs, the army could prevent nuclear escalation. It could deter Soviet aggression and, if the war occurred, defend NATO and secure peace on terms advantageous to the West.[47]

From its inception, "limited" or "tactical" atomic warfare—the terms were used interchangeably—presaged later postwar army transformation agendas by assuming that revolutionary technology would appear as needed. Gavin and his followers anticipated the imminent arrival of flying cargo containers and "convertaplanes" that could deliver troops and equipment; aerial combat vehicles; silicate-based tanks; and numerous other marvels.[48] Less than a year after Japan's surrender, Army planners outlined a modernization program that ranged from atomic warheads and missiles to body armor and recoilless artillery. In 1947 a series articles in *Infantry Journal* titled "Your Next War" envisioned drones able to scout hundreds of miles behind enemy lines; atomic missiles; helicopters; aerial assault vehicles; and rocket-propelled gliders.[49] This faith in technological miracles was bolstered by an equal conviction that these miracles would not only appear but also seamlessly integrate with each other and the tactical organizations. Thus the invention of a new missile would coincide with the simultaneous invention of guidance systems, transport, communications, and all other necessary supporting materiel—along with an abundance of skilled officers and enlisted personnel to operate them. To senior leadership, which came of age when the army was still using horses in significant military roles, the future offered limitless possibilities.

The army's enthusiasm for tactical atomic war was boosted by the apparently miraculous progress in the weapons to fight it. Fueled by massive increases in procurement funding for the Korean War, the army spent its millions on research and development for helicopters, armored personnel carriers, radios, computers, rifles, tanks, uniforms, and myriad other tools for future warfare. But the biggest incentive was what one participant cynically termed "the Army's attempts to get into the nuclear club."[50]

At least initially, the army smashed down the club's front door. In 1951 it deployed a 280mm cannon that could fire a Hiroshima-equivalent warhead fifteen miles downrange. This was shortly followed by missiles such as the Corporal, Honest John, and Redstone that provided atomic firepower to field forces; the Jupiter rocket powered the nation's first space flight, and Nike missiles defended cities from Soviet bombers. By the end of the decade the service had unveiled the Davy Crockett, a jeep-transportable tactical atomic weapon. These weapons were just the beginning: in 1959, *Army 1980* envisioned hovercraft tanks, flying jeeps, and a host of other weapons that would not have been out of place in the popular *Buck Rogers in the 25th Century* comic strip. In the process, the army learned that, like every other change, equipment modernization had unforeseen effects. During the mid-1950s, the "Pentomic" division restructuring required some infantry divisions to spend months inventorying new and old equipment, assimilate new Military Occupational Specialties personnel (MOSs) and dispatch surplus troops, and finally teach, train, and practice how to employ the restructured units. Among the stateside combat forces for much of this period, only the airborne divisions and the missile defenses would have been ready to fight.[51]

The army tested the tactics and materiel for atomic warfare with a variety of methods, but the large-scale exercises were the most studied and the most publicized. In 1947 the army held its first division exercise and a year later held joint exercises with the air force and navy. In 1949 Exercise Miki, a combined Army–Navy–Marines exercise, involved over 50,000 troops.[52] In 1952 Exercise Longhorn incorporated over 100,000 troops and incorporated "atomic play" on both sides. In common with its successors, Longhorn served as both a rehearsal for atomic war and a well-orchestrated publicity event—complete with parachute drops, tank battles, and the faux-communist occupation of a Texas town.

In many ways the atomic war exercises, despite their scale and scope, proved disappointing. The army's faith in technology to resolve decision-making and fire control problems turned out to be wishful thinking. Communications improved, but not enough for commanders to identify enemy formations in time to target them with atomics before they moved on. Airborne assaults—a feature of almost every exercise—did allow troops to land on the enemy's flanks and rear, but they were soon overrun and, even worse, became ideal targets for atomic counterstrikes. Soldiers and officers persistently failed to follow doctrine: instead of taking cover, they stood in the open and admired the special effects–generated explosions. But the most discouraging lesson from the exercise was that atomic warfare was limited *only* in comparison to strategic nuclear warfare. Commanders were soon calling for tactical atomics to dispel even minor threats. One 1956 exercise in Europe, had it been real, would have involved hundreds of atomic strikes causing almost five million casualties in the first week.[53]

The transition to atomic warfare led to a second question: What organization could most effectively employ it? In 1956 Chief of Staff Maxwell D. Taylor, overriding much of the evidence from army maneuvers, authorized the Reorganization of the Combat Infantry Division. With his customary flair for marketing, Taylor nicknamed the new unit the "Pentomic" division, the term being a mélange of five battle groups and atomic capability. The service's public relations emphasized the division's revolutionary break with the past. This was not yesterday's slug-it-out instrument of attrition but rather a small, light mobile force able to maneuver over vast distances, equipped with space-age technology, and packing devastating firepower. An episode of the army-sponsored television show *The Big Picture* traced the evolution of war from cavemen to the present, proving that Pentomic was the inevitable result of centuries of progress in weaponry, tactics, and organization.[54] But could this new model army attract a similarly evolved officer corps to lead it?

Post–World War II America witnessed the rise of the managerial class, or what one social critic termed the "Organization Man." One of the ringing messages of the 1955 novel (and subsequent movie) *The Man in the Gray Flannel Suit* was corporate America's desperate need for competent, ethical executives like Tom Rath.[55] The US Army had long been influenced by contemporary trends in the commercial sector, so much so that one Chief of Staff was moved to tell the Army War College in 1930 that "the nearest analogy to war, for us, is the business or industrial leader in peace."[56] Besides its perennial retention dilemma, the service now faced a problem shared with some technical industries: professional requirements might change over the course of a career. The army had long known that a man comfortable as a captain running an infantry company might flounder when promoted to major and expected to manage a garrison, serve on a staff, or even attend school. It also recognized that its field grades and generals, all educated in the pre-atomic era, need a crash course in recent theoretical and practical developments. Although much of this reeducation occurred in the service schools, the postwar army increasingly turned to civilian expertise. It dispatched some of its best and brightest for managerial training at such academic settings as Harvard's Advanced Management Program. It incorporated business manuals and models into its curriculum and methods and even changed its uniform to resemble a Wall Street suit. But as the employers of veteran–turned–PR flak Rath discovered, acquiring new talent while retaining existing expertise was a perpetual quandary.

At least initially, the post–World War II army appeared content to follow well-trod paths for its peacetime career officer corps. In June 1945 there were 891,663 army officers on active duty; in 1948 there were 68,178. The 1945 Regular Army Integration Program tried to retain the best of the wartime veterans from the Organized Reserves and National Guard. But of the 25,667 accepting active commissions, only 11,332 chose the army, leaving it 12 percent short of its authorized allotment. As after previous wars, most of these new Regular Army officers fell within a few years in age and had served in the combat arms. The majority, commissioned after a cram course at Officer Candidate School, were the famous "90-day wonders." Their strengths and limitations were summarized by one such graduate, James B. Vaught, who recalled that, although he was competent to lead a forty-man infantry platoon, "I hadn't been trained to know anything about the Army."[57] And as after previous wars, nearly all these incoming officers entered at the lowest grade: of the first 10,000 accepted, 7,000 were lieutenants. As since 1815, the postwar officer corps grew a generational "hump" in the company ranks: men of similar age, experience, and seniority. A dozen years after the war's termination, this group represented almost three out of every four serving officers. By 1960 this hump was so big that Congress intervened to move senior veterans into retirement.

World War II had revealed, at least to the service's leaders, one of its critical weaknesses to be its upper levels: too many survivors of the World War I "hump" had proved incapable of shifting from the routines of peacetime service to the challenges of war. Even before World War II began, Marshall felt compelled to push 600 officers out of uniform, and many others, including some of his protégés, would fail the test of combat.[58] With war scenarios against the Soviet Union predicated on armies in the millions for combat and occupation, the army desperately needed lieutenant colonels and colonels with managerial expertise. In 1938 roughly 20 percent of the officer corps were in these grades, but by December 1945 the Regular Army had more of them than it did captains and lieutenants combined. The postwar reduction boards adopted a simple seniority system similar to World War I: those commissioned in the Regular Army before 1930 kept their wartime promotions, whereas those coming after were reduced two or three grades. The impact of this concession to seniority was debatable: over two-thirds of these Old Army relics left the service within three years.[59]

The Officer Personnel Act of 1947 provided quotas for each grade, a promotion path, and retirement benefits. But how to ensure uniform competence given the disparate wartime experiences of field-grade and general officers? In one of its first career-management initiatives, the War Department rotated hundreds of officers who had spent the war stateside into overseas command and staff positions. A related project shifted fast-tracked officers—some of whom had risen from captain to colonel—to Leavenworth for a crash course in the responsibilities of their new ranks. Such Washington-imposed changes did little to dispel the deep animosity of many prewar regular officers toward OPA-47. They believed the act violated their previous guaranteed employment until sixty, politicized promotion, and encouraged "ticket-punching"—quick tours in high-prestige assignments to burnish the résumé. They argued that officership would be seen as a career, not as a lifetime calling, attracting those in search of steady paychecks and fast retirement. Such grousing was largely nostalgia for a fictive golden age of officer brotherhood. Since the Regular Army's inception, officers had accused others of politicking, avoiding troop service, transferring for promotion, and pulling strings to secure cushy assignments. Some of the service's most revered heroes—and most vocal exponents of duty, honor, and country—owed their advancement to relentless careerism and patronage as much as ability.

The real limits of OPA-47 were less cultural than practical and impacted regulars and reservists. Passed prior to the Cold War– Korean War buildup, the act anticipated an all-volunteer career force of 50,000 officers and 400,000 enlisted men. But a decade later, the army numbered 96,000 officers, with almost 900,000 in other ranks. Acknowledging the twin problems of the Korean mobilization and the necessity for large overseas deployments, Congress deferred to the armed forces' conviction that any future conflict would require, as had World War II, a host of senior managers to direct the nation's military mobilization and to command citizen-soldier armies deploying millions. Retaining top management inflated their numbers far beyond peacetime needs, forcing Congress to limit the number of senior grades in 1954.

OPA-47 created a further challenge in dealing with reserve officers returning to active duty: The act assumed they would be few and all of them specialists filling temporary vacancies, but at the start of 1947 they represented over half the officer corps. Persistent shortfalls in incoming regular officers and the unwillingness of ROTC graduates to make the service a career ensured their retention. A decade after war's end, those with reserve commissions from World War II still represented one-quarter of the active force. Most were too old to change careers; some were only a few years from the "million-dollar package" of benefits. But OPA-1947 denied them statutory tenure and made them an obvious target for any reductions.[60]

A final dilemma was that OPA-47 depended on a steady stream of second lieutenants intent on pursuing a military career, thereby filling in the bottom levels and keeping the career escalator moving smoothly.

But its authors did not anticipate the postwar army's unprecedented peacetime demands for entry-level leaders. In fiscal year 1925 the Regular Army commissioned 336 second lieutenants, nearly all from West Point; three decades later it commissioned over 15,000.[61] OPA-47 forced the army to establish a system to incorporate thousands of incoming officers who, unlike their wartime predecessors, would arrive with both the education to take on a multitude of administrative, technical, and leadership assignments and sufficient military socialization to immediately assume these responsibilities.

As had occurred after the previous world war, West Point emerged with a mixed reputation. The school took great pride in its role molding such leaders as MacArthur, Eisenhower, Patton, Ridgway, Collins, Gavin, and other stellar alumni. But some, including alumni, believed the school had been a haven for those avoiding national service. A survey of officer veterans revealed deep antipathy to Academy graduates, contempt for their educational qualifications, and a conviction that the "West Point Protective Association" ensured their promotion no matter how incompetent.[62] The Military Academy did itself no favors by its carelessness, or arrogance, in asserting its prerogatives even when they appeared counter to both service and national interests. Perhaps the most egregious example was promoting football coach Earl "Red" Blaik, who had all of two years of active service, to full colonel. It compounded this by commissioning many of his coaches, recruiting a stable of cadet-athletes, and claiming successive national championships. That almost a fifth of its for-the-duration cadets, including several prominent athletes, resigned once the fighting stopped gave further credence to its critics.[63]

Dispatched by Chief of Staff Eisenhower to reform both West Point and its reputation, Superintendent Taylor, a charismatic former paratroop general with a movie star's handsomeness, took over in 1946. He modernized the archaic curriculum, raised academic standards, and publicized its achievements. He also tried to reduce, if not eliminate, the notorious hazing that too often verged on torture. But Taylor could not overcome the school's primary drawback: the size of the postwar army meant that the school graduated barely 10 percent of the army's annual requirements for second lieutenants. Efforts to increase this output, such as increasing the cadet body to 2,500, were ineffective, given that most incoming classes met barely three-quarters of their quotas. Compounding the problem, West Point lost 10–15 percent of its student body annually, and between 1954 and 1960 one in five graduates resigned within ten years. An ineptly handled cheating scandal in 1951 involving Blaik's players and coaches damaged West Point's reputation as a bastion of honor. Even its supporters acknowledged the school's deteriorating facilities and unqualified instructors, and in 1962 one expert delivered the devasting judgement that "academically, West Point is a second-class college for first-class students."[64]

Fortunately for the army, a ready source of well-educated junior officers was on the horizon. Just as big business looked to the new state universities for talent, so too did the army. Even before World War II ended its leaders were determined to revive the moribund Reserve Officers Training Corps (ROTC) program. Broken into two two-year sections, the first provided basic military instruction; the second qualified candidates for a reserve commission and the possibility of active service. Ideally, the most distinguished ROTC graduates would accept Regular commissions and make a career in the service; the rest would provide the necessary thousands of company-level trainers, executives, and technicians in the event of war. Once reconstituted, ROTC expanded quickly, from 10,000 students at 129 colleges in 1946 to 100,000 at 190 just four years later, numbers owing much to the compulsory two-year program at many state universities. By the mid-1950s, 14,000 ROTC graduates were entering the US Army each year. The great majority took reserve commissions, but 525 of them would enter the Regular Army—substantially more than West Point's 355.[65]

The passage of the Selective Service Act of 1951, which exempted ROTC cadets from conscription (provisional on their commissioning as officers upon graduation) further increased its numbers. This exemption was not a complete blessing. It provided a surplus of entry-level second lieutenants of much higher education and technical skills. But it came at the cost of reducing the quality and quantity of the enlisted draftee pool. In 1951, one out of every six of those deferred from conscription were in ROTC programs.[66] Moreover, the annual influx of hundreds of ROTC graduates altered both the cultural and professional balance of the junior officer corps. The majority of these new second lieutenants had no intention of making soldiering a career. Over a third of ROTC's distinguished graduates refused to exercise their right to a Regular commission and, in common with their classmates, fulfilled the two-year active-duty obligation and then the bare minimum for reserve obligations.

The post–World War II army, and its Korean War successor, were soon caught in the familiar quality-versus-quantity trap. Conscription provided such a surplus of ROTC-generated second lieutenants that in the mid-1950s the service called up only a third of them for active duty, the majority for only six months. Small-level trainers, supervisors, and bureaucrats, they provided the minor management needed to keep the draftee army running. But they were easily replaced, and most of them lacked the ability to be anything more. The army wanted to retain the graduates of West Point and ROTC's Distinguished Military Graduate Program it had identified as possessing the potential for military careers. When the army complained about its retention problems, it was talking about this elite, not the transitory, obligated college graduate doing his two-year stint.

Why did the new generation of officers—those who missed combat in World War II or Korea—choose to remain in the postwar army? As in previous generations, the reasons were largely individual. Service life attracted those who wanted to lead, those who enjoyed the outdoors, and those who for religious, political, or family values were committed to duty, nation, and service. An idealistic, intelligent, and dedicated person looking for purpose could well find military life preferable to what he saw as the conformity, materialism, and rat race characterizing civilian life. He joined a unique community in intellectual ferment over important issues such as national security, military policy, and the nature of conflict. He had the camaraderie of his peers and inspiration from his superiors (all of whom were veterans) and responsibilities far greater than contemporaries trudging up the corporate ladder. How many men in their mid-twenties were paid to tour Europe or train with nuclear weapons? Rigidly authoritarian in some ways, the army was also democratic in its experiences. If a junior officer's quarters were inadequate, he knew his fellow officers had no better. And he soon learned from his commander, or the commander's spouse, how much worse the conditions were when they had first served. And if he was fortunate, he learned a soldier's trade from supremely competent noncoms and officers who were masters of the craft.[67]

Although the army anticipated a substantial intellectual boost from incoming college graduates, it faced the immediate educational deficit among its World War II veterans. Almost every officer who had entered between the end of World War I and the outbreak of World War II had been a college graduate. But in the expansion of 1947–1948, some 4,500 nongraduates were commissioned, in the process sacrificing their higher education through the G.I. Bill. As a result, the army's field grades contained a large number of experienced but (compared to equivalent civilian professions) uneducated members. One 1953 survey of lieutenant colonels available for battalion command in Europe found an average of 40 percent lacking a college degree—and among reserve officers it was 60 percent.[68]

As after previous wars, the army embarked on the mammoth task of cycling thousands of battlefield-commissioned officers back to school for the professional education needed for the peacetime duties of their war-accelerated ranks. The greatest burden fell on the branch schools for basic (lieutenant) and advanced (captain) instruction. These schools were rated highly by students, perhaps because so much of the curriculum was familiar to veterans. But even working overtime, the branch schools could not keep up with the demands of the World War II generation. Five years after the end of that war, they were still providing remedial education, and the Korean expansion ensured this effort would continue into the 1960s.[69]

The most significant differences between prewar and postwar professional education manifested slowly at the senior schools: the upgraded Command and General Staff College (CGSC) and the Army War College. They had provided a common springboard for the "Eisenhower generation," and the now senior leaders expected them to serve as intellectual centers of excellence for the army of the future. But the prewar system, intended to create a core of elite staff officers, was ill-suited to fulfill the postwar army's demands for hundreds of competent, if not exceptional, officer managers. Like the universities dealing with the flood of G.I. Bill students, the army expanded its classroom space and almost tripled the student body. It divided the colleges' responsibilities, with CGSC teaching leadership, the staff process, and combat fundamentals, and the War College covering international and domestic politics, strategic concepts, and future developments in technology and military organization. Throughout the postwar decade the army routinely added to these missions, most notably when it charged the faculty and staff of CGSC with writing doctrine and force structure for the atomic army.

Even more pronounced than quantity was the difference in quality. As the complexity and scope of war expanded, so did the curriculum. A decade after World War II ended, the school's commandant estimated that the course material and the student body had quadrupled. Whereas the prewar course had ended at the division level, students now had to learn corps and army functions, joint operations, the zone of the interior (continental United States), atomic and conventional warfare, and a variety of other subjects demanded by the Department of the Army or various headquarters. As before the war, there were complaints that instructors discouraged initiative and imposed the "school solution," while students became adept at scenarios in which, as one division commander complained, "units are always at full strength, commanders competent, supply levels up, troops well trained. In war, this is simply not so."[70] The prewar army had the luxury of selecting its 200-odd students and sending the best to choice assignments. The postwar army was desperate for middle managers, and by the mid-1950s Leavenworth classes ranged between 850 and 1,000, selected by quotas assigned to each branch and with career timelines established by OPA-47. As one historian discovered, since a graduate of CGSC was all but guaranteed to remain to collect his twenty-year pension and few students were allowed to fail, "selection to attend, rather than learning while in attendance, became a mark of professional achievement."[71]

Educating the midlevel wartime generation was one method to advance officer professionalism. Discharging those who could not maintain standards was another. The "deadwood" problem—a constant refrain in the reform agenda—was supposed to end with OPA-47's system of merit boards and up-or-out promotion. But, in fact, the army was reluctant to turn out its officers, especially once they reached the grade of major. Frustrated by the still-bloated officer corps, Congress mandated reductions between 1953 and 1957, eliminating 5,500 active-duty officers. But these draconian cuts may have actually increased the proportion of deadwood. One chief agent implementing the separation process estimated that the service could have purged over twice as many "at the bottom of the efficiency totem pole" had not "voluntary attrition [of] our most efficient officers" made their retention necessary.[72]

Without intending to, OPA-1947's emphasis on long-term career benefits may have fostered a culture that pushed out younger officers. OPA-47 compelled potential career officers to weigh their prospects at least twice before committing to a lifetime career, first as lieutenants upon completion of their ROTC or West Point obligations. There they confronted that their military pay—which as incoming second lieutenants had been comparable to a starting salary in the civilian world—now and long into the future would be only half of what they might earn in the commercial sector.[73] The second decision point came at the ten- to twelve-year mark on promotion from captain to major. As majors, most would enter, for at least a decade, the grade still overflowing with the World War II and Korean War "humps." Competition for advancement and good assignments would be ruthless, pay increases minimal, and opportunities limited. Majors were the

1950s army's workhorses, often assigned the drudge work, given little responsibility, and seldom receiving credit. Realists recognized that, after making their twenty years and retirement pay, they would enter a job market competing against civilians with probably more relevant occupational skills. When they looked at the booming economy of the 1950s, the seemingly limitless opportunities for those with university degrees, and the higher-paying and less transitory jobs their civilian peers enjoyed, it is not surprising that most decided to swap their uniforms for a three-piece suit.[74]

That officers weighed the career benefits of OPA-47 and found them wanting was apparent in 1953, when as part of the drawdown the service allowed officers to opt for early release. The immediate resignation of so many young company officers further increased the army's reliance on the dwindling wartime humps. In the ensuing years, despite the thousands of young officers commissioned annually into the US Army, the service failed to convince 85 percent to remain. Grizzled Old Army types blamed retention problems on selfish and immature youths, coddling parents and teachers, collapsing morality, and a distinct lack of patriotic spirit. But survey after survey revealed a primary reason for junior officer resignation was not low pay or danger but frustration. Company officers complained of their superiors' "snoopervision," having a multitude of responsibilities but little authority, and spending their time on dull, repetitive tasks rather than in command. A typical day might start with morning formation during which over a hundred soldiers were present, but by the time cooks, clerks, labor gangs, and others on detached duty had peeled off there might be only twenty or so left for training. A 1957 survey of senior officers revealed that their sons viewed the service as replete with "malpractices, irritations, harassments, and onerous obligations" and a consensus that "the docile conformists are the successful officers."[75] Vice Chief of Staff Lyman L. Lemnitzer suppressed the report on the ground that mentioning low morale encouraged low morale.

In 1958 a general in the personnel office summarized the army's great leadership dilemma. Over 70 percent of its career officers were part of the "hump" of World War II veterans with at least a dozen years in service. But behind them was the "valley behind the hump" of too few three- to twelve-year Regular Army officers. In the next few years, the hump generation would qualify for their twenty-year retirement pensions and, with a potential shortage of 5,000 experienced officers to replace them, "we are going to have a hell of a time manning this man's Army."[76] As one federal commission pointed out, the "critical shortage" of experienced company commanders meant that "the short-term, inexperienced officer is in most frequent contact with enlisted personnel. Thus, it is this very officer, continually preoccupied with 'getting out' and 'going home,' who exerts the greatest influence upon the enlisted men and his decision concerning re-enlistment."[77] Like Grisham's Law, bad senior leaders often drove out good junior ones, and inefficient or uncommitted junior officers drove out good enlisted personnel. Compounding the problem, the perennial shortage of senior lieutenants and captains meant the army had to keep the ones it had, even if that meant promoting mediocrities.

A decade after the end of World War II, the long-term benefits and costs of officer reform were manifest. The service had an abundance of field grades in the event of wartime mobilization—almost 6,000 officers at major and above in the Pentagon alone. But as had been true since 1815, the field companies and battalions were routinely short-staffed. The career escalator imposed by OPA-47 ensured that officers were generalists, at the cost of too few spending sufficient time in any one assignment—particularly troop command—to become expert. Knowing they would soon be rotated, suspecting that they would be micromanaged, and convinced that a mistake could kill their careers, too many officers devoted their brief tenures to flashy projects that made them, and their superiors, look good while avoiding the tough, unpopular steps necessary to resolve complicated problems.

In his 1955 War College thesis, Col. William G. Van Allen identified the changes he had witnessed in his own career: "The pre-war army of small posts and small units with direct operational leadership is gone, probably forever. Now the army's 'big business' and the opportunities for command leadership are very limited in the senior grades. There is an urgent need for 'executive leaders' who can control the more complex organization." The problem, as Van Allen recognized, was that, as was true in civilian businesses, the corporate heads were increasingly distanced from the workplace. As more and more authority was centralized further and further from the units who actually did the soldiering, there were ever-increasing demands for information, planning, and direction from ever-expanding staffs. The result was that field officers who should have been leading troops were instead co-opted into the "vicious circle of larger subordinate staffs, more detailed procedures and reporting and still closer supervision by the higher staff."[78] And at the bottom was the harassed junior officer, whose grim situation was described by one service historian: "Held on a very short leash and not allowed to exercise their judgment or initiative in their work . . . [they] were now required to attend to many housekeeping chores that have been left to corporals and sergeants in the interwar years . . . [and] found themselves working fifty, sixty, or even seventy hours a week, sacrificing their family life for the sake of their menial and oftentimes unnecessary duty."[79] Small wonder that too few, and often not the best, decided to remain in uniform.

In the decade after World War II, the army's soldiery experienced an even greater transformation than the officer corps. It was a transformation of both quantity and quality. In 1938 army enlisted personnel numbered barely 170,000, all of them volunteers and most drawn from the margins of society. A decade later enlisted strength topped 485,000; a decade further on it reached almost 800,000. This expansion was made possible by a radical shift in procurement: after 1948, conscription, or the threat of it, provided the great majority of incoming soldiers. As with American industry, the US Army faced the problem of not simply acquiring soldiers but of acquiring the right ones. The service's dilemma was encapsulated by a major general at the conclusion of a 1957 *Big Picture* episode: "Ours is a modern army, for and of the modern American soldier who was born into a land of applied science. Who cut his teeth on radio grids and model airplanes. Who grew up with mechanical marvels and electronic wonders as robust companions that he learned to adjust, maintain, and improve. To this resourceful soldier, we offer the army of the future today."[80]

As the *Big Picture* and other army publicity vehicles emphasized, not only was the service "modern, progressive, and forward thinking"; it now expected incoming soldiers to possess the crucial technical skills needed to maintain and employ that sophisticated equipment.[81] Army public relations rejected images that would tie the service to the past and always tried to portray soldiers riding helicopters, shooting missiles, operating computers and radios, and otherwise showing off the new model force's technical skill, education, and modernity.[82] But one unfortunate consequence was that many in senior leadership, who came of age in an era of far slower technological change, came to believe that incoming soldiers arrived with the high-tech skills the service required. Frustrated logisticians tried to explain that, contrary to officers' nostalgic memories of World War II, the jeep of the 1950s was so complicated that no GI could fix it with a screwdriver and that listening to rock and roll on a transistor did not qualify a teenager to operate a military radio. And as many officers have discovered since, the technical or educational skills a young postwar recruit brought in from the civilian world often did not compensate for his lack of other skills that earlier recruits had possessed.[83]

The *Big Picture*'s unspoken message was perhaps even more important. Whereas for over a century the army had, with the public's blessing, segregated its rankers from society, it now employed the latest media marvel—television—to urge Americans to send their best young men into uniform. The army's leadership knew how popular *Sergeant Bilko* and *Beetle Bailey* were and devoted enormous attention and resources to improving the service's image. The effort had two fronts: military personnel and civilians. The service conducted a host of surveys to detect sources of discontent, improve morale, and identify career incentives. The recruiting slogan "Join the Army and Secure Your Future" typically stressed the benefits of military service—education, vocational training, retirement, allowances, medical care—as far better than the uncertain public workplace. Army leaders adopted the language of Madison Avenue executives; Chief of Staff Eisenhower touted one recruitment campaign as "expertly handled and if salesmanship is firmly supported by the solid satisfaction of the buyer—that is, the soldier—permanent success is possible."[84]

The second front in army public relations was to secure public support for more personnel, bigger budgets, and an enhanced national security mission. Within months following World War II, the army selected J. Lawton Collins, an outstanding combat commander, to head a new public relations, or "information," branch. Courting civilian opinion, the army unleashed a full marketing and advertising arsenal: mottos such as "Mark of a Man" and "U.S. Army: Part of the Team for Security," drill exhibitions, radio shows, advertisements in magazines, parades, speeches to civic groups, declaring 6 April "Army Day," and so on. One of the most visible standard-bearers was the Women's Army Corps, whose designer uniforms, high education, and superior discipline made them favorites among the press and the public. Postwar army officers borrowed Madison Avenue's mantra that "this is an era of dynamic public relations," and the army like "any good product today must be 'sold' . . . or public opinion will not support that product."[85]

The postwar service stationed information officers at important headquarters to cultivate the media, plant favorable articles and kill negative ones, and publicize individual and unit accomplishments. This public relations campaign was just winning popular support when the Korean War sent the army's reputation into a tailspin. The service redoubled its efforts and throughout the 1950s sponsored radio and television programs, assisted in the production of movies (and edited their plots), participated in public events, worked with civic organizations, held sporting events, and marketed the new model army in dozens of other ways.[86] Rather than take pride in the wartime GI, the service's media campaigns sought to "associate the Army with the future [and] destroy any association with obsoleteness or decadence."[87]

The draftee-dependent army was a quantitative and qualitative transformation. At the time of Pearl Harbor only one in ten soldiers had a technical rating; by war's end that had doubled, and by 1957 it had nearly tripled. But maintaining that skilled labor force proved impossible without conscription. Barely six months after Japan surrendered, the secretary of war admitted that "many of our recruits are below the standard that should be set, [and] we dare not reject them for fear that better men will not be forthcoming."[88] In December 1947 a board created to investigate recruiting failures revealed what most enlisted personnel already knew: housing was abysmal, assignments unpredictable, working hours excessive, promotion slow, pay inadequate, and uniforms disliked. Recruiting violations abounded. Thousands assigned to the combat arms had enlisted for technical branches, and thousands more had failed to receive their promised vocational training. A 1948 survey revealed that a third had enlisted to better themselves (if not the service) through vocational education, a quarter because they could not find a job, and a sixth for such disparate motives as "to stop drinking," "get away from that damned whore," and "people telling lies in court tried to convict me."[89]

Despite, or perhaps because of, conscription, the post–World War II army had many of the same problems recruiting quality personnel as did its all-volunteer predecessors. Those who enlisted were usually motivated by notification of imminent conscription (i.e., they "volunteered to avoid the draft"), most were teenagers with little prospects for gainful employment, and not a few had joined as an alternative to prison. Category 4s—functionally illiterate and innumerate—represented on average a third of the enlisted ranks. In 1950 over half the inductees were in this group. Such unpromising personnel were useless in many of the army's hundreds of MOSs, some of which required over a year for qualification. Even those with potential for a military career required remedial schooling and extended training before they could perform at a level above manual labor. And many, after having achieved their vocational requirements, returned to civilian life. Much against its wish, the army was forced to rely on conscripts—usually older, better-educated, and work-experienced—to fill many of its skilled occupations. From the clerk who typed out company records for his semiliterate sergeant to the electronics whiz who maintained the Nike missile, the assurance of quality conscripts in sufficient numbers allowed the army to stick with a wasteful, high-turnover personnel system.[90]

Selective Service and desegregation made the army the most diverse social-economic, regional, and racial institution in the United States. Like the fictional squad in the comic strip *Beetle Bailey*—which debuted in 1950—a typical outfit might include a college dropout, a Category 4 illiterate, a gang member, an intellectual, and a hustler—all supervised by a tough, if overwhelmed, sergeant. An imaginative commander might find among those cast into his outfit by the personnel system an array of high-performing talent and an equal collection of unmotivated, feckless troublemakers. With over half its enlisted personnel under twenty-one, the army entered the 1950s as the first national agency required to deal with teenagers, described by one disgusted senior officer as "a parasitic-type of human who . . . is a radio-listening, game-attending, movie-going, auto-riding, television-watching creature who is rarely called upon to operate under his own power."[91]

The annual influx of draftees beginning their two-year obligation and the largely draft-motivated volunteers their three-year enlistment kept the enlisted lower ranks in perpetual turmoil. In FY 1956, which was not untypical, an army of 1,110,000 discharged 460,000 and enlisted 376,000.[92] Compounding this, the "pipeline"—processing, training, deployment, and discharge—swallowed one in four enlisted personnel. It was rare to get more than seventy-four "work" weeks out of a draftee's obligated 104. On the positive side, conscripts generally adjusted better to service life than their less-educated and often authority-resistant volunteer comrades. Their credo was summed up by their most famous member, Elvis Presley: "You can't fight them, so you can make it easy or you can make it hard for yourself. . . . If you are going to be an individual or try to be different you are going to go through two years of misery."[93] In common with the great majority of draftees, Elvis soldiered well.

Like Beetle Bailey's squad, the transient draftee privates often engaged in a generational war with "lifers" such as Sergeant Snorkel. Much as was true of the postwar officer corps, the postwar enlisted ranks were rank-heavy: in 1947 there was one sergeant for every two privates. But the prewar noncom had multiple enlistments, had extensive experience, and was a master of the soldier's trade, whereas the average postwar sergeant had limited schooling, was barely out of his teens, and owed his stripes to filling a job vacancy. He had learned on the job, perhaps as a capable tank mechanic, supply clerk, or squad leader, but he had neither experience nor training in the other duties of his rank. Even after being busted down a grade or two, such men still commanded rank, pay, and prestige far beyond what they might have acquired out of uniform; they and their Korean War successors would make the service a career.

The Enlisted Career Guidance Plan announced in January 1948 was a belated effort to create a new model sergeant for the new model army. Like OPA-47, it imposed standard personnel policies on all the armed forces, requiring the army to establish equivalences in MOSs, pay and benefits, and criteria for advancement. Through exemplary performance in the field, armywide competitions, and examination scores, a recruit might rise to the top levels (E-7) in six years, though ten was more common. Whereas prewar noncoms held their chevrons through the grace of their superior officers, their successors had a "travelling rating" that carried to subsequent assignments. And like officers, a career soldier could retire after twenty years' service with a lifetime pension, health benefits, and other perquisites. An important corollary was a reclassification program to weed out the unqualified, reduce the rank and authority of technicians, and restore primacy to troop leaders. The plan's implementation was halted by the Korean War, where the shortage of qualified noncoms resulted in men being promoted from corporal to master sergeant in barely three years.[94]

Despite some outstanding individual examples, there was a consensus among officers and soldiers that as a collective entity the postwar noncommissioned officer corps was not up to its responsibilities. Much of this was due to the persistent failure of the service to establish an enlisted education system to prepare noncoms for duties beyond their experience. The legacy of World War II and Korea further hampered rebuilding the noncom ranks. Many, if not most, who wore stripes had been spot-promoted to fill a specific task and had never received the training or education necessary to accomplish the multitude of tasks that went with the grade. Within a few years they had reached the highest levels (E-6 or E-7), but their skills remained limited to their individual experience. As the commandant of the Armor School explained in 1956, due to the "liberal promotion of enlisted men overseas to fill vacancies," the army has an excess of unqualified sergeants, and "we have to be ruthless in the application of our demands that the individual be competent in the grade that matches the stripes he wears. . . .

As long as the mediocre performance is our standard we will be stuck with this excess."[95] That year a sample of 2,350 sergeants revealed only 9 percent functioning at an eighth-grade education or above. The author of the survey noted that "we don't publicize it highly because we think it would reflect unfairly on the Army if it were generally known that one quarter of our NCO's could not reenlist without a waiver if they were privates."[96] The privates were not fooled: they labeled noncom remedial education "Ding-Dong School."

As in previous postwar eras, rebuilding the career ranks faced a number of persistent problems. One was that there was little incentive to remain in uniform until reaching the senior grades. A junior sergeant's pay and privileges were little better than a prewar private's—certainly not enough to support a family—and his path to promotion and a living wage were blocked by the hump of wartime veterans. These sergeants also had to tolerate the supervision of transitory junior-officer superiors who were usually ROTC graduates doing their obligatory two years of active service.[97] Perhaps even more of a burden were senior officers determined to enforce the discipline they remembered from the prewar force. "The enlisted man," Sgt. Harry Ryson opined, was "getting a bellyful of this close-order drill mentality. . . . [He] no longer cares about the glory of the regiment; that exists only for the tradition-minded commander standing on the reviewing stand who did not have to work the night before getting ready for the affair and did not have to endure the long, rigid hours spent waiting for the nightmare to get started and finished."[98]

Compounding the postwar noncom problem was that, like the officer corps, its ranks were so top-heavy there was insufficient work for them. The highest-ranking—first sergeants, sergeants major, platoon sergeants, and staff sergeants—used their traveling rating to avoid drudge assignments. Many others, like the *Soldier in the Rain*'s Master Sergeant William Maxwell, finagled assignments that required little work.[99] A not-untypical survey of one coveted post, the Armor School, revealed almost double the authorization for the top two grades and barely half for the lowest. In many "cushy" posts, Charles Williford declared, "it was not uncommon to find five or more master sergeants, ten or twelve technical sergeants, and staff sergeants by the numbers all assigned to one organization." Today's noncom, he asserted "is a security-conscious, cautious, and reluctant warrior. A man who works like a dog for master sergeant, avoids promotion to warrant officer, and then keeps his nose clean until his twenty years are in. Then he coasts, because from that day forward it is all gravy."[100]

Between the exigencies of the Korean War and the needs of the expanded draftee force, it took the US Army almost a decade after the end of World War II to give its full attention to improving the noncommissioned officer corps. Over a period of three years the army underwent a "dogged, unglamorous, unpopular, mandatory retraining and reclassification."[101] It booted out almost 60 percent of the wartime holdovers in the top three grades, improved the education of those who remained, and opened up promotion for the postwar generation. Congress aided matters by authorizing two new ranks of master sergeant (E-8) and sergeant major (E-9). Restricted to the top 2 percent, these grades were supposedly for those serving in combat units in the field, not deskbound intruders or bumbling Snorkels. To alleviate the long-standing problem of noncoms learning on the job or through impromptu crash courses, the army systemized the instructional curriculum. And in a vital step to retain occupational skills, Congress authorized proficiency pay for specialists, giving the best among them salaries several times above the rank on their sleeves.

As with earlier efforts, the initial success of the noncom reforms during the late 1950s was diluted by inflation. The noncom schools were chronically underfunded, and the respective branches and commanders were not willing to send their best sergeants to school when they were so desperately needed in the field. The ideal of restricting the top grades to the combat arms proved unworkable. Within a few years the E-8 and E-9 ranks were opened up to those the army needed to retain—technicians, bureaucrats, recruiters, ROTC cadre, and so forth—until within a decade some seventy-five MOSs qualified. One critic noted that at Fort Bragg and Fort Hood two out of every five E-9s were on desk duty; at Fort Lewis it was almost half. Fort Bragg alone boasted over 150 E-9s, including the head of its NCO mess.[102] The grade inflation was recognized inside and outside the service, most notably when television made the scheming Sergeant Ernie Bilko, chief of his post's motor pool, a master sergeant.

Closely related to the army's efforts to develop a competent, educated, and proficient noncommissioned officers corps was its efforts to improve the quality of enlisted force. In part this was due to the increased educational and technical demands of atomic age warfare, in part to the need to attract high-quality career soldiers, and in part to prove to the public and its members it deserved the right to conscript the nation's youths. Whereas the prewar US Army had been comfortable with semiliterate privates, the postwar army was one of the largest educational institutions in the nation. Academic offerings ranged from preliterate to university-level, with technical classes ranging from woodworking to rocket engines. The army's incessant quest to fill MOS positions meant that in some years as many as one in five soldiers enrolled in a specialist course. Some of the more technical occupations, particularly in electronics, required over a year for qualification. In the case of draftees, the army might reap only a few months of active duty before the soldier took his new skills to the civilian market. The ranks of the technical-administrative specialists continued to swell: by 1966 there were almost twice as many E-5s in specialist grades as in leadership positions.

In addition to education, the army also agreed to "assure the individual soldier and our total citizenry of the keen interest of the U.S. Army in wholesome and constructive social and recreational activities."[103] Its Character Guidance Program instructed soldiers in patriotism, morality, civics, anticommunism, obedience, and other societal virtues. But the service also sponsored a multitude of other activities to inform and entertain, underwriting the largest library system and movie theater chain in the world. Soldiers were encouraged to play sports, form musical combos, cultivate hobbies from photography to hot rods, travel, learn new languages, and in many other ways benefit from their time in uniform. Where postwar armies of the past had sought to segregate their privates from civilian society, the post–World War II conscript army tried to ensure connection. And to its credit, the service largely succeeded in convincing the American public that time in uniform benefited their sons. Even the nation's youths, most victimized by the draft, largely accepted it as yet another adult imposition and celebrated the hardships and occasional rewards of service life in the growing teen culture of music, comics, and television.[104]

By 1955 the US Army had undergone an unprecedented transformation from the force that had emerged from World War II. Its subordinate role in the Department of Defense bore almost no resemblance to the War Department bureaucracy that Secretary Calhoun had instituted and only a superficial one to that under Root. It had endured a personnel roller coaster—from 8.3 million in 1945 to 555,000 in 1948, then climbing to 1.6 million in 1953 before shedding 500,000 in the final two years. The service's concept of war still focused on large-scale conventional operations against a rival Great Power. But it now planned to fight this war with atomic warheads, missiles, helicopters, computers, and a host of other technological marvels. The army altered its social composition to an extent that would have amazed a prewar soldier. The majority of incoming officers, no longer the exclusive domain of West Pointers, now came from ROTC and served only a few years. And all officers advanced not according to seniority but through a career management system that plotted their assignments to ensure they emerged as generalists with experience in schooling, staff, training, and troops. But in many ways the career officers were reminiscent of their forebears. The majority of field-grade officers, and some company ones, were members of the traditional postwar "hump." Much of their social life—parades and ceremonies, formal calls on superiors, dances, sports, mess nights, and other customs and traditions—would have been familiar to officers fifty years earlier.

A decade after the end of World War II the traditional postwar army of lifetime privates drawn from the margins of society had vanished in favor of soldiers brought in through outright conscription or as volunteers avoiding the draft. For the overwhelming number of enlisted and officers, soldiering was a two-year gap marking the transition from adolescence to full citizenship and adulthood. Career enlisted personnel no longer spent the majority of their lives in one outfit; like officers they were shuffled from assignment to assignment. The service was not only desegregated and included women; it had a new mission almost as critical as defending the nation: as the inculcator of occupational skills and civic virtues in the nation's young people. The 1955 army was no longer the nation's employer of last resort. As Maj. Gen. Gilman C. Mudgett pointed out, it had become the organization with "the biggest employer-employee relationship program that exists in the United States today." Now the service had to overcome all the labor and management challenges of other megacorporations, from training, to equipping, to placement, to retention, to retirement—but with the unique problem "that 60% of our employees did not apply for their jobs."[105] And as had been true since the days of Secretary Elihu Root, the army was perennially short of skilled labor to maintain its machinery, facilities, and administration.

Despite the army's supreme efforts to transform itself for the atomic age, World War II's aftermath army had much in common with its postwar predecessors. Its missions had expanded—but they had after every war. And if the army replaced its prior commitment to defending the empire with new duties in Europe and Japan, it had almost the same proportion of its personnel deployed overseas as before World War II. The new weapons and materiel that featured so prominently in army claims of modernity were a thin veneer. In 1955 stateside soldiers wore uniforms, trained with weapons, and lived in barracks that were mostly indistinguishable from those of their wartime predecessors; the key difference was that their materiel was in far worse shape. Soldiers still spent much of their time laboring on tasks, from picking up cigarette butts to painting rocks, that were unrelated to their military duties. And in a complaint that might have dated from 1825, an officer told Chief of Staff Ridgway that the reason so many refused to reenlist was because "they joined the Army voluntarily or otherwise with the intent of soldiering and being led with firm and fair military discipline, and they ought to have been permitted to do the one and get the other."[106]

5

The Hollow Army after Vietnam, 1970–1980

In the stark words of one Vietnam War survivor: "We had a horrible Army after Vietnam. Poor leaders. Poor equipment. Terrible maintenance and logistics. Incredibly ill-disciplined, with racial and rampant drug problems."[1] Another veteran titled the chapter on the aftermath of that war "The Bad Years."[2] Although the last US Army combat unit would not depart South Vietnam until 1972, both physically and psychically the service had left the war much earlier. Physically US Army manpower had been cut from almost 1.6 million in 1968 to barely 800,000 in 1972. Psychically the Regular Army leadership had recognized that not only could they not win the war; it had caused a "collective nervous breakdown" that was destroying their service's discipline, personnel system, reputation, and identity.[3] Vietnam tarnished the army's reputation for decades. By war's end Americans were no longer willing to allow young men to be conscripted into military service. Many, if not the majority, of college-educated young people were openly hostile. Whether or not veterans were cursed and spat upon by antiwar advocates, many who served believed they had been. Politicians on both left and right withdrew their support and slashed budgets, the key difference being those on the right did so while claiming to support the troops. Between 1968 and 1978, personnel shrank by almost half, including a devastating purge of the officer corps. Racial tensions, indiscipline, violence, and substance abuse destroyed morale and cohesion, barracks were squalid, facilities and resources were patently inadequate, and equipment was obsolescent, damaged, unmaintainable, or unsuited for the army's postwar missions. In what immediately became iconic testimony, Chief of Staff Edward C. "Shy" Meyer warned Congress in June 1980 that the US Army was becoming a "hollow" force.[4]

How this dysfunctional organization transformed itself to the one that so decisively smashed the Iraqi army in 1991 has made it one of

the few of the army's postwar eras to generate an extensive literature. Some lionize the "visionary cohort of soldiers"—Creighton W.
Abrams, William E. DePuy, Paul F. Gorman, Donn A. Starry—who
anticipated and implemented a "revolution in military affairs" that resulted in the "certain victory" against Iraq in the Gulf War.[5] Other
authors have illuminated the institutional reforms and developments
in doctrine, recruitment, training, and materiel. Despite varied ap-
proaches, with few exceptions the histories of the post-Vietnam army
share a common narrative track and emphasis. After briefly cataloging
the sorry state of the aftermath force they rush to identify the individuals, organizations, policies, and materiel that set the US Army on
what one deterministic account titles the "road to victory in Desert
Storm."[6] Yet viewed from a longer duration, the post-Vietnam decade
conformed to traditional cycles and to traditional challenges. Moreover, far from being unique to the post-Vietnam army, the service's
dominant concerns were comparable to that experienced in every postwar decade since 1815.[7]

Even as the last troops were withdrawing in 1973, Chief of Staff Frederick C. Weyand proclaimed: "Men and women of the U.S. Army went
into Vietnam with their heads high and they came out with their heads
high—*Mission Accomplished!*"[8] Two decades later, the combat veteran
and future statesman Colin Powell encapsulated the Vietnam narrative
as well as its lesson when he wrote: "Many of my generation, the career
captains, majors, and lieutenant colonels seasoned in that war, vowed
that when our turn came to call the shots, we would not quietly acquiesce in halfhearted warfare for half-baked reasons that the American
people could not understand or support."[9]

If the career officer corps was seasoned by its experience in Vietnam,
the result was not the homogenous, professional, and stalwart force
that Powell extolled. As Meredith H. Lair has documented, during the
war the army channeled both individual and material resources into
lavish facilities in rear areas for the 75–90 percent of military personnel in noncombat assignments. These "REMFs" were provided gigan-
tic PXs stuffed with cheap electronics, swimming pools and basketball
courts, all-you-can-eat dining facilities, and an eight-hour workday
with weekends off. Many had a far easier and privileged life in the
wartime Vietnam army than they would in the later peacetime force.[10]

In the field, things were very different. Rather than keeping proven
combat leaders with the grunts, the army's personnel system rotated
them out of command at six months, and often less. Most then went

to staff and other, safer assignments to make a place for a new officer. Despite an officer-to-enlisted ratio of one-to-five, line units were skeletonized. Michael S. Davison recalled that it was common to find "a battalion commanded by a Lieutenant Colonel who had a Captain for an executive officer and Second Lieutenants for company commanders. The normal tenure for these inexperienced company commanders was three to four months, and the entire strength of the company turned over every nine to twelve months."[11]

The army's rotation policy kept the Regular Army's career ladder moving and allowed its members a chance to "punch a ticket" for promotion, although at substantial cost to morale, cohesion, and expertise in the combat forces. This lack of experienced leadership in the field was made even more serious by the retirement of many veteran noncoms and the fact that many others carried a "profile" that designated them unable for physical or personal reasons to deploy. Over the course of the Vietnam War, the historian and veteran Ronald Spector argued, the career army congregated in the rear, leaving the fighting to "draftees, one-term enlistees, instant NCOs, and OCS and ROTC graduates."[12] Even the fighting diminished dramatically: by the end of 1971 only 12,000 of the 157,00 soldiers in South Vietnam were in combat units. By August of the next year only support organizations remained.[13]

Within the army, the interpretation of the lessons of Vietnam began in controversy, and this remains so half a century later. The service, defense analysts, and contractors such as the legendary S. L. A. Marshall generated reams of information that appeared in journals, books, and intraservice publications intended for immediate application on tactics, equipment, operations, combat, and other relevant topics. The depth and breadth of the army analysis extended from company officers attending the Infantry School writing on their combat experiences to general officers analyzing airmobile and riverine operations in the *Vietnam Studies* series.[14] As had occurred after earlier conflicts, senior officers contributed their memoirs. Several embittered field officers criticized conduct of the war, their leaders, and the decline of the US Army's effectiveness. As in the aftermath of earlier wars, the postwar "battle of the books" exacerbated existing divisions and did little to heal the service.[15] But perhaps because so much of the literature inevitably brought to light individual and institutional failings, even more important than learning Vietnam's lessons was, in David Fitzgerald's apt phrase, "learning to forget."[16]

With the legacy of Vietnam so divisive, the service gladly moved on from the lost war. The intellectual flight was facilitated, as the officer-historian Robert Doughty recognized, by the "opportune occurrence" of the 1973 Yom Kippur War. The speed, lethality, and technological innovations revealed during that war "served to accelerate the transition from the previous focus on counterinsurgency to the new focus on conventional warfare."[17] Accelerating this pivot, army analyses concluded that their service's earlier technological and training superiority had dissipated during the Vietnam years. Soviet equipment was now as good as or better than its American equivalents, and their troops were far better trained than a decade prior. With the Warsaw Pact's rising strength added to the crippling lethality of conventional combat, American forces in Europe now faced the challenge encapsulated in the service's mantra—"to fight outnumbered and win."[18]

President Richard M. Nixon, as the usually reserved Gen. Bruce R. Palmer opined, "was a very devious person when it came to making and implementing decisions."[19] The newly elected commander in chief was determined to show he was strong on defense, but he was equally determined to withdraw from Vietnam and slash military spending. Proclaiming he had achieved peace with honor, during Nixon's five years in office army personnel fell from 1.5 million to 783,000.[20] Such a ruthless drawdown would have been traumatic enough, but the president's propensity to seek immediate political benefits at the cost of long-term strategic achievements compounded the trauma. In one not-untypical example, Nixon threw planning for the 1970 Cambodian incursion into turmoil when he pulled out marine units and increased army forces, simultaneously slashing draft calls from 114,000 to 10,000. Continental Army Command (CONARC), the mammoth organization responsible for recruiting, training, and deploying personnel, had to rush reinforcements to Vietnam, keep the overseas garrisons filled, and maintain its accessions and training schedules. Half a year later, CONARC's commander, reflecting on the dangerous gaps in stateside force structure, admitted that "we ate off the shelves which are now bare."[21] The president's willingness to sacrifice coherent manpower planning to political advantage was shared by Congress, which in September 1971 insisted the army cut 50,000 personnel within nine months, thereby sending the entire personnel management system into frantic improvisation.

The Vietnam drawdown was all the more traumatic because it corresponded with the momentous shift from the conscript experiment

to a volunteer force. A presidential commission under the former secretary of defense Thomas Gates soon split over whether the mandate
was to end the draft or to create effective, sustainable armed forces.
The army's leadership—almost unanimous in retaining Selective Service—tended to emphasize conscription's intangibles, such as the citizen's obligation to the nation and the service's connection with the
American public. More realistically, they feared a return to the army's
historic peacetime role as marginalized, dispersed, underfunded, and
unready. This apprehension underlay much of the service's insistence
that the nation establish a *modern* volunteer army: a force for the future and not a return to the past. These concerns were dismissed by the
academics and policymakers who advanced strictly rational (if wrong)
market economy arguments that better recruiting, increased pay,
subsidized medical care, housing, and other benefits would make the
armed forces competitive with private sector employers. With good
reason, most army officers who participated in the Gates Commission
were convinced that Nixon's insistence on ending the draft had sacrificed the army's prospects of recovery.[22]

The transition to the Modern Volunteer Army was complicated by
early decisions that, however wise they appeared in retrospect, were
calamitous in the ensuing decade. Of these, perhaps none was more
problematic than Chief of Staff Abrams's (1972–1974) arrangement to
increase active force structure without a concurrent increase in personnel. By mid-1973 the drawdown had hollowed out personnel; the
planners at Army Staff struggled to balance overly ambitious missions
with limited resources. Gen. William DePuy believed that the US
Army had sufficient personnel for only ten good divisions. Another
general pointed out that the FY 1973 estimates for thirteen active divisions could be accomplished only by cutting each division slice—the
total personnel required to keep a division functional—from 48,000 to
31,000.[23] In a bit of Pentagon legerdemain, military spokesmen waved
away such concerns with the claim that they could fill the divisions
with 221,000 reservists, downplaying the fact that reserve units were
neither organized to be part of the division slice nor ready for mobilization. When news broke that Congress required yet deeper cuts—
to 765,000 by mid-1974—planners concluded that, even by reducing
many units to skeleton formations and removing all personnel from
others ("zeroing out"), the service could sustain only a dozen active
divisions.

Without informing his own staff, Abrams met with his civilian
chiefs and brokered a personal agreement—sometimes termed the

"golden handshake"—that the army would increase the active force to sixteen divisions without any additional soldiers. Abrams's admiring biographer describes this "bombshell" as a crucial turning point in the army's recovery from Vietnam: stabilizing personnel, ensuring the activation of the Organized Reserves in a crisis, and, most important, altering how the US Army was perceived by the public and its own members.[24] A more sustainable argument is that of Dwight E. Phillips: "The roots of the 1970s' 'Hollow Army' began with Abrams pegging the Army to an unsustainable force structure."[25]

Much of Abrams's justification for an underpopulated sixteen-division active force rested on another Nixon-era initiative: the 1970 Total Force Concept, in which regulars, the National Guard, and the Organized Reserves would achieve the long-announced goal of being able to quickly mobilize in the event of war. Although it conformed to the political goals of Nixon and Congress, in the short term Total Force eviscerated postwar readiness. First, and perhaps foremost, reserve combat units—some twenty battalions in total—were assigned to "round out" nine understrength stateside divisions in the event of mobilizing for war. Second, it allowed the active force to dump its sustain-and-support units into the reserves and thus generate sufficient combat units to fill, at least partially, the promised sixteen divisions while complying with the 765,000-person limit on the active force. Some authors assert a third rationale: that Abrams deliberately organized Total Force to blend active and reserve forces so that it would be impossible for any politician to send the former to war without simultaneously mobilizing the latter. This last argument has found little documentary support, and Conrad Crane has argued convincingly that, if Abrams's goal was to usurp presidential powers, his initiative "failed miserably."[26]

Although with the benefit of hindsight Abrams's sixteen-division plan may have retained active divisions for the 1980s buildup, the results approached the "Total Farce" nickname bestowed by those who lived with its consequences.[27] The round-out initiative was plagued by equipment shortages, training lapses, and a great deal of creative accounting. In order to fight as part of a combat force, the Organized Reserves units had to have equivalent equipment and MOS-qualified personnel and be trained sufficiently to deploy immediately. They were expected to be as competent as soldiers who trained every day while also holding down full-time jobs in the civilian sector. This would have been a difficult task even in the best of times. But the Department of the Army in the 1970s could not meet even the unrealistic budget imposed by Congress to outfit Abrams's overexpanded active force. As a result, reserve units were under-resourced in equipment, personnel, and training. And given limited opportunities for the professional schooling needed to master their military skills, they could not improve. Moreover, the ending of conscription gutted reserve units even more than it did active forces. Many guardsmen and reservists had accepted a six-year commitment in the 1960s to avoid service in Vietnam. By FY 1976 almost 450,000—or 65,000 more than the entire National Guard—would be eligible for discharge.[28]

Shifting the bulk of support and logistic units to the Organized Reserves to fill active combat divisions had a similar Potemkin effect. It did allow the army to maintain the large overseas garrisons that the national security policy demanded, but it did *not* provide the means for those forces to fulfill their mission to fight and win the first battle. In Germany, 2nd Lt. Michael Toler's mechanized four-squad infantry platoon was authorized at fifty-two soldiers but seldom had more than thirty-six, including half his squad leaders. Lt. James Willbanks's platoon was so understrength that, when it deployed to its alert positions on the East German border, he would set out metal stakes signifying the missing troopers: "MG" for machine-gunner, "G" for grenadier, and so forth.[29] As one corps commander noted when he left Europe in 1980, without an immediate, massive, and near-impossible augmentation of the rounded out stateside divisions, the defenders "could do well the first day or two and then we would have shot our wad."[30]

In an effort to fill the army's depleted ranks, Abrams accelerated the full integration of women into the active force and accelerated the death of the Women's Army Corps. The 1970 Supreme Court ruling that married servicewomen had similar family entitlements, parity for jobs, promotion, and other equal rights was one strike against a segregated branch. The conservatism of some WAC leaders—one of whom allegedly tried to restrict WACs to MOSs in which they wore skirts—also generated demands from activist younger officers to, in the words of one *Army* contributor, "Go Ahead—Exploit Us!"[31] But Abrams and Army Staff recognized that women's participation was essential for the MVA's success. Between 1972 and 1974 the army removed the limits on promotion, increased the number of open MOSs from 173 to 430, awarded women full scholarships in the ROTC, and provided married women full spousal benefits. These years also saw the number of women increase to 26,000, exceeding army recruitment goals in both quantity and quality. Women had higher educational standards, exhibited fewer disciplinary problems, and were crucial for some MOSs. In 1975, with almost 40,000 women in uniform, the army formally requested that both the WAC and the separate promotion list be abolished.[32]

As was the case in the past, after a flurry of changes in the first postwar years, the rest of the decade witnessed consequences. Those who helmed the army in the postwar decade, Frederick C. Weyand (1974–1976), Bernard W. Rogers (1976–1979), and Edward C. Meyer (1979–1983), fit this historic pattern. All focused on managing the personnel, materiel, and force structure policies they inherited. Under their collective tenure the army reverted to its pre-Vietnam focus on large unit conventional warfare in Europe, building its doctrine, equipment procurement, and training around this scenario. Some of the issues most controversial at the time—particularly increasing minority accession and advancement, ending the Women's Army Corps, and admitting women to West Point—proved easier than expected. Others—such as delays in equipment modernization, recruiting and retention shortfalls, racial tensions, substance abuse, and the progressive deterioration of stateside forces—were not. By the time Meyer left in 1983, the postwar army had made great strides toward recovery, but as the conflict in Grenada demonstrated, it was not necessarily on the path to becoming the Desert Storm army of 1991.[33]

In the immediate post-Vietnam decade, the US Army underwent substantial administrative reform. Unlike previous postwar eras, this was less a politically imposed reorganization than an internal one. With the Pentagon's attention fixed on administering the aftermath army, the initiative for moving the service toward its future fell to two 1973 organizations carved out from CONARC. The US Army Forces Command (FORSCOM) managed stateside-based active and reserve personnel, infrastructure, and tactical and support units. But as was common with previous postwar administrative changes, the impact was not immediately apparent in the field. As had been the common pattern since 1815, soldiers struggled with the detritus of war: decaying installations and training facilities, broken equipment, insufficient and often unprepared troops, personnel turbulence, a dearth of personnel in high-skill MOSs, and many other issues. The US Army Training and Doctrine Command (TRADOC) took responsibility for small unit training, doctrine, the school system, and combat developments. Under its first commander, General DePuy (1973–1977), TRADOC became the center of a concerted effort to build a new model army, one that rejected the Vietnam experience and looked toward (or, more accurately, back to) the repulse of a Soviet attack on NATO.[34]

Reviewing the trauma that rocked the service in FY 1972, one of its historians asked the question that would dominate much of the 1970s: "How could the Army, on the heels of an unpopular war, in the face of antimilitary sentiment and social ferment, with reduced strength and appropriations, and without resort to the draft, maintain a strong, viable, and professional ground force to meet its current and future roles and missions?"[35] It was a question much easier to ask than to answer. With the return to the pre–World War II all-volunteer army establishment, the task of providing the training and management for a post–World War II mass-mobilization citizen-soldier army disappeared. Yet persisting against this diminution of responsibilities was the fact that the US Army's missions—Western Europe, the Far East, stateside-based rapid reaction force for emergencies—were still those of the post–World War II draftee force. In 1962 the conscript army of 1,066,000 officers and men could station 278,000 in Europe and 54,000 in Japan and Korea. A decade later, the transitioning volunteer force of 801,000 could maintain only 172,000 in Europe and 37,000 in the Far East—and those numbers were falling.[36] Compounding the manpower–mission disconnect was a much larger issue of whether in the aftermath of Vietnam committing ground forces seemed to promise little else than long, bloody, slugging matches in faraway places: easy to get into, but difficult to get out of. To a war-sick public and its representatives, now grappling with the economic and social consequences of Vietnam, it seemed better to build up the air force and navy to wage rapid, decisive, and bloodless (at least to Americans) operations.

The question of the post-Vietnam army's purpose so troubled the higher command that Chief of Staff Abrams commissioned a study with the appropriate title "Why Do We Need an Army?" Released in 1973, it was a fundamentally conservative manifesto that recycled many arguments made during the 1950s for countering a Soviet invasion of Western Europe. As its predecessors had maintained, it concluded that only in-place land forces could defeat the attack and secure a favorable resolution before nuclear escalation. The 1973 report not only provided a justification for the future new model army; it served to inspire a number of initiatives in training, doctrine, materiel, personnel, and motivation.[37]

TRADOC's commander, William DePuy, was convinced that drastic action was needed to prevent the army from continuing to agonize over Vietnam. He interpreted the 1973 Yom Kippur War as evidence of "a historic turning point in the evolution of Army forces," an imminent revolution in military affairs.[38] It was up to TRADOC to overhaul

US Army warfighting—from squad training, to tactics, to the procurement of new equipment, to force structure. He set about doing
this with a passion, efficiency, and bureaucratic ruthlessness that—at
least in TRADOC's histories and to those who drew their inspiration
from them—transformed the broken post-Vietnam force to the 1980s
"Army of Excellence."[39] Throughout the process the unifying intellectual framework was DePuy's managerial approach, in which all his priorities—materiel modernization, training, leadership, doctrine—were
conceptualized, tested, and evaluated to determine the best solution.
Once the general had decided on the correct course, he intended to
impose it on the rest of the army.

DePuy's primary vehicle for transforming the army was the 1975
doctrinal publication *FM 100–5: Operations*. In Paul H. Herbert's astute
summary, the general intended the manual as "an overarching concept
of warfare that would rationalize everything the Army did, from training recruits to designing tanks, in term of how the Army intended to
fight."[40] Written in simple language and replete with numerous illus-
trations, *FM 100–5* applied system analysis and cost-effectiveness to
what DePuy saw as both the primary threat and the primary impetus
to forcing change: a Soviet invasion of NATO. On one level, its central tactical concept—Active Defense—reflected a realistic if narrow
assessment of the tactical problem—simplified as "*prepare to win the
first battle of the next war.*"[41] It recognized that NATO would not be
allowed potentially better options such as a preventative spoiling attack or an extended defense-in-depth that abandoned West German
territory. The solution was to absorb the Soviet armored offensive,
channel it into kill zones, and stop the invaders at the border, in the
process inflicting such heavy casualties that the Soviets would have to
abandon the campaign.

His assessment of the postwar force left DePuy pessimistic about
the wartime capabilities of enlisted personnel and junior officers. In a
momentous intellectual shift, he abandoned a key army doctrinal assumption dating back at least to Pershing: that the initiative and intelligence of American soldiers made them qualitatively better than their
opponents. Instead, revitalizing a debate in army military thought
that continues to this day, he argued that war-winning quality would
be provided by superior American equipment. He saw in the army's
equipment procurement program—especially the new weapon systems
later made famous as the "Big Five"—a crucial opportunity for the
army to gain, for the first time, a decided weapon-to-weapon advantage over Soviet equivalents. Although his successors would return to

extolling the inherent qualities of American troops, DePuy's insistence on technological supremacy remains a foundation of not only doctrine but also army self-identity.[42]

By a fortuitous coincidence, DePuy's desire to create an army for high-intensity mechanized warfare in Europe coincided with what TRADOC historians termed the "training revolution" envisioned by Lt. Gen. Paul F. Gorman.[43] Like DePuy, Gorman wanted to build the force from the tactical units up, and like DePuy he applied systems analysis to the problem. His breakthrough was to recognize training as demonstrable mastery of a specific skill and not, as was common army practice, certifying a soldier's competence after completion of the requisite hours of instruction. In Gorman's performance-oriented training, each MOS task was broken into component bits; a soldier had to demonstrate proficiency at each level before moving forward. To train and test for MOS expertise, Gorman established the Skill Qualification Test (SQT). Noncommissioned officers would supervise SQTs, aided (or directed) by TRADOC-issued *Soldier's Manuals*. In keeping with TRADOC's systems-analysis approach, SQTs provided indices to measure the performance of individuals; the Army Training and Evaluation Program did so for organizations. Ultimately, Gorman envisioned one or more large training centers where brigade-size units would be able to maneuver and fire in realistic practice of TRADOC's tactics against a surrogate Soviet force.[44]

With the benefit of hindsight, augmented by TRADOC's own histories, there is a consensus that the morphing of DePuy's doctrine into AirLand Battle (along with the implementation of Gorman's reforms) set the stage for the four-day victory over Iraq in the 1991 Desert Storm campaign. But such a lineal, causal, and triumphalist narrative ignores the far more complicated two-decade transition of the post-Vietnam army. As DePuy acknowledged, TRADOC's initiatives in doctrine, procurement, and training began as individual projects; it is only in retrospect that they "took on the appearance of something designed whole from the beginning."[45] Perhaps more important, the claim by one of DePuy's admirers that the general "had an intellectual grasp that was so broad that it encompassed the whole Army [and] [t]hrough the power of his intellect[] the Army changed" fails to acknowledge the problems the army experienced implementing TRADOC's initiatives and the role of other commanders who pursued their own, equally important, initiatives.[46]

Under DePuy and Gorman TRADOC compensated for the post-war decade's transient enlisted and junior officer force by structuring rigid, lockstep, and mechanistic doctrine and training regimens. But Gen. Maxwell Thurman, who would later head TRADOC, identified the key weakness in the DePuy–Gorman agenda: "The concept was exactly on, but the people to execute it were exactly the opposite of the people necessary to take advantage of it."[47] Although TRADOC manuals were written at a sixth-grade level, soldiers in the units could not or would not read them, in part because a large number (2,000 in one division) lacked basic English literacy. Many of these problems were TRADOC's responsibility. Analysts found that the organization was failing to provide adequate basic training; soldiers arrived at their units with perhaps 60–70 percent of the skills they needed to perform their MOSs and required additional instruction from their already hard-pressed leaders to become proficient members of their squads.[48] Compounding the problem was the time and resources Gorman's program required and the long lag time between conception and implementation. It was not until 1979 that the first infantry battalion in Europe went through the SQT, and its implementation required 238 battalion staff man-days, 52 man-days for every company, and seven weeks of individual squad training.[49] Confronted with overwhelming evidence of failure to pass their SQTs—90 percent of nuclear specialists and 82 percent of air-defense missile crews—the army responded by dropping the passing score from 80 to 60. It was a solution, but one that accepted a D- grade as good enough.[50]

Another stumbling block for TRADOC's training revolution was personnel turbulence, particularly in the stateside combat units assigned to FORSCOM. One 1977 study of an infantry division revealed its combat squads averaging a 30 percent shortage in personnel and half its soldiers transferring out within a two-month period. Over that period's 40,000 man-days, only half were allocated to training, and even this was substantially reduced by headquarters-imposed garrison maintenance. Once in the field, soldiers spent much of their time either enroute to the training sites or standing around.[51] Two years later, analysts extended their assessment of training to five FORSCOM combat divisions. Not only did the average division suffer an annual turnover rate of 71 percent (one had 92 percent); each one had "critical shortages" in combat, supply, maintenance, and administrative personnel. Headquarters appropriated the best personnel, contributing to a "low-performance group norm"—and constantly interrupted training with short-notice assignments like maintaining ranges, restoring buildings, guard duty, ceremonies, and so forth. Between personnel turbulence and insufficient time and resources, inspectors found that "readiness reports are obsolete soon after they are completed." Committed officers and noncoms improvised by zeroing out partial units to create one at full strength, assigning bilingual instructors, and routinely working sixty-hour weeks. Despite TRADOC mandating progressive small-to-large training, the investigators found that "unit commanders paid the most attention to short term requirements and felt that at the company level nothing could be depended upon beyond 30 days out." Indeed, the consensus in every division was "collective training above the company level cannot be effectively performed." Neither was there much chance of improvement in the field forces, since "NCOs and officers get out of the Army because they are always handling the same crises and can't see any progress after hard work."[52]

Much of the army's recovery from Vietnam that is later ascribed to top-down directives owed its origins to field commanders who implemented rigorous, combat-focused, and innovative programs. During Maj. Gen. Henry E. Emerson's 1973–1975 command of the 2nd Infantry Division in Korea, each battalion rotated every three months for a ten-day nonstop tactics course, then shifted to night exercises. Officers and noncoms were expected to lead the program, and dozens who could not measure up were relieved.[53] In the 25th Infantry Division, Maj. Gen. Harry L. Brooks's program emphasized realistic, tough, stressful, and challenging combat training at the individual and small-unit levels that included the "Tropic Lighting Mile" (three miles), night operations, airmobile assaults, obstacle courses, and other realistic tests. In an indication that soldiers liked such tough soldiering, reenlistments increased, crime dropped, and substance-abuse cases declined.[54]

A good argument can be made that the army's most influential trainer in the immediate post-Vietnam era was Lt. Gen. Arthur S. "Ace" Collins, the deputy commander in United States Army Europe (USAREUR) between 1971 and 1973. Collins was more than a hands-on trainer, he was an intellectual with a gift for putting complex ideas into an understandable format and then devising methods to implement them. His *Common Sense Training: A Working Philosophy* became a canonical work for junior officers, selling over 100,000 copies.[55] Perhaps the best testimony to his impact on the forces in Germany was the decision by an officer who served with Collins to title his chapter "The Recovery."[56]

Collins had little patience with commanders who had given up on the postwar army. Typical was his directive to one unfortunate battalion commander to "get out of the office and get his officers out from behind their desks."[57] Visiting an artillery battery, he found a senior sergeant reading from a training manual to a large formation of soldiers. Collins summoned the battery command and tore into them for "poor, uninteresting, not properly prepared [training that] turns the troops against the Army."[58] Yet Collins was far from a martinet; his goal was always to improve the force. On one occasion a captain defended his soldiers and complained that on a recent visit to head-quarters he had seen "roomfuls of senior NCOs" that should be with the troops. Rather than slap this officer down for insubordination, Collins commended him.[59]

In common with DePuy and Gorman, Collins recognized that rebuilding soldier skills had to begin at the small-unit level, stress fundamentals, practice these skills constantly, and ensure they were supervised. But his view of training incorporated the unglamorous yet essential parts of soldiering such as administration, race relations, maintenance, morale, living conditions, and leadership. In a very un-DePuy initiative, Collins decentralized training responsibilities throughout USAREUR. He pushed it down to the unit command-ers, insisting that company commanders draw up their own training schedules, battalion commanders outline objectives and supervise, and senior commanders provide guidance, set priorities and resources, and assess overall effectiveness. He was also less focused on what the ideal soldier should be in the future and was more sensitive to the realities of the European battlefield of the early 1970s and the US Army that would have to fight on it. In his oral history, Michael S. Davison, USA-REUR commanding general, recalled how Collins inevitably returned from his training inspections shaking his head and beginning his report "you won't believe what I saw today." But by late 1973, Collins came back smiling, recognizing that USAREUR was on the way to recovery; Davison then "loosed the bonds" and moved from small-unit to bat-talion- and division-size training.[60]

The army in Europe predated and superseded TRADOC's influ-ence in many other ways. The Return of Forces to Germany (RE-FORGER) exercises provided the service with the only opportunity to practice large-scale tactical operations on the very battlefield DePuy envisioned. Maj. Gen. Thomas P. Lynch recalled his brigade's twenty-one-day ordeal in the 1974 REFORGER: "We ran our tanks some-thing like 200 miles in snow, ice and mud, and we tore up the ground and we were everywhere; from one end of that division area to an-other."[61] Lynch dismissed the "wimps" sent by TRADOC to explain the new doctrine: "They were all full of crap. . . . Christ we were already in the active defense—we didn't need a new name."[62] Perhaps most important, Germany was also where one of DePuy's disciples, Donn Starry, concluded that the doctrine did not work. On his return in 1977 to take control of TRADOC, Starry began a complete revision of *FM 100–5: Operations* that appeared in 1982. Referred to as "AirLand Battle," this doctrine was credited with directing the way the army employed forces against Iraq in 1991.[63]

As the US Army withdrew from Vietnam there was widespread recognition that the officer corps had lost much of its profession's ethics, expertise, and prestige—both inside and outside the service. Combat officers were simultaneously envious and outraged when they observed the bloated administrative and support headquarters, the polished boots and starched uniforms, the air-conditioning, the bulging PXs, and all the other comforts in the rear echelons. Their outrage might have been tempered by the knowledge that, due to the army's fixation on managing careers, within a few months they would share in such luxury.[64] By some accounts infantry commanders were so transitory that they had little opportunity to lead: squads and companies might have as many as four in a year while themselves going through a 200 percent change in personnel. Given these short tours and the industrial production of lieutenants through OCS and ROTC, many field-grade officers lacked confidence in their company-grade officers' tactical and leadership abilities. These subordinates were embittered by what they saw as superiors who were careerist, critical, risk-adverse, and micromanaging. A trope of Vietnam war stories was the skirmish in which "the battalion commander was circling; his brigade commander was circling; the division commander was circling; the corps commander was circling; and the poor [captain] wasn't allowed to do anything on his own initiative."[65] There was perhaps even greater anger at the senior leaders in Washington, who were blamed for not standing up to the politicians, not allowing the army to fight to win, and for all-around moral cowardice. Indeed, Chief of Staff Harold K. Johnson's alleged reason for not resigning—"that they'll just put somebody in who will vote the way they want him to"—provides a brutal assessment of himself, his fellow generals, and the decline in the profession's ethics.[66]

In a 1970 paper, Col. Robert E. McCord provided a grim view of the challenges his fellow officers faced in the coming decade. Since the war began, the "typical officer" had been shuttled from assignment to assignment, "constantly learning new duties" and concerned primarily "that nothing goes wrong during the period of his temporary tenure." McCord had been overseas twice in the last five years, enduring the emotional and financial costs of extended separations from his family. The next decade did not promise to alleviate this instability. Government accommodations were "woefully inadequate in quantity as well as quality," forcing many to "accept near slum-like housing." Fringe benefits were steadily eroding, medical and dental care for soldiers and their families was inadequate, shopping on posts was overcrowded, and recreational facilities were inadequate and often closed. The officer corps was suffering from collective burnout, manifested by high attrition among junior officers and "early retirement syndrome" among senior officers, many of whom spent their last years in uniform searching for a civilian job. Grim as McCord's view of the officer corps' prospects was, he probably would have concluded that it was overoptimistic had he anticipated the winnowing of its ranks that would soon occur.[67]

During his 1968–1972 tenure as Army Chief of Staff, William C. Westmoreland was profoundly shaken by what he termed the "terrible shame of My Lai and the failure of the officer leadership."[68] He was distraught not only by the massacre but also that the board headed by Lt. Gen. William R. Peers recommended that twenty-eight officers, including the division commander during My Lai, Samuel W. Koster, be charged with 224 military offenses. With this 15 May 1971 summation, Peers submitted a private memo to Westmoreland that identified a deep and pervasive moral rot within the army officer corps. The chief of staff ordered the Army War College to conduct a review of the officer corps' professionalism and was appalled when it confirmed Peers's assessment. Reflecting his personal and professional ideals, Westmoreland tasked the War College with preparing another study on the military leadership needed for the all-volunteer force of the next decade. Both reports revealed a consensus, from lieutenant to general, on the importance of professional standards, competence, and integrity, with far less consensus on whether the service was living up to these ideals.[69]

Although a direct cause-and-effect relationship is impossible to establish, the War College studies and Westmoreland's actions helped shift the definition of officer expertise toward leadership rather than management, inserted ethics training into school curriculums, focused attention on command climate, and fueled the impetus for dramatic change. Many of these reforms were credited with enhancing the professional standards and competence demonstrated in the Gulf War. But as the historian Dwight E. Phillips noted, the official Army histories, while quick to take credit for Desert Storm, "are largely silent on reforms that addressed [the] personnel management system, leadership practices, and organizational climate. . . . [perhaps because] a full explanation would uncomfortably highlight the poor state of the 1970s officer corps and how many human management goals have remained unrealized."[70]

One of the most traumatic of these human management goals was the reduction in force (RIF) that followed the Vietnam War. As with previous wars, Vietnam had accelerated officers' careers. In what became known as "shake-and-bake" promotions, it was rare for a lieutenant not to advance to captain within two years. If an officer remained on active duty and did a second tour of Vietnam, he might be a major after seven years and perhaps a lieutenant colonel within a dozen. The rampant inflation in rank did not necessarily correlate to combat experience. One survey of the infantry lieutenant colonels selected for colonel found that, in the previous decade, their average time in troop command was barely ten months.[71] By 1971 the army was so rank-heavy that for every two second lieutenants there was one lieutenant colonel, and for every three there were two majors. One brigadier general claimed, with no pride, that in the Pentagon alone there were 3,000 more colonels and ten more lieutenant generals than the combined American armed forces had required to wage World War II.[72]

Between FYs 1970 and 1976 the active-duty officer corps shrank from over 170,000 to 98,000. The process resembled what the future Chief of Staff Gordon R. Sullivan termed "a wholesale, big muscle movement release of people."[73] In 1969, recognizing the inevitability of the drawdown, the service began cutting accessions: the number of OCS graduates dropped by 350 percent in 1970 alone, and the ROTC graduates designated for active duty declined from 15,500 to 9,237. In FY 1971, 1,906 officers went before boards for inefficiency and nonperformance, with the recommendation that 1,218 be released. But that was a drop in the bucket in an officer corps required to rapidly shed tens of thousands.[74] Very quickly the boards, in Sullivan's words, "started getting into the meat" as they were forced to choose which of many highly qualified candidates would remain.[75]

With no apparent irony, Secretary of the Army Robert F. Froehlke, in a 1972 article on pride and integrity, justified the purge in brutally frank terms: they might have been good combat leaders, but "in the harsh light of competition[] we felt [they] would not measure up in the long haul."[76] Whereas previous postwar boards had privileged candidates with wartime experience, those of 1970s were under orders to identify the qualities that would be valuable for the future. However, as with previous drawdowns the cuts fell unevenly, with disproportionately more senior field grades retained under the rationale their experience and expertise were necessary in case of national mobilization.[77] In contrast, those of company-grade rank with less than eight years service took a very hard hit. Many of the junior officers targeted for involuntary release lacked the college degrees seen as necessary for the Modern Volunteer Army. One recent West Point graduate who joined the 101st Airborne Division watched an OCS graduate with years of service and a Silver Star struggling to obtain a night-school diploma so that he could remain an officer.[78] Another targeted group included career enlisted men who had been given direct commissions: The lucky ones were allowed to soldier on as sergeants until they qualified for retirement; many others were discharged short of their pensions. Lt. Gen. James B. Vaught recalled such examples—all outstanding combat leaders and only a few years from their twenty-year retirements: "They threw them out in the street. I didn't understand it then, and I don't understand it now. I think it was unnecessary, it was cruel, and it was wrong."[79] The boards also scythed hundreds of helicopter pilots whose careers reflected the unique needs of the Vietnam War. Most were enlistees or draftees sent directly from basic to flight school, assigned as warrant officer pilots in Vietnam, then commissioned as captains in return for a second tour—all within three years of entering the army. But then the hammer fell. Because aviation was not a distinct branch until 1983, the pilots were assigned to Infantry, Armor, or some other combat arm. Retention boards—noting that aviators had not completed the requisite branch schools and lacked unit leadership or staff assignments—recommended them for separation.[80]

In FY 1974 there was another, perhaps even more brutal budget-driven RIF. This reduction went after some 5,000 reserve captains and majors who had been retained on active duty. In December 1974, amid complaints that the service was protecting mediocre regulars and "riffing" superior reservists, Congress passed legislation that ensured career officers were included in the FY 1975 cut of 2,000 officers. Administrative shuffling rendered a further 4,500 officer positions superfluous and downgraded or converted to enlisted grade 4,700 slots. Such statistics give only a superficial picture of the personal and institutional trauma inflicted on the service. One CGSC student told Roger Spiller that half of the 163 who had attended his officers' basic course had been casualties in Vietnam and that two-thirds of those who remained had been riffed. James Willbanks was one of seven captains in a battalion; he arrived one day to find five of them had been cut. Michael Lee Lanning was at the Advanced Armor School when his class heard a monotone voice reading the names of officers who were to report immediately to the commandant. Soon one in every five officers had been expelled. The students who remained were so demoralized and resentful that some instructors simply gave up teaching.[81] This brutal downsizing finally ended in 1976, when the secretary of the army reported that the officer corps was at 98,600, a reduction of 43 percent since its Vietnam peak and its lowest level since 1950. There it would remain until a new buildup began in 1982.

Following on the defeat in Vietnam, the postwar RIFs had a deep and lasting impact on the service's internal cultures. They repudiated the implicit promise of tenure and job security in the Officer Career Act of 1947; downsizing might occur at any time. Those who were separated often left feeling betrayed, those who remained often suffered survivor's guilt, and those on the boards bore the anguish of deciding who among a group of committed, experienced, and dedicated soldiers must leave. For all the good intentions of the Pentagon and board members, this drastic downsizing instilled a mixed message of what would define excellence in the postwar force. Officers witnessed firsthand the penalties for a bad Officer Efficiency Rating, for taking risks that might displease a superior, or for being outside the accepted career pattern. Although professional standards increased, they too often took the form of box-checking. Selection to attend the staff or war colleges, not performance in the classroom, was essential. And for those passed over for the senior service college necessary for promotion to general—in 1975, over half of the army's 3,544 colonels—there was often little to look forward to but punching a clock until retirement at thirty years.

For at least one group of officers, the 1970s represented a period of turmoil and opportunity. Until the mid-1960s the number of officers in the Women's Army Corps was capped at 800, with the highest rank being colonel. Women could not command men, were segregated in administrative or medical occupations, and had to leave the service if pregnant. With the dissolution of the WAC in 1975, a host of opportunities suddenly opened. At the entry level, the army integrated the ROTC, transferred women into formerly closed occupations, and imposed gender limits on some traditional female specialties. One beneficiary was Lt. Col. Evelyn P. Foote, who, like many WACs, was advised by personnel officers to transfer into an administrative position in the Adjutant General's Corps. Foote, however, was determined to avoid being one of the "thundering herd of women" she believed would be "dumped [into] and mismanaged" by that bureau. When she learned the Military Police branch was negotiating to obtain a senior female officer, she applied to that branch. For several years her duties were confined to staff duties and the War College, but in 1983 she became the first woman to command a Military Police Group and retired as a brigadier general.[82]

In a 1970 *Army* article on "youth" as the "key challenge to to-day's army," Deputy Chief of Staff for Personnel Walter T. Kerwin emphasized that, to ensure high-quality officers for the MVA, the service had to overcome young Americans' perception that it was conservative, dictatorial, and resistant to any forms of individual initiative.[83] The service needed to not only attract second lieutenants; it had to retain a sufficient number who would rise in rank and maintain an active, energetic officer corps. This was no easy task. A survey of junior officers found that many believed the service had lost sight of its professionalism. Instead of membership in a warrior brotherhood, they perceived themselves members of "a conglomeration of ill-trained, poorly educated, and generally inexperienced officers."[84] The Pentagon team charged with studying major issues in the army identified significant retention problems including the propensity for senior officers to micromanage, overwork, and dole out capricious, career-killing assignments such as removing an infantry lieutenant from platoon command to manage base housing.[85]

To sustain its career ladder, the mid-1970s officer corps of 101,550 required an annual intake of 7,000 entry-level (nonspecialist) officers and needed to retain 40 percent of them. Although it had been a primary source for Vietnam-era officers, the Officers Candidate School was not considered to be a viable option in peacetime. Tainted by OCS-graduate officers' role in the My Lai Massacre, it was also costly, had a high failure rate, and limited its graduates' training to small-unit tactical command.[86] The service's managers believed that a university degree provided the intellectual foundation necessary to perform the wide variety of assignments in a professional military career. Personnel planners calculated that perhaps 800 would commission from the Military Academy annually, with a five-year obligation and the majority from ROTC scholarships that entailed one of three to four years.[87] But would these people come? The omens were not encouraging.

As had occurred in the aftermath of earlier wars, the 1970s were not good years for West Point. The decade began with the relief of Superintendent Koster for his role in the coverup of the My Lai Massacre. Koster's emotional speech, and the subsequent cadet parade in his support, were what one witness termed a "punctuation point" in the "siege mentality" that pervaded the school: a perception that it

was under attack from all sides.[88] Although no one could accuse the
Military Academy of sheltering draft dodgers, critics challenged the
school both academically and ethically, with one former faculty member declaring that "the malaise which afflicts [the army] today no doubt
owes a great deal to its West Point core."[89] In what may have been a
rejection of the permissiveness, corruption, and irresponsibility of civilian life, cadets on the honor board insisted on expelling their not-so-
upstanding peers. Many of these decisions were promptly reversed at
the Department of the Army level, with one such reversal prompting
the silencing of the returned cadet and further negative publicity. In
part to head off further interference, Superintendent Sidney Berry
formed a committee to examine the honor code. The initiative back-
fired when the committee discovered multiple infractions; the most
serious resulted in some 150 cadets facing expulsion for cheating on
a single exam. Recognizing that the situation was out of control, the
army appointed a special commission under the astronaut and retired
colonel Frank Borman (USMA Class of 1950). Under its tutelage and
some enlightened leadership, West Point restored much of its reputation by the mid-1980s.[90]

Perhaps creating the most angst among many graduates was the
admission of women to the USMA. Ignoring West Point's origins as
an engineering school and the wartime role of the OCS, the school's
board asserted that West Point's primary mission was to provide officers for the combat or combat support arms. Since women were not
at that time allowed in these branches, in this view it made no sense to
admit them. Berry considered resigning but decided he would do more
good ensuring that the program worked. Despite much fulminating
from some alumni, West Point's first women entered in 1976. Commandant Walter Ulmer played a crucial role in preparing the school,
visiting training camps and successful ROTC programs, and resolving
most of the difficult logistical and disciplinary questions. The experiences of the initial female cadets revealed their determination and
character. They withstood bullying, overbearing media coverage, inadequate facilities, and direct and inadvertent humiliation. By the early
1980s women accounted for a small—15 percent—but consistent part
of the corps of cadets.[91]

If Vietnam had a deleterious effect on West Point, it was more destructive to the ROTC. In 1966 there were 174,000 male cadets in
colleges; in 1974 there were only 30,000.[92] Many programs in elite
institutions were abolished, some not returning for decades. Critics
challenged the academic qualifications of cadre members, arguing that

vocational training should not receive college credit. Always small, the number of ROTC graduates who remained in uniform after their initial obligation shrank to barely one in five. In a significant change in priorities, the army shifted from commissioning thousands of short-service junior officers as the junior managers of transitory draftees to identifying those with the commitment to make the all-volunteer force a career.

Chief of Staff Westmoreland recognized that it was essential to improve the intellectual and professional rigor of the ROTC curriculum. The army initiated a number of progressive steps to heal relations with academia, including involving faculty in ROTC activities, sending senior chiefs and academics to attend summer training camps, and assigning officers with graduate degrees to the ROTC. One of the most imaginative and constructive programs was the USMA's summer seminar for faculty assigned to teach ROTC's required military history course. Over the next three decades, hundreds of academics completed the seminar with not only the intellectual foundation to teach cadets but also a personal connection to the army. Many of them shifted their research interests toward US Army history, defending ROTC and the service within their departments and schools.[93]

Westmoreland's enthusiasm for ROTC was shared by many officers, especially those who were from the program. They recognized that some of the academic critiques had merit, they did not pursue a confrontational approach or wallow in self-pity, and they focused on practical solutions. Col. Robert M. Carroll recommended that cadre cut back on drill and ceremonies, encourage academic excellence, seek faculty input, and emphasize that the program should draw its membership from across the nation, representing every race and social class and "providing a built-in safeguard against an in-bred military caste system."[94] At Ohio State University, the ROTC cadre responded to critics' demands for their expulsion with a report detailing its contributions, prompting a wave of student and faculty support and an endorsement from the school's Council on Academic Affairs.[95]

The enrollment of women and increasing minority representation were crucial to the ROTC's success. The army began testing gender integration in 1972, allowing programs at selected universities to develop their own policies and award four-year scholarships. At the University of Hawai'i, women made up almost 30 percent of the cadet body, took the same curriculum (including weapons), and outscored the males in several exercises. These early successes prompted army leadership to throw its full support into women's participation in May

1973. That year over 3,000 women were in ROTC, and the army announced that the program would be the source of all WAC officers. By the end of the 1970s, women made up a quarter of the cadet population. The army pursued increased minority participation in the ROTC even more enthusiastically. It opened programs at eighteen historically Black colleges and rewarded cadre for enrolling minority candidates. As with women, these initiatives were successful: in the first four years of the decade, minority representation in the ROTC increased from 14 percent to 22 percent and Black representation from 11 percent to 17 percent.[96]

The junior officer corps also experienced a generational shift during the 1970s. Much of this was due to the restoration of peacetime career paths. The early post-Vietnam generation had been driven at a frantic pace: in 1972 many second lieutenants advanced to first lieutenant within a year and to captain a year later. By the middle of the decade these promotion times had doubled. The extended time in grade allowed officers an opportunity to gain experience in their assignments (particularly troop command), a more stable home life, and greater socialization.[97] The two generations also had very different experiences. Those in the immediate aftermath of the war served in an army traumatized by substance abuse, racial tensions, RIFs, diminished training resources, broken equipment, bad housing, and limited family support. Perhaps not surprisingly, of the ROTC class that entered the army in 1971, 58 percent separated within three years, and another 16 percent separated within six; only 17 percent of that cohort was on duty in 1986. In contrast, those who enrolled in ROTC in the mid-1970s experienced a far more supportive campus climate and a more military-friendly environment. Commissioned at the end of the decade, they benefited from the rapid improvements that began with the increased budgets in the last years of the Jimmy Carter administration and accelerated under Ronald Reagan. Not surprisingly, they had more job satisfaction: among the class of 1980, only 16 percent chose to leave after their first three years.[98]

The lieutenants and captains who served during the first postwar years did not know that a decade later things would get better. They had to deal not only with the legacy of Vietnam but also with the culture wars, insubordination, substance abuse, racial violence, and myriad other social problems of the early 1970s. On any given day, they might have to conduct an armed search of their unit's barracks, lead a race relations "rap session," and supervise a hearing to discharge a problem soldier. Paul H. Herbert, a 1972 Military Academy graduate, recalled being pleasantly surprised receiving superior marks on his first efficiency rating but disconcerted that the rating was based on his platoon's low crime rate.[99]

Herbert and others noted a pronounced generation gap between their cohort and their seniors, one reflected not only in more liberal political views but in their higher expectations of their superiors. Unfortunately, in the first years after Vietnam there were persistent complaints that went unmet. Generals lecturing at the Command and General Staff College were appalled at the open animosity of mid-career officers. One 1973 survey of junior officers found that barely 1 percent cited leadership among the most satisfactory aspects of their career, in contrast to the 40 percent who ranked it worst.[100] In a 1975 private letter to Chief of Staff Weyand, General Davison warned that many company officers perceived "a lack of integrity among their seniors, not only generals but colonels, lieutenant colonels, and senior sergeants."[101] Mark S. Pernell, whose first assignment was as an armor officer in Germany in the early 1970s, recalled:

> Maintenance is everything in a tank battalion, and maintenance was flat on its ass. It hardly mattered that we were short of skilled labor when there were no spare parts available for that labor to use to keep the tanks at ESC [Equipment Serviceability Criteria] Green. An especially pernicious practice was lying to higher HQ about maintenance. A commander was judged on the number of tanks that were operational. The lie began with the platoon leader who succumbed to threats/blandishments from his company commander and reported, say, 3 tanks operational (ESC Yellow or Green) when only 2 were "up." The company commander then reported that, say, 12 of his 17 tanks were Green. The battalion commander would lean on the company commanders and the battalion motor officer and chief warrant officer maintenance tech to inflate the numbers so that the battalion, lo and behold, reported, say, 45 tanks operational out of 53. The real figure might have been 30. The worst part? Everyone at every level knew it was all a lie.[102]

As Pernell made clear, challenges faced by junior officers were armywide. There was a lack of resources necessary to perform the duties of being a soldier while dealing with what Herbert termed "the overwhelming administrative headache of making the all-volunteer army happen."[103] Because of the riffing of so many junior officers and the rapid promotion to field grade of so many others, a postwar infantry company might have only one of its three platoons commanded by a lieutenant. In addition to learning his own duties, that officer would usually be assigned all of the company's collective administrative responsibilities: customs officer, pay officer, physical security officer, entertainment officer, and on and on. A 1976 survey of company commanders found that they routinely worked over sixty hours a week.[104]

An ongoing source of discontent was that much of an officer's time was extraneous to what should have been the top priorities of maintenance, training, and caring for their soldiers. In a profession that makes integrity and character essential, it was excruciating to demand excellence from subordinates but be unable to provide them with such basic expectations as decent food, housing, and clothing, a safe working environment, continuing education, and, above all, realistic military training. Compounding the problem, and adding to the general frustration, was that the officer's superior might see a broken showerhead (months after spare parts had been ordered) and conclude that the unit had a discipline problem. Shortages of fuel, ammunition, spare parts, and competent technicians meant that units seldom realistically practiced the mechanized infantry tactics the service mandated to combat the Soviets in Europe. As one infantry lieutenant recalled: "We worshipped the vehicles in the motor pool[] but did not get to use them."[105] In such straitened circumstances, a community of peers and an inspirational, sympathetic, mentoring commander could make a difference in whether an officer remained or resigned. That so many good officers chose to remain and serve deserves far more acknowledgement—and far more study from the US Army—than it has received.

At the end of the 1970s the officer corps was still recovering from Vietnam, the RIFs, and a decade's worth of hardships. Although resignations were no longer as catastrophic as in the first half-decade—when 40 percent of Academy and 70 percent of ROTC graduates had left within six years—they remained unsustainable. Of those commissioned in 1975, a third of the West Pointers and almost half the ROTC graduates would depart within six years.[106] Junior officers still perceived, as Capt. Andrew J. Bacevich commented in 1979, a service in which "careerism has more than survived—it flourishes."[107] Gen. William R. Richardson, who took charge of the Command and General Staff College, complained that students were more interested in "getting the 'ticket punched'" and acquiring credentials for postretirement jobs than focusing on military subjects.[108] Despite a revived sense of mission, doctrinal and training reforms, and a greater distance from the trauma of Vietnam, the renaissance that later historians discerned was not apparent to the great majority of officers.

The successful transition from draftee to all-volunteer force rested on two interconnected issues: quality and quantity. As one retired brigadier general pointed out, Selective Service had provided a "nearly limitless source of talented manpower" among junior enlisted men (E-1 to E-4), allowing the army to waste personnel resources on a prodigious level.[109] For all the leadership's vocal concerns about shortages in the combat arms, roughly two-thirds of the army's almost 500 Military Occupation Specialties were not associated with combat status. Since conscription began, the service had demonstrated that it could train blue-collar tradesmen to maintain and operate tanks and trucks, cook meals, stock supply rooms, type, and so on. The great majority of such semiskilled laborers' service soon outlived their usefulness, and the service was happy to send them back to civilian employment. In contrast, even during the draft the army had devoted extensive efforts to recruit and retain a small cadre of soldiers who would make the service a lifetime occupation. This elite group of leaders, supervisors, and technicians often required advanced education and costly specialized training and were most in demand in the civilian market.[110]

The post-Vietnam army's personnel problems were coupled to the fact that its lowest-ranking enlisted force was in a state of flux. The Total Force policy required extensive recalibrating to shift support MOSs to the reserves and fill out the active units with more combat MOSs. This in turn required a massive shifting in training priorities. Compounding the challenge was that for much of the 1970s between a third and a half of enlisted ranks were stationed outside the continental United States. As a result, the army administration was nearly overwhelmed juggling recruiting, training, deployment, rotation, return, and discharging those who had completed their enlistments. This would have been an enormous challenge with a homogenous force, and that of the 1970s was anything but.

To his credit, and despite having opposed an all-volunteer force, Westmoreland began preparing for it almost immediately after Nixon's election. As part of the VOLAR (Volunteer Army) initiative, the army experimented at stateside posts by improving barracks and recreation, reducing inspections and fatigue duty, easing restrictions on hair, and instituting more liberal leave and work policies. The initial results of the VOLAR experiments were promising: a decline in AWOLs and disciplinary problems and improved retention.[111] The defenders of eyewash and chickenshit huffed mightily at initiatives such as beer in the barracks, longer hair, and release from fatigue duties. Exasperated at the outrage over KP being abolished, Westmoreland snapped back that "few infantrymen have been better soldiers because they learned to clean a grease trap."[112] More serious were complaints from officers, noncoms, and soldiers alike of arbitrary and capricious standards. The limits on haircuts, private rooms, posters, coffee shops, alcohol, counseling, and entertainment varied from post to post and from unit to unit. Much like the Universal Military Training Camp experiment after World War II, VOLAR proved too expensive, too labor-intensive, and too diffuse in its goals to provide a template for how the army should treat its new labor force.[113]

From the get-go, army leaders recognized that the service's draft-era message ("Choice, Not Chance"), miniscule budget (some $3 million in 1967), and reliance on public service messages would not meet the qualitative or quantitative needs of the Modern Volunteer Army. They also believed that the service needed to sell itself not only to recruits but also to the American public. The service threw itself into this effort, aided by a greatly increased advertising budget and recruiting staff and the opening or modernization of over 1,000 stations. The early 1970s army offered over forty enlistment options, including bonuses for combat arms or high-demand MOSs, choices on where or with what unit to serve, enlisting with friends, and delayed entry to complete schooling. Enticed with the recruiting slogan "The Army is Changing—For the Better," the new soldiers for the new model army enjoyed increased pay, educational benefits, and bonuses.[114]

At the local level, the service sponsored such initiatives as the Chicago–Milwaukee Recruiting Command's $800,000, monthlong "Three Hundred Jobs" campaign to sign contracts in high-skill MOSs. In another initiative, they sent a sergeant back to his hometown; using his local contacts with local clergy, teachers, and other influential figures, he returned with 161 enlistment contracts. As a testimony to his salesmanship, the town adopted his infantry battalion, ensuring even more volunteers.[115] Another commander authorized a "try the Army on for size" campaign in which young men from disadvantaged backgrounds received three days of basic training. Although many quit, the majority concluded that army life—food, challenges, leadership, job counseling, recreation—was much better than they had expected, and several enlisted. The pay and benefit increases and intense recruiting allowed the MVA to make a strong start: in FY 1972 the number of men enlisting in the combat arms rose from a few hundred to 5,411, even after entry-level education standards were raised to limit the more marginal categories to under 20 percent.[116]

Unfortunately, the army's early recruiting success did not continue in the ensuing five years. Even more unfortunate, the climate of optimism it engendered may have led senior leaders to ignore or push aside evidence of increasing troubles. As skeptics had predicted, by mid-decade the service showed every indication of returning to its previous postwar role as the nation's employer of last resort. The majority of recruits tested at the medium or low end, and over 40 percent lacked a high-school diploma. Too many enlistees were quickly diagnosed as physically, mentally, or socially incapable of service: in the first six months of 1973 the army gave early discharges to 29,000 such recruiting mistakes. Company commanders complained that soldiers arriving in their units from TRADOC basic training were so poorly prepared they had to establish programs to ensure functional literacy, adequate diets, medical treatment, and physical endurance—and even then transfer many out of the combat arms. There was also concern about the new model army's demographic composition: during the decade the proportion of Blacks doubled, and middle-class whites all but disappeared.[117]

The army blamed its early personnel failings on too few recruiters and promised to improve both their numbers and quality. But the problems were clearly greater than anticipated. In 1974, Congress, suspicious the army was sabotaging the MVA by recruiting poor soldiers, mandated that at least 55 percent of new enlistees have a high-school diploma and that 82 percent test in the top-three categories. The effect was immediate: in FY 1974 the army missed its enlistment quotas by 20,000. Those who did join that year often proved unsuitable, forcing the service to discharge 41,000 enlistees before they had completed training. Compounding the service's recruiting problems, Congress decided in 1976 to terminate the G.I. Bill. This misguided budget-trimming unleashed an immediate and devastating fall in enlistments from those the service most wanted to attract: high-school graduates seeking funding for college.[118]

As had occurred in prior postwar armies, soldiers often were employed in a variety of tasks with little direct bearing on preparation for war. "The biggest problem driving my men out," one company commander declared, was the persistent "malassignment" of soldiers from their MOS to another task, usually one that was both arduous and of little personal benefit.[119] His peers complained that both the army's personnel system and their superiors viewed their units as no more than work crews that could be shifted from job to job, broken up and reassembled with no perceived impact on cohesion, morale, group expertise, unit integrity, or individual discomfort. A particularly bitter grievance was the misuse of temporary duty by seniors. This often took the form of levies that transferred soldiers to other units or reassigned them for indefinite periods while nonetheless maintaining them on unit rolls and thus preventing their replacement. A survey at Fort Carson found that 4th Infantry Division's headquarters had levied 350 combat MOSs from their companies to assist in administration.[120] Service chiefs acknowledged a widespread "MOS-mismatch problem," but their "voluntary reclassification" was equally brutal: in FY 1976 alone some 50,000 support slots, including those of 14,000 sergeants, were reclassified as combat-arms MOSs.[121]

The dilemma of attracting recruits of quality was complicated by Carter's appointment of Clifford Alexander as secretary of the army in February 1977. Alexander had several attributes, among them his presence as a Black in the administration of a Southern president and his bona fides as a proponent for affirmative action and equal opportunity. Unfortunately, his attributes did not include much sympathy for, or even interest in, military realities. He insisted that the army's criteria for quality recruits—a high-school diploma and strong test scores—were inherently racist. To demonstrate his point, he ordered the destruction of 400,000 soldiers' test results.[122]

Despite persistent evidence of recruiting problems, senior military leaders throughout the decade asserted that shortfalls were temporary and that the service could fulfill its primary mission of defending NATO. But as had occurred after previous wars, the army was losing too many good soldiers and gaining too few with the potential for long service. In 1979 the crises finally broke. The service ended up more than 10 percent under its quota despite Recruiting Command's lowering minimum test scores from 59 to 31 (and to 16 for high-school graduates), reducing physical standards, allowing a two-year enlistment, and widening its pool to seventeen-year-olds. In violation of official policy, less than two-thirds of enlistees had high-school diplomas, half scored in the lowest mental category, and two out of every five were discharged for disciplinary, medical, or other unsuitability before completing their enlistments. These grim statistics were overtaken by the news that the Armed Services Vocational Aptitude Battery—the primary testing tool for assessing military potential—was grossly inaccurate. Tens of thousands of unqualified (or "misnormed") people had been admitted into the armed forces. Almost simultaneously, the

Recruiting Command was shaken by revelations of significant abuses: one investigation revealed that almost 40 percent of the 6,650 soldiers interviewed had been enlisted fraudulently.[123]

With the Vietnam War now over for half a decade, Chief of Staff Edward C. Meyer determined to stabilize the enlisted ranks. In November 1979 he placed Gen. Maxwell Thurman in charge of Recruiting Command with carte blanche to clean house. Thurman insisted that the army retain only high-school graduates and those who retested in the top half of mental aptitude. He would soon reform recruiting, adapt the "Be All You Can Be" advertising campaign, and set the service on a course to creating the high-quality force of the later 1980s. But one of the reasons Thurman's impact was so marked was that it came after a decade of misdirection, corruption, and drift.[124]

Both anecdotal and scholarly evidence recognized that many recruits entered the service in the post-Vietnam era with what the general in charge of personnel termed "no sense of belonging or empathy," and they often viewed themselves as cogs in the "Green Machine."[125] Although army leadership and the media focused on obvious friction points such as drugs, race, and lifer-draftees, those in the ranks saw a far more diverse, discordant, and divisive world—a world one private described as divided into "cliques" of "bookworms, hillbillies, juicers, etc. and they don't get involved with one another."[126] The sociologist Charles Moskos observed stronger white collar–blue collar segregation in the army than in civilian life. Administrative staff and line soldiers almost never mixed, they lived on separate sides of their barracks, and they referred to those in the opposite row as "animals" or "queers and fairies."[127]

As had been true of their postwar predecessors, as the war faded many enlisted personnel witnessed a progressive decline in the quality of their lives. The service began the 1970s with a shortfall of 136,000 housing units; three out of every four soldiers stateside lived in temporary or inadequate barracks, some dating back to the world wars. As part of the initiatives to raise morale in the volunteer force, some post commanders authorized dividing the open thirty-man barracks bays into individual cubicles and allowed decorations such as lamps, posters, and rugs. But a combination of conservatism, transient leadership, poor management, and lack of funding stopped many of these initiatives. Although Congress doubled a private's (E-2) pay in 1971 to $342 a month, this was soon overtaken by inflation. Already inadequate if the private was married, or had to live off post, or was stationed in Germany, the rankers' standard of living was further undercut by politicians chipping away at the benefits promised for the all-volunteer force by eliminating superior performance pay, household travel allowances, college funding, and so on. By the end of the decade the purchasing power of a sergeant's salary had dropped by 30 percent, and in some army communities one-third of junior enlisted families were eligible for food stamps.[128]

A consistent complaint among officers and noncoms was that they spent 90 percent of their time on the malcontented 10 percent and not on the 90 percent of their good soldiers.[129] While it is important not to downplay the army's internal troubles, it is even more important to recognize that their superiors were correct: 90 percent of those who served had the potential to be good soldiers. Two examples illustrate the positive influence of the army during the decade. The first example was the transition from a segregated to a gender-integrated force. At the end of 1974 four out of every five WACs were assigned to thirty MOSs, almost all related to clerical duties where, in conformance to the WAC leadership's wishes, they would wear skirts. To change this, the army deliberately channeled men into traditionally female MOSs, such as nursing, and pushed WACs into traditionally all-male branches. At least initially, the army tried to maintain the fiction that female soldiers were first and foremost ladies. Training was a particularly thorny issue, and it took several years for the service to develop a satisfactory mixed-gender basic course. Indicative of the army's conservatism, noncoms in the drill instructors course were required to wear skirts when marching in formation. Despite demands by male and female soldiers, women were initially excluded from survival and weapons instruction, though most gave up a weekend to qualify on rifles. Pregnancy was also a source of concern. In 1974 one of every three women who took early separation did so for "family reasons." But by 1976 42,000 women served in 371 MOSs. It was one of the army's greatest 1970s successes.[130]

The experience of Roger Goodell between 1973 and 1976 may typify the positive experience the majority of enlisted personnel received while in uniform. A self-confessed dopehead surfer from Hawaii, his high-school guidance counselor advised him to enlist to find some purpose in his life. His recruiter, impressed by his test scores, urged him to consider nursing because it would guarantee him a civilian job and "that's where the chicks are." Only later did he learn that the recruiter had misinformed him: as part of WAC integration, recruiters were funneling promising male recruits into traditionally female MOSs. The nearly one-year army schooling was rigorous—the class began with forty and graduated twenty-four—but it provided the equivalent of a civilian licensed practical nurse degree. Throughout his three-year tour Goodell experienced none of the horrors that figured so prominently in the literature of the 1970s army. His barracks were comfortable, his noncoms were proficient and fair, the officers were professionally competent and treated subordinates with respect, and his unit was cohesive and racially tolerant. Goodell's three years in uniform not only gave him purpose and self-discipline; it provided him with essential qualifications for his subsequent careers with the Honolulu Fire Department and later as a nurse practitioner. Looking back, he views joining the army as turning his life around.[131]

Goodell was a one-term soldier: He filled an essential slot, and he returned to the civilian world with a skill of great benefit to society. But when he left, the service lost a year's worth of educating him and two years of experience. In this respect he represented the vast majority of his comrades: only 6 percent of the enlisted force remained in uniform until their twenty-year retirement.[132] A 1976 study found that, as had always been the case, individuals enlisted less for patriotism than for practical reasons: to acquire technical skills or college funds or to be paid while they gained maturity and decided on their careers. Most had achieved these goals when they were eligible for discharge, and the study concluded that "a fundamental problem handicapping reenlistment is that, typically, young men do not particularly like the Army or Army life."[133]

Even before the withdrawal from Vietnam, the army's career noncommissioned corps and its program to recruit their replacements had all but collapsed. Not only did most World War II and Korean War veterans reach retirement age; there were 25 percent declines in the prewar reenlistment rates of the E-5 and E-6 grades. By 1970 the army was short roughly 250,000 experienced noncommissioned officers. To replace them, the service rushed promising first-term enlisted men through a twelve-week course to make sergeant. These "shake-and-bake" sergeants rotated back to Vietnam on so many tours that a private might rise to E-6 in three years, a rank that in the prewar force had been the normal grade at retirement.[134] By 1970 the MOS system was in such turmoil that the army undertook a compete revision of its cataloging, only to impose a "reclassification moratorium" two years later to determine what "personnel assets" it had left.[135] Indicative of the confusion, in that year the service inexplicably discharged 4,500 senior sergeants, cutting a swath through its already insufficient reserve of experienced technicians and troop leaders and probably convincing many more to get out.[136]

In common with many junior officers, the army recognized that, while shake-and-bake sergeants provided capable small-unit tactical leadership, few developed either the occupational ethos or skills for peacetime service. Officers complained that, as a class, their sergeants were unable or unwilling to train their units or to resolve racial, generational, and discipline disputes. Compounding the problem was the lack of mentoring from senior master sergeants and sergeant majors, who one general characterized as prone "to sit in big offices [or] ride in the back end of a quarter-ton [truck] and patronize the commander."[137] Infantry officer Gordon Rudd recalled that in the elite airborne units—where light infantry skills most replicated the Vietnam experience—between a third and a half the sergeants were good. But in the mechanized units, where noncoms had to master not only the new battlefield of Europe but also maintain their vehicles, it was more like one-tenth. He had to fire several master sergeants incapable of performing their motor-pool duties.[138] From the perspective of forty years, Richard C. Hall remembered that as a company officer "I greatly resented that I was put in the position of having to yell at older and much more experienced soldiers for doing so many stupid things."[139] His more unpleasant memories included disciplining a senior sergeant for fornicating in a public railcar and kicking out another for sneaking prostitutes into the barracks.

The inexperience of junior noncoms and the congregation of so many senior sergeants homesteading in cushy jobs far from the troops accelerated the service's already oppressive proclivity toward officer micromanagement, further reducing troops' respect for squad leaders. The process was self-reinforcing and unending, and it continued throughout the decade despite constant demands by higher headquarters to decentralize. Harassed by his superiors and lacking a qualified, experienced sergeant, the junior officer was often in the position of Edward G. Miller, a lieutenant in a tank unit:

> We became specialists at eyewash, and following up on everything the NCOs did because everyone thought everyone else had to watch over what we were all doing. The NCOs resented it, we resented it, I'm sure the soldiers resented it. . . . We just managed the BS and decided it was a game we had to play. It was a merry-go-round we couldn't escape because of worry that a mistake or two could derail a career.[140]

In the wake of the Vietnam War, service leaders recognized that rebuilding the career noncommissioned officer corps was essential to the success of the Modern Volunteer Army. There would be no return to the illiterate, profane Sergeant Orville Snorkels or lifetime Private Beetle Baileys. The Enlisted Qualitative Management Program reimposed restrictions on reenlistment to career soldiers who had been denied promotion or who were found unqualified for advancement. The army also withdrew a commander's prerogative to fill local vacancies through spot promotions. In September 1970 the first centralized board for promotions to E-7 evaluated 10,977 E-6 candidates and selected 3,240. A few months later, another board took on the promotions to E-6, and in June the process was extended to promotions to E-5 grades. Unfortunately, the service's enthusiasm for tests and interviews was not matched by commensurate enthusiasm to implement their results: nine months after the board had met, barely half the E-7s had their new stripe.[141]

As part of the effort to improve its sergeants, the army in 1971 opened two schools: a basic for entry-level E-5s, and an advanced for E-6s and above. Soon afterward, the army established the Command Sergeant Majors Academy for its top performers. The initial results were disappointing: Of the 3,792 who entered the basic school, only 1,182 passed; perhaps even more depressing, only 529 of 1,182 graduated from the advanced course. Frustrated by this showing, the general in charge accused commanders of dumping their worst performers into the schools.[142] Although they gradually improved, the NCO schools remained understaffed and unable to take more than a fraction of the applicants. And despite the allegedly higher standards for both promotion and retention, a commander in the technically sophisticated Signal Corps reported in 1976 that over half his sergeants lacked high-school credentials.[143]

A decade after the last soldiers left Vietnam, the army was still struggling to attract high-quality enlistees and build a new career noncommissioned cadre. There were some visible successes. During the 1970s the number of Black NCOs almost doubled, and a 1979 survey found they were "highly integrated into the career enlisted force" and satisfied with their occupation, responsibilities, and advancement.[144] But against this must be set documentary and anecdotal evidence of continued problems with quality and retention. Despite the supposed improvements of the Enlisted Qualitative Management Program, officers complained that "my privates are brighter than my sergeants."[145] A 1980 survey of the stateside combat divisions revealed that the administrative staff had appropriated almost all the senior grades, and those who remained with the troops were "in a constant state of crisis management."[146] And in an equally serious consequence, once having witnessed the frustration and overwork of their noncoms, first-enlistment soldiers declined to make the service a career. The cumulative effect of turmoil in the ranks was apparent by the end of the decade when Chief of Staff Meyer referenced the 10,000 shortfall in noncoms as evidence of the "hollow" army.[147]

As had its predecessors, the post-Vietnam army was expected to serve as a combat force and as a pathway to citizenship, education, and job skills for the more than 90 percent who left before retirement. To some, the service's obligation was restricted to sufficient education and skills to allow soldiers to perform their MOSs. To others—perhaps the majority—any efforts at improving enlisted life had to come after ridding the service of malcontents, incompetents, and the maladjusted. Still others, more sensitive to the social changes sweeping the nation and its youths, believed with Maj. Gen. Harry W. Brooks that "combat preparedness has been[] and continues to be our primary concern, but the volunteer Army has clearly assigned us a social role as well." For such officers, it was imperative the service provide a holistic experience for those "already headed towards mediocrity." Those entering with "loser attitudes [and] low self-esteem as a result of repeated failures in civilian life" would leave with discipline, purpose, and confidence from an army-based foundation of physical, educational, and ethical improvement.[148]

One issue on which both conservatives and reformers agreed was crucial to the success of the postwar volunteer army: an educated workforce. Indeed, the very metrics that the army used to define a "quality" recruit were a high-school diploma and above-average test scores. Dropouts were the worst disciplinary problems, accounting for 70 percent of courts-martial. In 1972, CONARC announced that, as part of the volunteer army incentives, enlisted personnel could take duty time on post to work on a general education certificate, high-school diploma, or vocational certification. In a November 1974 message to his 2nd Infantry Division officers, Emerson declared that "every one of us must recognize that the educational program is an important part of the informal contract we establish with our soldiers."[149] Under Emerson, each soldier was granted eighteen hours of duty time for education a week, and those completing high school were allotted eight straight weeks of study. The general ordered that every officer with a master's degree was required to teach classes at night or on Saturdays, and he taught one himself. With a similar view, Brooks informed his 25th Infantry Division officers: "I see education as an integral part of our soldier's military life style," and it was an essential part of the army's duty to "return a better citizen to civilian life than the young man who entered."[150] The general established "Tropic Lightning Universities" that by the end of 1974 enrolled half the division's enlisted personnel in vocational and educational courses. Participants could work toward their high-school diplomas or MOS skills tests, learn English as a Second Language, or begin a college degree.

Despite these incentives, throughout the decade there were persistent complaints that recruiters and basic training dispatched people to field units who were simply too uneducated to soldier effectively. Lt. Daniel M. Caughey reported in 1974 that over half his infantry battalion's soldiers lacked high-school qualifications. He dismissed as "absurd" official claims based on manipulated recruitment statistics when the service had "lower[ed] education standards to the brink of disgrace." Political and military leaders had to face a hard fact—"an Army of dropouts cannot possibly be in the nation's interest"—and decide whether the service was a combat organization or a reform school.[151]

For many military and civilian observers, the drug problem was the unifying and most important social reform project. As late as 8 February 1970, the deputy commanding general in Vietnam declared that the primary problem was marijuana and that a combination of enforcement, suppression, and education was bringing it "under control."[152] But in 1971 Davison, then commander of II Field Force, Vietnam, declared that "the dimensions of the heroin problem are so enormous that they tend to sublimate any concern one might entertain about marijuana."[153] Both then and later, commentators on the left interpreted narcotic and marijuana use as emblematic of resistance to the war; those on the right saw it as yet another symptom of the nation's precipitous moral decline. In doing so, both downplayed or ignored entirely what may have been soldiers' far greater use of what at the time were then socially accepted drugs such as amphetamines, depressants, and alcohol. Was there really an "addicted army"? Or was there, as Moskos's research indicated, a distinct marijuana-smoking GI culture in which "heroin use is definitely regarded as deviant behavior even by most users"?[154] Later scholarship has added nuance and context to what contemporaries too often viewed as a monolithic problem—but with equally dissenting conclusions.[155]

In the prewar army, drugs were a nonissue. Between 1956 and 1960 only 160 soldiers were discharged for drug offenses; in 1960 there were only thirty-nine marijuana-related arrests in the entire continental United States. The last major survey before the large-scale commitment of troops to Southeast Asia reported that "narcotics activity in Hawaii, Okinawa, and Vietnam is virtually negative" and "extremely low" in Europe.[156] This optimistic appraisal owed much to the Uniform Code of Military Justice's failure to specify drug use as a chargeable offense until the mid-1960s. Unless a soldier had obvious needle marks or was found in possession, substance abuse could seldom be detected. Given both the severity of the punishment—up to ten years' imprisonment—and that the majority arrested for drug offenses were prior users, poorly educated, and chronic discipline problems, commanders found it easier to administratively discharge offenders. And since the army kept no records on drug-related administrative discharges, the true extent of substance abuse is impossible to determine. Further complicating the picture, until the mid-1960s amphetamines and barbiturates were not classified as controlled substances. The former were sometimes doled out by noncoms prior to maneuvers; Elvis Presley reputedly acquired them by the quart when stationed in Germany.[157]

The day after President Nixon's 17 June 1971 declaration that drugs were "public enemy Number One," the army instituted urinalysis testing for opiates for all soldiers departing Vietnam and, revealingly, all those seeking extended tours. This was extended to barbiturates and amphetamines in August, then to all overseas returnees, and later to spot-checks on individuals and units. In what was to become a common problem in assessing the nature and extent of substance abuse, initial results indicated a 5 percent positivity rate for heroin among troops leaving Vietnam, but retesting brought this to 2 percent, a figure that continued for most of 1972.[158] Another study revealed that all of the positive drug tests in Southeast Asia involved opiates, but in Europe this was only 11 percent and in Korea barely 5 percent. And whereas Vietnam's tests revealed no barbiturate or amphetamine abusers, barbiturates accounted for 30 percent of Europe's positive results and 88 percent of Korea's.[159] Yet could this data be trusted? Captain Bacevich's 1972 article argued—as some scientific experiments indicated—that biochemical tests failed to detect cocaine, marijuana, or LSD. Reflecting a common perspective among junior officers in the field, Bacevich accused the army leadership of citing misleading urinalysis tests to demonstrate its success in eliminating substance abuse.[160] Another officer, writing three years later, had an opposite complaint: half those testing positive were shown to be drug-free upon retesting.[161]

Brig. Gen. Robert G. Gard outlined the army's multistep response to the "Other War" in November 1972: prevention, identification, rehabilitation, evaluation, and research.[162] The army opened drug-treatment facilities as early as 1970, and by 1973 it boasted over 2,600 counselors, sixty detoxification centers, and forty halfway houses that collectively administered to some 62,000 patients, of which 17,841 abused alcohol. But these priorities were interpreted in a variety of ways, and many commanders and noncoms—frustrated with the attitude, criminality, inefficiency, indiscipline, and dangerous behavior that accompanied drug use—continued to implement punitive measures that would, if nothing else, get offenders out of their units and allow them to focus on soldiering. In a revealing insight into the service's internal contradictions and the stress imposed on its few experts, Maj. William L. Schwartz complained of having his work rehabilitating drug users constantly frustrated by noncoms who wanted them prosecuted, by medical personnel who covered for them, and by commanders who viewed drug treatment programs as a black mark on their careers.[163]

In the first half of the 1970s Europe emerged as the primary theater for the army's war on drugs. In large measure this was due to the leadership of General Davison, the USAREUR commander from 1971 to 1975. Davison later opined that the army's heroin problem, at its worst, was less than that of most contemporary cities. But he also believed that it was the army's responsibility "to protect our soldiers and dependents from the dangers of drug abuse, and to help, where possible, those who have become involved with illicit drug use."[164] Perhaps more important, he viewed substance abuse, like racial tensions, as symptomatic of an overall malaise in USAREUR that was disrupting its primary mission of NATO defense. From the beginning, the general pursued a broad variety of programs, some directly addressing drug and alcohol abuse and others focusing on contributing factors such as race relations, family housing, decent barracks, better equipment, realistic training, wholesome recreation, and responsive leadership.

Davison's emphasis on awareness, policing, and reintegration of drug users was neither consistent nor uniformly successful. There were lawsuits over the army conducting illegal searches in the barracks; the German authorities were often lethargic about closing down drug venues; and thorny issues had to be resolved such as whether soldiers who turned themselves in would be reduced in rank and lose their security clearances. Fortunately, Davison was an imaginative, adaptive, and compassionate leader who was willing to try new solutions, adjust them as necessity demanded, and not lose sight of his mission to restore USAREUR. The general spent long hours with his legal officers to ensure that commanding officers could rapidly discharge their malcontents. Although he was probably overly optimistic in seeing a decisive turning point as early as 1973, his success was validated not only by his successors but also by the army itself adapting many of his policies.[165]

Given the suddenness with which it captured the service's consciousness, the army's war on drugs was far more successful than the five-decade national debacle that Nixon initiated. The service ultimately developed a holistic approach that educated soldiers about the dangers (physical, legal, career) of drugs, that tested and identified users, and that rehabilitated or discharged offenders. However, much of this success was undercut by the recognition that "alcohol abuse was then, and still is, the chief drug problem in the Army." One mid-1970s study of installations located in the contiguous United States found that 32 percent of the enlisted force were "heavy" drinkers, 35 percent were "problem" drinkers, and that among the rest "whatever they do to relieve their boredom usually involves drinking."[166] Having purged its "dopers," the army would spend over a decade trying to rehabilitate or kick out its "juicers."

Next to narcotics, the most publicized postwar social problem centered on racial tensions that escalated into violent altercations. Both then and later, much attention was focused on Black militants demanding an end to individual and institutionalized racism. But perhaps even more disruptive was the "almost armed warfare between black and white soldiers" described by Maj. Gen. Frederic E. Davison on his arrival in Germany in 1971: "In Baumholder, as an example, just prior to my arrival there had been four or five hundred soldiers, primarily in the 8th Division, who were in the streets with bunk adapters, chains fighting in a pitched battle. In Mainz, fights in the barracks; soldiers thrown down steps. In Stuttgart . . . [w]e had what we called the Knights of the Chain Gang—a gang of soldiers who went around with chains terrorizing the barracks and the local community."[167] A Black officer, Davison believed that racial divisions were "superimposed" on a variety of other issues, most notably a collective "failure of command" and the fact that "living conditions for all enlisted troops in Europe were abominable." The fighting in Baumholder was in large measure due to troops crowded into barracks with broken lights, doors, and windows, unreliable heating, and a single working shower and toilet.

Much of the army's response to what it termed the "racial problem" consisted of continuing the arguments it had made since integration of being a merit-based, color-blind organization with equality in testing,

training, and promotion. Those who entered with the requisite qualifications would find themselves put through demanding training and
assigned an appropriate MOS. Tens of thousands of Blacks and other
minorities had done this—as the soldiers could see on a daily basis in
the faces of their sergeants. The aftermath army's challenge was to
make minority soldiers believe that the Big Green Machine treated
them equally, without the US Marine Corps addendum that all were
treated equally badly. That it did so is evidenced that between 1968 and
1977 the proportion of Black enlisted personnel more than doubled,
from 12 percent to 26 percent.[168]

Drug treatment and race relations were parts of a much larger reform
process: pulling the service out of the demoralization, indiscipline, dis-
sidence, and outright crime that had accelerated during the Vietnam
War and continued long afterward. The service faced continuous pressure from Congress to retain soldiers and to tighten discipline. Leaders from sergeants to generals complained that they were hamstrung
by the Uniform Code of Military Justice (UCMJ) and "long-haired
junior JAG officers" who had stripped commanders of their historic
right to discipline their troops.[169] Capt. Robert B. Killebrew, who commanded an infantry company, declared in 1971 that the "present system
of military justice serves neither discipline nor justice."[170] He estimated
it took over three months for a commander to receive authorization
to even fine a misfit, and the restrictions on pretrial confinement allowed bullies to intimidate their barracks mates for weeks. Others
complained it required but thirty minutes to reenlist a good soldier
while, "to be successful in an elimination or reduction action, a unit
commander must spend hours carefully gathering his evidence, hold
and record numerous counseling sessions with the soldier, coordinate
the activities of psychiatrists, physicians, legal counsel, witnesses and
his own clerks in preparing a lengthy packet of documentation."[171]

Over time it became clear that the problem was less that military
law restricted the application of discipline than that most officers did
not understand the UCMJ. The average company commander in the
Vietnam era had no more than four years in uniform and was rushed
through the professional schooling needed for garrison duty. As late
as 1976 a survey of company commanders disclosed that, of the top-
ten tasks they felt had been inadequately covered in their training,
half dealt with the administration of military justice.[172] Too many of
them, frustrated by indiscipline and what they perceived as lack of support from their noncoms and superiors, sought to resolve their problems by either courts-martial or such extrajudicial means as putting

troublemakers in pretrial confinement without filing charges. Such abuses prompted one officer to comment that "commanders who resort to military justice as a substitute for their own inadequacies" were "unfit to lead."[173] There was some merit in this accusation, for as Killebrew later admitted, "the most striking thing is that the UCMJ is generally adequate to enforce a much stricter degree of discipline than the one somebody is usually griping about."[174] The message appears to have sunk in and, together with better education of the benefits and obligations of military law, between fiscal years 1974 and 1976 the number of courts-martial shrank from 21,987 to 10,494.[175]

As had occurred after previous wars, most disciplinary problems resolved themselves in the second half of the decade. In part this was because the volunteer army not only removed recalcitrant draftees; it began to attract people willing to accept discipline, order, and structure. Two programs introduced late in 1973 and expanded over the next years were particularly effective. The Trainee Discharge Program monitored recruits in their first six months, expelling those consistently unable to fulfill their duties and thereby raising the quality of those sent into the field forces. In the program's first six months of operation almost one in ten recruits was flushed. The Expeditious Discharge Program allowed commanders to offer an incorrigible the option to waive an administrative board—and the threat of punitive sanctions—in return for an honorable discharge. As outlined by Emerson: "The goal is to [e]nsure that the leaders spend most of their time with the 99% of the soldiers who exhibit interest in self-improvement and adapt to the military environment. We do not want to waste time with the incorrigible man by building a case against him—we simply eliminate him as quickly as possible with as little trauma on both sides as possible."[176] The army was increasingly less interested in redeeming American youth and more interested in getting back to soldiering.

Chief of Staff Meyer's May 1980 reference to a "hollow Army" in his testimony to a congressional subcommittee created a national sensation.[177] Coming five months after the Soviet invasion of Afghanistan and barely a month after the disastrous Iran hostage rescue operation, "hollow Army" quickly became a buzzword for the precipitous decline in the nation's military power. Yet what did Meyer mean? He may have been responding to a specific question about conditions in tank companies at Fort Hood and been drawn into a larger comment on manpower shortages in stateside units. But very quickly the phrase expanded from one of continental manpower to much larger, more politically charged references to army unreadiness, national strategy, and America's apparent decline as a military power. Much of this was Washington political theater, a stage on which to attack President Jimmy Carter. But the phrase "hollow Army" resonated within the service and became iconic within army memory for encapsulating its worst of times.

The apparent transformation in the years immediately following Meyer's testimony have been the subject of numerous studies, few of which agree on the decisive turning point. In his 25 February 1983 testimony, Meyer highlighted some of the more important changes since his "hollow Army" comments—$153 billion in funding, better-quality recruits, retention of midlevel leadership—which were providing a "solid base on which to build the Army of the Future."[178] Gen. John M. Shalikashvili gave credit to President Reagan: "Overnight the morale changed. . . . We all of a sudden had a lot of money coming in to build new facilities and everyone felt like the Dark Ages were coming to an end. It had an impact on how we felt about ourselves and how the public felt about us."[179] Others have traced the transformation to the fulfillment of the DePuy–Gorman vision of a doctrinally united, highly trained, technically competent combat force armed with the most modern weapons. Still others have located the army's recovery in General Thurman's recruiting reforms that attracted top-quality, educated, and motivated enlistees. Whatever their interpretation, they all agree that by the early 1980s a turning point had arrived and that the army was on the way to recovery.

The "certain victory" of the Gulf War was far from Meyer's own bleak vision of the service's future. His 1983 testimony emphasized repeatedly how many problems remained: soldiers were driving military vehicles older than themselves, the Organized Reserves were understrength and underequipped, and over half the active force was deployed overseas. Even minimal congressional budget cuts would send the army quickly back to the dark days of the 1970s. The Grenada invasion of 1983 revealed alarming problems in leadership, equipment, training, communications, and above all working with other services. Surveys of volunteer soldiers found many were still turned off by the poor quality of their NCOs and the indifference among their officers; retention of high-quality, trained enlisted personnel was a critical issue. Promotion and separation inequities and the service's inability to reduce its rank-heavy officer corps prompted legislative restrictions. After the big boost in pay with the start of the MVA, salaries had not kept up with the cost of living, and junior enlisted personnel could not support their families.[180]

To someone unaware of the imminent changes of the 1980s, the army a decade after the majority of its forces had left Vietnam had much in common with its predecessors in the aftermath of every war. After the characteristic cycle of rapid institutional changes in the first years, it was slowly transitioning from a postwar force to the peacetime establishment that it would remain until the end of the Cold War. Like its predecessors, it was overcommitted and could not fulfill its missions. It was understrength and underequipped. In many places, its personnel were inadequately housed, underpaid, and devoting as much or more time on post maintenance as on combat training. The army was still undergoing doctrinal upheaval as it transitioned from Active Defense to AirLand Battle. TRADOC's new training and testing program was still in its infancy and encountering numerous problems, even after drastically lowering standards. The army of the late 1970s was no longer losing high-quality soldiers and officers at the unsupportable rates of the early postwar era, but it was still having problems with recruiting and retention. In many ways it was less a "modern volunteer army" than it was a force reminiscent of the decade after the War of 1812, or the Spanish–American War, or World War I, or every other war. The great constant remained: soldiering in the aftermath of war was a tough business.

Conclusion

The Aftermath Army in Perspective

Shortly after I began my tenure as a visiting professor at the Army War College in 1999 the newly confirmed Army Chief of Staff, Eric K. Shinseki, exhorted the students to remember that Secretary of War Elihu Root's "broad and general conclusions are as applicable today as they were 100 years ago."[1] Quoting Root's inaugural message to Congress, Shinseki highlighted two timeless truths: "The real object of having an Army is to provide for war," and "the regular establishment . . . will never be the whole machine with which any war will be fought." Root might have accepted the acknowledgement, but whether he would have recognized that his first priority could be simplified to "warfighting remains job #1" is far more problematic. And had he been able to understand the jargon, Root would probably have been aghast that his second priority, intended as a reference to a mass citizen-soldier army, was now interpreted as "the active Army will not go it alone. . . . This multicomponent integrated force[] can expect to operate as part of a joint and combined team, capable of commanding multinational operations." Shinseki recognized that his military audience's familiarity with Root's transformation of a century earlier would make them more receptive to his proposed Army Transformation Initiative.[2] And, by implication, anyone not on board the "transformation train" was the modern equivalent of the wrong-thinking recalcitrant who had opposed Root. Like other military leaders, Shinseki presented a "selective and heroic view of the past" to secure support and suppress dissent—or what Michael Howard termed a "myth."[3]

Army leaders may believe that, when it comes to history, to paraphrase the conclusion of the film *The Man Who Shot Liberty Valance*: "This is the US Army. When the legend becomes fact, print the legend."[4] As Howard observed, myths that are told within the service have practical value. Recruits will probably be better disciplined and more willing to persevere if they believe that they have joined an elite unit with a glorious past. Senior leaders may be better able to inspire their subordinates by references to previous eras in which the service overcame difficulties and emerged victorious. But as the narrative arc of *Liberty Valance* underscores, legends can be dangerous to those who inspired them and to their tellers. Whether or not intentionally, it was hard to miss the message that, a decade after the Cold War's victorious end, the Army Chief of Staff and Washington leaders viewed not only its equipment and organizations as a soon-to-be-shed legacy but also its personnel.

Today's readers, especially members of the armed forces and the defense community's intellectual leaders, probably have limited interest in mythology. They would be justified in asking whether a historical analysis based on the US Army's postwar experience in its first sixteen decades has any relevance to the last five. Given the enormous amount of reading and practice required just to keep up to date with the army's current requirements, why does this history matter? Why read *Real Soldiering* rather than one of three dozen other books on how to fight wars, all of which are on the Chief of Staff's reading list? What are, to use a Pentagon phrase, the "deliverables"? These are all legitimate questions. I know, because they have all been asked of me by four generations of serious, dedicated professionals who want to do their best for their service and for their nation. And perhaps the best way to answer them is to provide, in conclusion, a brief overview of the US Army in the post–Cold War decade and an even briefer one of the post–Middle East conflicts that illustrate the similarities to the other eras studied more closely in *Real Soldiering*.

For many, including the US Army's own historians, the "certain victory" against Iraq in 1991 marks the transition from the wreckage of the Vietnam-era army to the "Army of Excellence."[5] That Cold War force, structured to defeat a Soviet invasion of Western Europe, had won its war with the Soviet collapse in 1989. Desert Storm and the chest-thumping and credit-hogging that followed that campaign only obscured, at least for a few years, the fact that, by the time this "whirlwind war" occurred, the service had already entered its familiar postwar cycle.[6]

From the perspective of Washington and the higher command, the 1990s had much in common with previous postwar decades. The first years were absorbed in top-down management of force structure, doctrine, equipment, and personnel, much of which later evolved, or was bundled into, "transformation." As the army's history of this period reveals, to varying extents most of these initiatives were to varying degrees overtaken by events, were delayed or revised, or died aborning. Underlying the entire decade was the frustration of defining the service's purpose. How could it be ready if neither its political nor its military leaders could explain what the army needed to be prepared for?[7]

As had occurred previously, the immediate aftermath of the Gulf War featured significant administrative reforms intended to set the army on a course to meet the challenges of the future. Of these, among the most significant was the George H. W. Bush administration's acceptance of the Base Force plan supported by Chairman of the Joint Chiefs of Staff Colin Powell and the heads of the armed forces. This postulated that the nation's military forces must be shifted from containing the Soviet Union in Europe toward responding to two major regional contingencies. A second significant change emerged with the election of President Bill Clinton and the Bottom-Up Review that promised a complete reassessment of the nation's military. This fizzled out, in part due to the incessant commitment of military forces for what became known as "military operations other than war," in part because of Clinton's character, and in part because the military chiefs remained steadfast in their adherence to the Base Force and to the Cold War force structure. Doctrine remained derivative of the Cold War AirLand Battle's focus on large-scale, combined arms warfare against a peer opponent; with the post–Gulf War hubris, the ideal was now "full-spectrum dominance." The service reduced its active divisions from FY 1989's eighteen to FY 1996's ten, and it cut the new organizations by 3,000 personnel, although in their configuration and training they were very much like their predecessors. Throughout the decade there was much talk of "transformation" and "revolutions in military affairs," of "Force XXI" and the "Army After Next" and the "Future Combat System," but the army that entered the twenty-first century—in its organization, concept of war, equipment, and personnel system—was essentially the same as during the Cold War.[8]

With the lessening and then elimination of the decades-long Soviet threat, American political leaders and the public demanded a "peace dividend" and a reduction of defense costs. Between 1989 and 1995 army manpower was cut by a third, from 780,000 to 508,000; by 1999 it was under 480,000. The pace of reductions was dizzying. In the two years after the Gulf War over 35,000 soldiers were released prior to their contracts, 50,000 career soldiers received a buyout, and tens of thousands of others transferred to the Organized Reserves. The ease of the reduction was aided immeasurably by two factors unique to the 1991 Gulf War. First, Congress authorized very generous benefits for those who left. Second, the brevity of the Desert Storm operation did not result in a substantial group of war-tested, rapidly promoted junior officers and noncoms who had entered at the onset of hostilities and wanted to remain in uniform. There was no postwar "hump." Although benign compared to the post-Vietnam RIFs, the army instituted Selective Early Retirement Boards (SERBs) that separated 1,745 officers involuntarily in FY 1992 alone, with 800 more planned for the next year. Those who were "SERBed" lost many of the benefits given to those who left willingly, which no doubt contributed to the success of the buyout program. As it had in previous force reductions, the army tried to preserve its senior managerial talent and remove the suboptimal—the career captains and majors, and those, like Russia or nuclear specialists, whose skills were not seen as crucial in the twenty-first century. In the first half of the decade the reductions pushed out those with insufficient commitment or talent to be career officers and retained a core of the dedicated, experienced, and proficient. However, as had occurred previously, in the second half of the 1990s a valley emerged behind the hump of Cold War veterans as too few high-quality lieutenants and captains remained in uniform.[9]

In a familiar pattern, the postwar army assumed new missions even as it struggled to disentangle itself from older ones. When Army Chief of Staff Gordon R. Sullivan assumed office in 1991 the US Army's primary overseas commitment was tidying up after the Gulf War; the most onerous of these missions was Provide Comfort, a predominantly US Air Force–Marine Corps operation in which the army deployed only a few military police, construction, and civil affairs units, many of them reservists. By the time Sullivan left office in 1994, Provide Comfort remained active, but it was dwarfed by far larger troop commitments in Somalia and the Balkans. Two years later his successor, Gen. Dennis J. Reimer, revealed that the average soldier assigned to a troop unit averaged 138 days on deployment.[10]

The multinational humanitarian relief in Somalia, the tragic Battle of Mogadishu in October 1993, and the subsequent evacuation prompted service-wide frustration and bitterness. The Clinton administration deservedly took the brunt of this, but self-reflective officers recognized that their own leadership, tactical performance, and ability to adapt had all been found wanting.[11] The Balkan commitment, which was supposed to be short-term but extended for most of the 1990s, was almost as embittering. A series of factors contributed to demoralization: the controversial leadership of Gen. Wesley K. Clark, the delays accompanying Task Force Hawk, a profound distaste for the region's bigotry and bloodthirstiness, and the collective inability of either the service or the political leadership to define the mission or its end state. But most embarrassing was the contrast with allied forces and the US Marine Corps, which mixed with local populations to alleviate tensions while the army leadership, apparently obsessed with avoiding casualties, insisted that soldiers stay in a luxurious base camp (termed "Disneyland") and emerge only for brief forays in armored convoys.[12] At the end of the 1990s, an army of 475,000 had a third of its troops overseas, and the pace of operations had produced individual and collective frustration and exhaustion.

The quick tempo of deployments was only one factor aggravating the army's increasing problems manning its units. According to a report by the chairman of the House Committee on National Security, the service had a personnel turnover (or churn) of 40 percent of its enlisted personnel each year; one division had a turnover average of 10 percent each month. The service had to shift soldiers out of MOSs to meet more urgent demands; tank sergeants were sent to lead infantry platoons. And yet the service reported that the equivalent of a division's worth of infantry squads were unmanned and that other units were skeletonized or had a high proportion of untrained soldiers.[13]

As during previous postwar eras, the decade after the end of the Cold War placed great stresses on the officer corps. Contributing to this was the familiar generation gap. The senior leadership still shared many Old Army characteristics familiar to their predecessors. In their view, they had pulled the army out of the Vietnam doldrums, fended off the Soviet threat, and won the Gulf War. But too many had become complacent and had little patience with what they viewed as political interference from Washington and carping from junior officers who hadn't lived through the tough times. Moreover, in the early tenure of these Old Army stalwarts, the indices used to evaluate success— morale, readiness, retention, maintenance, education—were positive overall. But midway through the postwar decade, a survey of 24,000 active and reserve officers forced Army Chief of Staff Reimer to acknowledge in 1996 that "the state of ethical conduct is abysmal. . . . There is a return to the 'zero defects' and ticket-punching mentality of the 1960s and 1970s that nearly destroyed the officer corps."[14] Reimer's efforts to teach better leadership to the senior grades did not resolve the problem. Whereas in the five years prior to 1997 only four lieutenant colonels declined command, in the following three years 108 did so.[15] One study by a retired Regular Army officer found that junior officers often referred to their superiors as occupying "echelons above reality" and "looking good—not being good."[16]

Many officers were not content to merely grouse: in the last half of the 1990s resignations increased to unsupportable levels. The most serious were those at captain grade, which doubled in the five years prior to 1999, leading to a shortage of 3,000 by the end of that year. In part this represented a shift in the culture of the officer corps. As had been the case in the past, male West Point graduates often married into military families whose spouses were accustomed to the obligations, lifestyle, and ambitions of a career officer's wife. But ROTC graduates during the 1990s often married fellow university graduates who had the skills for their own careers. Having experienced a few years as unpaid den mothers, hostesses, "voluntary" post committee members, and other expected obligatory roles, they offered their spouses a simple choice: the army or me. The inability to retain sufficient junior officers, in turn, meant that too many were pulled out of troop command into headquarters staffs, which probably contributed to additional resignations. At the other end of the career trajectory, more and more field officers were retiring early.[17]

General Shinseki's 1999 exhortation to the students and faculty at the Army War College to recall the transformation wrought by Elihu Root was delivered as the full impact of the postwar decade hit the service. Despite accusations of dropping standards, the force had missed its recruiting goals and, with an active force of 479,000, was unable to fill its combat units. Officer resignations and command declinations continued. The Government Accounting Office reported that the negative results on unit performance from persistent overseas deployments was being underreported. Congress was holding hearings on the army leadership's complicity in suppressing readiness or, more accurately, unreadiness reports.[18]

Would it have helped inspire his audience to greater heights had Shinseki explained that, a decade after the Root era's transformation, the reforms had been confined largely to Washington and a few model programs? Or that congressional and army opposition would soon prompt a serious attempt to dismantle much of Root's legacy? Or that in 1911 a secretary of war would tell Congress: "We have scattered our Army over the country as if it were merely groups of local constabulary instead of a national organization. The result is an Army which is extraordinarily expensive to maintain; and whose efficiency for the main purpose of its existence has been nullified so far as geographical location can nullify it"?[19] Perhaps not. But it might also have mitigated some of the cynicism that much of General Shinseki's own transformation plan—from issuing berets to undertaking the Future Combat System—proved neither essential nor appropriate for the wars in Iraq and Afghanistan in the early 2000s.[20]

It is clearly too early to attempt an evaluation on the current US Army in the aftermath of the Middle East wars. And as someone who bought a Macintosh 128K computer but not Apple stock years ago, I know the limits of my predictive abilities. Yet it is hard not to draw parallels that situate the current US Army as being midway through its ten-year postwar cycle.

As after previous wars, the senior leadership set out to learn the lessons of Iraq and Afghanistan. As with every war, there was the familiar "battle of the books" as various generals—or admiring subordinates and journalists—rushed to extoll heroes, denigrate rivals, and avert blame. Reviewing the tomes and articles collectively, it is hard to believe these officers served in the same wars—or even the same countries. Many of their claims have been undercut if not refuted by the release, only under pressure, of the two internal histories of the wars and a trove of self-studies, documents, and interviews.[21] And as with Vietnam, the army's leadership, having largely acknowledged long before the official ending of hostilities that both wars were unwinnable, repudiated the recently approved counterinsurgency doctrine and turned back to large-scale, mobile, high-tempo combined arms warfare against a peer opponent such as Russia or China. The resulting doctrine—Multi-Domain Operations—draws inspiration from World War II and especially the evolution of AirLand Battle; as with DePuy's post-Vietnam efforts, doctrine justifies a massive equipment modernization program.[22]

As with Vietnam, even as the US Army was wrapping up the conflict in Iraq and waging war in Afghanistan, it was downsizing from 546,000 in 2011, to 487,000 in 2015, to 472,000 in 2018. As in previous wars, the postwar army had to lower its standards to obtain soldiers. "High-quality" accessions declined from 60 percent in 2003 to 44 percent in 2007. The postwar service in the twenty-first century, like its predecessors, inherited a substantial "hump" of experienced, rapidly promoted wartime junior officers and noncoms who have sometimes proven ill-suited for garrison service. Indicative of the continuing impact of the war on personnel are high rates of prescription drug misuse and sexual assault and the troubling rise of white supremacist gangs. The service also faces the perennial dilemma of competing for skilled labor, illustrated by its simultaneous "Warriors Wanted" recruiting slogan while offering enlistment bonuses of $5,000 to a combat arms trooper and $40,000 to a satellite communications systems operator.[23]

The Iraq and Afghanistan conflicts also exacerbated the post–Cold War failure to retain sufficient high-quality company officers to serve as future leaders. By FY 2007 the service faced a shortfall in excess of 3,000 career officers and anticipated that similar shortfalls would continue for at least six years. The postwar half-decade has continued this trend among potential career officers. Faced with unrealistic schedules for "generating" their commands, personnel churn that stripped returning units to a skeleton within three months, broken equipment and insufficient funding or skilled personnel to fix it, training schedules and personnel appropriated for post maintenance or headquarters duty, and a litany of complaints familiar to all their predecessors, too many have resigned.[24]

These brief summaries indicate that the post–Cold War and the post–Iraq/Afghanistan periods conform to the historic pattern that the ten years after each war provided the US Army distinct tests: creating an army for coast defense and frontier pacification after 1815; balancing imperial protection with preparation for modern war in the early 1900s; confronting the Soviets in the 1950s and 1970s; dealing with the post–Cold War world; and confronting Russian aggression. But each postwar decade has also presented the same challenges as those faced in previous eras: assessing the lessons of the last war; administrative reform; new missions; preparing for future conflict; developing the officer corps; and rebuilding the enlisted ranks. Most studies of peacetime forces focus only on the resolution of the first four of these challenges, and most of these are acted upon, if not resolved, in the first five years after each conflict. In the process, scholars tend to ignore the consequences of those resolutions over the second half of the postwar decade, particularly for the officers and rankers who lived through them.

This blinkered focus on top-down policy rather than people contributes to four major fallacies common to any large bureaucracy, from corporations to universities. *The first fallacy is that policy equals implementation*, to assume wherever Washington directs the field forces follow. *The second fallacy is assuming that, even if they wished to comply, the individuals tasked with executing policy have the intellectual, materiel, or other resources needed for implementation.* Often they do not. *The third fallacy is that the past yields clear lessons that can be applied to present problems if only the leaders have sufficient vision, the resources are abundant, and the subordinates dutifully salute and obey.* Predicting the future by copying the past is risky. It is even more risky when combined with the conviction that military expertise in one task automatically conveys expertise in another. As was once said about Gen. Bruce C. Clarke, the army lost a damn good sergeant when they made him a general. To these common institutional fallacies add a fourth: by confusing a *postwar* force with a *prewar* force and assessing it largely on its performance in a future war, the potential for misunderstanding and misinterpreting the distinct identities of aftermath armies is limitless.

William Lassiter recognized the essential dilemma of an army recovering from war. Observing the 1st Cavalry Division's 1929 maneuvers, he was appalled: their idea of tactics was "a confused medley of horsemen galumphing along, easy prey to a few cool[-]headed machine gunners posted on the ridge they were approaching." How could such an anachronism exist in an army that, barely ten years earlier, had mobilized and deployed millions across the Atlantic, employed thousands of tanks, airplanes, cannons, and all the other implements of modern war, and waged the greatest land battle in the nation's history? The answer, the general believed, lay in recognizing that the aftermath of war formed an army with a distinct character, distinct problems, and distinct realities. The 1st Cavalry Division was a hollow force, a division in name only, and its commanders, including some relics who served in the Spanish–American War, were "obsessed with the idea that they must charge" and refused to accept the fact that "modern weapons will not permit them to charge." Like the rest of the army in the years after World War I, the cavalry was in limbo; it was undergoing a slow and incomplete transition from the changes wrought by the last conflict toward preparation for an unknown, and probably faraway, future war.[25] In common with many postwar leaders dating back to 1815, Lassiter would have appreciated Gen. Matthew B. Ridgway's warning a decade after World War II that "it is not the dangerous days of battle which most strongly test the soldier's resolution, but the years of peace."[26] The US Army is right to celebrate its wartime exploits, but it would do well to remember that, despite the inefficiency, uncertainty, and under-resourcing emblematic of postwar eras, the service owes its continued existence to those forgotten legions that have done its "real soldiering" in war's aftermath.

Notes

Abbreviations Used in Notes and Bibliography

ACS	Assistant/Acting Chief of Staff
AFHRA	US Air Force Historical Research Agency, Montgomery, AL.
AG	Adjutant General
AGO	Adjutant General's Office File Number
AHEC	US Army Heritage and Education Center, Carlisle, PA
ANJ	*Army and Navy Journal*
AWC	Army War College
CAJ	*Coast Artillery Journal/Journal of the United States Artillery*
CARL	Combined Arms Research Library, Fort Leavenworth, KS
CFJ	*Combat Forces Journal*
CG	Commanding General
CGSC	Command and General Staff College/Command and General Staff School
CJ	*Cavalry Journal*
CSA	Chief of Staff, US Army
DCS	Deputy Chief of Staff, US Army
DOAHR	*Department of the Army Historical Reports*
DTIC	Defense Technical Information Center
E	Record Group Entry, National Archives
FAJ	*Field Artillery Journal*
FY	Fiscal Year
GSM/AWCCA	General Staff Memoranda, AWC Curricular Archives, AHEC
HD	Hawaiian Department/Hawaiian Division
IG	Inspector General
IJ	*Infantry Journal*
JMSI	*Journal of the Military Service Institute of the United States*
MCEL	Maneuver Center of Excellence Libraries, Donovan Research Library, Fort Benning, GA
MDLOC	Manuscripts Division, Library of Congress, Washington, DC
MID	Military Information/Intelligence Division
MOS	Military Occupation Specialization
MR	*Military Review*
NA	National Archives
PD	Philippine Department/Philippine Division

PF	Project File
R	Microfilm Roll
RCS	*Report of the Chief of Staff*
RG	Record Group, National Archives
RSW	*Report of the Secretary of War*
SAMS	School of Advanced Military Studies, Command and General Staff College
SP	Student Paper
USAREUR	US Army Europe
USMAL	US Military Academy Library, West Point, NY
WD	*Report of the War Department*
WDGS	War Department General Staff
WPD	War Plans Division, General Staff

Preface: The Aftermath Army

1. Michael S. Davison, "Address to the Information Officer's Conference," 8 March 1972, box 5, Michael S. Davison Papers, AHEC.

2. Davison, "Address to the Information Officer's Conference."

3. Thomas Hardy, *The Dynasts*, part 2, scene 5.

4. Christopher Bassford, *The Spit-Shine Syndrome: Organizational Irrationality in the American Field Army* (Westport, CT: Praeger, 1988).

5. Public Opinion Surveys, *Attitude of Adult Civilians Toward the Military Service as a Career* (Princeton, NJ: Public Opinion Surveys, 1955); Charles C. Moskos, Jr., *The American Enlisted Man: The Rank and File in Today's Military* (New York: Russell Sage Foundation, 1970), 1–36.

6. James Jones, *From Here to Eternity*, ed. George Hendrick (1951, ebook, New York: Open Road, 2011), 50. For an engaging nonfictional account, see Henry G. Gole, *Soldiering: Observations from Korea, Vietnam, and Safe Places* (Dulles, VA: Potomac Books, 2005).

7. William A. Ganoe, *The History of the United States Army* (New York: D. Appleton-Century Co., 1942), 298–354. Ganoe's term referred specifically to the post–Civil War decade, but he accorded a similarly pessimistic appraisal of the decades after the Spanish–American War and World War I.

8. Oliver L. Spaulding, *The U.S. Army in War and Peace* (New York: G. P. Putnam's Sons, 1937), vii.

9. John R. Dabrowski, ed., *An Oral History of General Gordon R. Sullivan* (Carlisle Barracks, PA: US Army War College, 2009), 71.

10. Spaulding, *U.S. Army*, viii.

11. Roy K. Flint, "Task Force Smith and the 24th Division: Delay and Withdrawal, 5–19 July, 1950," in *America's First Battles, 1776–1965*, ed. Charles E. Heller and William A. Stofft (Lawrence: University Press of Kansas, 1986), 266–299; John Garrett, "Task Force Smith: The Lesson Never Learned," 2000, SP, SAMS; Gordon Sullivan, "No More Task Force Smiths," in Gordon R. Sullivan, *The Collected Works of the Thirty-Second Chief of Staff, United States Army, 1991–1995* (Washington, DC: Department of the Army, 1996), 73–79. On peacetime military innovation, see

Barry Posen, *The Sources of Military Innovation: France, Britain, and Germany Between the Two World Wars* (Ithaca: Cornell University Press, 1984); Stephen Peter Rosen, *Winning the Next War: Innovation and the Modern Military* (Ithaca: Cornell University Press, 1991); Adam Grissom, "The Future of Military Innovation Studies," *Journal of Strategic Studies* 29 (October 2006): 905–934.

12. Among many examples that challenge era exceptionalism, see J. P. Clark, *Preparing for War: The Emergence of the Modern U.S. Army, 1815–1917* (Cambridge, MA: Harvard University Press, 2017); Edward M. Coffman, *The Old Army: A Portrait of the American Army in Peacetime, 1784–1898* (New York: Oxford University Press, 1986); Edward M. Coffman, *The Regulars: The American Army, 1898–1941* (Cambridge, MA: Harvard University Press, 2004); Carol Reardon, *Soldiers and Scholars: The U.S. Army and the Uses of Military History, 1865–1920* (Lawrence: University Press of Kansas, 1990); Robert Wooster, *The United States Army and the Making of America: From Confederation to Empire, 1775–1903* (Lawrence: University Press of Kansas, 2021).

13. Quoted in L. Michael Allsep, Jr., "New Forms of Dominance: How a Corporate Lawyer Created the American Military Establishment" (PhD diss., University of North Carolina at Chapel Hill, 2008), 203.

14. See, for example, John L. Romjue, Susan Canedy, and Anne W. Chapman, *Prepare the Army for War: A Historical Overview of Training and Doctrine Command* (Fort Monroe: TRADOC, 1993). Having worked with them for four decades, my experience has been that the TRADOC's and the US Army's historians as a group are distinguished in their professionalism and research skills from their academic peers only by the fact that they tend to work more productively.

15. *It's the Old Army Game*, directed by Eddie Sutherland (Los Angeles, CA: Paramount, 1926), www.youtube.com/watch?v=jkhWPRqeBxQ.

16. John Sloan Brown, *Kevlar Legions: The Transformation of the U.S. Army, 1989–2005* (Washington, DC: Center of Military History, 2011). During my 2003–2007 tenure on the Department of the Army Historical Advisory Committee, I was made well aware that the deterioration of recordkeeping and cataloging, the bizarre and counterproductive federal security classification system, software updates, and the drastic cuts in archival resources and staff had all made it virtually impossible for even the US Army's official historians to access the service's records. This point is made by one such scholar, Robert T. Davis II, in *The Challenge of Adaptation: The U.S. Army in the Aftermath of Conflict, 1953–2000* (Fort Leavenworth, KS: Combat Studies Institute, 2008), ii. 5, 101. Interviews with both service and federal archivists convinced me that the post-2005 situation is even worse.

17. Oral History, 2:317, Arthur S. Collins Papers, AHEC.

Chapter 1. The Nineteenth-Century Aftermath Army

1. Zachary Taylor to Thomas Jesup, 18 September 1820, digital images 23–25, at www.loc.gov/resource/mss42440.001_0027_0913/?sp=23.

2. Ulysses S. Grant, *Memoirs and Selected Letters* (New York: Library of America, 1990), 69.

3. K. Jack Bauer, *Zachary Taylor: Soldiers, Planter, Statesman of the Old Southwest*

(Baton Rouge: Louisiana State University Press, 1985); Coffman, *Old Army*, 198; Hamilton Holman, *Zachary Taylor*, vol. 1 (Indianapolis: Bobbs-Merrill, 1941).

4. This work will use both "Regular Army" and "US Army" as the organizational title of the nation's active standing military forces. On early American military history to the War of 1812, see Allan R. Millett, Peter Maslowski, and William Feis, *For the Common Defense: A Military History of the United States of America, 1607–2012*, 3rd ed. (New York: Free Press, 2012), 1–95. On the War of 1812 establishing permanent foundations of the standing army, see Clark, *Preparing for War*; Coffman, *Old Army*; William B. Skelton, *An American Profession of Arms: The Army Officer Corps, 1784–1861* (Lawrence: University Press of Kansas, 1992); Samuel J. Watson, "Surprisingly Professional: Trajectories in Army Officer Corps Drawdowns, 1783–1848," in *Drawdown: The American Way of Postwar*, ed. Jason W. Warren (New York: New York University Press, 2016), 73–106.

5. Ganoe, *History*, 79.

6. Richard H. Kohn, *Eagle and Sword: The Beginnings of the Military Establishment in America* (New York: Free Press, 1975); Russell F. Weigley, *History of the U.S. Army* (New York: Macmillan, 1967), 74–98.

7. Theodore J. Crackel, *Mr. Jefferson's Army: Political and Social Reform of the Military Establishment, 1801–1809* (New York: New York University Press, 1989); Lawrence D. Cress, *Citizens in Arms: The Army and the Militia in American Society to the War of 1812* (Chapel Hill: University of North Carolina Press, 1982). The Federalists conceived of the army's internal security duties as a means to control political adversaries. Later political and military leaders would broaden the army's internal security duties to the control of racial groups, economic classes, and ideological opponents. I am grateful to Ian Hope for bringing this distinction to my attention.

8. Robert S. Browning III, *Two if by Sea: The Development of American Coastal Defense Policy* (Westport, CT: Greenwood Press, 1983), 1–18; Clark, *Preparing for War*, 10–17; Coffman, *Old Army*, 1–41; Walter E. Kretchik, *U.S. Army Doctrine: From the American Revolution to the War on Terror* (Lawrence: University Press of Kansas, 2011), 22–45; Francis Paul Prucha, *The Sword of the Republic: The United States Army on the Frontier, 1783–1846* (Bloomington: Indiana University Press, 1977), 1–118; Skelton, *An American Profession*; Richard W. Stewart, ed., *American Military History*, vol. 1, *The United States Army and the Forging of a Nation, 1775–1917* (Washington, DC: Center of Military History, 2005), 131–157; Samuel J. Watson, *Jackson's Sword: The Army Officer Corps on the American Frontier, 1810–1821* (Lawrence: University Press of Kansas, 2012), 1–61; Weigley, *History of the U.S. Army*, 74–118.

9. Clark, *Preparing for War*, 17–24; Harry Coles, *The War of 1812* (Chicago: University of Chicago Press, 1965); Donald Hickey, *The War of 1812: A Forgotten Conflict* (Urbana: University of Illinois Press, 1989); Millett, Maslowski, and Feis, *For the Common Defense*, 95–107; Wayne E. Lee, "Plattsburgh, 1814: Warring for Bargaining Chips," in *Between War and Peace: How America Ends Its Wars*, ed. Matthew Moten (New York: Free Press, 2011), 43–63; Stewart, *American Military History*, 131–157.

10. James Monroe to House of Representatives, 30 January 1824, in *The New*

American State Papers, Naval Affairs, vol. 1, *General Naval Policy and Defense*, ed. K. Jack Bauer (Wilmington, DE: Scholarly Resources, 1981), 107–108.

11. John C. Calhoun to John W. Taylor, 12 December 1820, *The Papers of John C. Calhoun*, vol. 5, *1820–1821*, ed. W. Edwin Hemphill (Columbia: University of South Carolina Press, 1971), 482.

12. "Annual Report of the Secretary of War Showing the Operations of that Department in 1831," 21 November 1831, in *American State Papers: Documents, Legislative and Executive of the Congress of the United States: Military Affairs*, 7 vols. (Washington, DC: Gales and Seaton, 1832–1861), 4:712–713.

13. Sydney [pseud.], "Thoughts on the Organization of the Army," *Military and Naval Magazine of the United States* 2 (December 1833): 198. Henry W. Halleck, *Elements of Military Arts and Science . . . and Engineers* (1846; repub. Westport, CT: Greenwood Press, 1971), 48, 140–141.

14. James S. Pettit, "How Far Does Democracy Affect the Organization and Discipline of Our Armies and How Can Its Influence Be Most Effectually Utilized," *JMSI* 38 (January–February 1906): 14.

15. J. C. A. Stagg, "United States Army Officers in the War of 1812: A Statistical and Behavioral Portrait," *JMH* 76 (October 2012): 1001–1034. I am indebted to Samuel J. Watson for the information on British-American socializing on the border.

16. On War Department bureaucratic reforms, see Clark, *Preparing for War*, 24–30; Skelton, *An American Profession*, 109–130; Stewart, *American Military History*, 159–166; Weigley, *History of the U.S. Army*, 132–143.

17. Jean-Pierre Beugoms, "The Logistics of the United States Army, 1812–1821" (PhD diss., Temple University, 2018), 194–286.

18. David A. Clary and Joseph W. A. Whitehorne, *The Inspectors General of the United States Army, 1777–1903* (Washington, DC: Center of Military History, 1987), 114–120; Mark A. Smith, "The Politics of Military Professionalism: The Engineer Company and the Political Activities of the Antebellum U.S. Army Corps of Engineers," *JMH* 80 (April 2016): 355–387.

19. The Bragg incident is cited in Coffman, *Old Army*, 66. Charles Francis O'Connell, "The United States Army and the Origins of Modern Management, 1818–1860" (PhD diss., Ohio State University, 1982).

20. Ganoe, *History*, 146. Weigley, *History of the U.S. Army*, 139–140; Francis B. Heitman, *Historical Register and Dictionary of the United States Army*, vol. 1 (orig. pub. 1903, repr., Urbana: University of Illinois Press, 1963), 50–64, 81–96.

21. Ganoe, *History*, 143–151; Kretchik, *U.S. Army Doctrine*, 50–55.

22. What today are termed the "combat arms" in the nineteenth century were termed "branches." Officers were commissioned in a branch—the infantry, artillery, and later cavalry—but there was no peacetime organization higher than the regiment. Officers often stayed with a regiment their entire careers, though in some cases they would transfer to another regiment or, rarely, to another branch.

23. Clary and Whitehorne, *Inspectors Generals*, 151–162; Weigley, *History of the U.S. Army*, 138–139; William B. Skelton, "The Commanding General and the Problem of Command in the U.S. Army, 1821–1841," *Military Affairs* 34 (December 1970): 117–122.

24. Samuel J. Watson, *Peacekeepers and Conquerors: The Army Officer Corps on the American Frontier, 1821–1846* (Lawrence: University Press of Kansas, 2013), 18, 41–42.

25. Cited in Walter Millis, ed., *American Military Thought* (Indianapolis: Bobbs-Merril Co., 1962), 89.

26. "Fortifications," 12 February 1821, 16th Cong, 2nd Sess., #206, in *American State Papers*, 3:304–310. The Fortification Board was alternatively known as the Board of Engineers for Fortifications and the Board of Fortifications.

27. On coastal defense policy, see Browning, *Two if by Sea*; David A. Clary, *Fortress America: The Corps of Engineers, Hampton Roads, and United States Coastal Defense* (Charlottesville: University Press of Virginia, 1990); Ian C. Hope, *A Scientific Way of War: Antebellum Military Science, West Point, and the Origins of American Military Thought* (Lincoln: University of Nebraska Press, 2015), 31–33, 47–57; Brian McAllister Linn, *The Echo of Battle: The Army's Way of War* (Cambridge, MA: Harvard University Press, 2007), 10–39; Jamie W. Moore, *The Fortifications Board 1816–1828 and the Definition of National Security* (Charleston: Citadel Press, 1981); Samuel J. Watson, "Knowledge, Interest, and the Limits of Military Professionalism: The Discourse on American Coast Defense, 1815–1860," *War in History* 5 (Fall 1998): 280–307.

28. Edmund P. Gaines to John C. Calhoun, 28 July 1823, *American State Papers*, 2:579. Francis Paul Prucha, *Broadax and Bayonet: The Role of the United States Army in the Development of the Northwest, 1815–1860* (orig. publ. 1953; repr., Lincoln: University of Nebraska Press, 1995), 16–25; Watson, *Jackson's Sword*, 123–187.

29. On the Arikara expedition, see Prucha, *Sword of the Republic*, 153–157. On the importance of Native American allies and intratribal conflict, see John W. Hall, *Uncommon Defense: Indian Allies in the Black Hawk War* (Cambridge, MA: Harvard University Press, 2009).

30. Hope, *Scientific Way of War*, 134.

31. On the army's role as agent of federal authority and control, see Watson, *Peacekeepers and Conquerors*; Andrew J. Polsky and Willian D. Adler, "The State in a Blue Uniform," *Polity* 40 (July 2008): 348–354. For an example of an officer's peacetime duties on the frontier, see Roger L. Nichols, "Stephen H. Long," in *Soldiers West: Biographies from the Military Frontier*, ed. Paul Andrew Hutton (Lincoln: University of Nebraska Press, 1987), 24–41.

32. Michael A. Bonura, *Under the Shadow of Napoleon: French Influence on the American Way of Warfare from the War of 1812 to the Outbreak of WW II* (New York: New York University Press, 2012), 55–66; Ganoe, *History*, 143–146, 164–166; Kretchik, *U.S. Army Doctrine*, 50–59; Wayne W. Hsieh, *West Pointers and the Civil War: The Old Army in War and Peace* (Chapel Hill: University of North Carolina Press, 2009), 34–53. I am indebted to J. P. Clark for his insight into Scott's generation's conflation of command, drill, and tactics.

33. Skelton, *American Profession of Arms*, 249–252.

34. William B. Skelton, "High Army Leadership in the Era of the War of 1812," *William and Mary Quarterly* 51 (April 1994): 253–274.

35. Robert M. Utley, *Frontiersmen in Blue: The United States Army and the Indian, 1848–1865* (orig. publ. 1967; repr., Lincoln: University of Nebraska Press, 1981), 32.

36. Watson, "Surprisingly Professional," 86.

37. John C. Calhoun to John W. Taylor, 12 December 1820, *Papers of John C. Calhoun*, 5:482.

38. Watson, "Surprisingly Professional," 87–96. Michael S. Fitzgerald, "Rejecting Calhoun's Expansible Army Plan: The Army Reduction Act of 1821," *War in History* 3 (1996): 161–185.

39. Skelton, *An American Profession*, 138–139.

40. Clark, *Preparing for War*, 22.

41. Hope, *Scientific Way of War*, 1–11, 59–75, 146–160; James L. Morrison, *"The Best School in the World": West Point, the Pre-Civil War Years, 1833–1866* (Kent, OH: Kent State University Press, 1986).

42. Clark, *Preparing for War*, 38–41; Timothy D. Johnson, *Winfield Scott: The Quest for Military Glory* (Lawrence: University Press of Kansas, 2006), 67–103; Allan Peskin, *Winfield Scott and the Profession of Arms* (Kent, OH: Kent State University Press, 2003).

43. Clary and Whitehorne, *Inspectors Generals*, 151–154, 172–174. James W. Silver, *Edmund Pendleton Gaines: Frontier General* (Baton Rouge: Louisiana State University Press, 1949).

44. Hope, *A Scientific Way of War*, 77–105.

45. Prucha, *Sword of the Republic*, 174–192; Polsky and Adler, "State in a Blue Uniform"; Robert P. Wettemann, "West Point, the Jacksonians, and the Army's Controversial Role in National Improvements," in *West Point: Two Centuries and Beyond*, ed. Lance Betros (Abilene, TX: McWhiney Foundation Press, 2004): 144–166.

46. Ricardo A. Herrera, *For Liberty and the Republic: The American Citizen as Soldier, 1775–1861* (New York: New York University Press, 2015).

47. Dale R. Steinhauer, "'Sogers': Enlisted Men in the U.S. Army, 1815–1860" (PhD diss., University of North Carolina at Chapel Hill, 1992), 68–114.

48. Prucha, *Sword of the Republic*, 174–192; Prucha, *Broadax and Bayonet*, 34–188.

49. Lorien Foote, *The Gentlemen and the Roughs: Violence, Honor, and Manhood in the Union Army* (New York: New York University Press, 2010).

50. Steinhauer, "'Sogers,'" 232–276. J. C. A. Stagg, "Freedom and Subordination: Disciplinary Problems in the U.S. Army in the War of 1812," *JMH* 78 (April 2014): 537–574.

51. Skelton, *An American Profession*, 270–278; Coffman, *Old Army*, 193–197; Mark A. Vargas, "The Military Justice System and the Use of Illegal Punishments as Causes of Desertion in the U.S. Army, 1821–1835," *JMH* 55 (January 1991): 1–19.

52. Watson, *Peacekeepers and Conquerors*, 41.

53. Watson, *Peacekeepers and Conquerors*, 266–270; Steinhauer, "'Sogers,'" 192–231.

54. Steinhauer, "'Sogers,'" 332–356.

55. Weigley, *History of the U.S. Army*, 188–196. Stewart, *American Military History*, 190–194.

56. K. Jack Bauer, *The Mexican War, 1846–1848* (orig. publ. 1974; repr., Lincoln: University of Nebraska Press, 1992); Joseph G. Dawson III, "The U.S. War with Mexico: The Difficulties of Concluding a Victorious War," in Moten, *Between War and Peace*, 85–106; Ganoe, *History*, 196–228; Hsieh, *West Pointers*, 54–74; Hope,

Scientific Way of War, 161–168; Kretchik, *U.S. Army Doctrine*, 59–62; Timothy D. Johnson, *A Gallant Little Army: The Mexico City Campaign* (Lawrence: University Press of Kansas, 2007); Richard Bruce Winders, *Mr. Polk's Army: The American Military Experience in the Mexican War* (College Station: Texas A&M University Press, 1997).

57. Skelton, *An American Profession*, 294–295.

58. John C. Pinheiro, *Manifest Ambition: James K. Polk and Civil-Military Relations During the Mexican War* (Westport, CT: Praeger Security International, 2007). On US Army interpretations of the war's lessons, see Clark, *Preparing for War*, 57–71; Linn, *Echo of Battle*, 21–22.

59. Coffman, *Old Army*, 58; Durwood Ball, *Army Regulars on the Western Frontier, 1848–1861* (Norman: University of Oklahoma Press, 2001), xx.

60. Ethan Allen Hitchcock, *Fifty Years in Camp and Field* (orig. publ. 1909; repr., Freeport, NY: Books for Libraries Press, 1971), 391.

61. Bonura, *Under the Shadow*, 94–96; Clark, *Preparing for War*, 60–63; Hseih, *West Pointers*, 75–90; Kretchik, *U.S. Army Doctrine*, 63–70.

62. Browning, *Two if by Sea*, 108–123; Linn, *Echo of Battle*, 25–29; Watson, "Knowledge, Interest," 280–307.

63. "Letter from Major General Scott," 3 November 1849, 31st Cong., 1st Sess., H. Executive Docs, v. 3, p. 98.

64. Halleck, *Elements of Military Arts and Science* (orig. publ. 1846; repr., Westport, CT: Greenwood Press, 1971), 145.

65. On the Army's adaptation to Native American warfare, see Skelton, *An American Profession*, 255–256; Samuel J. Watson, "Military Learning and Adaptation Shaped by Social Context: The U.S. Army and Its 'Indian Wars,' 1790–1890," *JMH* 82 (April 2018): 371–412. On Mahan's contribution, see Clark, *Preparing for War*, 32–35; Hope, *Scientific Way of War*, 195–200.

66. Quoted in Coffman, *Old Army*, 58. Matthew Moten, *The Delafield Commission and the American Military Profession* (College Station: Texas A&M University Press, 2000), 6–15; Samuel J. Watson, "Continuity in Civil-Military Relations and Expertise: The U.S. Army during the Decade before the Civil War," *JMH* 75 (January 2011): 221–250.

67. Hope, *Scientific Way of War*, 174–177, 260.

68. Poussin, *United States*, 393–394.

69. Utley, *Frontiersmen in Blue*, 40–41.

70. Edward B. Hunt, *Modern Warfare: Its Science and Art* (New Haven: T. J. Stafford, 1860), 916.

71. Ganoe, *History*, 298–364; Huntington, *The Soldier and the State*, 226–246.

72. Ganoe, *History*, 306–309. On Black regiments on the frontier, see William A. Dobak and Thomas D. Phillips, *The Black Regulars, 1866–1898* (Norman: University of Oklahoma Press, 2001); James N. Leiker, *Racial Borders: Black Soldiers Along the Rio Grande* (College Station: Texas A&M University Press, 2002).

73. *RSW 1870*, vi; Clayton R. Newell and Charles R. Shrader, "The U.S. Army's Transition to Peace, 1865–66," *JMH* 77 (July 2013): 867–894. On the postwar army, see Clark, *Preparing for War*, 99–162; Coffman, *Old Army*, 215–404; Joseph G. Glatthaar, "The Civil War: A New Definition of Victory," in *Between War and Peace*, 107–128; Stewart, *American Military History*, 303–319; Robert M. Utley,

Frontier Regulars: The United States Army and the Indian, 1866–1891 (New York: Macmillan, 1973); Weigley, *History of the U.S. Army*, 257–283; Robert Wooster, *The Military and United States Indian Policy, 1865–1903* (New Haven: Yale University Press, 1988); Mark R. Grandstaff, "Preserving the 'Habits and Usages of War': William T. Sherman, Professional Reform, and the U.S. Army Officer Corps, 1865–1881," *JMH* 62 (July 1998): 521–545.

74. Ganoe, *History*, 244–297; Weigley, *History of the U.S. Army*, 199–200.

75. Brian W. Dippie, "George A. Custer," in Hutton, *Soldiers West*, 101–102. On Upton, see David John Fitzpatrick, *Emory Upton: Misunderstood Reformer* (Norman: University of Oklahoma Press, 2017), 182–207.

76. John C. Sparrow, *History of Personnel Demobilization in the United States Army* (Washington, DC: Department of the Army, 1952), 5.

77. Barbara A. Gannon, *The Won Cause: Black and White Comradeship in the Grand Army of the Republic* (Chapel Hill: University of North Carolina Press, 2011); Russell F. Weigley, *Towards an American Army: Military Thought from Washington to Marshall* (New York: Columbia University Press, 1962), 106–113.

78. Donald B. Connelly, *John M. Schofield and the Politics of Generalship* (Chapel Hill: University of North Carolina Press, 2006), 148–155; Stephen Cushman, *The General's Civil War: What Their Memoirs Can Teach Us Today* (Chapel Hill: University of North Carolina Press, 2021); Paul Andrew Hutton, *Phil Sheridan and His Army* (Lincoln: University of Nebraska Press, 1985), 148–151; Reardon, *Soldiers and Scholars*, 14, 35–49.

79. Clark, *Preparing for War*, 93–109; Fitzpatrick, *Emory Upton*, 91–95; Kretchik, *U.S. Army Doctrine*, 78–88.

80. Spaulding, *U.S. Army*, 340. For similar views, see Ganoe, *History*, 298. On Reconstruction, see Mark L. Bradley, *The Army and Reconstruction, 1865–1877* (Washington, DC: Center of Military History, 2015); Joseph G. Dawson, *Army Generals and Reconstruction: Louisiana, 1862 to 1877* (Baton Rouge: Louisiana State University Press, 1982); Andrew Lang, *In the Wake of War: Military Occupation, Emancipation, and Civil War America* (Baton Rouge: Louisiana State University Press, 2017); James E. Sefton, *The United States Army and Reconstruction, 1865–1877* (Baton Rouge: Louisiana State University Press, 1967).

81. Jerry M. Cooper, *The Army and Civil Disorder: Federal Military Intervention in Labor Disputes, 1877–1900* (Westport, CT: Greenwood Press, 1980).

82. Wooster, *The United States Army and the Making of America*, 198–266.

83. Hutton, *Phil Sheridan*, 110, 245–261; Wooster, *Military and United States Policy*, 144–173.

84. Browning, *Two if by Sea*, 136–141; Linn, *Echo of Battle*, 29–31. Some artillery units were sent to the frontier where they often served as infantry.

85. Coffman, *Old Army*, 216–222. On postwar officers, see Coffman, *Old Army*, 215–286; Clark, *Preparing for War*, 99–162.

86. Clark, *Preparing for War*, 100–102; Coffman, *Old Army*, 230–235; Dippie, "George A. Custer," 100–114; William B. Hazen, *The School and the Army in Germany and France, with a Diary of Siege Life at Versailles* (New York: Harper and Brothers, 1872), 226–238.

87. Kevin Adams, *Class and Race in the Frontier Army: Military Life in the West, 1870–1890* (Norman: University of Oklahoma Press, 2009), 31. Samuel P.

Huntington, *The Soldier and the State: The Theory and Politics of Civil-Military Relations* (New York: Vintage Books, 1957), 222–237. There is an extensive and disputatious literature on the causes, evolution, and extent of military professionalism in the latter part of the nineteenth century; see James L. Abrahamson, *America Arms for a New Century: The Making of a Great Military Power* (New York: Free Press, 1981); Clark, *Preparing for War*, 129–162; Coffman, *Old Army*, 269–286; John M. Gates, "The Alleged Isolation of U.S. Army Officers in the Late-19th Century," *Parameters* 10 (1980), 32–45; Huntington, *The Soldier and the State*, 223–246; Ronald G. Machoian, *William Harding Carter and the American Army* (Norman: University of Oklahoma Press, 2006), 3–97; Rory McGovern, *George W. Goethals and the Army: Change and Continuity in the Gilded Age and Progressive Era* (Lawrence: University Press of Kansas, 2019), esp. xv–xxvii; Weigley, *History of the U.S. Army*, 264–292.

88. Emory Upton to Francis V. Greene, 25 January 1879, box 2, Francis Vinton Greene Papers, Manuscripts and Archives Division, New York Public Library, New York, New York. Kevin Adams, *Class and Race*, 163–193; Coffman, *Old Army*, 266–269; Dobak and Phillips, *Black Regulars*, 146–149; Hutton, *Sheridan's Army*, 71–72; Charles M. Robinson, *General Crook and the Western Frontier* (Norman: University of Oklahoma Press, 2001); Robert W. Utley, *The Commanders: Civil War Generals Who Shaped the American West* (Norman: University of Oklahoma Press, 2018); Robert Wooster, *Nelson Miles and the Twilight of the Frontier Army* (Lincoln: University of Nebraska Press, 1993).

89. "Report of the Board of Visitors," *WD 1869*, 479–494.

90. "Personal Memoranda of Major General Eben Swift," Eben Swift Papers, USMAL.

91. Robert G. Carter, *The Art and Science of War Versus the Art of Fighting* (Washington, DC: National Publishing, 1922), 4. On West Point, see Coffman, *Old Army*, 269–271; Connolly, *John M. Schofield*, 224–233; Fitzpatrick, *Emory Upton*, 128–148; Walter Scott Dillard, "The United States Military Academy, 1865–1900: The Uncertain Years" (PhD diss., University of Wisconsin, 1972).

92. Timothy K. Nenninger, *The Leavenworth Schools and the Old Army: Education, Professionalism, and the Officer Corps of the United States Army, 1881–1918* (Westport, CT: Greenwood Press, 1978).

93. On enlisted men, see Adams, *Class and Race*, 11–29, 37–72; Coffman, *Old Army*, 328–399; Douglas C. McChristian, *Regular Army O! Soldiering on the Western Frontier, 1865–1891* (Norman: University of Oklahoma Press, 2017); Don Rickey, Jr., *Forty Miles a Day on Beans and Hay: The Enlisted Soldier Fighting the Indian Wars* (Norman: University of Oklahoma Press, 1963), 85–87; Utley, *Frontier Regulars*, 69–79.

94. Martin Pegler, *U.S. Cavalryman, 1865–1890* (London: Osprey, 1993), 10.

95. Hazen, *School and the Army*, 224.

96. John G. Bourke, *On the Border with Crook* (orig. publ. 1891; repr., Lincoln: University of Nebraska Press, 1971), 7.

97. *Report of the General of the Army, 1870*, 4–5.

98. Dippie, "George A. Custer," 103–104; McChristian, *Regular Army O!*, 410–423; Rickey, *Forty Miles*, 148–155; [Edward N. Woodbury], "A Study of Desertion," [1920], AHEC.

Chapter 2. Postscript to the Imperial Wars

1. "Notes and Diaries," 16–20, box 1, William Lassiter Papers, USMAL.

2. Graham A. Cosmas, *An Army for Empire: The United States Army in the Spanish-American War* (Columbia: University of Missouri Press, 1971).

3. Clarence C. Clendenen, *Blood on the Border: The United States Army and the Mexican Irregulars* (London: Macmillan Company, 1969), 139.

4. Douglas A. Macgregor, "Resurrecting Transformation for the Post-Industrial Era," *Defense Horizons* 2 (September 2001): 13. The post-1898 decade has inspired an extensive and disputatious historical literature; see Abrahamson, *America Arms for a New Century*, 66–73; Clark, *Preparing for War*, 163–230; Coffman, *The Regulars*, 10–195; Ganoe, *History*, 397–423; Huntington, *The Soldier and the State*, 247–254; Machoian, *William Harding Carter*; Weigley, *History of the U.S. Army*, 313–342; Allsep, "New Forms of Dominance"; Barrie M. Zais, "The Struggle for a Twentieth Century Army: Investigation and Reform of the United States Army After the Spanish-American War, 1989–1903" (PhD diss., Duke University, 1981).

5. Vincent Cirillo, *Bullets and Bacilli: The Spanish American War and Military Medicine* (New Brunswick, NJ: Rutgers University Press, 2004); Richard Severo and Lewis Milford, *The Wages of War: When America's Soldiers Came Home—From Valley Force to Vietnam* (New York: Simon and Schuster, 1989), 193–210. On the Spanish–American War, see David F. Trask, *The War with Spain in 1898* (New York: Macmillan, 1981).

6. Celwyn E. Hampton, "The Experiences of our Army Since the Outbreak of the War with Spain: What Practical Use has been Made of Them, and How May They be Further Utilized to Improve Its Fighting Efficiency," *JMSI* 36 (May–June 1905): 402.

7. John Bigelow, *Reminisces of the Santiago Campaign* (New York: Harper & Brothers, 1899), 126.

8. Brian McAllister Linn, *The Philippine War, 1899–1901* (Lawrence: University Press of Kansas, 2000); David J. Silbey, *A War of Frontier and Empire: The Philippine-American War, 1899–1902* (New York: Hill and Wang, 2007).

9. Pettit, "How Far Does Democracy Affect . . .," 27–28.

10. Matthew Forney Steele, *American Campaigns*, 2 vols. (orig. publ. 1909; repr., Washington, DC: US Infantry Association, 1922), 2:620.

11. Robert L. Bullard, "The Citizen Soldier—The Volunteer," *JMSI* 39 (September–October 1906): 153–167; Brian McAllister Linn, "The Impact of the Philippine Wars (1898–1913) on the U.S. Army," in *Colonial Crucible: Empire in the Making of the Modern American State*, ed. Alfred McCoy and Francis Scarano (Madison: University of Wisconsin Press, 2009), 460–472.

12. Clark, *Preparing for War*, 197; see also 182–230. William H. Carter, "Elihu Root—His Services as Secretary of War," *North American Review* 178 (January 1904): 110–121; Machoian, *William Harding Carter*, 98–198.

13. *RSW 1899*, 45.

14. George C. Marshall, "The Development of the General Staff" (lecture, 19 September 1922, AWC), AHEC; James Parker, *The Old Army: Memories, 1872–1918*

(Philadelphia: Dorrance, 1929), 391; "Personnel of the Army General Staff," *ANJ* 41 (2 January 1904). Not until 1914 did the army require that appointees to General Staff who were not staff college graduates pass an entrance exam.

15. Quotation from Clark, *Preparing for War*, 194. Machoian, *William Harding Carter*, 225–242.

16. 27 April 1909 diary entry, Wood Papers. Harry P. Ball, *Of Responsible Command: A History of the U.S. Army War College* (Carlisle Barracks, PA: Alumni Association of the U.S. Army War College, 1983), 41–119; Johnson Hagood, *The Services of Supply: A Memoir of the Great War* (Boston: Houghton Mifflin, 1927), 21; McGovern, *George W. Goethals*, 74–83.

17. "From Reveille to Retreat," 188, Eli Helmick Papers, AHEC. Mabel E. Deutruch, *Struggle for Supremacy: The Career of General Fred C. Ainsworth* (New York: Public Affairs Press, 1962); Jack C. Lane, *Armed Progressive: General Leonard Wood* (San Rafael, CA: Presidio Press, 1978), 156–170; Weigley, *History of the U.S. Army*, 328–341.

18. Robert L. Bullard, "The Army in Cuba," *JMSI* 41 (September–October 1907): 152. *Five Years of the War Department Following the War with Spain* (Washington, DC: US War Department, 1904), 147, 326; *RSW 1907*, 3.

19. On the National Guard, see Jerry C. Cooper, *The Rise of the National Guard: The Evolution of the American Militia, 1865–1920* (Lincoln: University of Nebraska Press, 1997), 108–152; Michael D. Doubler, *I Am the Guard: A History of the Army National Guard, 1636–2000* (Washington, DC: Department of the Army, 2001), 148–153,

20. Brian McAllister Linn, *Guardians of Empire: The U.S. Army and the Pacific, 1902–1940* (Chapel Hill: University of North Carolina Press, 1997), 51–113.

21. "Manoeuvres on the Massachusetts Coast: Their Purpose and Value," [1910], box 50, Leonard Wood Papers, MDLC. "Our Army at Peace," *ANJ* 41 (7 May 1904). Dollars are in 1900–1910 values.

22. Steven T. Ross, *American War Plans, 1890–1945* (Portland, OR: Frank Cass, 2002), 1–53.

23. Hugh S. Johnson, "The Lamb Rampant," *Everybody's Magazine* 18 (March 1908): 291–301. Linn, *Echo of Battle*, 93–15.

24. "General Chaffee's Views on War," *ANJ* 47 (2 October 1909).

25. US War Department, *Field Service Regulations, United States Army, 1905* (Washington, DC: GPO, 1905), 104. On the impact of the Russo–Japanese War, see Brent L. Sterling, *Other People's Wars: The US Military and the Challenge of Learning from Foreign Conflicts* (Washington, DC: Georgetown University Press, 2021), 58–136.

26. *RSW WD 1899*, 45–46. Kretchik, *U.S. Army Doctrine*, 107–116; Nenninger, *The Leavenworth Schools*, 88–93.

27. Arthur S. Wagner, "The Fort Riley Maneuvers," *JMSI* 32 (January–February 1903): 70–93; Charles Douglas McKenna, "The Forgotten Reform: Field Maneuvers in the Development of the United States Army, 1900–1920" (PhD diss., Duke University, 1981).

28. Manoeuvres on the Massachusetts Coast: Their Purpose and Value," [1910], box 50, Wood Papers. William H. Carter, "Camps of Instruction," *Reader* 10 (July 1907): 114–121; Helen F. Sanders, "When Uncle Sam Plays at War," *Overland*

Monthly 48 (October 1906): 259–275; John P. Wisser, "The Coast Joint Manoeuvers—1902," *JMSI* 31 (November 1902): 837–879.

29. HQ, Philippine Department, "Secret Service File, 1909," AWC 6595, E 296, RG 165; Hugh Straughn, "History of the Intelligence Office, Philippine Department," 1919, MID 10560-152-187, RG 165; Joan M. Jensen, *Army Surveillance in America, 1775–1980* (New Haven: Yale University Press, 1991), 88–108; Alfred W. McCoy, *Policing America's Empire: The United States, the Philippines, and the Rise of the Surveillance State* (Madison: University of Wisconsin Press, 2009), 59–267.

30. Adna R. Chaffee to Henry C. Corbin, 9 December 1901, box 1, Henry C. Corbin Papers, MDLC. *RSW WD 1900*, 4:56; Clark, *Preparing for War*, 173–177. Statistics on officer casualties from "Regular Army Promotion List," enc. in A. S. Conklin, "To Determine Whether or Not There Will Be in the Future a Surplus of Air Service Officers in the Higher Grades," 24 December 1924, SP, AWC, AHEC. In 1890 the army began requiring annual efficiency reports and examinations for promotion up to major—thus grandfathering in the Civil War veterans. Any officer who failed his examination lost his place on the seniority list; if he failed again he was discharged.

31. George Bridges Rodney, *As a Cavalryman Remembers* (Caldwell, ID: Caxton Press, 1944), 85. Forrest C. Pogue, *George C. Marshall: Education of a General, 1880–1939* (New York: Viking Press, 1963), 58–69.

32. Edward Hunter, "Our Military Judicial System," *JMSI* 32 (March–April 1903): 234.

33. "Report of the Philippines Department," *WD 1906*, 3:212. Oswald Garrison Villard, "New Army of the United States," *Atlantic Monthly* 89 (April 1902): 450; "Eliminating Army Officers," *The Nation* 82 (February 1906): 110–111; "The Question of Army Morals," *The Nation* 81 (October 1905): 333–334;

34. The schools at Fort Leavenworth went through several designations. In 1901 the Infantry and Cavalry School was renamed the General Service School. Three years later the curriculum was split into two courses. The first year was termed the Infantry and Cavalry School, and the top graduates remained for the Staff College. In 1907 the Infantry and Cavalry School was renamed the School of the Line; the Staff College kept its name, but both schools were combined as the Army Service School. On the Leavenworth schools and their teachings, see T. R. Brereton, *Educating the U.S. Army: Arthur L. Wagner and Reform, 1875–1905* (Lincoln: University of Nebraska Press, 2000); Nenninger, *The Leavenworth Schools*.

35. McGovern, *George W. Goethals and the Army*, 15. Paul B. Malone, "The Army School of the Line," *IJ* 6 (January 1910): 511–532; Clark, *Preparing for War*, 200–215.

36. Parker Hitt, "A Brief History of the School of Musketry," at http://1-22infantry.org/history3/musketry.htm. David A. Armstrong, *Bullets and Bureaucrats: The Machine Gun and the United States Army, 1861–1916* (Westport, CT: Praeger, 1982).

37. T. Bentley Mott to C/S, Memo: "The West Point Military Academy," December 1913, box 6, Francis Vinton Greene Papers, Manuscripts and Archives Division, New York Public Library, New York, NY; Lance Betros, *Carved from Granite: West Point Since 1902* (College Station: Texas A&M University Press, 2012), 22–24, 31–41, 78–83, 112–118; Dillard, "The United States Military Academy, 1865–1900," 334–355.

38. "Service Reminiscences of Lt. Gen. John C. H. Lee," 7–9, John C. H. Lee Papers, Hoover Institute Archives, Stanford University, Palo Alto, CA.

39. *RSW WD 1912*, 8.

40. Captain Peter Traub, "Esprit de Corps—How It May Be Strengthened and Preserved in Our Army Under the Present Organization and Method of Promotion," *JMSI* 34 (March–April 1904): 195–196.

41. I. B. Holley, *General John M. Palmer, Citizen Soldiers, and the Army of a Democracy* (Westport, CT: Greenwood Press, 1982), 189. This tribalism may have been better than the current system in which officers are rapidly transferred from unit to unit.

42. An Army Officer, "The Uplift Hits the Army," *American Mercury* 5 (June 1925): 139.

43. "An Army without Officers," *ANJ* 46 (13 February 1909). J. Franklin Bell, "The Evil of Detached Service and a Bill to Remedy the Matter by Creating Additional Officers of the Regular Army," Appendix A, *WD 1907*, 61–65.

44. "Report of the Inspector General," *WD 1909*, 268.

45. "An Army Wife," *ANJ* 43 (21 October 1905); "Another Army Wife," *ANJ* 43 (25 November 1905); Coffman, *Regulars*, 55–60; Linn, *Guardians of Empire*, 61–71.

46. Lloyd Buchanan, "Army as a Career," *World's Work* 11 (February 1906): 7236–7238; *RSW WD 1906*, 12; *RSW WD 1908*, 78–90.

47. "Questions by a Doughboy," *ANJ* 47 (17 April 1909).

48. Johnson Hagood, *Circular Relative to Pay of Officers and Enlisted Men of the Army* (Washington, DC: GPO, 1907), 25–26, 39.

49. Reardon, *Soldiers and Scholars*, 21–25, 103–105. Eben E. Swift, "Remarks on the Course of Instruction" (lecture, 1 September 1907, AWCCA), AHEC.

50. F. M. Lewis, "Discipline—Its Importance to an Armed Force and the Best Means of Promoting It and Maintaining It in the United States Army," *JMSI* 28 (May 1901): 331.

51. Hunter Liggett, *A.E.F: Ten Years Ago in France* (New York: Dodd, Mead and Co., 1928), 259. David C. Shanks, "Administration and the Management of Men," *IJ* 13 (November–December 1916): 276–289; Henry C. Davis, "Joint Exercises," *Journal of the United States Artillery (Coast Artillery Journal)* 28 (November–December 1907): 286–290.

52. D. Clayton James, *The Years of MacArthur*, vol. 1, *1880–1941* (Boston: Houghton Mifflin, 1970), 87–135.

53. Pogue, *Education*, 70–108.

54. "Rooseveltism in the Army," *ANJ* 44 (3 November 1906).

55. James G. Harbord, "Theodore Roosevelt and the Army," *Review of Reviews* 69 (1924): 66. Ronald J. Barr, *The Progressive Army: US Army Command and Administration, 1870–1914* (New York: St. Martin's Press, 1998), 169–170, 186–193; Mathew Oyos, *In Command: Theodore Roosevelt and the American Military* (Lincoln, NE: Potomac Books, 2018).

56. Henry O. S. Heistand to C. L. Humphries, 3 September 1903, E 2065, RG 395.

57. *RSW WD 1906* 1:12.

58. "Report of the Philippines Department," *WD 1909*, 3:201. Robert H. Noble, "Selection Versus Seniority," *IJ* 6 (July 1909): 63–77.

59. *RSW WD 1912*, 9.

60. "The President's Warning," *ANJ* 42 (15 July 1905).

61. "Y" to Editor, *ANJ* 46 (9 January 1909).

62. William H. Carter, "A General Staff for the Army," *North American Review* 175 (October 1902): 564. On Carter's politicking, see Machoian, *William Harding Carter*, 214–216.

63. Donald Smythe, *Guerrilla Warrior: The Early Life of John J. Pershing* (New York: Scribner's Sons, 1973), 125–127.

64. "The Koehler Court-Martial" *ANJ* 44 (30 March 1907). "The Case of Captain Koehler," *ANJ* 43 (8 November 1906). On Wood, see John D. Eisenhower, *Teddy Roosevelt and Leonard Wood: Partners in Command* (Columbia: University of Missouri Press, 2014); Lane, *Armed Progressive*; Jack McCallum, *Leonard Wood: Rough Rider, Surgeon, Architect of American Imperialism* (New York: New York University Press, 2006).

65. LeRoy Eltinge, *Psychology of War* (Fort Leavenworth: Army Service Schools Press, 1911); Carl Reichmann, "In Pace Para Bellum," *IJ* 2 (January 1906): 3–19; John H. Parker, "The Military Education of the Youth of this Country for a Period of at Least One Year as a Means of Developing the Military Spirit of this Country for National Defense," *JMSI* (March–April 1912): 153–172; Linn, *Echo of Battle*, 100–113.

66. Joseph J. O'Connell, "Comment and Criticism: The Moral Preparation of the Soldier," *JMSI* 32 (January–February 1902): 120.

67. Hugh M. Kelly, "The Heritage of Ham," *Munsey's Magazine* 31 (July 1908): 282.

68. Hamilton M. Higday, "A Day in the Regular Army: The Life of a Private Cavalryman from Reveille to Taps in a Western Military Post," *World's Work* 5 (January 1903): 3011.

69. Edgar Allen Forbes, "Trouble with the Army: From the Standpoint of the Enlisted Man," *World's Work* 13 (April 1907): 8772.

70. *RCS WD 1904*, 226. "Report of the Military Secretary," *WD 1904*, 1:254–256; Traub, "Esprit de Corps," 181–217.

71. Hagood, *Circular*, 14. John F. Madden to Adjutant, 29th Infantry Regiment, 1 August 1907, Briant H. Wells Papers, AHEC.

72. R. H. Kelly, "Recruiting," *IJ* 11 (July–August 1914): 54; E. Anderson, "Pay of Our Soldiers as Affecting Desertion and Reenlistment," *Review of Reviews* 33 (March 1906): 330–334; Melbourne C. Chandler, *Of Garryowen in Glory: The History of the Seventh United States Cavalry Regiment* (Annandale, VA: Turnpike Press, 1960), 120–121; "The Question of Army Morals," *Nation* 81 (October 1905): 333–334.

73. "Color Line in the Army," *ANJ* 44 (29 December 1906); Oswald Garrison Villard, "Negro in the Regular Army," *Atlantic Monthly* 91 (April 1903): 721–729; Garna L. Christian, *Black Soldiers in Jim Crow Texas, 1899–1917* (College Station: Texas A&M Press, 1995), 69–91; Coffman, *Regulars*, 126–133; Marvin Fletcher, *The Black Soldier and Officer in the United States Army, 1891–1917* (Columbia: University of Missouri Press, 1974), 119–160; John D. Weaver, *The Brownsville Raid* (New York: W. W. Norton, 1970).

74. J. Franklin Bell, "The Army as a Life Occupation for Enlisted Men," 1 September 1907, in Appendix B, *WD 1907*, 76. Alfred Reynolds, *The Life of an Enlisted Soldier in the United States Army* (Washington, DC: GPO, 1904).

75. "Reflections and Suggestions: An Address by General J. Franklin Bell" (Fort Leavenworth, KS: N.p., 1906), 5. I am indebted to J. P. Clark for a copy of this manuscript.

76. "Reflections and Suggestions," 5.

77. "Reflections and Suggestions," 3.

78. Charles Burnett, "Efficient War Soldiers," *CAJ* 54 (April 1921): 63–65; Louis M. Hamilton, "The Training of the Non-Commissioned Officer," *JMSI* 35 (September–October 1904): 260–264; Arthur P. S. Hyde, "The Training of the Non-Commissioned Officer," *JMSI* 35 (November–December 1904): 386–391; Shanks, "Administration and the Management of Men."

79. Offnere Hope, "The Mechanical Specialist, Coast Artillery Corps," *Journal of the United States Artillery (Coast Artillery Journal)* 34 (November–December 1910): 245. On the coast artillery and skilled labor, see George M. Brooke, "Present Needs of Coast Artillery," *JMSI* 36 (March–April 1905): 257–274; Hagood, *Circular*, 10–11; Edwin Landon, "The Needs of the Coast Artillery," *Journal of the United States Artillery (Coast Artillery Journal)* 25 (March–April 1906): 143–148.

80. "An Act Making Appropriation for the support of the Army for the fiscal year ending June 30, 1909," 11 May 1908, 60th Congress, Session 1, HR 17288, 109–110; *RCS WD 1908*, 352–353; [Edward N. Woodbury], "A Study in Desertion," [1920], AHEC.

81. Frederick Funston, "Army Life and Discipline," *World's Work* 14 (May 1907): 8897.

82. R. L. Bullard, "In Times of Peace," *Overland Monthly* 47 (February 1906): 108. Frederick Funston, "Army Life and Discipline," *World's Work* 14 (May 1907): 8897; Jesse M. Lee, "Personal Memorandum Submitted to the Honorable, the Secretary of War," 21 March 1907, AGO 1250150, RG 94.

83. Leonard Wood, "Why We Have No Army," *McClure's* 38 (April 1912): 678.

84. Reynolds, *The Life of an Enlisted Soldier*, 19–20.

85. Bailey Millard, "The Shame of our Army," *Cosmopolitan* 49 (September 1910): 411–420.

86. Anderson, "Pay of Our Soldiers as Affecting Desertion and Reenlistment"330–334; Forbes, "Trouble with the Army."

87. Dana T. Merrill, "Desertions from the Army," *IJ* 3 (October 1906): 84–87; "Report of the Adjutant General," *WD 1908*, 294–295; "Report of the Judge Advocate," *WD 1914*, 276.

88. Hagood, *Circular Relative to Pay*, 14–15.

89. "Report of the Judge Advocate General," *WD 1903*, 478. [Woodbury], "A Study of Desertion."

90. Will Adams, "The Education of Trooper Brown," *Century* 74 (May 1907): 10–18. Eli A. Helmick, "How May Public Opinion Concerning the Army and Navy Be so Educated as to Secure to the Soldier and Sailor in Uniform the Consideration Ordinarily Accorded to the Civilian," *JMSI* 42 (January–February 1908): 1–12; C. McK. Saltzman, "How May Public Opinion Concerning the Army and Navy Be so Educated as to Secure to the Soldier and Sailor in Uniform the Consideration Ordinarily Accorded to the Civilian," *JMSI* 42 (January–February 1908): 13–21.

91. Henry B. Sullivan to Editor, *New York Sun*, 23 September 1910, cited in

"Report of the Adjutant General," *WD 1910*, 182. Second Relief (pseud.), "The Deserter," *ANJ* 42 (17 June 1905): 1134.

92. *RCS WD 1911*, 161. James W. Pope, "Three States of Army Penology," *JMSI* 35 (July–August 1904): 37–42; "Report of the Judge Advocate," *WD 1911*, 286–287.

93. [Woodbury], "A Study of Desertion;" "Report of the Department of Mindanao," *WD 1910*, 247–248; Millard, "Shame."

94. Henry Swift, "Drunkenness in the Army," *JMSI* 30 (March 1902): 242.

95. E. G. Eberle and Frederick T. Gordon, "Report on the Committee of the Acquirement of Drug Habits," *American Journal of Pharmacy* 75 (October 1903): 474–488.

96. Forbes, "Trouble with the Army." Anni Baker, "The Abolition of the U.S. Army Canteen, 1898–1914," *JMH* 80 (July 2016): 697–724.

97. William Conant Church, "Increasing Desertions and the Army Canteen," *North American Review* 177 (December 1903): 858. Higday, "A Day in the Regular Army," 3012.

98. Hagood, *Circular*, 14. On the baneful effects of prohibition, see the extensive military correspondence in AGO 361008, RG 94.

99. [Woodbury], "A Study of Desertion."

100. "Manila's Greatest Need," *ANJ* 42 (12 August 1905). "Report of the Judge Advocate," *WD 1909*, 306–308; Coffman, *Regulars*, 78–80.

101. James H Blount, "Army Morals and the Canteen," *North American Review* 193 (March 1911): 409–421.

102. Circular 10, 18 March 1902, reprinted in *ANJ* 39 (29 March 1902): 747. "Question of Army Morals"; *RSW WD 1905*, 8; "Report of the Surgeon General," *WD 1908*, 2:96; Coffman, *Regulars*, 80–81.

103. *RSW WD 1912*, 11.

104. Andrew Byers, *The Sexual Economy of War: Discipline and Desire in the U.S. Army* (Ithaca: Cornell University Press, 2019), 56–92; Linn, *Guardians of Empire*, 127–129.

105. William H. Carter, "Military Preparedness," *North American Review* 191 (May 1910): 636–643.

106. Mathew E. Hanna, "Our Army a School," *JMSI* 41 (September–October 1907): 143–151; M. B. Stewart, "The Army as a Factor in the Upbuilding of Society," *JMSI* 36 (May–June 1905): 391–398; Coffman, *Regulars*, 139–140.

107. Day Allen Willey, "Spirit of Sport in the Army," *Harper's Weekly* 50 (4 August 1906): 1100–1101. Edward L. King, "Athletics for the Physical Betterment of the Enlisted Man of the Army," *Outing* 39 (January 1902): 432–436; Herman J. Koehler, "Physical Training in the Army," *IJ* 1 (July 1904): 8–13.

108. Arthur Brown Ruhl, "Army-and-Navy Game," *Outing* 49 (December 1906): 305–314. Garrett Gatzemeyer, *Bodies for Battle: Physical Culture and Systematic Training, 1885–1957* (Lawrence: University Press of Kansas, 2021).

109. Edmund Luther Butts, "Soldierly Bearing, Health and Athletics," *Outing* 43 (March 1904): 707–711. Bowers Davis, "A System for Army Athletics," *IJ* 3 (October 1906): 79–83.

110. "Army Field Day at Portland, Ore.," *ANJ* 42 (6 May 1905): 970–971;

William W. Wotherspoon, "Training of the Efficient Soldier," *Annals of the American Academy of Political and Social Science* 26 (July 1905): 149–160.

111. James Chester, "The Army Uniform and Its Protection," and "Comment and Criticism," *JMSI* 33 (July–August 1903): 53–55, 83–90; I. L. Hunt, "Public Opinion and the American Army," *IJ* 3 (January 1907): 64–88; Helmick, "How May Public Opinion"; Hugh M. Kelly, "Protecting the Uniform," *IJ* 4 (July 1907): 231–234.

112. Robert L. Bullard, "A Moral Preparation for the Soldier for Service and Battle," *JMSI* 31 (November 1902): 779–792, 782. "The Army's Influence on Society," *ANJ* 42 (6 May 1905).

113. Coffman, *Regulars*, 194.

114. Reynolds, *The Life of an Enlisted Soldier*; Thomas F. Ryan, *The United States Army as a Career* (Washington, DC: War Department, 1913).

115. There are great discrepancies in personnel statistics due to different methods of counting discharges, transients, recruits, desertions, indigenous forces, etc., I have based my figures on *Reports of the Adjutant General*, 1900–1912 and on *RWD 1903*, 150, *RWD 1907*, 3; *RWD 1909*, 8–9; *RWD 1912*, 8. Different manpower statistics can be found in Weigley, *History of the U.S. Army*, 368.

116. William J. Woolley, *Creating the Modern Army: Citizen-Soldiers and the American Way of War, 1919–1939* (Lawrence: University Press of Kansas, 2022), 10–14.

117. *RSW WD 1912*, 7–8. These represented the actual strength of the Regular Army as of 30 June 1912. Its authorized strength was 4,812 officers and 81,409 enlisted men. These figures do not include the Philippine Scouts.

118. *RSW WD 1911*, 14.

119. "Report of the Inspector General," *WD 1911*, 268; Machoian, *William Harding Carter*, 222–243.

120. Linn, *Echo of Battle*, 103–115.

121. Doubler, *I Am the Guard*, 150–156; Mahon, *History of the Militia*, 141–147.

122. "Report of the Inspector General," *WD 1911*, 271.

123. Entry 18 April 1915, "Notes and Diaries," box 2, William Lassiter Papers, USMAL.

Chapter 3. The Aftermath Army in the Decade after World War I

1. "Notes and Diaries, 1916–1917," box 3, William Lassiter Papers, USMAL. For overviews on the postwar US Army, see Coffman, *Regulars*, 202–424; Robert K. Griffith, Jr., *Men Wanted for the U.S. Army: America's Experience with an All-Volunteer Army Between the World Wars* (Westport, CT: Greenwood Press, 1982); J. E. Kaufman and H. W. Kaufman, *The Sleeping Giant: American Armed Forces Between the Wars* (Westfield, CT: Praeger, 1996); Linn, *Echo of Battle*, 116–150; Ronald M. Spector, "The Military Effectiveness of the US Armed Forces, 1919–39," in *Military Effectiveness*, vol. 2, *The Interwar Period*, ed. Allan R. Millett and Williamson Murray (orig. publ. 1988; repr., New York: Cambridge University Press, 2010), 70–97.

2. "Annual Report of the Chief of Field Artillery for 1923–1924," *FAJ* 15 (January–February 1925): 1.

3. "Post War Reflections and Occupations," 47, box 3, Lassiter Papers.

4. An Army Officer, "An Army of Amateurs," *American Mercury* 6 (October 1925): 188. On the Revolution in Military Affairs and history, see Colin Gray, *Strategy for Chaos: Revolutions in Military Affairs and the Evidence of History* (Portland: Frank Cass, 2002); Macgregor Knox and Williamson Murray, *The Dynamics of Military Revolution, 1300–2050* (New York: Cambridge University Press, 2001).

5. Theodore M. Knappen, "The Army as a School," *American Review of Reviews* 63 (June 1921): 628.

6. Frederic Logan Paxson, *The Great Demobilization and Other Essays* (Madison: University of Wisconsin Press, 1941), 7.

7. Sparrow, *History of Personnel Demobilization*, 11–19.

8. "Post War Reflections and Occupations," 39. On AEF operations and Pershing, see Edward M. Coffman, *The War to End All Wars: The American Military Experience in World War I* (orig. publ. 1968; repr., Lexington: University Press of Kentucky, 1998); Mark E. Groteleuschen, *The AEF Way of War: The American Army and Ground Combat* (New York: Cambridge University Press, 2006); Timothy K. Nenninger, "American Military Effectiveness in the First World War," in *Military* Effectiveness, vol. 1, *The First World* War, ed. Allan R. Millett and Williamson Murray (orig. publ. 1988; repr., New York: Cambridge University Press, 2010), 116–156; Donald Smythe, *Pershing: General of the Armies* (Bloomington: Indiana University Press, 1983); David F. Trask, *The AEF and Coalition Warmaking, 1917–1918* (Lawrence: University Press of Kansas, 1993); David R. Woodward, *The American Army and the First World War* (New York: Cambridge University Press, 2014).

9. Cited in E. F. Rice et al., "Morale in Armies," 24 October 1928, AHEC. James J. Cooke, *Pershing and His Generals: Command and Staff in the AEF* (Westport, CT: Praeger, 1997).

10. "Conference—Morale, Paris," 19 March 1919, box 10, John L. Hines Papers, MDLOC.

11. Richard S. Faulkner, *Pershing's Crusaders: The American Soldier in World War I* (Lawrence: University Press of Kansas, 2017), 612–617; Jennifer D. Keene, *Doughboys, the Great War, and the Remaking of America* (Baltimore: Johns Hopkins University Press, 2001), 132–140; Smythe, *Pershing*, 249–255, 269–273.

12. Keene, *Doughboys*, 137–140; Sparrow, *History of Personnel Demobilization*, 11–18. On troop welfare in World War I, see Mark T. Hauser, "'A Violent Desire for the Amusements': Boxing, Libraries, and the Distribution and Management of Welfare During the First World War," *JMH* 86 (October 2022): 833–913.

13. "Post War Reflections and Occupations," 30.

14. Faulkner, *Pershing's Crusaders*, 130, 135–137, 260–280; Keene, *Doughboys*, 135–137.

15. William Hazlett Upson, "Good Old Army! Good Old War!" *Saturday Evening Post* 198 (5 June 1926): 237. For frank explanation of veterans' bitterness at the Regular Army by a general officer, see Eli A. Helmick, "Leadership" (lecture, AWC, 17 May 1924), AHEC.

16. Doubler, *I Am the Guard*, 172–184; Faulkner, *Pershing's Crusaders*, 537–539, 662–665; John K. Mahon, *History of the Militia and the National Guard* (New York: Macmillan, 1983), 158–164; Les Andrii Melnyk, "A True National Guard: The Development of the National Guard and its Influence on Defense Legislation, 1915–1933" (PhD diss., City University of New York, 2004), 115–138.

17. Theodore Roosevelt, Jr., *Average Americans* (New York: G. P. Putnam's Sons, 1919). Keene, *Doughboys*, 165–170; William Pencak, *For God and Country: The American Legion, 1919–1941* (Boston: Northeastern University Press, 1989), 46–77; Sebastian H. Lukasik, "Doughboys, the YMCA, and the Moral Economy of Sacrifice in the First World War," *JMH* 84 (July 2020): 774–797.

18. John Gary Clifford, *The Citizen Soldiers: The Plattsburg Training Camp Movement, 1913–1920* (Lexington: University Press of Kentucky, 1972), 263.

19. I. B. Holley, *General John M. Palmer, Citizen Soldiers, and the Army of a Democracy* (Westport, CT: Greenwood Press, 1982), 400, 402–526. Brian F. Neumann, "A Question of Authority: Reassessing the March-Pershing 'Feud' in the First World War," *JMH* 73 (October 2009): 1117–1142.

20. "Notes and Diaries," 12.

21. Walter Lippman, "Leonard Wood," *New Republic* (17 March 1920): 80. On the Pershing–March–Wood imbroglio, see Smythe, *Pershing*, 81–86.

22. The 1920 National Defense Act identified the combat or line branches as the Infantry, Cavalry, Field Artillery, Coast Artillery, Air Service, and Chemical Warfare Service.

23. George C. Marshall, "The Development of the National Army" (lecture, AWC, 10 September 1923), AHEC.

24. US Infantry Association, *National Defense: A Compilation of Opinions* (Washington, DC: US Infantry Assoc., 1924), 111. On the National Defense Act of 1920, see Edward M. Coffman, *The Hilt of the Sword: The Career of Peyton C. March* (Madison: University of Wisconsin Press, 1966), 173–211; Griffith, *Men Wanted*, 1–84; Smythe, *Pershing*, 255–263; Melnyk, "A True National Guard," 139–270; Russell F. Weigley, *History of the U.S. Army* (Bloomington: Indiana University Press, 1984), 396–404; William J. Woolley, *Creating the Modern Army: Citizen-Soldiers and the American Way of War, 1919–1939* (Lawrence: University Press of Kansas, 2022), 22–28.

25. Woolley, *Creating*, 28.

26. William A. Ganoe, *The History of the United States Army* (New York: D. Appleton-Century, 1942), 479.

27. K. L. Simpson, "Importance, Means and Methods of Publicity for the Army" (lecture, AWC, 23 May 1922), AHEC.

28. D. Clayton James, *The Years of MacArthur*, vol. 1, *1880–1941* (Boston: Houghton Mifflin, 1970), 366–368.

29. William Mitchell, "Preliminary Report of Inspection of Air Service Activities in the Hawaiian Department," 10 December 1923, box 24, William Mitchell Papers, MDLOC. James J. Cooke, *Billy Mitchell* (Boulder, CO: Lynn Rienner, 2002), 107–219; David E. Johnson, *Fast Tanks and Heavy Bombers: Innovation in the U.S. Army, 1917–1945* (Ithaca: Cornell University Press, 1998), 50–53, 81–84, 91.

30. Sherman Miles, "More Perfect Peace," *North American Review* 214 (November 1921): 580.

31. Dean A. Nowowiejski, *The American Army in Germany, 1918–1923: Success against the Odds* (Lawrence: University Press of Kansas, 2021).

32. "Doughboys and Brides Back from the Rhine," *Literary Digest* 76 (3 March 1923): 43.

33. Robert L. Eichelberger to Dearest Emmalina, 5 January 1920, box 6, Robert L. Eichelberger Papers, Perkins Library, Duke University, Durham, NC. John M. House, *Wolfhounds and Polar Bears: The American Expeditionary Force in Siberia, 1918–1920* (Tuscaloosa: University of Alabama Press, 2016).

34. Mark G. Brislawn, "Allied Intervention in Russia," SP CGSC, 1932, CARL.

35. Marlborough Churchill, "The Military Intelligence Division, General Staff," *Journal of the United States Artillery (Coast Artillery Journal)* 52 (April 1920): 294. Jensen, *Army Surveillance*, 160–177; Joshua E. Kastenberg, *To Raise and Discipline an Army: Major General Enoch Crowder, the Judge Advocate General's Office, and the Realignment of Civil and Military Relations in World War I* (Dekalb: Northern Illinois Press, 2017), 200–251; McCoy, *Policing America's Empire*, 293–347; Roy Talbert, Jr., *Negative Intelligence: The Army and the American Left, 1917–1940* (Jackson: University of Mississippi Press, 1991), 1–135.

36. Clayton Laurie and Ronald H. Cole, *The Role of Federal Military Forces in Domestic Disorder, 1877–1945* (Washington, DC: Center of Military History, 1997), 327; see also 329–336. William G. Haan to AGO, Sub: War Plan—White, 24 May 1920, AGO 381 (5–24–20), box 52, E 37B, RG 407; General Staff College, Memo for Director, WPD, Sub: War Plan—White: Estimate of the Situation, 24 December 1920, War Plans Course File, AHEC.

37. Talbert, *Negative Intelligence*, 213. Estimate of the Situation, Emergency Plan—White, 1923, AGO 381 (8–24–22), box 44, E 37B, RG 407. G-2 Annex, Emergency Plan—White, 9th Corps Area, 1923, AGO 381 (8–24–22), box 45, E 37B, RG 407.

38. Francis H. French to AG, Sub: Annual Report, FY ending 30 June 1919, 26 July 1919, AGO 319.12, E 37, RG 407.

39. An Army Officer, "The Uplift Hits the Army," *American Mercury* 5 (June 1925): 140. Dennis E. Nolan, "The Military Intelligence Division of the General Staff" (lecture, AWC, 6 September 1921), AHEC; Jensen, *Army Surveillance*, 198–201.

40. Weston Jenkins, "What Gave Birth to 'What Price Glory,'" *IJ* 30 (January 1927): 8–13. Jack Capps, "The Literature of the AEF: A Doughboy Legacy," in *Unknown Soldiers: The American Expeditionary Forces in Memory and Remembrance*, ed. Mark A. Snell (Kent, OH: Kent State University Press, 2008), 195–237; Jess Nevins, *The Encyclopedia of Pulp Heroes* (Amazon Digital Services, 2017); Steven Trout, *On the Battlefield of Memory: The First World War and American Remembrance, 1919–1941* (Tuscaloosa: University of Alabama Press, 2010). For an example of a narrow focus on postwar elite modernist writers, Hazel Hutchinson, *The War That Used Up Words: American Writers and the First World War* (New Haven, CT: Yale University Press, 2015). I am indebted to Steven Trout for his insights into postwar popular literature

41. Linn, *Guardians of Empire*, 165–183.

42. "Military Policy," [1918], box 9, Hines Papers.

43. The New Infantry Drill Regulations," *IJ* (November 1919): 375. AEF, *Report of the Superior Board on Organization and Tactics*, 27 April 1919, AHEC.

44. On "open warfare," see John J. Pershing, *My Experiences in the World War*, 2 vols. (orig. publ. 1931; repr., Blue Ridge Summit, PA: TAB Books, 1989), 2:358; Groteleuschen, *AEF Way of War*, 30–31, 48–49; Woodward, *American Army*, 119–122, 199–200.

45. [William G. Haan], "A Positive System of Coast Defense (Army)," in Joint Army and Navy Board, *Joint Army and Navy Action on Coast Defense* (Washington, DC: GPO, 1920), 38–51.

46. Bradford G. Chynoweth, "Tank Infantry," *IJ* 18 (May 1921): 504. Dwight D. Eisenhower, "A Tank Discussion," *IJ* 17 (November 1920): 453–458; A. C. Cron, "The Tank," *CAJ* 61 (November 1924): 383–395.

47. A. J. Tittinger, "The Future of Cavalry," *CJ* 29 (April 1920): 69.

48. C. M. Bundel, "Is the Study of Military History Worthwhile," *IJ* 34 (March 1929): 238.

49. William O. Odom, *After the Trenches: The Transformation of U.S. Army Doctrine, 1918–1939* (College Station: Texas A&M University Press, 1999), 77.

50. Peter J. Schifferle, *America's School for War: Fort Leavenworth, Officer Education, and Victory in World War II* (Lawrence: University Press of Kansas, 2010), 36–52.

51. Elbridge Colby, "Cavalry in Recent War," *IJ* 16 (July 1919): 37. Matthew D. Morton, *Men on Iron Ponies: The Death and Rebirth of the Modern U.S. Cavalry* (DeKalb: Northern Illinois University Press, 2009); Bryon E. Greenwald, "Understanding Change: An Intellectual and Practical Study of Military Innovation: The U.S. Army Antiaircraft Artillery and the Battle for Legitimacy, 1917–1945" (PhD diss., Ohio State University, 2003).

52. HQ 8th Army Corps Area, Sub: Notes on Training, 20 November 1929, box 5, Lassiter Papers. James Scott Wheeler, *The Big Red One: America's Legendary 1st Infantry Division from World War I to Desert Storm* (Lawrence: University Press of Kansas, 2007), 117–124.

53. Jeffrey W. French, "Intellectual Discourse During the Interwar Years: A Content Survey of the United States *Infantry Journal* (1919–1939)" (masters thesis, Texas A&M University, 2000).

54. "Notes Taken During the Conference at the President's Rapidan Camp, May 9, 1931," box 4, Campbell B. Hodges Papers, Special Collections, USMAL. C. C. Benson, "Mechanization—Aloft and Alow," *CJ* 38 (January 1929): 58–62; Johnson, *Fast Tanks*, 95–100; Woolley, *Creating*, 206–215, 223–239.

55. Conclusions of the Chief Umpire, Joint Army and Navy Problem Two, 24 January 1924, box 40, Hines Papers; Holley, *General John M. Palmer*, 529–536.

56. Linn, *Guardians of Empire*, 198–200.

57. Diary Entry, 20 October 1929, box 5, Lassiter Papers.

58. "An Army of Amateurs," 188. *RSW WD 1921*, 11l; *RSW WD 1925*, 3–4; *RCS WD 1926*, 43.

59. J. L. DeWitt to CS, Sub: Report of the Operations and Training Division, General Staff, 17 December 1923, WPD 1549, RG 165. Committee No. 4, "Training," 2 December 1924; R. W. Hardenbergh, "The Capacity of the Regular Army at Its Present Strength to Train the Civilian Components," SP AWC, 1929, both in AHEC.

60. Editorial "Go to It," *IJ* 17 (August 1920): 184. On the prewar strength of the officer corps, see "AWC Graduates in the World War," 1926, file 68–58, Record Section, AHEC.

61. Griffith, *Men Wanted*, 21.

62. Committee No. 2, "Promotion and Retirement in the Regular Army," 12 October 1926, AHEC; Carlo D'Este, *Eisenhower: A Soldier's Life* (New York: Henry Holt, 2002); D. Clayton James, *Years of MacArthur*, 240–241, 261–265; Smythe, *Pershing*, 266.

63. Wilson B. Burtt, "The Fighting Unit," *IJ* 29 (September 1926): 241. *RSW WD 1921*, 11. The 1920 defense act did exempt all colonels, chaplains, and doctors, as well as those above captain in some technical and administrative branches from the single list.

64. "Oral History," 1981, John C. Arrowsmith Papers, AHEC.

65. *RSW WD 1928*, 187.

66. George S. Simonds, Memo for CSA, Sub: Promotion and Pay for the Army, 20 October 1930, box 4, Charles P. Summerall Papers, MDLOC. The sources differ on the size and the composition of the 1919–1920 augmentation and the consequences of the 1920 defense act and subsequent reductions; see Committee No. 2, "Promotion and Retirement in the Regular Army"; Clifford Jones, "The Personnel Outlook as Viewed from the Office of the Chief of Coast Artillery," *CAJ* 66 (January 1927): 30–43; Arthur T. Coumbe, *A History of the U.S. Army Officer Corps, 1900–1990* (Carlisle, PA: Strategic Studies Institute, 2014), 6–9.

67. Schifferle, *America's School for War*, 22.

68. Conklin, "To Determine Whether or Not,'" and James D. Taylor, "Determination of Whether There Will Be a Surplus of Air Service Officers in the Higher Grades," both SP AWC, 1924, AHEC; Mason G. Patrick to John L. Hines, 10 May 1922, box 6, Hines Papers. The War College was not being facetious in its estimates of pilot attrition. In one six-month period there were 150 airplane crashes resulting in forty-one fatalities and eighteen critically injured; see "Excerpts from Annual Report of the Chief of Air Service," *WD 1921*, 189.

69. *RSW WD 1928*, 219–220; *RSW WD 1929*, 196; Johnson, *Fast Tanks*, 90–92.

70. John L. Hines to James G. Harbord, 2 and 10 September 1922, box 2, Hines Papers.

71. *RSW 1922*, 19–20.

72. Harry R. Yarger, "Army Officer Personnel Management: The Creation of the Modern American System to 1939" (PhD diss., Temple University, 1995), 256–259.

73. J. C. F. Tillson, "Efficiency Reports: How May the Present Report be Improved?" SP AWC 193; Kerr T. Riggs, "Officers' Efficiency Reports: How Can the Present System Be Improved?," SP AWC 1932, both in AHEC.

74. "Post War Reflections and Occupations," 30–31. Neumann, "A Question of Authority."

75. Interview with Irving J. Phillipson, 2 December 1947, Harold Dean Cater Interviews, Office of Chief of Military History Collection, AHEC. Cooke, *Pershing and His Generals*, 149–151.

76. Interview with Charles H. Bridges, 13 October 1947, Cater Interviews. Charles Pelot Summerall, *The Way of Duty, Honor, Country: The Memoir of General*

Charles P. Summerall, ed. Timothy K. Nenninger (Lexington: University Press of Kentucky, 2010), 194–195, 233. On the Pershing–MacArthur mistress allegations, see James, *Years of MacArthur*, 291–293; Smythe, *Pershing*, 276–277.

77. Omar N. Bradley and Clay Blair, *A General's Life* (New York: Simon & Schuster, 1983), 70; James, *Years of MacArthur*, 435–437; Pogue, *George C. Marshall*, 294–296.

78. James G. Harbord to John L. Hines, 29 June 1921, box 2, John L. Hines Papers, MDLOC.

79. Douglas MacArthur, *Reminisces* (New York: Fawcett Crest, 1965), 101. This story may be apocryphal.

80. James, *Years of MacArthur*, 350–376; Linn, *Guardians of Empire*, 174–177.

81. "Faith in and a Doctrine for the Cavalry Service," *CJ* 36 (April 1927): 228. On the postwar army education system, see Ball, *Of Responsible Command*, 147–233; Schifferle, *America's School*. On the school's role in war planning, see Henry G. Gole, *The Road to Rainbow: Army Planning for Global War, 1931–1940* (Annapolis, MD: Naval Institute Press, 2003).

82. Harold H. Martin, *Soldier: The Memoirs of Matthew B. Ridgway* (New York: Harper & Brothers, 1956), 33. Betros, *Carved from Granite*, 119, 207–209; J. Lawton Collins, *Lightning Joe: An Autobiography* (Baton Rouge: Louisiana State University Press, 1979), 43. On Military Academy graduate deaths in combat, see *RSW WD 1928*, 228. For an angry response to the charge that West Pointers "shirked" combat, see "West Point Deaths Led," *IJ* 16 (October 1919): 254. On the officers' training schools, see Faulkner, *Pershing's Crusaders*, 261–264.

83. Frank L. Winn to James W. McAndrew, 25 February 1919, box 4, William G. Haan Papers, Wisconsin Historical Society, Madison, WI. C. S. Farnsworth, "Object, Scope, and System of Training for the Infantry," 26 April 1921 (lecture, AWC, 26 April 1921), AHEC.

84. Grantland Rice, "The Greatest Show on Earth," *Colliers* 76 (28 November 1925): 28, 173. On MacArthur's influence at West Point, Betros, *Carved from Granite*, 120–126, 173–177, 219–221; Coffman, *Regulars*, 225–227; James, *Years of MacArthur*, 259–294; Roger H. Nye, "The United States Military Academy in an Era of Educational Reform" (PhD diss., 1968, Columbia University), 263–348.

85. C. W. Christenberry, "American Militarism a Myth—Protective Preparedness a Necessity," *IJ* 33 (September 1928): 235.

86. Oral History, 7, George H. Decker Papers, AHEC. Ralph Parker, "The Reserve Officers Training Corps: Its Problems and Development," SP AWC, 1929, AHEC; Michael S. Neiberg, *Making Citizen Soldiers: ROTC and the Ideology of American Military Service* (Cambridge: Harvard University Press, 2000), 22–31.

87. Oral History, 13–14, Herbert B. Powell Papers; C. D. Arrowsmith et al., "Training for the Army of the United States," SP AWC, 1926; W. R. Gruber, "The Army School System," SP AWC 1929, AHEC, all in AHEC.

88. Bradley and Blair, *A General's Life*, 63–70; Collins, *Lightning Joe*, 47–55; Pogue, *George C. Marshall*, 247–269.

89. Ball, *Of Responsible Command*, 165–208; Schifferle, *America's School*; Timothy K. Nenninger, "Leavenworth and Its Critics: The U.S. Army Command and General Staff School, 1920–1940," *JMH* 58 (April 1994): 199–231. In the 1920s the

Command and Staff School was a one-year course, but in 1928 it was divided into a two-year course, with only the best going on to the second year.

90. "The Monkeys Have No Tails in Zamboanga," Charles F. Ivins Papers, AHEC.

91. On Eisenhower's interwar career, see D'Este, *Eisenhower*, 161–258. On the lack of troop command, see Committee No. 7, "Our Existing Training System and Methods: The Salient Difficulties and Deficiencies Resulting Therein, and Recommendations for Their Correction [or] Amelioration," 24 November 1925; Paul C. Paschal, "Rotation of Officers of Combat Arms on Duty with Troops of Their Own Arm," SP AWC, 1929, both in AHEC.

92. Russel Grigeler, "MS Biography of Orlando Ward," Orlando Ward Papers, AHEC; *RSW WD 1925*, 17–18; Anon., "Necessity for Construction at Fort Benning," *IJ* 27 (December 1925): 701–707; A. J. Dougherty, "Some of the Problems of a Regimental and Post Commander and How They Were Met," *IJ* 33 (November 1928): 460–471; D'Este, *Eisenhower*, 164–167.

93. "Go to It," 185.

94. Willard A. Holbrook, "Object, Scope, and System of Training for the Cavalry" (lecture, AWC, 4 May 1921), AHEC.

95. Bertram Frankenberger, "Are Army Officers Too Conservative, as Sometimes Hinted in the Press?" SP CGSC, 1930. H. C. Gilchrist, "The Responsibility of Senior Officers in Instructing Junior Officers in the Preparation of Their Future Career as an Officer of the Army," SP CGSC, 1930, both in CARL.

96. Oral History, 13–14, Powell Papers.

97. "Excerpts from the Annual Report of the Chief of the Personnel Division, General Staff," *WD 1922*, 130; *RCS WD 1926*, 51; Douglas McCaskey, "Resignation of Second Lieutenants, Regular Army, Who Have Less Than Four Years of Commissioned Service," SP AWC, 1928, AHEC; Coffman, *Regulars*, 225.

98. Bradley and Blair, *A General's Life*, 58; Assistant Chief of Staff for Military Intelligence, HQ, Hawaiian Division, *Digest of Information—The Hawaiian Department and the Territory of Hawaii* (Honolulu: Army Printing Office, 1930).

99. James, *Years of MacArthur*, 280.

100. Decker Oral History, 4. Wanda E. Wakefield, *Playing to Win: Sports and the American Military, 1898–1945* (Albany: State University of New York Press, 1997), 59–66.

101. D'Este, *Eisenhower*, 164, 175–176, 185–186.

102. *FAJ* 20 (May–June 1930): 345–356.

103. James G. Harbord to John L. Hines, 12 August 1921, box 2, Hines Papers.

104. Guy V. Henry to Frank Parker, 7 May 1931, file 123, box 7, Frank Parker Papers, Southern Historical Collection, University of North Carolina-Chapel Hill, Chapel Hill, NC.

105. George S. Simonds, Memo for CSA, Sub: Promotion and Pay for the Army; Paschal, "Rotation of Officers."

106. "Who's in the Army Now?" *Fortune Magazine* (September 1935): 39–49, 126–144.

107. Dougherty, "Some of the Problems"; A. J. Dougherty, "To What Pay Is an Officer Entitled?" *IJ* 34 (May 1929): 451–461, and A. J. Dougherty, "The Standard of Living and Officers' Pay?" *IJ* 35 (August 1929): 162–169.

108. "Annual Report of the Chief of Field Artillery," 9. Dana T. Merrill to Commanding General, Hawaiian Department, Sub: Survey and Inspection of Harbor Defenses of Honolulu, 30 June 1928 and Joseph P. Aleshire to CG, HD, Sub: Economic Survey, Schofield Barracks, 10 August 1928, both in E 333.1, RG 159.

109. Gerald Egan, "The Recruiting Problem," *IJ* 17 (September 1920): 216.

110. Griffith, *Men Wanted*, 9–30.

111. Edward N. Woodbury, "Morale: Improving the Standard of the Enlisted Many," 28 February 1931, #377–83, General Staff Memoranda, AHEC.

112. Eli A. Helmick, "The Relation of Psychology to Leadership" (lecture, AWC, 26 March 1925), AHEC. [Edward N. Woodbury], "A Study of Desertion," [1920], AHEC; Committee No. 2, "Recruitment by Voluntary Enlistment," 22 October 1928, AHEC.

113. John W. Heavey, "Universal Military Training," *IJ* 17 (July 1920): 27. Arthur Barbeau and Florette Henri, *The Unknown Soldiers: Black American Troops in World War I* (1974, New York: De Capo Press, 1996); Faulkner, *Pershing's Crusaders*, 206–208, 243–249; Keene, *Doughboys*, 82–104, 126–130, 164–166; Bernard C. Nalty, *Strength for the Fight: A History of Black Americans in the Military* (New York: Free Press, 1989), 107–124; Chad Williams, *Torchbearers of Democracy: African-American Soldiers in the World War I Era* (Chapel Hill: University of North Carolina Press, 2010).

114. Committee #7, "Organization, Training, and Military Use of Negroes," 2 May 1921, AHEC. Stanley C. Vestal, "The Use in Battle of Allies, Auxiliaries, Colored Troops, and Troops Raised in Insular Possessions," (lecture, AWC, 30 April 1924), AHEC.

115. Dougherty, "Some of the Problems," 460–471. Nalty, *Strength for the Fight*, 128–129.

116. J. M. Churchill, "Shall the Enlistment Allowance Be Abolished in the Interest of Economy?" SP AWC, 1925, and J. E. Munroe, "Desirability of Use of Terms Master Sergeant and Technical Sergeant Replacing Old Name of Sergeant Major," SP AWC, 1925, both in AHEC; Benjamin F. Cooling, "Enlisted Grade Structure and the Army Reorganization Act of 1920," *Military Affairs* 31 (December 1967): 187–194.

117. *RSW WD 1929*, 198–210.

118. J. G. Hill, "Peace-Time Morale," *IJ* 34 (April 1929): 404.

119. James Jones, *From Here to Eternity*, ed. George Hendrick (1951, ebook, New York: Open Road, 2011).

120. Otto P. Weyand Oral History, K239.0152–813, AFHRA.

121. John M. Collins, "Depression Army," *Army* 22 (January 1972): 10–11. For similarly critical views, see R. John West, "Leadership Applied," *IJ* 35 (July 1929): 75; H. E. Knight, "The Morale of the Regular Army," SP AWC, 17 March 1928), AHEC.

122. E. M. Lewis to AG, sub: Annual Report, Hawaiian Department, FY 1926, 30 June 1926, 319.12 HD (6–30–26), RG 407. *RSW WD 1924*, 161; *RSW WD 1929*, 242; Frank L. Purdon, "A Study to Cover Our Present System of Procurement, Treatment, Welfare, Separation, etc. of Enlisted Men With a View to Evolving a Better System Which Would Tend to Raise the Standard of Enlisted Personnel," SP AWC, 1932, AHEC.

123. Committee No. 2, "Recruitment by Voluntary Enlistment," *RSW WD*

1929, 199; H. K. Loughry, "Present Desertion Rates," SP AWC, 1926, AHEC; Griffith, *Men Wanted*, 97–101.

124. Bernard S. McMahan, "The Effect of the Uniform on Morale," SP AWC, 1926, AHEC.

125. Office of the Quartermaster General to AG, 28 January 1925, HD 319.12, E 37, RG 407.

126. Lucian K. Truscott, Jr., *The Twilight of the U.S. Cavalry: Life in the Old Army, 1917–1942* (Lawrence: University Press of Kansas, 1989), 36; G. L. Febiger to CG, HD, Sub: Annual Inspection, Schofield Barracks, 24 June 1931, 333.1, box 276, E 11, RG 159; Dennis C. Pillsbury, "Why Not Dress Up the Soldier?" *IJ* 33 (July 1928): 74–75.

127. Grigeler, "MS Biography of Orlando Ward," 5: 1–5; Orlando Ward Papers, AHEC.

128. Carl M. Ulbaker, "Mess Management in the 29th Infantry," *IJ* 34 (April 1929): 344–346. Coffman, *Regulars*, 305; Griffith, *Men Wanted*, 95–97.

129. HQ, IG, HD to IG, Sub: Annual Report, 31 June 1930, HD, RG 338; "Occupations," box 3, Lassiter Papers; Truscott, *Twilight*, 28.

130. John B. Brooks, "A Study of the Present Desertion Rates with Recommendations for Bringing About a Reduction of the Same," SP AWC, 1926, AHEC. Coffman, *Regulars*, 312–314; Griffith, *Men Wanted*, 43–47, 94–101.

131. Loughry, "Present Desertion Rates"; George Grunert, "Desertion in the United States Army," 1932, SP CGSC, CARL.

132. Woodbury, "Morale." T. L. Ames, "A Study of the Present Desertion Rates with Recommendations for Bringing About a Reduction of the Same," SP AWC, 1926; Robert G. Kirkwood, "Present Desertion Rates in the Army," SP AWC 1926, both in AHEC.

133. H. K., "Present Desertion Rates: Excerpts from Annual Report of the Judge Advocate General," *WD 1922*, 235–226; *RSW WD 1925*, 157; *RSW WD 1928*, 238.

134. Dougherty, "Some of the Problems," 460–471. Grigeler, "MS Biography of Orlando Ward," 5: 2–3.

135. WDGS to CS, Memo: Points of special interest in the Hawaiian Department . . . , 2 April 1925, box 39, Hines Papers.

136. J. H. McRae, "The Personnel Division, G-1" (lecture, AWC, 27 February 1922), AHEC. F. E. Charlton, "Athletics in the Army," *IJ* 21 (November 1922): 629–632.

137. HQ, HD, Bulletin No. 4, 25 November 1924, E 6071, RG 395.

138. James Jones, *From Here to Eternity*, ed. George Hendrick (1951, ebook, New York: Open Road, 2011).

139. Byers, *The Sexual Economy of War*, 181–190.

140. Chyoweth, *Bellamy Park*, 122–123. "On the Edge: Personal Recollections of an American Officer" (1934), Cornelis de Witt Willcox Papers, USMAL; *RSW WD 1927*, 202–203; Virginia Conner, *What Father Forbad* (Philadelphia: Dorrance, 1951), 155–159.

141. C. H. Conrad to CG, PD, Sub: Annual Inspection of Post of Manila, 19 May 1924, box 133, AG 333.1, RG 159.

142. Oral History, 18–19, Paul D. Adams Papers, AHEC. J. F. Siler et al., "Marijuana Smoking in Panama," *Military Surgeon* 73 (July–December 1933): 269–280.

143. Egan, "The Recruiting Problem," 216. Ernest J. Carr, "Americanization in the Army," *IJ* 23 (January 1921): 31–33.

144. Quoted in Coffman, *Regulars*, 293.

145. Faulkner, *Pershing's Crusaders*, 620–622; Mark Meigs, *Optimism at Armageddon: Voices of American Participants in the First World War* (New York: New York University Press, 1997), 189–193.

146. AGO, *The Educational System of the United States Army: The Army as a National School* (Washington, DC: Adjutant General of the Army, 1920), 21. On the army education system, see Adna R. Chaffee et al., "Enlisting, During Peace, Aliens Who Can Not Read, Write, or Speak English," SP AWC, 1924, AHEC; Charles Berry, "Some Problems of Americanization as Seen by an Army Psychologist," *School and Society* 13 (22 January 1921): 97–104; Z. T. Egardner, "Adult Education in the Army," *School Review* 30 (April 1922): 255–267.

147. Knappen, "The Army as a School," 628. Allan D. Albert, "Building Character in the Army," *Scribner's Magazine* 65 (January 1919): 117–122.

148. George Pattulo, "Selling the Army to the People," *Saturday Evening Post* 193 (21 August 1920): 14–15.

149. William G. Haan, "War Plans Division of the General Staff: Its Aims and the Scope of Its Work and Problems" (speech, General Staff College, 7 November 1919), box 7, Haan Papers.

150. Knappen, "The Army as a School," 628.

151. An Army Officer, "The Uplift Hits the Army," 140.

152. Mason G. Patrick to John L. Hines, 10 May 1922. William J. Snow to John L. Hines, 29 August 1922, both in box 6, Hines Papers.

153. H. H. Slaughter, "The Working Out of the National Defense Act of 1920" (SP AWC 1931, AHEC; *RSW WD 1929*, 196–198.

154. William P. Screws, "Civilian Components," SP, CGSC, 24 May 1929, AHEC. James E. Bayliss, "R.O.T.C. Units: Considered from the Viewpoint of the Procurement of Officers in the Event of General Mobilization, What Types of R.O.T.C. Units Should be Maintained?" SP AWC, 1931; Hardenbergh, "The Capacity of the Regular Army."

155. Collins, "Depression Army," 12.

156. *RSW WD 1929*, 199.

157. Albert N. Garland, "Motivate Me," *Army* 21 (December 1971): 43.

158. Johnson, *Fast Tanks*, 86.

159. William Lassiter to Commandant, 14th Naval District, 26 March 1931, box 14, Entry 284, RG 165. On Lassiter's Philippine plan, see William Lassiter to George S. Simonds, 28 December 1928, box 4, Lassiter Papers.

160. 28 December 1929 Diary, Lassiter Papers.

161. 4 May 1929 Diary, Lassiter Papers.

Chapter 4. The Aftermath Army of World War II and Korea

1. Harold H. Martin, "Paratrooper in the Pentagon," *Saturday Evening Post* 227 (28 August 1954): 81.

2. Martin, "Paratrooper in the Pentagon," 83. On Gavin, see T. Michael Booth

and Duncan Spencer, *Paratrooper: The Life of General James M. Gavin* (New York: Simon & Schuster, 1994).

3. "Foreign Affairs," *ANJ* 83 (3 November 1945). The similarities between post–world war demobilizations were recognized at the time and later; for a summary, see John F. Shortal, "20th Century Demobilization Lessons," *MR* 78 (September–November 1998): 58–63.

4. Susan L. Carruthers, *The Good Occupation: American Soldiers and the Hazards of Peace* (Cambridge, MA: Harvard University Press, 2016), 111–150, 191–226; Sparrow, *History of Personnel Demobilization*; Daniel Eugene Garcia, "Class and Brass: Demobilization, Working Class Politics, and American Foreign Policy between World War and Cold War," *Diplomatic History* 34 (September 2010): 681–698; Alton Lee, "The Army 'Mutiny' of 1946," *Journal of American History* 53 (December 1966): 555–571; Bert Marvin Sharp, "'Bring the Boys Home': Demobilization of the United States Armed Forces After World War II" (PhD diss., Michigan State University, 1977).

5. For overviews of post–World War II national defense issues and their impact on the US Army, see Millett, Maslowski, and Feis, *For the Common Defense: A Military History of the United States of America from 1607 to 2012* (New York: Free Press, 2012), 440–453; Richard W. Stewart, ed., *American Military History*, vol. 2, *The United States Army in a Global Era, 1917–2003* (Washington, DC: Center of Military History, 2005), 199–215; Weigley, *The History of the U.S. Army*, 485–504.

6. Carl H. Builder, *The Masks of War: American Military Style in Strategy and Analysis* (Baltimore: Johns Hopkins University Press, 1989), 38.

7. "Text of Biennial Report of the Chief of Staff of the Army," *ANJ* 83 (13 October 1945).

8. For a sample of the assimilation of World War II lessons, see "Historical Example: Battle of the Ardennes, #6414," CGSC 1955–56, CARL; Committee No. 2, Course 4, Problem # 4A: German Invasion of Russia, 21 November 1951, AHEC; HQ, ETO, "Combat Observations," Corps File 1960.88.382–450, George A. Taylor Collection, 1st Division Museum, Cantigny, IL; *U.S. War Department Equipment Board Report*, 29 May 1946, UC 463.U56 1946, AHEC; Richard D. Adamczyk and Morris J. Macgregor, eds., *United States Army in World War II: Reader's Guide* (Washington, DC: Center of Military History, 1992); Edward J. Drea, "Change Becomes Continuity: The Start of the U.S. Army's 'Green Book' Series," in *Essays on Official History in the United States and British Commonwealth*, ed. Jeffrey Grey (Westport, CT: Praeger, 2003), 83 104; Kretchik, *U.S. Army Doctrine*, 145–164; Linn, *Echo of Battle*, 156–161; Robert Smelser and Edward J. Davies II, *The Myth of the Eastern Front: The Nazi-Soviet War in American Popular Culture* (New York: Cambridge University Press, 2007); Robert W. Hutchinson, "The Weight of History: Wehrmacht Officers, the U.S. Army Historical Division, and U.S. Military Doctrine, 1945–1956," *JMH* 78 (October 2014): 1321–348.

9. William C. Westmoreland, "Our Twentieth Century Army" (speech, Airborne Conference, 7 May 1957), box 1, William C. Westmoreland Papers, USMAL.

10. Frazier Hunt, *MacArthur and the War Against Japan* (New York: Charles Scribner's, 1944). An indication of the self-censorship that constrained the memoirs of MacArthur's subordinates can be found by comparing Robert L. Eichelberger, *Our Jungle Road to Tokyo* (New York: Viking, 1950) with Robert L.

Eichelberger, *Dear Miss Em: General Eichelberger's War in the Pacific, 1942–1945*, ed. Jay Luvaas (Westport, CT: Greenwood, 1972).

11. Omar Bradley, *A Soldier's Story* (New York: Henry Holt, 1951); Dwight D. Eisenhower, *Crusade in Europe* (New York: Doubleday, 1948); George S. Patton, *War as I Knew It* (New York: Houghton Mifflin, 1947); Lucian K. Truscott, *Command Missions: A Personal Story* (New York: E. P. Dutton, 1954). Andrew J. Huebner, *The Warrior Image: Soldiers in American Culture from the Second World War to Vietnam* (Chapel Hill: University of North Carolina Press, 2008); Charles D. MacDonald, *Company Commander: The Infantry Classic of World War II* (orig. publ. 1947; repr., New York: Ballentine Books, 1972); Audie Murphy, *To Hell and Back* (New York: Henry Holt, 1949); Ernie Pyle, *Brave Men* (New York: Henry Holt, 1944).

12. Bill Mauldin, *Up Front* (New York: Henry Holt, 1944), 182. On the page displaying this cartoon, Mauldin commented: "Too many mess sergeants with thirty years in the army have been made temporary majors and lieutenant colonels, and they are making the most of their moments of glory."

13. *Battleground* (1947, directed by William Wellman, Metro-Goldwyn-Mayer, 2017), DVD; *Breakthrough* (1950, directed by Lewis Seiler, Warner Brothers, 2010), DVD; *Go for Broke* (1951, directed by Robert Pirosh, Metro-Goldwyn-Mayer, 2005), DVD.

14. John Hersey, *A Bell for Adano* (New York: Albert Knopf, 1944); Vern J. Sneider, *The Teahouse of the August Moon* (New York: Putnam, 1951).

15. Oral History, 119, Eugene P. Forrester Papers, AHEC. "A Tentative Basis for a Joint Defense Plan," 17 February 1947, file 381, box 12, E 54, RG 337; NSC 30, "United States Policy on Atomic Warfare," 10 September 1948, at https://history.state.gov/historicaldocuments/frus1948v01p2/d41; Stephen Ross, *American War Plans, 1945–1950* (Portland, OR: Frank Cass, 1996).

16. HQ, Eighth Army Korea (EUSAK), "Special Problems in the Korean Conflict," 1952, CARL. Thomas E. Hanson, *Combat Ready? The Eighth U.S. Army on the Eve of the Korean War* (College Station: Texas A&M University Press, 2010).

17. Arthur W. Connor, "The Tank Debacle in Korea, 1950: Implications for Today," *Parameters* 22 (July 1992): 66–76. On many works on Korean War operations, William M. Donnelly, *Under Orders: The Army National Guard During the Korean War* (College Station: Texas A&M University Press, 2001); Allan R. Millett, *The War for Korea, 1950–1951: They Came from the North* (Lawrence: University Press of Kansas, 2011); Matthew B. Ridgway, *The Korean War* (Garden City, NY: Doubleday, 1967).

18. John B. Tanzer, "Analysis and Comparison of Williston Birkhimer Palmer, General, USA and James Hilliard Polk, General, USA," 10 April 1973, AHEC.

19. *Semiannual Report of the Secretary of the Army, January 1 to June 30 1950* (Washington, DC: GPO, 1950): 67.

20. Roy K. Flint, "Task Force Smith and the 24th Division: Delay and Withdrawal, 5–19 July, 1950," in *America's First Battles, 1776–1965*, ed. Charles E. Heller and William A. Stofft (Lawrence: University Press of Kansas, 1986), 266–299.

21. Matthew B. Ridgway, "The Indispensable Weapon," *CFJ* 4 (January 1954): 9. William M. Donnelly, "Bilko's Army: A Crisis in Command?" *JMH* 75 (October 2011): 1183–1188.

22. James M. Gavin, *War and Peace in the Space Age* (New York: Harper & Brothers, 1958), 155.

23. Thomas D. Boettcher, *First Call: The Making of the Modern U.S. Military, 1945–1953* (Boston: Little, Brown, 1992); James E. Hewes, *From Root to McNamara: Army Organization and Administration, 1900–1963* (Washington, DC: Center of Military History, 1975), 57–215.

24. Matthew W. Markel, "The Organization Man at War: Promotions Policies and Military Leadership" (PhD diss., Harvard University, 2000), 200–206. On the impact of careerism, see Donnelly, "Bilko's Army."

25. "Lesson Plan: Character Guidance," in OCAFF to Commandants, et al., 7 April 1953, Sub: Character Guidance Program, box 3, E UD3, RG 546. Christopher S. DeRosa, *Political Indoctrination in the U.S. Army From World War II to the Vietnam War* (Lincoln: University of Nebraska Press, 2006); Anne C. Loveland, "Character Education in the U.S. Army, 1947–1977," *JMH* 64 (July 2000): 795–818.

26. George Q. Flynn, *The Draft, 1940–1973* (Lawrence: University Press of Kansas, 1993), 88–109; Amy J. Rutenberg, *Rough Draft: Cold War Military and Manpower Policy and the Origins of the Vietnam-Era Draft Resistance* (Ithaca: Cornell University Press, 2019), 38–68; William Taylor, *Every Citizen a Soldier: The Campaign for Universal Military Training After World War II* (College Station: Texas A&M University Press, 2014).

27. Oral History, 105, William J. McCaffrey Papers, AHEC. Doubler, *I Am the Guard*, 199–231.

28. George W. Sinks, "Reserve Policy for the Nuclear Age: The Development of Post-War American Reserve Policy, 1943–1955" (PhD diss., Ohio State University, 1985).

29. Edward F. Witsell to Office of the Army Comptroller, et al., 28 April 1948, Sub: Plan for expansion of the Army, box 26, E 32B, RG 337.

30. Sinks, "Reserve Policy," 217–233.

31. Rutenberg, *Rough Draft*, 72–95. John Michael Kendall, "An Inflexible Response: United States Army Manpower Policies, 1945–1957" (PhD diss., Duke University, 1982), 99–112.

32. Michael Cullen Green, *Black Yanks in the Pacific: Race in the Making of American Military Empire After World War II* (Ithaca: Cornell University Press, 2010), 8. Nalty, *Strength for the Fight*, 235–269.

33. Mary A. Hallaren, "The Women's Army Corps Becomes Permanent," *MR* 28 (March 1949): 8–13. Bettie J. Morden, *The Women's Army Corps, 1945–1978* (Washington, DC: Center of Military History, 1990).

34. HQ 8th Army to All Members of 8th Army, 21 January 1947, box 11, Robert L. Eichelberger Papers, Perkins Library, Duke University, Durham, NC. *Annual Report of the Secretary of the Army, 1948* (Washington, DC: GPO, 1949), 35–36; David T. Fautua, "The 'Long Pull' Army: NSC 68, the Korean War, and the Creation of the Cold War U.S. Army," *JMH* 61 (January 1997): 93–120.

35. "Proceedings of a Board of Officers Appointed to Study Human Relations Within the USA and the USAF," 11 February 1948, AHEC.

36. *National Security Act of 1947*, Sec. 303, 607. "Complete Revision of the 'Joint Action of the Army and Navy, 1935,'" JCS 370.26 (6-3-48), box 130, RG 218; J. M.

Kimbrough, "Roles and Missions of the Armed Forces" (lecture, 19 November 1953, AWC), AHEC.

37. J. Lawton Collins, "The Role of the Army in Future Warfare" (lecture, Air War College, 5 October 1948), box 43, J. Lawton Collins Papers, DDEL; Eliot V. Converse III, *History of Acquisition in the Department of Defense*, vol. 1, *Rearming for the Cold War, 1945–1960* (Washington, DC: Historical Office, Office of the Secretary of Defense, 2012), 170–173.

38. Carruthers, *The Good Occupation.* John Gimbel, *The American Occupation of Germany: Politics and the Military, 1945–1949* (Stanford, CA: Stanford University Press, 1968)

39. Wheeler, *The Big Red One*, 393–397.

40. [Robert Lee Eichelberger] to Houston Harte, 17 March 1948, box 12, Eichelberger Papers.

41. Tab G: Briefing at GHQ, Report of the Department of the Army Training Inspection: FECOM, 24 September to 29 October 1949, box 7, E 1, RG 337. Hanson, *Combat Ready?*.

42. James P. O'Donnell, "The World's Newest Army," *Saturday Evening Post* 228 (1 October 1955): 119. Donald A. Carter, *Forging the Shield: The U.S. Army in Europe, 1951–1962* (Washington, DC: Center of Military History, 2015), 1–142; Ingo Trauschweizer, *The Cold War U.S. Army: Building Deterrence for Limited War* (Lawrence: University Press of Kansas, 2008), 18–113; William M. Donnelly, "The Best Army That Can Be Put in the Field in the Circumstances: The U.S. Army, July 1951–July 1953," *JMH* 71 (July 2007): 809–847.

43. Introductory Narrative, Summary of Major Events and Problems, FY 1955, FY 1957, FY 1958 all in TRADOC Archives, Fort Eustis, VA; Jean E. Keith and Howard K. Butler, *The US Army Combat Developments Experimentation Command: Origin and Formation* (Fort Belvoir, VA: US Army Combat Developments Experimentation Command, 1972).

44. J. Lawton Collins, Background Material for the War Department Presentation to the Committee on the Armed Services, 11 February 1947, N-15083-C, CARL. On the US Army and atomic war, see Andrew J. Bacevich, *The Pentomic Era: The U.S. Army Between Korea and Vietnam* (Washington, DC: National Defense University Press, 1986); Linn, *Echo of Battle*, 151–192; Brian McAllister Linn, *Elvis's Army: Cold War GI's and the Atomic Battlefield* (Cambridge, MA: Harvard University Press, 2016), 73–98; Trauschweizer, *Cold War U.S. Army*, 48–80; Don Alan Carter, "From G.I. to Atomic Soldier: The Development of U.S. Tactical Doctrine, 1945–1956" (PhD diss.: Ohio State University, 1987; Paul C. Jussel, "Intimidating the World: The United States Atomic Army, 1956–1960" (PhD diss., Ohio State University, 2004).

45. James M. Gavin, *Airborne Warfare* (Washington, DC: Infantry Journal Press, 1947). James M. Gavin, "The Airborne Armies of the Future," *IJ* 60 (January 1947): 21–25; James M. Gavin, "Cavalry and I Don't Mean Horses," *Harper's* 208 (April 1954): 54–60; James M. Gavin, "The Future of Airborne Operations," *MR* 27 (December 1947): 3–8.

46. Office of the Chief of Army Field Forces, "Tactical Employment of the Atomic Bomb," 7 October 1951, 000.9/35, box 4, E 55B, RG 337.

47. I am indebted for this analysis to Dwight E. Phillips, Jr., "Reengineering

Institutional Culture and the American Way of War in the Post-Vietnam U.S. Army, 1968–1989" (PhD diss., University of Chicago, 2014), 38–41.

48. Gavin, *Airborne Warfare*, 181–183; "Gavin Says Air Mechanization Will Win Wars of the Future," *Army and Navy Bulletin* 3 (5 April 1947): 3.

49. Fred L. Walker, Jr., "Your Next War," *IJ* 60 (June 1947): 10–14, 61 (July 1947): 32–36; (August 1947): 41–45.

50. "The Regulars," 606, box 8, Donald A. Seibert Papers, AHEC. James M. Gavin, "The Tactical Use of the Atomic Bomb," *CFJ* 1 (November 1950): 9–11; George C. Reinhardt and W. R. Kintner, *Atomic Weapons in Land Combat* (Harrisburg, PA: Military Service Pub., 1953).

51. Linn, *Elvis's Army*, 126–128.

52. Report of Visit by D/A Inspection Team to USARPAC in Observing Exercise MIKI, 19 December 1949, box 22, E 1, RG 337; Jean R. Moenk, *A History of Large-Scale Army Maneuvers in the United States, 1935–1964* (Fort Monroe, VA: HQ CONARC, 1969); Historical Division, *Air Force Participation in Joint Army-Air Force Training Exercises, 1947–1950* (Maxwell AFB, AL: Air University, 1955).

53. Don Allan Carter, "War Games in Europe: The U.S. Army Experiments with Atomic Doctrine," in *Blueprints for Battle: Planning for War in Central Europe, 1948–1968*, ed. Jan Hoffenaar and Dieter Krüger (Lexington: University Press of Kentucky, 2012), 131–153.

54. *The Big Picture*, Episode 394: *The Pentomic Army*, 1957, ARC Identifier 2569662, National Archives and Records Administration.

55. Sloan Wilson, *The Man in the Gray Flannel Suit* (New York: Simon & Schuster, 1955).

56. Charles P. Summerall, "Morale and Leadership" (lecture, AWC, 16 October 1930), AHEC.

57. Oral History, 58, James B. Vaught Papers, AHEC. *RSA 1948*, 84; "Army Commissions," *ANJ* 83 (29 December 1945): 583; "Select Regular Appointments," *Army and Navy Bulletin* 3 (4 January 1947): 2; Separation of Officers," *ANJ* 83 (2 March 1946): 872; George Mather, "Military Personnel Policies and Procedures" (lecture, Armored School, 30 September 1958), box 34, E UD 10, RG 546; Ed Drea, "Historical Perspectives on Reductions in Force," 1989, CMH.

58. Thomas E. Ricks, *The Generals: American Military Command from World War II to Today* (New York: Penguin, 2012), 32–35.

59. "Army Defends High Percentage of Colonels in Peacetime Force," *Army and Navy Bulletin* 3 (22 February 1947). 2; *RSW 1938*, 53; Committees #10 and #11, "Forced Retirement of Colonels at 30 Years Commissioned Service," 12 October 1950, AHEC.

60. "Bombshell," *Armed Force* 5 (27 August 1949): 2. Charles W. G. Rich, "Reserve Officer Career Program," SP AWC, 1953, AHEC.

61. *RSW 1925*, 143; R. N. Young, "Responsibilities and Problems of the Army G-1" (lecture, AWC, 18 November 1953), AHEC.

62. "Voluntary Comments about 'The Army.'" Oral History, 178–183, Arthur S. Collins Papers, AHEC; Oral History, 28, James B. Vaught Papers, AHEC; Lewis Sorley, *Thunderbolt: General Creighton Adams and the Army of His Times* (orig. publ. 1992; repr., Bloomington: Indiana University Press, 2008), 355.

63. Oral History, 33–35, Eugene P. Forrester Papers, AHEC; John M. Taylor,

General Maxwell Taylor: The Sword and the Pen (New York: Doubleday, 1989), 150. For one West Point graduate and combat veteran's view of Blaik and his wartime football program, see Robin Olds with Christina Olds and Ed Rasimus, *Fighter Pilot: The Memoirs of Legendary Ace Robin Olds* (New York: St. Martin's Press, 2010), 148–149.

64. David Boroff, "West Point: Ancient Incubator for a New Breed," *Harper's Magazine* 225 (December 1962): 59. Ingo Trauschweizer, *Maxell Taylor's Cold War: From Berlin to Vietnam* (Lexington: University Press of Kentucky, 2019), 13–36; James A. Blackwell, *On Brave Old Army Team: The Cheating Scandal That Rocked the Nation: West Point, 1951* (Novato, CA: Presidio Press, 1996). On hazing, see Oral History, 20–22, box 59, Sidney B. Berry Papers, AHEC; Oral History, 24, Donald R. Keith Papers, AHEC.

65. Robert N. Young, "The ROTC Pays Off," *Army* 7 (September 1956): 14. Bernd G. Baetcke, "The Reserve Officers' Training Corps," SP AWC, 1951, AHEC; Tom Barratt, "The Officer Personnel Act of 1947," SP AWC, 1953, AHEC; Ivan W. Elliott, "The Officer Personnel Act of 1947," SP AWC, 1953, AHEC.

66. Neiberg, *Making Citizen Soldiers*, 35–83; Joe E. Burke et al., "The Future of Army ROTC," SP AWC, 1974, AHEC.

67. On service life as a junior officer, see John R. Galvin, *Fighting the Cold War: A Soldier's Memoir* (Lexington: University of Kentucky Press, 2015); Michael D. Mahler, *Tales from the Cold War: The U.S. Army in West Germany* (Dahlonega: University of North Georgia Press, 2021), 1–86; Gaines Post, Jr., *Memoirs of a Cold War Son* (Iowa City: University of Iowa Press, 2000).

68. Memo: Items for CINFO to Cover in Visits to Commands, Visits 1953 file, box 435, E 287, RG 319. Arthur T. Coumbe, *Army Officer Retention: Historical Context* (Carlisle, PA: Strategic Studies Institute, 2010), 4.

69. "Infantry Instructors Conference, 16–21 June 1952 Report," DLFB; Office of Chief of Army Field Forces, *Infantry School, Fort Benning* (1952), box 30, E UD-9, RG 546; "Army School Commandant's Conference," 4 February 1954, box 6, E UD-4, RG 546.

70. HQ, 101st Airborne Division to CG, CGSC, 28 March 1958, box 35, E NC3–338–81–14, RG 338. Garrison H. Davidson, "After-Action Report," 9 July 1956, N-13423.02, CARL; Students Summary of the 1954–1955 Regular Command and General Staff Officer Course, box 18, E UD3, RG 546; "Career Management and Your Future: Who Goes to School?" *CFJ* 4 (September 1953): 34–35.

71. Michael David Stewart, "Raising a Pragmatic Army: Officer Education at the U.S. Army Command and General Staff College, 1946–1986" (PhD diss., University of Kansas, 2010), 306.

72. Young, "Responsibilities and Problems of the Army G-1."

73. *Report of the Defense Advisory Committee on Professional and Technical Compensation*, vol. 1, *Military Personnel* (Washington, DC: GPO, 1957), 91–93.

74. James F. Collins, "Army Manpower" (lecture, AWC, 14 May 1958), AHEC; Charles Holmes, "Dollars Won't Make Good Soldiers," *American Mercury* 83 (August 1958): 143–146; J. Robert Moskin, "Our Military Manpower Scandal," *Look* 22 (18 March 1958): 27–33.

75. Donnelly, "Bilko's Army," 1202. *What the 1956 Soldier Thinks: A Digest of Attitude and Opinion Studies* (Washington, DC: US Army Adjutant General's Office,

1957); James A. Alger, "Procurement and Distribution of Manpower" (lecture, AWC, 7 November 1955), AHEC: William S. McElhenny, "Problems Confronting the United States Army," SP AWC, 1959, AHEC; Coumbe, *Army Officer Retention*, 3–4; Oral History, box 1, Cosbie E. Saint Papers, AHEC.

76. Mather, "Military Personnel Policies and Procedures." Thomas F. Cole, "Brevet Promotions and the Hump," SP AWC, 1969, AHEC; Max L. Pitney, "Retention of Junior Officers," SP AWC, 1959, AHEC.

77. *Report of the Defense Advisory Committee*, 108–109. Don A. Carter, *The U.S. Army Before Vietnam, 1953–1965* (Washington, DC: Center of Military History, 2015), 17–18.

78. William G. Van Allen, "Revitalization of Senior Army Leadership," SP AWC, 1955, AHEC. "Career Management and Your Future: Selection for General Staff Duty," *CFJ* 4 (January 1954): 32.

79. Coumbe, *Army Officer Retention*, 5–6.

80. *The Big Picture, The Pentomic Army*.

81. John W. Lemza, *The Big Picture: The Cold War on the Small Screen* (Lawrence: University Press of Kansas, 2021); Jeffrey Crean, "Something to Compete with 'Gunsmoke': The *Big Picture* Television Series and Selling a 'Modern, Progressive and Forward Thinking' Army to Cold War America," *War and Society* 35 (2016): 204–218.

82. R. Weaver, "Remarks Before Army Information Officers' Conference, 1–3 December 1958," 337 file, box 28, CINFO 1958, E UD-84, RG 319.

83. Linn, *Elvis's Army*, 99–131.

84. Dwight D. Eisenhower to Willis D. Crittenberger, 25 July 1947, box 32, Willis D. Crittenberger Papers, AHEC. Mark R. Grandstaff, "Making the Military American: Advertising, Reform, and the Demise of the Antistanding Army Tradition, 1945–1955," *JMH* 60 (April 1996): 299–232.

85. Remarks by Major General H. P. Storke, Army Commanders Conference, 3 December 1958, 337 file, box 28, E UD-84, RG 319.

86. Linn, *Elvis's Army*, 230–267.

87. Office of Chief of Information, Presentation to VCS on Execution of PI Segment of Command Program Management, 10 February 1957, box 3, E 55A, RG 319.

88. Robert P. Patterson to President, Sub: Increase in Pay for the Armed Forces, 18 February 1946, in Strategy and the Army files, box 1, RG 319.

89. Special Staff, US Army, Information and Education Division, Troop Attitude Research Branch, "Attitudes of New Recruits in the Army," 15 January 1948, report 50–314Ra, box 1006, E 93, RG 330. Rocco M. Paone, "The Last Volunteer Army," *MR* 49 (December 1969): 9–17.

90. "BG Mather's Remarks at the MOS Proficiency Test Conference, 19 December 1956," box 11, E UD-7, RG 546. John R. Smoak, "Procurement of Personnel with Qualifications for Combat," SP AWC, 1956, AHEC; "Men of Quality," *CFJ* 1 (April 1951): 9–11.

91. Colonel Hutton, "Recruiting Standards," WAC Staff Adviser Conference, 12–16 September, 1949, box 55, E 145, RG 319. Jacob Devers, *Report of Activities of Army Field Forces, 1945–1949*," 30 September 1949, 319.1 File, box 41, E 32B, RG 337.

92. Maxwell D. Taylor, "The Army at Home and Abroad," 10 December 1956, box 1, Winant Sidle Papers, AHEC.

93. Elvis Presley interview, 8 March 1960, on www.youtube.com/watch?v= 1MyrPxU6Ruo.

94. Course 5, Committee #10, "Enlisted Personnel Management," 17 December 1954, AHEC.

95. "Notes on Commanders Conference," Armor School, 5 October 1956, box 27, E UD-10, RG 546. DOA, "Enlisted Grade Structure Study," vol. 6, Annex E (July 1967), www.ncohistory.com/files/EGSS.pdf; Mather, "Military Personnel Policies and Procedures."

96. Byron K. King, "NCO Education Program," 17 January 1956, Organization Planning Files #337/250/16, box 531, E 2135, RG 549. Henry Gole is the source for "Ding Dong School."

97. Robert F. Hallock, "Drill," *CFJ* 2 (March 1952): 34.

98. Harry Ryson, "Bellyful," *CFJ* 2 (March 1952): 6. Captain Artillery [pseud.], "Noncoms," *CFJ* 2 (November 1951): 6–8; Hamilton H. Howze, "The Mishandling of Noncoms," *CFJ* 1 (February 1951): 37–38; Archibald Stuart, "The Training of Noncommissioned Offers During Mobilization and War," SP AWC, 1951, AHEC; John M. Collins, "The Care and Cleaning of NCOs: Policies and Practice, 1939–1969" (unpublished ms, courtesy of author) also at www.ncohistory.com /CareCleaning.html.

99. William Goldman, *Soldier in the Rain* (New York: Dell, 1960); *Soldier in the Rain*, directed by Ralph Nelson (1963; Burbank, CA: Warner Brothers Archive Collection, 1991), DVD. Moskos, *American Enlisted Man*, 16–17, 22.

100. Charles Willeford, "A Reflection on Retirement," *CFJ* 3 (August 1952): 40. Moskos, *American Enlisted Man*, 16–17; Armor School, Staff and Commanders Conference, 10 February 1956, box 27, E UD-10, RG 546; Mather, "Military Personnel Policies and Procedures."

101. Roy Moore, "Quality Manpower and the Modern Army," *Armor* 66 (July–August 1957): 22–23.

102. Collins, "The Care and Cleaning of NCOs," 125–128; David W. Hogan, Arnold G. Fisch, and Robert K. Wright, eds., *The Story of the Noncommissioned Officers Corps: The Backbone of the Army* (Washington, DC: Center of Military History, 2003), 42.

103. John T. English, "Protection of Moral Standards," 17 October 1958, box 558, E 1, RG 247.

104. DeRosa, *Political Indoctrination*; Linn, *Elvis's Army*, 268–297.

105. Gilman C. Mudgett, "CINFO Remarks on PI and TI&E," 1955, AGO 350, box 21, E NND 957387, RG 319.

106. John D. Austin to Matthew B. Ridgway, 3 May 1954, 220.3 file, box 3, E 55F, RG 337.

Chapter 5. The Hollow Army after Vietnam, 1970–1980

1. Michael M. Toler questionnaire, 3 January 2020.

2. Mahler, *Tales from the Cold War*, 87–99.

3. Ronald H. Spector, "The Vietnam War and the Army's Self Image," in *The Second Indochina War*, ed. John Schlight (Washington, DC: Center of Military

History, 1986), 170. On contemporary perceptions of the post-Vietnam US Army, see Zeb B. Bradford and Frederic J. Brown, *America's Army in Transition* (Beverly Hills, CA: Sage, 1973); William L. Hauser, *America's Army in Crisis: A Study of Civil-Military Relations* (Baltimore: Johns Hopkins University Press, 1973); Haynes Johnson and George C. Wilson, *Army in Anguish* (New York: Pocket Books, 1972); George Walton, *The Tarnished Shield: A Report on Today's Army* (New York: Dodd, Mead & Co., 1973); John P. Lovell, "No Tunes of Glory: America's Military in the Aftermath of Vietnam," *Indiana Law Journal* 49 (Summer 1974): 698–717.

4. "Pentagon Press Group," 13 June 1980, Edward C. Meyer, *E. C. Meyer, General, United States Army Chief of Staff, June 1979–June 1983* (Washington, DC: Department of the Army, 1984), 98. Frank L. Jones, *A "Hollow Army" Reappraised: President Carter, Defense Budgets, and the Politics of Military Readiness* (Carlisle, PA: Strategic Studies Institute, 2012); Polly Peyer, "Hollow Force: Scare or Dare?," SP Industrial College of the Armed Forces, 1994, DTIC; Jerry Lembcke, *The Spitting Image: Myth, Memory, and the Legacy of Vietnam* (New York: New York University Press, 1998).

5. Robert H. Scales, Jr., *Certain Victory: The US Army in the Gulf War* (Washington, DC: Office of the Chief of Staff, 1993), 5. James Kitfield, *Prodigal Soldiers: How the Generation of Officers Born of Vietnam Revolutionized the American Style of War* (Washington, DC: Brassey's, 1995); Henry G. Gole, *General William E. DuPuy: Preparing the Army for Modern War* (Lexington: University Press of Kentucky, 2008); Mike Guardia, *Crusader: General Donn Starry and the Army of his Times* (Haverton, PA: Casemate, 2018); Al Santoli, *Leading the Way: How Vietnam Veterans Rebuilt the U.S. Military: An Oral History* (New York: Ballantine, 1994). For an overview of postwar US Army historiography, see Dwight E. Phillips, Jr., "Re-engineering Institutional Culture and the American Way of War in the Post-Vietnam U.S. Army, 1968–1989" (PhD diss., University of Chicago, 2014), viii–xxxvi.

For a succinct treatment of the Gulf War literature, see Stephen Biddle, "Victory Misunderstood: What the Gulf War Tells Us About the Future of Conflict," *International Security* 21 (Fall 1996): 139–179.

6. Gregory Fontenot, *The 1st Infantry Division and the US Army Transformed: Road to Victory in Desert Storm, 1970–1991* (Columbia: University of Missouri Press, 2017). TRADOC, *Transforming the Army: TRADOC's First Thirty Years, 1973–2003* (Fort Monroe, VA: TRADOC, 2003); Paul H. Herbert, *Deciding What Has to Be Done: General William E. DePuy and the 1976 Edition of FM 100–5 Operations* (Fort Leavenworth, KS: Combat Studies Institute, 1988); Roger J. Spiller, *In the School of War* (Lincoln: University of Nebraska Press, 2010), 220–257; Richard Lock-Pullan, "'An Inward Looking Time': The United States Army, 1973–1976," *JMH* 67 (April 2003): 483–511; Frank N. Scubert and Theresa L. Kraus, eds., *The Whirlwind War: The United States Army in Operations Desert Shield and Desert Storm* (Washington, DC: Center of Military History, 1995), 24–40. On the shift from a conscript to volunteer force, see Beth Bailey, *America's Army: Making the All-Volunteer Force* (Cambridge, MA: Harvard University Press, 2009); Robert K. Griffith, *The U.S. Army's Transition to an All-Volunteer Force, 1968–1974* (Washington, DC: Center of Military History, 1997).

7. For a condensed version of this argument, see John F. Shortal, "20th Century Demobilization Lessons," *MR* 78 (September–November 1998): 58–64.

8. Frederick C. Weyand, "The Army in the Pacific is a Visible Presence for Peace," *Army* 23 (October 1973): 48.

9. Colin Powell with Joseph E. Persico, *My American Journey*, rev. ed. (New York: Ballantine, 2003), 144–145.

10. Meredith H. Lair, *Armed with Abundance: Consumerism & Soldiering in the Vietnam War* (Chapel Hill: University of North Carolina Press, 2011).

11. "Address at the Command and General Staff College, Fort Leavenworth, Kansas," 10 April 1972, box 5, Michael S. Davison Papers, AHEC.

12. Spector, "The Vietnam War," 178. For an essential work on the OCS officers by a veteran, see Ron Milam, *Not a Gentleman's War: An Inside View of Junior Officers in the Vietnam War* (Chapel Hill: University of North Carolina Press, 2009). For a personal view of the rotation policy's impact at the small-unit level, see James R. McDonough, *Platoon Leader: A Memoir of Command in Combat* (New York: Random House, 1985), 229–241.

13. Andrew J. Birtle and John R. Maass, *The Drawdown, 1970–1971* (Washington, DC: Center of Military History, 2019), 68.

14. For a sample of wartime studies by army officers and observers, see Zeb B. Bradford, "US Tactics in Vietnam," *MR* 52 (February 1972): 63–76; Robert E. Edwards, "Operations of the 1st Battalion, 7th Cavalry, 1st Cavalry Division (Airmobile), in the Airmobile Assault of Landing Zone X-Ray, Ia Drang Valley, Republic of Vietnam, 14–16 November 1965 (Personal Experience of a Company Commander)," 6 February 1968, MCEL; William B. Fulton, *Riverine Operations, 1966–1969* (Washington, DC: Department of the Army, 1973); S. L. A. Marshall, *Ambush and Bird: Two Vietnam Battle Narratives* (New York: Doubleday, 1969); John J. Tolson, *Airmobility, 1961–1971* (Washington, DC: Department of the Army, 1973).

15. For a sample of the generals' analysis, see David R. Palmer, *Summons of the Trumpet: U.S.-Vietnam in Perspective* (San Rafael, CA: Presidio, 1978); Bruce R. Palmer, *The Twenty-Five Year War: America's Military Role in Vietnam* (Lexington: University Press of Kentucky, 1984); Lewis W. Walt, *Strange War, Strange Strategy: A General's Report on Vietnam* (New York: Funk and Wagnalls, 1970); William C. Westmoreland, *A Soldier Reports* (New York: Dell, 1976). On field officer critiques, see Bradford and Brown, *America's Army in Transition*; Hauser, *America's Army in Crisis*; Edward L. King, *The Death of the Army: A Pre-Mortem* (New York: Saturday Review Press, 1972).

16. Fitzgerald, *Learning to Forget: US Army Counterinsurgency and Practice from Vietnam to Iraq* (Stanford, CA: Stanford University Press, 2013). For a sample of the debate on the US Army's assimilation of the perceived lessons of Vietnam, see Guenter Lewy, *America in Vietnam* (New York: Oxford University Press, 1978); Andrew F. Krepinevich, Jr., *The Army and Vietnam* (Baltimore: Johns Hopkins University Press, 1986); Dale Andrade, "Westmoreland Was Right: Learning the Wrong Lessons from the Vietnam War," *Small Wars & Insurgencies* 19 (September 2008), 145–181; Gregory A. Daddis, *Westmoreland's War: Reassessing American Strategy in Vietnam* (New York: Oxford University Press, 2014); John P. Lovell, "Vietnam and the U.S. Army: Learning to Cope with Failure," *Democracy, Strategy, and Vietnam: Implications for American Policymaking*, ed. George K. Osborn et al. (Lexington, MA: Lexington Books, 1985), 121–154; George C. Herring, "Preparing

Not to Fight the Last War: The Impact of Vietnam on the U.S. Military," in *After Vietnam: Legacies of a Lost War*, ed. Charles E. Neu (Baltimore: Johns Hopkins University Press, 2000), 56–84; Conrad C. Crane, *Avoiding Vietnam: The U.S. Army's Response to Defeat in Southeast Asia* (Carlisle, PA: Strategic Studies Institute, 2002); James H. Willbanks, "The Legacy of the Vietnam War for the U.S. Army," in *America and the Vietnam War: Re-examining the Culture and History of a Generation*, ed. Andrew Weist, Mary Kathryn Barbier, and Glenn Robins (New York: Routledge, 2010), 271–288.

17. Robert A. Doughty, *The Evolution of U.S. Army Tactical Doctrine, 1946–1976* (Fort Leavenworth, KS: Combat Studies Institute, 1976), 41. "Middle East War—1973," *MR* 54 (February 1974): 48–49.

18. R. Z. Alessi-Friedlander, "Learning to Win When Fighting Outnumbered: Operational Risk in the U.S. Army, 1973–1982, and the Influence of the 1973 Arab-Israeli War" (masters thesis, GGSC, 2016). Sterling, *Other People's Wars*, 189–272; Herbert, *Deciding What Has to Be Done*, 29–39; Donn A. Starry, "A Perspective on American Military Thought," *MR* 69 (July 1989): 2–11.

19. Bruce R. Palmer Oral History, 9, AHEC. *DOAHR FY 71*, 6 and 48–49; *DOAHR FY 72*, 59.

20. Statistics from *DOAHR FY 74*, 51; Trauschweizer, *Cold War U.S. Army*, 241. On Nixon and the withdrawal from the war, see James H. Willbanks, *Abandoning Vietnam: How America Left and South Vietnam Lost its War* (Lawrence: University Press of Kansas, 2004).

21. James K. Woolnough, "Higher Priority to Be Given to Troop Morale and Welfare," *Army* 20 (November 1970): 37. Lloyd Norman, "Turbulence and Army Readiness," *Army* 21 (July 1971): 10–14.

22. Flynn, *The Draft, 1940–1973*, 224–277; Rutenberg, *Rough Draft*, 157–187.

23. Lynn D. Smith, "A Question of Purpose," *Army* 23 (May 1973): 11–15; M. Wade Markel et al., *The Evolution of U.S. Military Policy from the Constitution to the Present*, vol. 4, *The Total Force Policy Era, 1970–2015* (Santa Monica, CA: RAND, 2020), 32.

24. Lewis Sorley, *Thunderbolt: General Creighton Abrams and the Army of His Times* (1992, Bloomington: Indiana University Press, 2008), 363. John B. Wilson, *Maneuver and Firepower: The Evolution of Divisions and Separate Brigades* (Washington, DC: US Army Center of Military History, 1998), 353–373.

25. Phillips, "Reengineering Institutional Culture," 41. Jones, *A "Hollow Army" Reappraised*, 15.

26. Conrad C. Crane, "Post-Vietnam Drawdown: The Myth of the Abrams Doctrine," in *Drawdown: the American Way of Postwar*, ed. James W. Warren (New York: New York University Press, 2016), 241. On Total Force, see Markel et al., *Evolution of U.S. Military Policy*, 7–38.

27. Doubler, *I Am the Guard*, 281; see also 279–286. John K. Mahon, *History of the Militia and the National Guard* (New York: Macmillan, 1983), 248–257; William J. Moran, "Total Force Concept Requires Doers'—Not Advisors," SP AWC, 1973, AHEC; Phillips, "Reengineering Institutional Culture," 319–322.

28. Gustavo A. Leon, "Total Force Concept: Reality or Myth," SP AWC, 1975, AHEC. Doubler, *I Am the Guard*, 275.

29. Toler questionnaire; Willbanks interview.

30. Oral History of Sidney B. Berry [hereafter Berry Oral History], 1077, Mississippi Oral History Program, box 59, Sidney B. Berry Papers, AHEC.

31. Karen McKay, "Go Ahead—Exploit Us!," *Army* 22 (April 1972): 21–25.

32. Bailey, *America's Army*, 136–171; Morden, *The Women's Army Corps, 1945–1978*, 390–395; Tanya L. Roth, *Her Cold War: Women in the U.S. Military, 1945–1980* (Chapel Hill: University of North Carolina Press, 2020), 159–214.

33. William Gardner Bell, *Commanding Generals and; Chiefs of Staff, 1775–2013* (Washington, DC: Center of Military History, 2013), 152–156.

34. Jean R. Moenk, *Operation Steadfast Historical Summary: A History of the Reorganization of Continental Army Command (1972–1973)* (Fort Monroe, VA: TRADOC, 1973).

35. *DOAHR FY 71*, 3.

36. Trauschweizer, *Cold War U.S. Army*, 241.

37. Harry G. Summers, "The Astarita Report: A Military Strategy for the Multipolar World" (Carlisle, PA: Strategic Studies Institute, 1981); Phillips, "Reengineering Institutional Culture," 38–40.

38. William E. DePuy to Fred C. Weyand, 18 February 1976, in William E. DePuy, *Selected Papers of General William E. DePuy: First Commander, U.S. Army, Training and Doctrine Command*, ed. Donald L. Gilmore and Carolyn D. Conway (Fort Leavenworth, KS: Combat Studies Institute, 1994), 180. Phillips, "Reengineering Institutional Culture," 47–66.

39. TRADOC, *Transforming the Army*; John L. Romjue, *The Army of Excellence: The Development of the 1980s Army* (Fort Monroe, VA: TRADOC, 1998).

40. Herbert, *Deciding What Has to Be Done*, 1.

41. HQ, Department of the Army, *FM 100–5: Operations* (1 July 1976), 1. On Active Defense, see Herbert, *Deciding What Has to Be Done*; Kretchik, *U.S. Army Doctrine*, 197–202; John L. Romjue, *From Active Defense to AirLand Battle: The Development of Army Doctrine, 1973–1982* (Fort Monroe, VA: TRADOC, 1984); Jonathan Lee Due, "Seizing the Initiative: The Intellectual Renaissance That Changed U.S. Army Doctrine, 1970–1982" (PhD diss., University of North Carolina at Chapel Hill, 2007), 36–64.

42. David C. Trybula, "'Big Five' Lessons for Today and Tomorrow," 2012, SP AWC, AHEC.

43. Anne W. Chapman, *The Army's Training Revolution, 1793–1990: An Overview* (Fort Monroe, VA: TRADOC, 1991), 3–10.

44. Paul F. Gorman, "TRADOC Training," November 1973, CARL; Phillips, "Reengineering Institutional Culture," 52–55.

45. Gole, *General William E. DuPuy*, 242. Romjue, *Army of Excellence*; Romjue, *From Active Defense to AirLand Battle*.

46. Oral History, 113, Louis E. Menetrey Papers, AHEC.

47. DCS Resource Management, March 1975 to Apr 1977, Maxwell Thurman Papers, AHEC.

48. Benjamin Bonner, "A Survey of USAREUR Entry Level Skills in the 11B Infantryman" (Alexandria, VA: US Army Human Resources Research Organization, 1979), DTIC.

49. Louise G. Yates, "The Estimated Impact of SQT on USAREUR Infantry Units: Survey Results" (Alexandria, VA: US Army Human Resources Research Organization, 1979), DTIC.

50. Bailey, *America's Army*, 127; Steven L. Funk, et al., "Training Detractors in FORSCOM Divisions and How They are Handled" (Alexandria, VA: US Army Research Institute, 1980), DTIC.

51. Hilton R. Beliak, "Personnel Turbulence and Time Utilization in an Infantry Division" (Alexandria, VA: US Army Human Resources Research Organization, 1977), DTIC.

52. Funk et al., "Training Detractors."

53. Oral History, 82–91, Henry E. Emerson Papers, AHEC; Richard G. Stilwell "Pro-Life Is Key in Korea," *Army* 24 (October 1974): 109–111; Powell with Persico, *My American Journey*, 179–204.

54. Harry W. Brooks, Jr., to All Commanders, Sub: Taking Care of Business, 23 August 1974 in Annual Historical Supplement, 25th Division, 1974, Tropic Lighting Museum, Schofield Barracks, HI; Bernard S. Pergerson, Jr., "Modern Volunteer Army: The 25th Infantry Division," SP AWC, 1974, AHEC.

55. Arthur S. Collins, Jr., *Common Sense Training*. Collins's reports on training and conditions in USAREUR can be found in boxes 3 and 4, Arthur S. Collins Papers, AHEC. On Collins's direction of USAREUR's training program, see Michael S. Davison, "Remarks at the Annual Meeting, European Department, AUSA," 1 June 1972, box 5, Michael S. Davison Papers.

56. Mahler, *Tales from the Cold War*, 100–121.

57. "Memorandum for Record: DCINCUSAREUR Trip to Bamberg and Schweinfurt 27 October 1971," 29 October 1971, box 4, Collins Papers.

58. "Memorandum for Record: DCINCUSAREUR Visit to the Schweinfurt Area, 28 February 1974," 4 March 1974, box 4, Collins Papers.

59. "DCINCUSAREUR Trip to Mainz 2 February 1972," 7 February 1972, box 3, Collins Papers.

60. Oral History, 5:16–17, Michael S. Davison Papers.

61. Oral History, 610, Thomas P. Lynch Papers, AHEC. *Reforger V After Action Report* (15 January 1974), AHEC.

62. Oral History, 614–615, Lynch Papers.

63. Kretchik, *U.S. Army Doctrine*, 193–211.

64. On base camp luxury, see Lair, *Armed with Abundance*.

65. Oral History, 144, Louis C. Wagner, Jr., Papers, AHEC. Bradford and Brown, *America's Army*, 237–38 Galvin, *Fighting the Cold War*, 133–141.

66. Lewis Sorley, *Honorable Warrior: General Harold K. Johnson and the Ethics of Command* (Lawrence: University Press of Kansas, 1998), 268.

67. Robert E. McCord, "The Challenge to Military Professionalism," SP AWC, 1970, AHEC.

68. William C. Westmoreland, *A Soldier Reports* (New York: Dell, 1980), 462–463.

69. *Leadership for the 1970s: USAWC Study of Leadership for the Professional Soldier* (Carlisle Barracks, PA: Army War College, 1971); *Study on Military Professionalism* (Carlisle Barracks, PA: Army War College, 1970); Samuel Zaffiri, *Westmoreland: A Biography of General William C. Westmoreland* (New York: William Morrow, 1994), 334–336, 343–345.

70. Phillips, "Reengineering Institutional Culture," xiv.

71. George B. Bartel, "Are the Troops Getting Enough Officer Duty?," *Army* 23 (September 1973): 41–42.

72. Smith, "A Question of Purpose"; Dandridge M. Malone, "The Prize," *Army* 23 (March 1973): 24–31; *Hearings Before the Special Subcommittee of Manpower in the Military of the Committee on Armed Services*, House of Representatives, 92nd Congress, 1st and 2nd Sessions, HASC No, 92–51 (Washington, DC: GPO, 1972), 12241–12242.

73. Dabrowski, ed., *An Oral History of General Gordon R. Sullivan*, 61. Drea, "Historical Perspectives on Reductions in Force," 13. CMH. I am indebted to Shane P. Reilly for locating this source.

74. Office of the Deputy Chief of Staff for Personnel, Annual Historical Summary FY 1972, 50–51, AHEC. I am indebted to William Donnelly for locating these reports.

75. *Oral History . . . Sullivan*, 62. Office of the Deputy Chief of Staff for Personnel, Annual Historical Summary FY 1971, 44, AHEC; *DOAHR FY 76*, 40–41; James H. Hayes, *The Evolution of Military Officer Personnel Policies: A Preliminary Study with Parallels from Industry* (Santa Monica, CA: RAND, 1978).

76. Robert F. Froehlke, "Peace-Keeping with Pride and Integrity," *Army* 22 (November 1972): 17.

77. Howard H. Callaway to CSA, 21 January 1975, Sub: Secretary of the Army's Top 5, box 10: "Analysis of the Brehm Initiative on Officer and Civilian Grade Reductions," 7 May 1976, box 14, both in Frederick C. Weyand Papers, AHEC.

78. Paul Herbert interview, 20 February 2021.

79. Oral History, 90–91, James V. Vaught Papers, AHEC.

80. Andrew Bacevich email, 3 March 2021; Richard G. Trefry interview 25 February 2021; Theodore Stroup email, 23 February 2021; Harley Mooney interview, 25 February 2021.

81. Michael Lee Lanning, *The Battles of Peace* (New York: Ivy Books, 1992), 9–10; James Willbanks phone conversation, 12 August 2021; Stroup email; Spiller, *In the School of War*, 226.

82. Oral History, 2:129–132, Evelyn P. Foote, AHEC.

83. Walter T. Kerwin, "Youth's 'Why' Key Challenge in Today's Army," *Army* 20 (November 1970): 70.

84. Cited in Colin O. Halvorson, "Motivation and Job Satisfaction for Middle Level Career Army Officers" (masters thesis, CGSC, 1975), 4.

85. Franklin M. Davis, Sub: Project Seventy Action, 13 March 1970, Major Issues Facing Army (Project Seventy Actions) file, William J. McCaffrey Papers, AHEC. Robert W. Berry, "Why They Quit," *Army* 20 (December 1970): 3–4, William J. Hauser, "Professionalism and the Junior Officer Drain," *Army* 20 (July 1970): 17–22.

86. Office of the Deputy Chief of Staff for Personnel, Annual Historical Summary 1 July 1968 to 30 June 1969, AHEC. The majority of OCS candidates in the later stages of the war had some college credit.

87. In FY 1976 the US Army brought on active duty 854 USMA graduates, 5,385 ROTC, 463 OCS, 168 Voluntary Active, and 643 WACs (mostly ROTC); see Office of the Deputy Chief of Staff for Personnel, Annual Historical Summary FY 1976, AHEC. Specialist officer acquisitions were usually direct commissions, numbered about 2,000, and included chaplains, medical, and legal officers.

88. Paul Herbert interview, 13 March 2021.

89. Richard C. U'Ren, *Ivory Fortress: A Psychiatrist Looks at West Point* (Indianapolis: Bobbs-Merrill Co., 1974), 142. K. Bruce Galloway and Robert B. Johnson II, *West Point: America's Power Fraternity* (New York: Simon & Schuster, 1973; Joseph J. Ellis and Robert Moore, *School for Soldiers: West Point and the Profession of Arms* (New York: Oxford University Press, 1974); Ward Just, *Military Men* (New York: Alfred A. Knopf, 1970), 15–52.

90. Betros, *Carved from Granite*, 57–59, 284–289. Berry Oral History, 146–161. Berry recalled that as a cadet, when he heard that World War II had ended, his first reaction was, "Well, I *am* a draft dodger"; see Berry Oral History, 30.

91. Betros, *Carved from Granite*, 97, 147–150, 252–254; Berry Oral History, 149–153; Lance Janda, *Stronger Than Custom: West Point and the Admission of Women* (Westport, CT: Praeger, 2002); Roth, *Her Cold War*, 202–210; Lia Daphne Winfield, "Claiming Their Place: Women's Integration into the U.S. Army, 1970–1989" (PhD diss., University of California Davis, 2013), 58–91.

92. William R. Calhoun, "Bullish on ROTC," *Army* 24 (May 1974): 36–38; Ward Elliott, "The Assault on ROTC," *Army* 21 (February 1971): 35–38; Neiberg, *Making Citizen Soldiers*, 112–150.

93. Westmoreland, *A Soldier Reports*, 452. T. R. McNeill, "An Up-to-Date System for Procuring Officers," *Army* 21 (June 1971): 32–33; Deputy Chief of Staff for Personnel, Annual Historical Summary FY 1970, AHEC; R. E. Morris, "Improving the Infantry Image Among Today's ROTC Cadets," *Army* 21 (March 1971): 56–57; CONARC/ARRED Annual Historical Summary, FY 1972, TRADOC Archives, Fort Eustis, VA; USMA Department of History, *Perspectives* (West Point, New York, US Military Academy History Department, 1980). I am indebted to Sam Watson for information on the USMA Summer Seminar in 1988. Among the West Point instructional faculty were several future generals and many lifetime friends.

94. Robert M. Carroll, "Army ROTC: The Future on the Campus," SP AWC, 1970, AHEC. Robert L. Goldrich, "The Art of Winning Friends on Campus," *Army* 21 (January 1971): 24–29; George B. Gray, "ROTC: Military Training or University Military Science Education?" SP AWC, 1970, AHEC.

95. John T. Bonner, "ROTC's Battle and Survival," *Army* 22 (February 1972): 40–44.

96. Neiberg, *Making Citizen Soldiers*, 157–170.

97. Office of the Deputy Chief of Staff for Personnel, Annual Historical Summary FY 1974, AHEC. Arthur J. Cornelson, "The Talent Drain," *Army* 22 (April 1972): 48.

98. Fumiyo T. Hunter, *Tenure Patterns of U.S. Commissioned Officers in the 1970s and 1980s* (Alexandria, VA: U.S. Army Research Institute of the Behavioral and Social Sciences, 1988), 14.

99. Paul Herbert interview, 13 March 2021.

100. Robert G. Gard, "The Direction of Army Leadership in the 1970s" (lecture, CONARC Training to Lead Conference, 14–18 May 1973), DTIC. Anneliese M. Steele, "Are the Relationships Between Junior and Senior Officers in the U.S. Army Officer Corps Dysfunctional?" SP SAMS, 2001, CARL.

101. Michael S. Davison to Frederick C. Weyand, 10 June 1975, box 6, Davison Papers.

102. Mark S. Pernell questionnaire, 15 July 2021. One officer recalled that in order to find out the true state of readiness the higher headquarters would send inspectors to count how many vehicles had been left behind during alerts. Enterprising junior officers would foil such oversight by towing disabled vehicles with them when they went to the field. Robert Griffith email, 21 August 2021.

103. Herbert interview.

104. Steven R. Stewart, Chester I. Christie, and T. O. Jacobs, "Leadership Tasks Performed by U.S. Army Company Commanders in Europe" (Alexandria, VA: US Army Research Institute for the Behavioral and Social Sciences, 1976).

105. E. Mike Perry questionnaire, 19 December 2019. Herbert interview; Pernell questionnaire.

106. Hunter, *Tenure Patterns*, 18.

107. Andrew J. Bacevich, Jr., "Progressivism, Professionalism, and Reform," *Parameters* 9 (March 1979): 69.

108. Oral History, 2, William R. Richardson Papers, AHEC.

109. William A. Patch, "Professional Development of Today's NCO," *Army* 24 (November 1974): 16.

110. Linn, *Elvis's Army*; Harold Wool, *The Military Specialist: Skilled Manpower and the Armed Forces* (Baltimore: Johns Hopkins University Press, 1968).

111. William E. Datel, "Final Evaluation Report on Fort Ord Project VOLAR," 4 August 1972, Walter Reed Army Institute of Research, DTIC; L. James Binder, "The Now Is Very in at Fort Benning," *Army* 21 (April 1971): 22–29; Richard S. Wadleigh, "The Now and VOLAR," *Army* 21 (June 1971): 5–6; "Barracks Life Now a Little Brighter," *Army* 21 (January 1971): 6–8.

112. William C. Westmoreland, "Straight Talk from the Chief," *Army* 21 (May 1971): 13. JBS [pseud.], "Beer in the Barracks Is Bad?" *Army* 21 (May 1971): 8–9; US Army Infantry School, *The Benning Plan for a Modern Volunteer Army*, 27 January 1971, DLFB.

113. For the views of VOLAR's primary implementer, see Oral History, George I. Forsythe Papers, AHEC. On VOLAR, see Bailey, *America's Army*, 52–65; Griffith, *U.S. Army's Transition*, 81–114.

114. *DOAHR FY 72*, 76. On US Army advertising, see Bailey, *America's Army*; Jeremy K. Saucier, "Mobilizing the Imagination: Army Advertising and the Politics of Culture in Post-Vietnam America" (PhD diss., University of Rochester, 2010).

115. Jack K. Wagstaff, "Army of the People," *Army* 22 (December 1972): 2. *DOAHR FY 74*, 52; Walter T. Kerwin, Jr., "Far-Flung Command Stays Combat Ready," *Army* 24 (October 1974): 34–38.

116. *DOAHR FY 72*, 77. Tom Hamrick, "Trying the Army on for Size," *Army* 22 (August 1972): 37–40; Robert M. Lee, "Flagging Vigilance: The Post-Vietnam 'Hollow Army'" (master's thesis, Texas A&M University, 2001), 27–29.

117. Charles C. Moskos and John Sibley Butler, *All That We Can Be: Black Leadership and Racial Integration the Army Way* (New York: Basic Books, 1996), 33; Robert B. Killebrew, "Where the Squad Leader Makes a Difference," *Army* 24 (March 1974): 33–37; John F. Shortal, "20th Century Demobilization Lessons," *MR* 78 (September–November 1998): 58–63; Lee, "Flagging Vigilance," 28–30.

118. *1976 Annual Report: Comptroller General of the United States* (Washington,

DC: GPO, 1977), 130–131; *DOAHR FY 74*, 51–52; *DOAHR FY 75*, 38; John R. Prosser, "Reforming Military Justice," *Army* 23 (April 1973): 38–42; James H. Powers, "The Volunteer Soldier—A Self-Portrait," SP AWC, 1980, AHEC.

119. Robert B. Killebrew, "Volunteer Army: How it Looks to a Company Commander," *Army* 21 (March 1971): 19. Office of Personnel Operations, "Survey Estimate of Retention of Army Personnel" 31 August 1971, DAPO-PMP Report #2-72-E, CARL; Norman, "Turbulence and Army Readiness."

120. US GAO, *The Army Can Improve Peacetime Use of Deployable Enlisted Personnel* (7 September 1978).

121. Bernard W. Rogers, "People the Key in the New Army," *Army* 23 (October 1973): 22–26. *DOAHR FY 76*, 18; "Army Will Retrain 14,000 NCOs to Fill Combat Unit Slots," *Army* 26 (January 1976): 10.

122. Bailey, *America's Army*, 117–120.

123. *DOAHR FY 79*, 49–53; Shortal, "20th Century Demobilization Lessons." For a detailed treatment of the ASVAB scandal, see Lee, "Flagging Vigilance," 86–93.

124. Bailey, *America's Army*, 178–190.

125. Norman, "Turbulence and Army Readiness," 14. Tom Hamrick, "Sophisticated Basic Trainees," *Army* 21 (September 1971): 39; R. A. Weaver, "What Must We Do to Understand [a] New Soldier?" *Army* 21 (April 1971): 62.

126. Memorandum for Record: DCINCUSAREUR Visit to 3rd Infantry Division 1 and 6 April 1971, box 4, Collins Papers.

127. Moskos, *The American Enlisted Man*, 74. Larry H. Ingraham, *The Boys in the Barracks: Observations on American Military Life* (Philadelphia: Institute for the Study of Human Issues, 1984).

128. Harold G. Moore, "On Pay and Benefits, A Balanced Approach," *Army* 26 (October 1976): 100–102; Eric C. Ludvigsen, "Army Tightens Belt Against Inflation from Munitions to Maple Syrup," *Army* 24 (November 1974): 12–13; "Times Are Perilous for 'Contractual Rights,'" *Army* 26 (January 1976): 6–8; *DOAHR FY 79*, 91–92.

129. Alexander M. S. McColl, "On Restoring Discipline," *Army* 23 (July 1973): 3–4; Killebrew, "Volunteer Army," 21; *DOAHR FY 70*, 61. The 90 percent figure was apocryphal but accurate; see Prosser, "Reforming Military Justice," 38–42.

130. Anne W. Chapman, *Mixed-Gender Basic Training: The U.S. Army's Experience, 1973–1985* (Fort Monroe, VA: TRADOC, 1991), 33–56; Mildred C. Bailey, "Army Women and a Decade of Progress," *Army* 24 (October 1974): 85–91; Tom Hamrick, "The Drill Sergeant Wore Skirts," *Army* 22 (September 1972): 38–42; John H. Batts, et al., "The Roles of Women in the Army and Their Impact on Military Operations and Organizations," SP AWC, 1975, AHEC.

131. Roger Goodell interviews, 30 December 2020 and 30 June and 2 July 2021.

132. Maxwell R. Thurman, "Sustaining the All-Volunteer Force 1983–1992: The Second Decade," in *The All-Volunteer Force After a Decade: Retrospect and Prospect*, ed. William Bowman, Roger Little, and G. Thomas Scilia (Washington, DC: Pergamon-Brassey's, 1986), 267.

133. "Attitudes and Motivations of First Termers Toward Reenlistment," January 1976, box 11A, Weyand Papers.

134. William A. Patch, "Professional Development of Today's NCO," *Army* 24 (November 1974): 15–20; Joseph B. Love, "Optimum Career Content of Selected Military Occupational Specialties," SP, AWC, 27 February 1969, AHEC.

135. Office of the Deputy Chief of Staff for Personnel, Annual Historical Summary FY 1972, 56, AHEC.

136. Office of the Chief of Staff for Personnel, Annual Historical Summary, 1 July to 30 June 1969, AHEC *DOAHR FY 69*, 36; *DOAHR FY 70*, 57.

137. Oral History, 3:71, Lynch Papers.

138. Gordon Rudd Oral interview, 26 May 2021.

139. Richard C. Hall email, 16 September 2019.

140. Edward G. Miller email, 31 May 2020.

141. Office of the Deputy Chief of Staff for Personnel, Annual Historical Summary FY 1972, 48–49, AHEC.

142. CONARC/ARRED Annual Historical Summary, FY 1972, TRADOC Archives, Fort Eustis, VA. *DOAHR FY 72*, 57–60, 81.

143. R. E. Funderburk, "Six-Hour Day: Equal Training, Less Time," *Army* 26 (July 1976): 51–52.

144. John D. Blair, Richard C. Thompson, and David Segal, *Race and Job Satisfaction in the U.S. Army*, December 1979 (Alexandria, VA: US Army Research Institute for the Behavioral and Social Sciences), DTIC. Moskos and Butler, *All That We Can Be*, 34.

145. Arthur T. Hadley, *The Straw Giant: Triumph and Failure: America's Armed Forces* (New York: Random House, 1986), 251.

146. Funk et al., "Training Detractors."

147. Meyer, *E. C. Meyer*, 147. Powers, "The Volunteer Soldier."

148. Harry W. Brooks, Jr., to All Commanders, Sub: Taking Care of Business, 23 August 1974, in Annual Historical Supplement, 25th Division, 1974, Tropic Lightning Museum, Schofield Barracks, HI.

149. Henry Emerson to All Commanders, Sub: Pro-Life Program, 5 November 1974, Pro-Life File, box 21, Richard G. Stilwell Papers, AHEC.

150. Brooks to Commanders, Sub: Taking Care of Business.

151. Daniel M. Caughey, "The Higher Standards," *Army* 24 (December 1974): 5. *DOAHR FY 73*, 63–64; *DOAHR FY 74*, 51–52; CONARC/ARRED Annual Historical Summary, FY 1972, TRADOC Archives, Fort Eustis, VA.

152. Frank T. Mildren, "US Army Vietnam for Period 22 June 1968 to 1 July 1970," 2 February 1970, DTIC.

153. Debriefing Report, Michael S. Davison, CG II Field Force Vietnam, 15 April 1970–26 May 1971, 26 May 1971, Davison Papers.

154. Charles C. Moskos, Jr., "Coping in Europe: Shorter Tours May be the Answer," *Army* 23 (November 1973): 13.

155. Jeremy Kuzmarov, *The Myth of the Addicted Army: Vietnam and the Modern War on Drugs* (Amherst: University of Massachusetts Press, 2009); Alexander Vazansky, *An Army in Crisis: Social Conflict and the U.S. Army in Germany, 1968–1975* (Lincoln: University of Nebraska Press, 2019), 161–227. On American drug policy, see Katherine J. Freydl, *The Drug Wars in America, 1940–1973* (New York: Cambridge University Press, 2013).

156. Morris J. Lucree to OSD (Manpower), Sub: Armed Forces Narcotics Activity, 23 May 1962, AGO 250.1, box 23, RG 407.

157. Peter Guralnick, *Careless Love: The Unmaking of Elvis Presley* (Boston: Little Brown and Company, 1999), 21; Glen A. Hill, "Control of Narcotic and Dangerous

Drug Abuse Among Army Troops Stationed in the Continental United States," SP AWC, 1970, AHEC. I am indebted to Dr. Fred Borch of the US Army Judge Advocate's School for his insights on drug use and military law.

158. Robert G. Gard, Jr., "The 'Other War' on Drugs, Alcohol," *Army* 22 (October 1972): 107–108.

159. William R. Porter, "The Problem of Drug Abuse in the Army," SP AWC, 1972, AHEC.

160. Andrew J. Bacevich, "A 'Grass Roots' Look at the Drug Problem," *Army* 22 (November 1972): 25–28. Ingraham, *Boys in the Barracks*, 8–10.

161. James M. Krebs, "New Directions for Army Alcohol and Drug Abuse Control," SP AWC, 1975, AHEC.

162. Gard, "'Other War.'" By June 1971 the Department of the Army avowed that the service was committed to a "compassionate" policy to detoxify and rehabilitate drug-dependent personnel and sponsored drug treatment centers at several bases; see *DOAHR FY 71*, 63.

163. William L. Schwartz, "Dealing with Drug, Alcohol Abuse: Good Vibes, Bad Vibes," *Army* 24 (May 1974): 29–34.

164. Michael S. Davison (untitled speech, Woodrow Wilson Center, 25 March 1972), box 5, Davison Papers.

165. Michael S. Davison (untitled speech, Heidelberg, Germany, 17 March, 1972), and "Remarks at Judge Advocates' Conference," Berchtesgaden, Germany, 4 May 1972, both in box 5, Davison Papers; Oral History, 5:11, Davison Papers, AHEC; Vazansky, *An Army in Crisis*, 183–227.

166. E. A. Lawrence, "The Alcohol Problem and What the Army Is Doing About It," *Army* 26 (August 1976): 25.

167. Oral History, 215, Frederic E. Davison Papers, AHEC. My views on army race policy is informed by Beth Bailey, *An Army Afire: How the US Army Confronted Its Racial Crisis in the Vietnam Era* (Chapel Hill: University of North Carolina Press, 2023).

168. Blair, Thompson, and Segal, *Race and Job Satisfaction*.

169. Albert N. Garland, "Military Justice Before the Bar," *Army* 22 (January 1972): 27–29. On Vietnam-era indiscipline, see *DOAHR FY 73*, 4–5. *DOAHR FY 71*, 64; George Lepre, *Fragging: Why U.S. Soldiers Assaulted Their Officers in Vietnam* (Lubbock: Texas Tech University Press, 2011); David Cortright, *Soldiers in Revolt: The American Military Today* (New York: Anchor Press, 1975).

170. Killebrew, "Volunteer Army," 21. For a response, see Joseph W. Sutton to Ed., *Army* 21 (June 1971): 4; AWC Study Leadership, CONARC Training to Lead Conference.

171. Stephen D. Turner, "New Army Has No Room for Duds," *Army* 23 (September 1973): 43. Donald M. Miller to Ed., *Army* 21 (June 1971): 4.

172. Stewart et al., "Leadership Tasks." David T. Bryant, "The 1969 Manual for Courts-Martial: A Guide for Commanders," SP AWC, 1968, AHEC.

173. "Only a Leader Can Command a Company," *Army* 21 (November 1971): 58–59.

174. Killebrew, "Where the Squad Leader Makes a Difference," 37.

175. *DOAHR FY 75*, 51; *DOAHR FY 76*, 49–50.

176. Emerson to All Commanders, Sub: Pro-Life Program. *1976 Annual Report: Comptroller General of the United States* (Washington, DC: GPO, 1977), 137.

177. Hearings Before the Senate Armed Services Committee, 25 February 1983, Meyer, *E. C. Meyer*, 146. "Pentagon Press Group," 13 June 1980, Meyer, *E. C. Meyer*, 98. On Meyer's intentions and the response, see Jones, *A "Hollow Army" Reappraised*.

178. Hearings Before the Senate Armed Services Committee, 25 February 1983, Meyer, *E. C. Meyer*, 366.

179. *Oral History of General John M. Shalikashvili*, 35, 2006, AHEC.

180. *DOAHR FY 80*, 118. Bernard Rostker, et al., *The Defense Officer Personnel Management Act of 1980: A Retrospective Assessment* (Santa Monica, CA: RAND, 1992); Thomas J. Horner, "Killers, Fillers, and Fodder," *Parameters* 12 (September 1982): 27–34: Powers, "The Volunteer Soldier."

Conclusion: The Aftermath Army in Perspective

1. In contrast to past practice, the Army War College does not keep transcripts of speeches. However, most of the speech at the AWC appears in Eric K. Shinseki, "Address to the Eisenhower Luncheon" (speech, 12 October 1999, 45th Annual Meeting of the Association of the US Army), box 85, Eric K. Shinseki Papers, AHEC. I am grateful to Michael Lynch for providing a copy of this document at the last moment.

2. For army analysis of the problems in implementing the Transformation Plan, see Robert D. Bradford III, "What Happened to FCS: An Organizational Change Case Study," 2011, AWC, DTIC; Mark T. Calhoun, "Complexity and Innovation: Army Transformation and the Reality of War," 2004, SAMS, CARL.

3. Michael Howard, "The Use and Abuse of Military History," *Parameters* 11 (1981): 10.

4. *The Man Who Shot Liberty Valance*, directed by John Ford (1962; Hollywood, CA: Paramount DVD, 2001). I am indebted to Brian Donlon for this allusion.

5. Scales, *Certain Victory*; Romjue, *The Army of Excellence*.

6. On traditional postwar "battle of the books" that followed Desert Storm, see Michael R. Gordon and Bernard E. Trainor, *The Generals' War: The Inside Story of the Conflict in the Gulf* (Boston: Little, Brown, 1995), 463–468.

7. For a useful summary of the debate over post–Cold War doctrine, see Davis II, *The Challenge of Adaptation*, 86–96.

8. On army downsizing, see David McCormick, *The Downsized Warrior: America's Army in Transition* (New York: New York University Press, 1998), esp. 63–116. For overviews, see Bart Brasher, *Implosion: Downsizing the U.S. Military, 1987–2015* (Westport, CT: Greenwood, 2000); Richard A. Lacquement, "Preaching After the Devil's Death: U.S. Post–Cold War Drawdown," in *Drawdown: the American Way of Postwar*, ed. James W. Warren (New York: New York University Press, 2016), 267–290.

9. General Accounting Office, *Military Downsizing: Balancing Accessions and Losses is Key to Shaping the Future Force* (1993), 25–38, DTIC.

10. Dennis R. Reimer, "Leadership for the 21st Century: Empowerment, Environment, and the Golden Rule," *MR* 76 (January–February 1997): 51; Gordon R.

Sullivan, *The Collected Works of the Thirty-Second Chief of Staff, United States Army, 1991–1995* (Washington, DC: Department of the Army, 1996), 452–455.

11. Robert Baumann, Lawrence Yates, and Versalle F. Washington, *My Clan Against the World: US and Coalition Forces in Somalia, 1992–1994* (Fort Leavenworth, KS: Combat Studies Institute, 2004); Mark F. Duffield, "Into the Beehive: The Somali Habr Gidr Clan as an Adaptive Enemy," 17 December 1999, SP, SAMS; Timothy M. Karcher, "Understanding the 'Victory Disease:' From the Little Bighorn, to Mogadishu, to the Future," 22 May 2003, SP, SAMS. For overviews, see David Halberstam, *War in Time of Peace: Bush, Clinton, and the Generals* (New York: Simon and Schuster, 2001); Richard Lock-Pullan, *U.S. Intervention Policy and Army Innovation: From Vietnam to Iraq* (New York: Routledge, 2006), 133–158; Dana Priest, *The Mission: Waging War and Keeping Peace with America's Military* (New York: W. W. Norton, 2003). On the Battle of Mogadishu, see Jonathan Carroll, "Courage Under Fire: Re-evaluating Black Hawk Down and the Battle of Mogadishu," *War in History* 29 (September 2022): 704–726.

12. Richard A. Lacquement, "The Casualty-Aversion Myth," *Naval War College Review* 57 (Winter 2004): 39–57; Morris T. Goins, "Does the Perception of Casualties Affect Military Operations in the 1990's," 31 December 1999, SP, SAMS; Timothy S. Mundy, "Casualty Aversion: Dispelling the Myth," 31 December 1999, SP, SAMS; Perry Rearick, "Force Protection and Mission Accomplishment in Bosnia and Herzegovina" (masters thesis, CGSC, 2001).

13. Floyd D. Spence, *Military Readiness 1997: Rhetoric and Reality*, 9 April 1997, DTIC.

14. Reimer, "Leadership for the 21st Century," 47.

15. David W. Burwell, "Morale as a Principle of War," 2000, SP SAMS; Steele, "Are the Relationships Between Junior and Senior Officers in the U.S. Army Officer Corps Dysfunctional?"; John Philip Scholesser, "Officer Trust in Army Leadership" (PhD diss., University of Oklahoma, 2003), 54.

16. Scholesser, 177–178.

17. Burwell, "Morale as a Principle of War"; Steele, "Are the Relationships Between Junior and Senior Officers in the U.S. Army Officer Corps Dysfunctional?"; Scholesser, "Officer Trust," 54.

18. William M. Donnelly, *Army Readiness Reporting Systems, 1945–2003* (Washington, DC: Center of Military History, 2018), 144–149.

19. *RSW WD 1911*, 11.

20. Thomas K. Adams, *The Army After Next: The First Postindustrial Army* (Stanford, CA: Stanford University Press, 2008); David Jablonsky, "Army Transformation: A Tale of Two Doctrines," *Parameters* 31 (Autumn 2001): 43–62: GAO, *Army Has a Comprehensive Plan for Managing Its Transformation but Faces Major Challenges* (November 2001).

21. For a sample of the "battle of the books," see Tommy Franks with Malcolm McConnell, *American Soldier* (New York: Regan Books, 2004); Fred Kaplan, *The Insurgents: David Petraeus and the Plot to Change the American Way of War* (New York: Simon and Schuster, 2013); Stanley McChrystal, *My Share of the Task: A Memoir* (New York: Portfolio/Penguin, 2013); Ricardo S. Sanchez with Donald T. Phillips, *Wiser in Battle: A Soldier's Story* (New York: HarperCollins, 2008). For an

insightful commentary on such memoirs, see Andrew J. Bacevich, "A Modern Major General," *New Left Review* 29 (September–October 2004): 123–134. On institutional histories and a recent release of documents, see Edmund J. Degen and Mark J. Reardon, *Modern War in an Ancient Land: The United States*, 2 vols. (Washington, DC: Center of Military History, 2021); Joel D. Rayburn and Frank K. Sobchak, eds., *The U.S. Army in the Iraq War*, 2 vols. (Carlisle, PA: US Army War College Press, 2019); Craig Whitlock, *The Afghanistan Papers: A Secret History of the War* (New York: Simon and Schuster, 2021).

22. *The U.S. Army in Multi-Domain Operations, 2028* (Fort Eustis, VA: TRADOC, 2020). For a provocative critique by an officer instrumental in the development of AirLand Battle, see Huba Wass de Czege, *Commentary on "The US Army in Multi-Domain Operations in 2028"* (Carlisle Barracks, PA: Strategic Studies Institute, 2020)

23. Matthew Cox, "Army Launches New 'Warriors Wanted' Campaign Aimed at Generation Z," 19 October 2018, *Military.Com*; Army bonuses from www.goarmy.com/benefits/money/bonuses-earning-extra-money.html; Drug Facts: Substance Abuse in the Military, 2019, at www.drugabuse.gov/publications/drugfacts/substance-use-in-military-life; Office of the Under Secretary of Defense, Personnel and Readiness, *Population Representation in the Military Services, 2019*, at cna.org/pop-rep/2019/contents; James V. Marrone et al., *Organizational and Cultural Causes of Army First-Term Attrition* (Santa Monica, CA: RAND, 2021); Miriam Matthew et al., *Organizational Characteristics Associated with the Risk of Sexual Harassment in the U.S Army* (Santa Monica, CA: RAND, 2021).

24. Charles A. Henning, *Army Officer Shortages: Background and Issues for Congress* (Washington, DC: Congressional Research Service, July 2006). Thomas D. Koh, "Army Officer Retention: How to Retain the Best and Brightest" (masters thesis, John Hopkins University, 2018); Michael J. Slocum, "Maintaining the Edge: A Look At Army Officer Retention," SP AWC, 2012.

25. 20 October 1929, Diary, box 5, William Lassiter Papers, USMAL. Brian McAllister Linn, "The U.S. Army's Postwar Recoveries," *Parameters* (Autumn 2016): 13–22.

26. Matthew B. Ridgway as told to Harold H. Martin, *Soldier: The Memoirs of Matthew B. Ridgway* (New York: Harper & Brothers, 1956), 286.

Bibliography

Archival Collections

National Archives Record Groups
    RG 94   Records of the Adjutant General's Office, 1780–1917
    RG 107   Records of the Office of the Secretary of War
    RG 153   Records of the Office of the Judge Advocate General (Army)
    RG 159   Records of the Office of Inspector General
    RG 218   Records of the US Joint Chiefs of Staff
    RG 319   Records of the Army Staff
    RG 331   Records of Allied Operational and Occupation Headquarters, WW2
    RG 337   Records of Headquarters Army Ground Forces
    RG 338   Records of US Army Operational, Tactical, and Support Organizations
    RG 389   Records of the Provost Marshal General
    RG 407   Records of Adjutant General's Office
    RG 546   Records of US Army Continental Army Command
    RG 547   Records of US Army Forces in Alaska
    RG 548   Records of US Army Forces in the Caribbean
    RG 549   Records of US Army Europe
    RG 550   Records of US Army Pacific
    RG 551   Records of US Army Military District of Washington
CONARC/TRADOC Archives, Fort Eustis, VA
Duke University Library, Special Collections, Durham, NC
    Robert L. Eichelberger Papers
Dwight D. Eisenhower Library, Abilene, KS
    Joseph Lawton Collins Papers
    Lauris Norstad Papers
Hoover Institute Archives, Stanford University, Palo Alto, CA
    John C. H. Lee Papers
Ike Skelton Combined Arms Research Digital Library, Fort Leavenworth, KS
    Command and General Staff College Student Papers
    Command and General Staff School Student Papers
    Paul Gorman Papers
    Obsolete Military Manuals Collection
    School of Advanced Military Studies Monographs
Library of Congress Manuscripts Division
    Henry T. Allen Papers
    Tasker Bliss Papers

Robert L. Bullard Papers
William H. Carter Papers
Henry C. Corbin Papers
James G. Harbord Papers
John L. Hines Papers
William Mitchell Papers
George Van Horn Mosely Papers
George S. Patton Papers
John J. Pershing Papers
Charles P. Summerall Papers
Leonard Wood Papers
Maneuver Center of Excellence Libraries, Donovan Research Library,
    Fort Benning, GA
George C. Marshall Library, Virginia Military Institute, Lexington, VA
    James A. Van Fleet Papers
New York Public Library, Rare Books and Manuscript Division, NY
    Francis V. Greene Papers
South Carolina Historical Society, Charleston, SC
    Johnson Hagood Papers
Southern Historical Collections, University of North Carolina, Chapel Hill, NC
    Frank Parker Papers
Special Collections, US Military Academy Library, West Point, NY
    Frank William Gilbreath Papers
    Guy V. Henry Papers
    Campbell B. Hodges Papers
    William Lassiter Papers
    John Henry Parker Papers
    Charles D. Rhodes Papers
    Eben Swift Papers
    William C. Westmoreland Papers
    Cornelis de Witt Willcox Papers
Tropic Lightning (25th Infantry Division) Museum, Schofield Barracks, HI
    Annual Historical Supplement, 25th Division, 1974
    Tropic Lightning News
US Army Heritage and Educational Center, Carlisle, PA (AHEC)
    Paul D. Adams Papers
    Edward M. Almond Papers
    John C. Arrowsmith Papers
    Sidney B. Berry Papers
    Tasker H. Bliss Papers
    William E. Carraway Papers
    Bradford G. Chynoweth Papers, AHEC
    Arthur S. Collins Papers
    Willis Crittenberger Papers
    Benjamin O. Davis, Sr. Papers
    Frederic E. Davison Papers
    Michael S. Davison Papers, AHEC

George H. Decker Papers
Hugh A. Drum Papers
Henry E. Emerson Papers
Evelyn P. Foote Papers
Eugene P. Forrester Papers
George I. Forsythe Papers
James M. Gavin Papers
Eli Helmick Papers
Charles F. Ivins Papers
Walter T. Kerwin Papers
Thomas P. Lynch Papers
William J. McCaffrey Papers
Louis E. Menetrey Papers
Herbert B. Powell Papers
William R. Richardson Papers
 Matthew B. Ridgway Papers
Donald A. Seibert Papers
Winant Sidle Papers
Richard G. Stilwell Papers
Maxwell Thurman Papers
James B. Vaught Papers
Louis C. Wagner, Jr., Papers
Orlando Ward Papers
Briant H. Wells Papers
Frederick C. Weyand Papers
Wisconsin Historical Society, Madison, WI
 William G. Haan Papers

Published Government Documents

Department of the Army Historical Reports
Annual Reports of the Secretary of the Army
Reports of the Secretary of War
The New American State Papers, Naval Affairs. 7 vols. Edited by K. Jack Bauer.
 Wilmington, DE: Scholarly Resources, 1981.

Service Publications

Army
Army and Navy Journal
Cavalry Journal
Field Artillery Journal
Infantry Journal
Journal of the Military Service Institute of the United States
Journal of the United States Artillery (Coast Artillery Journal)

Books

Abrahamson, James L. *America Arms for a New Century: The Making of a Great Military Power*. New York: Free Press, 1981.

Adams, Kevin. *Class and Race in the Frontier Army: Military Life in the West, 1870–1890*. Norman: University of Oklahoma Press, 2009.

Adams, Thomas K. *The Army After Next: The First Postindustrial Army*. Stanford, CA: Stanford University Press, 2008.

Armstrong, David A. *Bullets and Bureaucrats: The Machine Gun and the United States Army, 1861–1916*. Westport, CT: Praeger, 1982.

Bailey, Beth. *America's Army: Making the All-Volunteer Force*. Cambridge, MA: Harvard University Press, 2009.

Bailey, Beth. *An Army Afire: How the US Army Confronted Its Racial Crisis in the Vietnam Era*. Chapel Hill: University of North Carolina Press, 2023.

Ball, Durwood. *Army Regulars on the Western Frontier, 1848–1861*. Norman: University of Oklahoma Press, 2001.

Barbeau, Arthur, and Florette Henri. *The Unknown Soldiers: Black American Troops in World War I*. 1974, New York: De Capo Press, 1996.

Barr, Ronald J. *The Progressive Army: US Army Command and Administration, 1870–1914*. New York: St. Martin's Press, 1998.

Bassford, Christopher. *The Spit-Shine Syndrome: Organizational Irrationality in the American Field Army*. Westport, CT: Praeger, 1988.

Bauer, K. Jack. *The Mexican War, 1846–1848*. Originally published 1974. Reprint, Lincoln: University of Nebraska Press, 1992.

Bauer, K. Jack. *Zachary Taylor: Soldiers, Planter, Statesman of the Old Southwest*. Baton Rouge: Louisiana State University Press, 1985.

Betros, Lance. *Carved from Granite: West Point Since 1902*. College Station: Texas A&M University Press, 2012.

Bigelow, John. *Reminisces of the Santiago Campaign*. New York: Harper & Brothers, 1899.

Blackwell, James A. *On Brave Old Army Team: The Cheating Scandal That Rocked the Nation: West Point, 1951*. Novato, CA: Presidio Press, 1996.

Boettcher, Thomas D. *First Call: The Making of the Modern U.S. Military, 1945–1953*. Boston: Little, Brown, 1992.

Bonura, Michael A. *Under the Shadow of Napoleon: French Influence on the American Way of Warfare from the War of 1812 to the Outbreak of WWII*. New York: New York University Press, 2012.

Booth, T. Michael, and Duncan Spencer. *Paratrooper: The Life of General James M. Gavin*. New York: Simon & Schuster, 1994.

Bourke, John G. *On the Border with Crook*. Originally published 1891. Reprint, Lincoln: University of Nebraska Press, 1971.

Bradford, Zeb B., and Frederic J. Brown. *America's Army in Transition*. Beverly Hills, CA: Sage, 1973.

Bradley, Omar. *A Soldier's Story*. New York: Henry Holt, 1951.

Bradley, Omar N., and Clay Blair. *A General's Life*. New York: Simon and Schuster, 1983.

Brasher, Bart. *Implosion: Downsizing the U.S. Military, 1987–2015*. Westport, CT: Greenwood, 2000.

Brereton, T. R. *Educating the U.S. Army: Arthur L. Wagner and Reform, 1875–1905*. Lincoln: University of Nebraska Press, 2000.

Browning, Robert S., III. *Two if by Sea: The Development of American Coastal Defense Policy*. Westport, CT: Greenwood Press, 1983.

Builder, Carl H. *The Masks of War: American Military Style in Strategy and Analysis*. Baltimore: Johns Hopkins University Press, 1989.

Byers, Andrew. *The Sexual Economy of War: Discipline and Desire in the U.S. Army*. Ithaca: Cornell University Press, 2019.

Carruthers, Susan L. *The Good Occupation: American Soldiers and the Hazards of Peace*. Cambridge, MA: Harvard University Press, 2016.

Carter, Robert G. *The Art and Science of War Versus the Art of Fighting*. Washington, DC: National Publishing Co., 1922.

Chandler, Melbourne C. *Of Garryowen in Glory: The History of the Seventh United States Cavalry Regiment*. Annandale, VA: Turnpike Press, 1960.

Christian, Garna L. *Black Soldiers in Jim Crow Texas, 1899–1917*. College Station: Texas A&M Press, 1995.

Cirillo, Vincent. *Bullets and Bacilli: The Spanish American War and Military Medicine*. New Brunswick, NJ: Rutgers University Press, 2004.

Clark, J. P. *Preparing for War: The Emergence of the Modern U.S. Army, 1815–1917*. Cambridge, MA: Harvard University Press, 2017.

Clary, David A. *Fortress America: The Corps of Engineers, Hampton Roads, and United States Coastal Defense*. Charlottesville: University Press of Virginia, 1990.

Clendenen, Clarence C. *Blood on the Border: The United States Army and the Mexican Irregulars*. London: Macmillan Company, 1969.

Clifford, John Gary. *The Citizen Soldiers: The Plattsburg Training Camp Movement, 1913–1920*. Lexington: University Press of Kentucky, 1972.

Coffman, Edward M. *The Hilt of the Sword: The Career of Peyton C. March*. Madison: University of Wisconsin Press, 1966.

Coffman, Edward M. *The Old Army: A Portrait of the American Army in Peacetime, 1784–1898*. New York: Oxford University Press, 1986.

Coffman, Edward M. *The Regulars: The American Army, 1898–1941*. Cambridge, MA: Harvard University Press, 2004.

Coffman, Edward M. *The War to End All Wars: The American Military Experience in World War I*. Originally published 1968. Reprint, Lexington: University Press of Kentucky, 1998.

Coles, Harry. *The War of 1812*. Chicago: University of Chicago Press, 1965.

Collins, Arthur S., Jr. *Common Sense Training: A Working Philosophy for Leaders*. Originally published 1978. Reprint, Novato, CA: Presidio Press, 1998.

Collins, J. Lawton. *Lightning Joe: An Autobiography*. Baton Rouge: Louisiana State University Press, 1979.

Connelly, Donald B. *John M. Schofield and the Politics of Generalship*. Chapel Hill: University of North Carolina Press, 2006.

Cooke, James J. *Billy Mitchell*. Boulder: Lynn Rienner, 2002.

Cooke, James J. *Pershing and his Generals: Command and Staff in the AEF*. Westport, CT: Praeger, 1997.

Cooper, Jerry C. *The Rise of the National Guard: The Evolution of the American Militia, 1865–1920*. Lincoln: University of Nebraska Press, 1997.

Cooper, Jerry M. *The Army and Civil Disorder: Federal Military Intervention in Labor Disputes, 1877–1900*. Westport, CT: Greenwood Press, 1980.

Cortright, David. *Soldiers in Revolt: The American Military Today*. New York: Anchor Press, 1975.

Cosmas, Graham A. *An Army for Empire: The United States Army in the Spanish-American War*. Rev. ed. College Station: Texas A&M Press, 1994.

Crackel, Theodore J. *Mr. Jefferson's Army: Political and Social Reform of the Military Establishment, 1801–1809*. New York: New York University Press, 1989.

Cress, Lawrence D. *Citizens in Arms: The Army and the Militia in American Society to the War of 1812*. Chapel Hill: University of North Carolina Press, 1982.

Daddis, Gregory A. *Westmoreland's War: Reassessing American Strategy in Vietnam*. New York: Oxford University Press, 2014.

Dawson, Joseph G. *Army Generals and Reconstruction: Louisiana, 1862 to 1877*. Baton Rouge: Louisiana State University Press, 1982.

DeRosa, Christopher S. *Political Indoctrination in the U.S. Army from World War II to the Vietnam War*. Lincoln: University of Nebraska Press, 2006.

D'Este, Carlo. *Eisenhower: A Soldier's Life*. New York: Henry Holt, 2002.

Deutruch, Mabel E. *Struggle for Supremacy: The Career of General Fred C. Ainsworth*. New York: Public Affairs Press, 1962.

Dobak, William A. and Thomas D. Phillips. *The Black Regulars, 1866–1898*. Norman: University of Oklahoma Press, 2001.

Donnelly, William M. *Under Orders: The Army National Guard During the Korean War* College Station: Texas A&M University Press, 2001.

Eisenhower, Dwight D. *Crusade in Europe*. New York: Doubleday, 1948.

Eisenhower, John D. *Teddy Roosevelt and Leonard Wood: Partners in Command*. Columbia: University of Missouri Press, 2014.

Ellis, Joseph J., and Robert Moore. *School for Soldiers: West Point and the Profession of Arms*. New York: Oxford University Press, 1974.

Faulkner, Richard S. *Pershing's Crusaders: The American Soldier in World War I*. Lawrence: University Press of Kansas, 2017.

Fitzgerald, David. *Learning to Forget: US Army Counterinsurgency and Practice from Vietnam to Iraq*. Stanford, CA: Stanford University Press, 2013.

Fitzpatrick, David John. *Emory Upton: Misunderstood Reformer*. Norman: University of Oklahoma Press, 2017.

Fletcher, Marvin. *The Black Soldier and Officer in the United States Army, 1891–1917*. Columbia: University of Missouri Press, 1974.

Flynn, George Q. *The Draft, 1940–1973*. Lawrence: University Press of Kansas, 1993.

Fontenot, Gregory. *The 1st Infantry Division and the US Army Transformed: Road to Victory in Desert Storm, 1970–1991*. Columbia: University of Missouri Press, 2017.

Foote, Lorien. *The Gentlemen and the Roughs: Violence, Honor, and Manhood in the Union Army*. New York: New York University Press, 2010.

Fox, Aimée. *Learning to Fight: Military Innovation and Change in the British Army, 1914–1918*. New York: Cambridge University Press, 2018.

Franks, Tommy, with Malcolm McConnell. *American Soldier*. New York: Regan Books, 2004.

Freydl, Katherine J. *The Drug Wars in America, 1940–1973*. New York: Cambridge University Press, 2013.

Galloway, K. Bruce, and Robert B. Johnson II. *West Point: America's Power Fraternity*. New York: Simon & Schuster, 1973.

Galvin, John R. *Fighting the Cold War: A Soldier's Memoir*. Lexington: University Press of Kentucky, 2015.

Gannon, Barbara A. *The Won Cause: Black and White Comradeship in the Grand Army of the Republic*. Chapel Hill: University of North Carolina Press, 2011.

Ganoe, William A. *The History of the United States Army*. New York: D. Appleton-Century Co., 1942.

Gatzemeyer, Garrett. *Bodies for Battle: U.S. Army Physical Culture and Systematic Training, 1885–1957*. Lawrence: University Press of Kansas, 2021.

Gavin, James M. *War and Peace in the Space Age*. New York: Harper & Brothers, 1958.

Gimbel, John. *The American Occupation of Germany: Politics and the Military, 1945–1949*. Stanford, CA: Stanford University Press, 1968.

Goldman, William. *Soldier in the Rain*. New York: Dell, 1960.

Gole, Henry G. *General William E. DuPuy: Preparing the Army for Modern War*. Lexington: University Press of Kentucky, 2008.

Gole, Henry G. *The Road to Rainbow: Army Planning for Global War, 1931–1940*. Annapolis, MD: Naval Institute Press, 2003.

Gole, Henry G. *Soldiering: Observations from Korea, Vietnam, and Safe Places*. Lincoln, NE: Potomac Books, 2005.

Gordon, Michael R., and Bernard E. Trainor. *The Generals' War: The Inside Story of the Conflict in the Gulf*. Boston: Little, Brown, 1995.

Gray, Colin. *Strategy for Chaos: Revolutions in Military Affairs and the Evidence of History*. Portland, OR: Frank Cass, 2002.

Green, Michael Cullen. *Black Yanks in the Pacific: Race in the Making of American Military Empire After World War II*. Ithaca: Cornell University Press, 2010.

Griffith, Robert K., Jr. *Men Wanted for the U.S. Army: America's Experience with an All-Volunteer Army Between the World Wars*. Westport, CT: Greenwood Press, 1982.

Groteleuschen, Mark E. *The AEF Way of War: The American Army and Ground Combat*. New York: Cambridge University Press, 2006.

Guardia, Mike. *Crusader: General Donn Starry and the Army of his Times*. Haverton, PA: Casemate, 2018.

Guralnick, Peter. *Careless Love: The Unmaking of Elvis Presley*. Boston: Little Brown and Company, 1999.

Hadley, Arthur T. *The Straw Giant: Triumph and Failure: America's Armed Forces* New York: Random House, 1986.

Halberstam, David. *War in Time of Peace: Bush, Clinton, and the Generals*. New York: Simon & Schuster, 2001.

Hall, John W. *Uncommon Defense: Indian Allies in the Black Hawk War*. Cambridge, MA: Harvard University Press, 2009.

Halleck, Henry W. *Elements of Military Arts and Science and Engineers; or, Course of Instruction in Strategy, Fortification, Tactics of Battles, etc.; Embracing the Duties of Staff, Infantry, Cavalry, Artillery, and Engineers.* Orig. pub. 1846. Rept. Westport, CT: Greenwood Press, 1971.

Hanson, Thomas E. *Combat Ready? The Eighth U.S. Army on the Eve of the Korean War.* College Station: Texas A&M University Press. 2010.

Hauser, Mark T. "'A Violent Desire for the Amusements': Boxing, Libraries, and the Distribution and Management of Welfare During the First World War." *Journal of Military History* 86 (October 2022): 833–913.

Hauser, William L. *America's Army in Crisis: A Study of Civil-Military Relations.* Baltimore: Johns Hopkins University Press, 1973.

Hazen, William B. *The School and the Army in Germany and France, with a Diary of Siege Life at Versailles.* New York: Harper and Brothers, 1872.

Heitman, Francis B. *Historical Register and Dictionary of the United States Army.* Vol. 1. Orig publ. 1903. Reprint, Urbana: University of Illinois Press, 1963.

Hemphill, W. Edwin. *The Papers of John C. Calhoun.* Vol. 5, *1820–1821.* Columbia: University of South Carolina Press, 1971.

Herrera, Ricardo A. *For Liberty and the Republic: The American Citizen as Soldier, 1775–1861.* New York: New York University Press, 2015.

Hersey, John. *A Bell for Adano.* New York: Albert Knopf, 1944.

Hickey, Donald. *The War of 1812: A Forgotten Conflict.* Urbana: University of Illinois Press, 1989.

Hitchcock, Ethan Allen. *Fifty Years in Camp and Field.* Originally published 1909. Reprint, Freeport, NY: Books for Libraries Press, 1971.

Holley, I. B. *General John M. Palmer, Citizen Soldiers, and the Army of a Democracy.* Westport: Greenwood Press, 1982.

Holman, Hamilton. *Zachary Taylor.* Vol. 1. Indianapolis, IN: Bobbs-Merrill, 1941.

Hope, Ian C. *A Scientific Way of War: Antebellum Military Science, West Point, and the Origins of American Military Thought.* Lincoln: University of Nebraska Press, 2015.

House, John M. *Wolfhounds and Polar Bears: The American Expeditionary Force in Siberia, 1918–1920.* Tuscaloosa: University of Alabama Press, 2016.

Hsieh, Wayne W. *West Pointers and the Civil War: The Old Army in War and Peace.* Chapel Hill: University of North Carolina Press, 2009.

Huebner, Andrew J. *The Warrior Image: Soldiers in American Culture from the Second World War to Vietnam.* Chapel Hill: University of North Carolina Press, 2008.

Hunt, Edward B. *Modern Warfare: Its Science and Art.* New Haven: T. J. Stafford, 1860.

Hunt, Frazier. *MacArthur and the War Against Japan.* New York: Charles Scribner's, 1944.

Huntington, Samuel P. *The Soldier and the State: The Theory and Politics of Civil-Military Relations.* New York: Vintage Books, 1957.

Hutchinson, Hazel. *The War That Used Up Words: American Writers and the First World War.* New Haven, CT: Yale University Press, 2015.

Hutton, Paul Andrew. *Phil Sheridan and His Army.* Lincoln: University of Nebraska Press, 1985.

Ingraham, Larry H. *The Boys in the Barracks: Observations on American Military Life.* Philadelphia: Institute for the Study of Human Issues, 1984.

James, D. Clayton. *The Years of MacArthur*. Vol. 1, *1880–1941*. Boston: Houghton Mifflin, 1970.

Janda, Lance. *Stronger Than Custom: West Point and the Admission of Women*. Westport, CT: Praeger, 2002.

Jensen, Joan M. *Army Surveillance in America, 1775–1980*. New Haven: Yale University Press, 1991.

Johnson, David E. *Fast Tanks and Heavy Bombers: Innovation in the U.S. Army, 1917–1945*. Ithaca: Cornell University Press, 1998.

Johnson, Haynes, and George C. Wilson. *Army in Anguish*. New York: Pocket Books, 1972.

Johnson, Timothy D. *A Gallant Little Army: The Mexico City Campaign*. Lawrence: University Press of Kansas, 2007.

Johnson, Timothy D. *Winfield Scott: The Quest for Military Glory*. Lawrence: University Press of Kansas, 2006.

Just, Ward. *Military Men*. New York: Alfred A. Knopf, 1970.

Kaplan, Fred. *The Insurgents: David Petraeus and the Plot to Change the American Way of War*. New York: Simon & Schuster, 2013.

Kaufman, J. E., and H. W. Kaufman. *The Sleeping Giant: American Armed Forces Between the Wars*. Westfield, CT: Praeger, 1996.

Keene, Jennifer D. *Doughboys, the Great War, and the Remaking of America*. Baltimore: Johns Hopkins University Press, 2001.

King, Edward L., *The Death of the Army: A Pre-Mortem*. New York: Saturday Review Press, 1972.

Kitfield, James. *Prodigal Soldiers: How the Generation of Officers Born of Vietnam Revolutionized the American Style of War*. Washington, DC: Brassey's, 1995.

Knox, Macgregor, and Williamson Murray. *The Dynamics of Military Revolution, 1300–2050*. New York: Cambridge University Press, 2001.

Kohn, Richard H. *Eagle and Sword: The Beginnings of the Military Establishment in America*. New York: Free Press, 1975.

Krepinevich, Andrew F., Jr. *The Army and Vietnam*. Baltimore: Johns Hopkins University Press, 1986.

Kretchik, Walter E. *U.S. Army Doctrine: From the American Revolution to the War on Terror*. Lawrence: University Press of Kansas, 2011.

Kuzmarov, Jeremy. *The Myth of the Addicted Army: Vietnam and the Modern War on Drugs*. Amherst: University of Massachusetts Press, 2009.

Lair, Meredith H. *Armed with Abundance: Consumerism and Soldiering in the Vietnam War*. Chapel Hill: University of North Carolina Press, 2011.

Lane, Jack C. *Armed Progressive: General Leonard Wood*. San Rafael, CA: Presidio Press, 1978.

Lang, Andrew. *In the Wake of War: Military Occupation, Emancipation, and Civil War America*. Baton Rouge: Louisiana State University Press, 2017.

Lanning, Michael Lee. *The Battles of Peace*. New York: Ivy Books, 1992.

Leiker, James N. *Racial Borders: Black Soldiers Along the Rio Grande*. College Station: Texas A&M University Press, 2002.

Lembcke, Jerry. *The Spitting Image: Myth, Memory, and the Legacy of Vietnam*. New York: New York University Press, 1998.

Lemza, John W. *The Big Picture: The Cold War on the Small Screen*. Lawrence: University Press of Kansas, 2021.

Lepre, George. *Fragging: Why U.S. Soldiers Assaulted Their Officers in Vietnam*. Lubbock: Texas Tech University Press, 2011.

Lewy, Guenter. *America in Vietnam*. New York: Oxford University Press, 1978.

Liggett, Hunter. *A.E.F: Ten Years Ago in France*. New York: Dodd, Mead and Co., 1928.

Linn, Brian McAllister. *The Echo of Battle: The Army's Way of War*. Cambridge, MA: Harvard University Press, 2007.

Linn, Brian McAllister. *Elvis's Army: Cold War GI's and the Atomic Battlefield*. Cambridge, MA: Harvard University Press, 2016.

Linn, Brian McAllister. *Guardians of Empire: The U.S. Army and the Pacific, 1902–1940*. Chapel Hill: University of North Carolina Press, 1997.

Lock-Pullan, Richard. *U.S. Intervention Policy and Army Innovation: From Vietnam to Iraq*. New York: Routledge, 2006.

Mahler, Michael D. *Tales from the Cold War: The U.S. Army in West Germany, 1960–1975*. Dahlonega: University of North Georgia Press, 2021.

Markel, M. Wade, et al. *The Evolution of U.S. Military Policy from the Constitution to the Present*. Vol. 4, *The Total Force Policy Era, 1970–2015*. Santa Monica, CA: RAND, 2020.

Mauldin, Bill. *Up Front*. New York: Henry Holt, 1945.

McCallum, Jack. *Leonard Wood: Rough Rider, Surgeon, Architect of American Imperialism*. New York: New York University Press, 2006.

McChristian, Douglas C. *Regular Army O! Soldiering on the Western Frontier, 1865–1891*. Norman: University of Oklahoma Press, 2017.

McChrystal, Stanley. *My Share of the Task: A Memoir*. New York: Portfolio/Penguin, 2013.

McCormick, David. *The Downsized Warrior: America's Army in Transition*. New York: New York University Press, 1998.

McCoy, Alfred W. *Policing America's Empire: The United States, the Philippines, and the Rise of the Surveillance State*. Madison: University of Wisconsin Press, 2009.

McDonough, James R. *Platoon Leader: A Memoir of Command in Combat*. New York: Random House, 1985.

Meigs, Mark. *Optimism at Armageddon: Voices of American Participants in the First World War*. New York: New York University Press, 1997.

Milam, Ron. *Not a Gentleman's War: An Inside View of Junior Officers in the Vietnam War*. Chapel Hill: University of North Carolina Press, 2009.

Millett, Allan R. *The War for Korea, 1950–1951: They Came from the North*. Lawrence: University Press of Kansas, 2011.

Millett, Allan R., Peter Maslowski, and William Feis. *For the Common Defense: A Military History of the United States of America, 1607–2012*, 3rd ed. New York: Free Press, 2012.

Millis, Walter, ed. *American Military Thought*. Indianapolis: Bobbs-Merril Co., 1962.

Moore, Jamie W. *The Fortifications Board 1816–1828 and the Definition of National Security*. Charleston, SC: Citadel Press, 1981.

Morrison, James L. *"The Best School in the World": West Point, the Pre-Civil War Years, 1833–1866*. Kent, OH: Kent State University Press, 1986.

Moskos, Charles C. *The American Enlisted Man: The Rank and File in Today's Military*. New York: Russell Sage Foundation, 1970.

Moskos, Charles C., and John Sibley Butler. *All That We Can Be: Black Leadership and Racial Integration the Army Way*. New York: Basic Books, 1996.

Moten, Matthew. *The Delafield Commission and the American Military Profession*. College Station: Texas A&M University Press, 2000.

Murphy, Audie. *To Hell and Back*. New York: Henry Holt, 1949.

Murray, Williamson, and Allan R. Millett, eds. *Military Innovation in the Interwar Period*. Originally published 1988. Reprint, New York: Cambridge University Press, 1996.

Muth, Jörg. *Command Culture: Officer Education in the U.S. Army and the German Armed Forces, 1901–1940, and the Consequences for World War II*. Denton: University of North Texas Press, 2011.

Nalty, Bernard C. *Strength for the Fight: A History of Black Americans in the Military*. New York: Free Press, 1986.

Neiberg, Michael S. *Making Citizen Soldiers: ROTC and the Ideology of American Military Service*. Cambridge: Harvard University Press, 2000.

Nenninger, Timothy K. *The Leavenworth Schools and the Old Army: Education, Professionalism, and the Officer Corps of the United States Army, 1881–1918*. Westport, CT: Greenwood Press, 1978.

Nevins, Jess. *The Encyclopedia of Pulp Heroes*. Amazon Digital Services, 2017.

Nowowiejski, Dean A. *The American Army in Germany, 1918–1923: Success against the Odds*. Lawrence: University Press of Kansas, 2021.

Odom, William O. *After the Trenches: The Transformation of US Army Doctrine, 1918–1939*. College Station: Texas A&M University Press, 1999.

Olds, Robin, Christina Olds, and Ed Rasimus. *Fighter Pilot: The Memoirs of Legendary Ace Robin Olds*. New York: St. Martin's Press, 2010.

Oyos, Mathew. *In Command: Theodore Roosevelt and the American Military*. Lincoln, NE: Potomac Books, 2018.

Parker, James. *The Old Army: Memories, 1872–1918*. Philadelphia: Dorrance, 1929.

Paxson, Frederic Logan. *The Great Demobilization and Other Essays*. Madison: University of Wisconsin Press, 1941.

Pegler, Martin. *U.S. Cavalryman, 1865–1890*. London: Osprey, 1993.

Pencak, William. *For God and Country: The American Legion, 1919–1941*. Boston: Northeastern University Press, 1989.

Pershing, John J. *My Experiences in the World War*, 2 vols. Originally published 1931. Reprint, Blue Ridge Summit, PA: TAB Books, 1989.

Peskin, Allan. *Winfield Scott and the Profession of Arms*. Kent, OH: Kent State University Press, 2003.

Pinheiro, John C. *Manifest Ambition: James K. Polk and Civil-Military Relations During the Mexican War*. Westport, CT: Praeger Security International, 2007.

Pogue, Forrest C. *George C. Marshall: Education of a General, 1880–1939*. New York: Viking Press, 1963.

Posen, Barry. *The Sources of Military Innovation: France, Britain, and Germany Between the Two World Wars*. Ithaca: Cornell University Press, 1984.

Powell, Colin, with Joe E. Persic. *My American Journey: An Autobiography*. New York: Random House, 1995.

Priest, Dana. *The Mission: Waging War and Keeping Peace with America's Military*. New York: W. W. Norton, 2003.

Prucha, Francis Paul. *Broadax and Bayonet: The Role of the United States Army in the Development of the Northwest, 1815–1860*. Originally published 1953. Reprint, Lincoln: University of Nebraska Press, 1995.

Prucha, Francis Paul. *The Sword of the Republic: The United States Army on the Frontier, 1783–1846*. Bloomington: Indiana University Press, 1977.

Pyle, Ernie. *Brave Men*. New York: Henry Holt, 1944.

Reardon, Carol. *Soldiers and Scholars: The U.S. Army and the Uses of Military History, 1865–1920*. Lawrence: University Press of Kansas, 1990.

Reinhardt, George C., and W. R. Kintner. *Atomic Weapons in Land Combat*. Harrisburg, PA: Military Service Pub., 1953.

Rickey, Don Jr. *Forty Miles a Day on Beans and Hay: The Enlisted Soldier Fighting the Indian Wars*. Norman: University of Oklahoma Press, 1963.

Ridgway, Matthew B. *The Korean War*. Garden City, NY: Doubleday, 1967.

Ridgway, Matthew B., and Harold H. Martin. *Soldier: The Memoirs of Matthew B. Ridgway*. New York: Harper & Brothers, 1956.

Robinson, Charles M. *General Crook and the Western Frontier*. Norman: University of Oklahoma Press, 2001.

Roosevelt, Theodore Jr. *Average Americans*. New York: G.P. Putnam's Sons, 1919.

Rosen, Stephen P. *Winning the Next War: Innovation and the Modern Military*. Ithaca: Cornell University Press, 1991.

Ross, Stephen T. *American War Plans, 1890–1945*. Portland, OR: Frank Cass, 2002.

Ross, Stephen T. *American War Plans, 1945–1950*. Portland, OR: Frank Cass, 1996.

Roth, Tanya L. *Her Cold War: Women in the U.S. Military, 1945–1980*. Chapel Hill: University of North Carolina Press, 2020.

Rutenberg, Amy J. *Rough Draft: Cold War Military and Manpower Policy and the Origins of the Vietnam-Era Draft Resistance*. Ithaca: Cornell University Press, 2019.

Sanchez, Ricardo S., with Donald T. Phillips, *Wiser in Battle: A Soldier's Story*. New York: HarperCollins, 2008.

Santoli, Al. *Leading the Way: How Vietnam Veterans Rebuilt the U.S. Military: An Oral History*. New York: Ballantine, 1994.

Schifferle, Peter J. *America's School for War: Fort Leavenworth, Officer Education, and Victory in World War II*. Lawrence: University Press of Kansas, 2010.

Sefton, James E. *The United States Army and Reconstruction, 1865–1877*. Baton Rouge: Louisiana State University Press, 1967.

Severo, Richard, and Lewis Milford. *The Wages of War: When America's Soldiers Came Home—From Valley Force to Vietnam*. New York: Simon & Schuster, 1989.

Silbey, David J. *A War of Frontier and Empire: The Philippine-American War, 1899–1902*. New York: Hill and Wang, 2007.

Silver, James W. *Edmund Pendleton Gaines: Frontier General*. Baton Rouge: Louisiana State University Press, 1949.

Skelton, William B. *An American Profession of Arms: The Army Officer Corps, 1784–1861*. Lawrence: University Press of Kansas, 1992.

Smythe, Donald. *Guerrilla Warrior: The Early Life of John J. Pershing*. New York: Scribner's Sons, 1973.

Smythe, Donald. *Pershing: General of the Armies*. Bloomington: Indiana University Press, 1983.

Sneider, Vern J. *The Teahouse of the August Moon*. New York: Putnam, 1951.

Sorley, Lewis. *Honorable Warrior: General Harold K. Johnson and the Ethics of Command*. Lawrence: University Press of Kansas, 1998.

Sorley, Lewis. *Thunderbolt: General Creighton Abrams and the Army of His Times*. 1992, Bloomington: Indiana University Press, 2008.

Spaulding, Oliver L. *The U.S. Army in War and Peace*. New York: G. P. Putnam's Sons, 1937.

Sterling, Brent L. *Other People's Wars: The US Military and the Challenge of Learning from Foreign Conflicts*. Washington, DC: Georgetown University Press, 2021.

Summerall, Charles Pelot. *The Way of Duty, Honor, Country: The Memoir of General Charles P. Summerall*. Edited by Timothy K. Nenninger. Lexington: University Press of Kentucky, 2010.

Talbert, Roy Jr. *Negative Intelligence: The Army and the American Left, 1917–1940*. Jackson: University of Mississippi Press, 1991.

Taylor, John M. *General Maxwell Taylor: The Sword and the Pen*. New York: Doubleday, 1989.

Taylor, William. *Every Citizen a Soldier: The Campaign for Universal Military Training After World War II*. College Station: Texas A&M University Press, 2014.

Trask, David F. *The AEF and Coalition Warmaking, 1917–1918*. Lawrence: University Press of Kansas, 1993.

Trask, David F. *The War with Spain in 1898*. New York: Macmillan, 1981.

Trauschweizer, Ingo. *The Cold War U.S. Army: Building Deterrence for Limited War*. Lawrence: University Press of Kansas, 2008.

Trauschweizer, Ingo. *Maxwell Taylor's Cold War: From Berlin to Vietnam*. Lexington: University Press of Kentucky, 2019.

Trout, Steven. *On the Battlefield of Memory: The First World War and American Remembrance, 1919–1941*. Tuscaloosa: University of Alabama Press, 2010.

Truscott, Lucian K. *Command Missions: A Personal Story*. New York: E. P. Dutton, 1954.

Truscott, Lucian K., Jr. *The Twilight of the U.S. Cavalry: Life in the Old Army, 1917–1942*. Lawrence: University Press of Kansas, 1989.

U'Ren, Richard C. *Ivory Fortress: A Psychiatrist Looks at West Point*. Indianapolis: Bobbs-Merrill Co., 1974.

Utley, Robert M. *The Commanders: Civil War Generals Who Shaped the American West*. Norman: University of Oklahoma Press, 2018.

Utley, Robert M. *Frontier Regulars: The United States Army and the Indian, 1866–1891*. New York: Macmillan, 1973.

Utley, Robert M. *Frontiersmen in Blue: The United States Army and the Indian, 1848–1865*. Originally published 1967. Reprint, Lincoln: University of Nebraska Press, 1981.

Vazansky, Alexander. *An Army in Crisis: Social Conflict and the U.S. Army in Germany, 1968–1975*. Lincoln: University of Nebraska Press, 2019.

Wakefield, Wanda E. *Playing to Win: Sports and the American Military, 1898–1945*. Albany: State University of New York Press, 1997.

Walton, George. *The Tarnished Shield: A Report on Today's Army*. New York: Dodd, Mead, 1973.

Watson, Samuel J. *Jackson's Sword: The Army Officer Corps on the American Frontier, 1810–1821*. Lawrence: University Press of Kansas, 2012.

Watson, Samuel J. *Peacekeepers and Conquerors: The Army Officer Corps on the American Frontier, 1821–1846*. Lawrence: University Press of Kansas, 2013.

Weaver, John D. *The Brownsville Raid*. New York: W. W. Norton, 1970.

Weigley, Russell F. *History of the U.S. Army*. New York: Macmillan, 1967.

Weigley, Russell F. *The History of the U.S. Army*. Bloomington: Indiana University Press, 1984.

Weigley, Russell F. *Towards an American Army: Military Thought from Washington to Marshall* New York: Columbia University Press, 1962.

Wheeler, James Scott. *The Big Red One: America's Legendary 1st Infantry Division from World War I to Desert Storm*. Lawrence: University Press of Kansas, 2007.

Whitlock, Craig. *The Afghanistan Papers: A Secret History of the War*. New York: Simon & Schuster, 2021.

Willbanks, James H. *Abandoning Vietnam: How America Left and South Vietnam Lost its War*. Lawrence: University Press of Kansas, 2004.

Woolley, William J. *Creating the Modern Army: Citizen-Soldiers and the American Way of War, 1919–1939*. Lawrence: University Press of Kansas, 2022.

Articles and Book Chapters

Adams, Will. "The Education of Trooper Brown." *Century* 74 (May 1907): 10–18.

Albert, Allan D. "Building Character in the Army." *Scribner's Magazine* 65 (January 1919): 117–122.

An Army Officer. "An Army of Amateurs." *American Mercury* 6 (October 1925): 184–189.

An Army Officer. "The Uplift Hits the Army." *American Mercury* 5 (June 1925): 136–141.

"An Army Wife." *Army and Navy Journal* 43 (21 October 1905).

"An Army without Officers." *Army and Navy Journal* 46 (13 February 1909).

Anderson, E. "Pay of Our Soldiers as Affecting Desertion and Reenlistment." *Review of Reviews* 33 (March 1906): 330–334.

Andrade, Dale. "Westmoreland Was Right: Learning the Wrong Lessons from the Vietnam War." *Small Wars & Insurgencies* 19 (September 2008): 145–181.

"Annual Report of the Chief of Field Artillery for 1923–1924." *Field Artillery Journal* 15 (January–February 1925): 1–30.

"Another Army Wife." *Army and Navy Journal* 43 (25 November 1905).

"Army Commissions." *Army and Navy Journal* 83 (29 December 1945).

"Army Defends High Percentage of Colonels in Peacetime Force." *Army and Navy Bulletin* 3 (22 February 1947).

"Army Field Day at Portland, Ore." *Army and Navy Journal* 42 (6 May 1905).

"Army Morals." *The Nation* 81 (October 1905): 333–334.

"The Army's Influence on Society." *Army and Navy Journal* 42 (6 May 1905).

"Army Will Retrain 14,000 NCOs to Fill Combat Unit Slots." *Army* 26 (January 1976): 10.

Bacevich, Andrew J. "A 'Grass Roots' Look at the Drug Problem." *Army* 22 (November 1972): 25–28.

Bacevich, Andrew J. "A Modern Major General." *New Left Review* 29 (September–October 2004): 123–134.

Bacevich, Andrew J. "Progressivism, Professionalism, and Reform." *Parameters* 9 (March 1979): 66–71.

Bailey, Mildred C. "Army Women and a Decade of Progress." *Army* 24 (October 1974): 85–91.

Baker, Anni. "The Abolition of the U.S. Army Canteen, 1898–1914." *Journal of Military History* 80 (July 2016): 697–724.

Bartel, George B. "Are the Troops Getting Enough Officer Duty?" *Army* 23 (September 1973): 41–42.

Benson, C. C. "Mechanization—Aloft and Alow." *Cavalry Journal* 38 (January 1929): 58–62.

Berry, Charles. "Some Problems of Americanization as Seen by an Army Psychologist." *School and Society* 13 (22 January 1921): 97–104.

Biddle, Stephen. "Victory Misunderstood: What the Gulf War Tells Us About the Future of Conflict." *International Security* 21 (Fall 1996): 139–179.

Binder, L. James. "The Now Is Very in at Fort Benning." *Army* 21 (April 1971): 22–29.

Blount, James H. "Army Morals and the Canteen." *North American Review* 193 (March 1911): 409–421.

"Bombshell." *Armed Force* 5 (27 August 1949): 2.

Bonner, John T. "ROTC's Battle and Survival." *Army* 22 (February 1972): 40–44.

Boroff, David. "West Point: Ancient Incubator for a New Breed." *Harper's Magazine* 225 (December 1962): 51–59.

Bradford, Zeb B. "US Tactics in Vietnam." *Military Review* 52 (February 1972): 63–76.

Brooke, George M. "Present Needs of Coast Artillery." *Journal of the Military Service Institute of the United States* 36 (March–April 1905): 257–274.

Buchanan, Lloyd. "Army as a Career." *World's Work* 11 (February 1906): 7236–7238.

Bullard, Robert L. "The Army in Cuba." *Journal of the Military Service Institute of the United States* 41 (September–October 1907): 152–157.

Bullard, Robert L. "The Citizen Soldier—The Volunteer." *Journal of the Military Service Institute of the United States* 39 (September–October 1906): 153–167.

Bullard, Robert L. "In Times of Peace." *Overland Monthly* 47 (February 1906): 101–113.

Bullard, Robert L. "A Moral Preparation for the Soldier for Service and Battle." *Journal of the Military Service Institute of the United States* 31 (November 1902): 779–792.

Burnett, Charles. "Efficient War Soldiers." *Coast Artillery Journal* 54 (April 1921): 63–65.

Burtt, Wilson B. "The Fighting Unit." *Infantry Journal* 29 (September 1926): 237–241.

Butts, Edmund Luther. "Soldierly Bearing, Health and Athletics." *Outing* 43 (March 1904): 707–711.

Calhoun, William R. "Bullish on ROTC." *Army* 24 (May 1974): 36–38.

Capps, Jack. "The Literature of the AEF: A Doughboy Legacy." In *Unknown Soldiers: The American Expeditionary Forces in Memory and Remembrance.* Edited by Mark A. Snell. Kent, OH: Kent State University Press, 2008, 195–237.

Captain Artillery [pseud.]. "Noncoms." *Combat Forces Journal* 2 (November 1951): 6–8.

"Career Management and Your Future: Selection for General Staff Duty." *Combat Forces Journal* 4 (January 1954): 32.

Carr, Ernest J. "Americanization in the Army." *Infantry Journal* 23 (January 1921): 31–33.

Carroll, Jonathan. "Courage Under Fire: Re-evaluating Black Hawk Down and the Battle of Mogadishu." *War in History* 29 (September 2022): 704–726.

Carter, Don Allan. "War Games in Europe: The U.S. Army Experiments with Atomic Doctrine." In *Blueprints for Battle: Planning for War in Central Europe, 1948–1968.* Edited by Jan Hoffenaar and Dieter Krüger. Lexington: University Press of Kentucky, 2012, 131–153.

Carter, William H. "Camps of Instruction." *The Reader* 10 (July 1907): 114–121.

Carter, William H. "Elihu Root—His Services as Secretary of War." *North American Review* 178 (January 1904): 110–121.

Carter, William H. "A General Staff for the Army." *North American Review* 175 (October 1902): 558–565.

Carter, William H. "Military Preparedness." *North American Review* 191 (May 1910): 636–643.

"The Case of Captain Koehler." *Army and Navy Journal* 43 (8 November 1906).

Caughey, Daniel M. "The Higher Standards." *Army* 24 (December 1974): 5.

Charlton, F. E. "Athletics in the Army." *Infantry Journal* 21 (November 1922): 629–632.

Chester, James. "The Army Uniform and Its Protection" and "Comment and Criticism." *Journal of the Military Service Institute of the United States* 33 (July–August 1903): 53–55, 83–90.

Christenberry, C. W. "American Militarism a Myth—Protective Preparedness a Necessity." *Infantry Journal* 33 (September 1928): 229–237.

Church, William Conant. "Increasing Desertions and the Army Canteen." *North American Review* 177 (December 1903): 855–863.

Churchill, Marlborough. "The Military Intelligence Division, General Staff." *Journal of the United States Artillery (Coast Artillery Journal)* 52 (April 1920): 293–315.

Collins, John M. "Depression Army." *Army* 22 (January 1972): 8–14.

"Color Line in the Army." *Army and Navy Journal* 44 (29 December 1906).

Connor, Arthur W. "The Tank Debacle in Korea, 1950: Implications for Today." *Parameters* 22 (July 1992): 66–76.

Cooling, Benjamin F. "Enlisted Grade Structure and the Army Reorganization Act of 1920." *Military Affairs* 31 (December 1967): 187–194.

Cornelson, Arthur J. "The Talent Drain." *Army* 22 (April 1972): 48.

Cox, Matthew. "Army Launches New 'Warriors Wanted' Campaign Aimed at Generation Z." Military.com, 19 October 2018.

Crane, Conrad C. "Post-Vietnam Drawdown: The Myth of the Abrams Doctrine."

In *Drawdown: the American Way of Postwar*. Edited by James W. Warren. New York: New York University Press, 2016, 241–252.

Crean, Jeffrey. "Something to Compete with 'Gunsmoke': The *Big Picture* Television Series and Selling a 'Modern, Progressive and Forward Thinking' Army to Cold War America." *War and Society* 35 (2016): 204–218.

Davis, Bowers. "A System for Army Athletics." *Infantry Journal* 3 (October 1906): 79–83.

Davis, Henry C. "Joint Exercises." *Journal of the United States Artillery (Coast Artillery Journal)* 28 (November–December 1907): 286–290.

Dawson, Joseph G., III. Joseph G. Dawson III, "The U.S. War with Mexico: The Difficulties of Concluding a Victorious War." In *Between War and Peace: How America Ends its Wars*, ed. Matthew Moten. New York: Free Press, 2011, 85–106.

Dippie, Brian W. "George A. Custer." In *Soldiers West: Biographies from the Military Frontier*, ed. Paul Andrew Hutton (Lincoln: University of Nebraska Press, 1987), 100–114.

Donnelly, William M. "The Best Army That Can Be Put in the Field in the Circumstances: The U.S. Army, July 1951–July 1953." *Journal of Military History* 71 (July 2007): 809–847.

Donnelly, William M. "Bilko's Army: A Crisis in Command?" *Journal of Military History* 75 (October 2011): 1183–1188.

Donnelly, William M. "Professionalism and the Officer Personnel Management System." *Military Review* 93 (May–June 2013): 16–23.

"Doughboys and Brides Back from the Rhine." *Literary Digest* 76 (3 March 1923): 43.

Dougherty, A. J. "Some of the Problems of a Regimental and Post Commander and How They Were Met." *Infantry Journal* 33 (November 1928): 460–471.

Dougherty, A. J. "The Standard of Living and Officers' Pay?" *Infantry Journal* 35 (August 1929): 162–169.

Dougherty, A. J. "To What Pay Is an Officer Entitled?" *Infantry Journal* 34 (May 1929): 451–461.

Drea, Edward J. "Change Becomes Continuity: The Start of the U.S. Army's 'Green Book' Series." In *Essays on Official History in the United States and British Commonwealth*. Edited by Jeffrey Grey (Westport, CT: Praeger, 2003), 83–104.

Eberle, E. G., and Frederick T. Gordon. "Report on the Committee of the Acquirement of Drug Habits." *American Journal of Pharmacy* 75 (October 1903): 474–488.

Editorial. "Go to It." *Infantry Journal* 17 (August 1920): 184.

Egan, Gerald. "The Recruiting Problem." *Infantry Journal* 17 (September 1920): 214–218.

Egardner, Z. T. "Adult Education in the Army." *School Review* 30 (April 1922): 255–267.

"Eliminating Army Officers." *The Nation* 82 (February 1906): 110–111.

Elliott, Ward. "The Assault on ROTC." *Army* 21 (February 1971): 35–38.

"Faith in and a Doctrine for the Cavalry Service." *Cavalry Journal* 36 (April 1927): 227–231.

Fautua, David T. "The 'Long Pull' Army: NSC 68, the Korean War, and the Creation of the Cold War U.S. Army." *Journal of Military History* 61 (January 1997): 93–120.

Fitzgerald, Michael S. "Rejecting Calhoun's Expansible Army Plan: The Army Reduction Act of 1821." *War in History* 3 (1996): 161–185.

Flint, Roy K. "Task Force Smith and the 24th Division: Delay and Withdrawal, 5–19 July, 1950." In *America's First Battles, 1776–1965*. Edited by Charles E. Heller and William A. Stofft. Lawrence: University Press of Kansas, 1986, 266–299.

Forbes, Edgar Allen. "Trouble with the Army: From the Standpoint of the Enlisted Man." *World's Work* 13 (April 1907): 8763–8775.

"Foreign Affairs." *Army and Navy Journal* 83 (3 November 1945).

Froehlke, Robert F. "Peace-Keeping with Pride and Integrity." *Army* 22 (November 1972): 16–19.

Funderburk, R. E. "Six-Hour Day: Equal Training, Less Time." *Army* 26 (July 1976): 51–52.

Funston, Frederick. "Army Life and Discipline." *World's Work* 14 (May 1907): 8896–8897.

Garcia, Daniel Eugene. "Class and Brass: Demobilization, Working Class Politics, and American Foreign Policy between World War and Cold War." *Diplomatic History* 34 (September 2010): 681–698.

Gard, Robert G., Jr. "The 'Other War' on Drugs, Alcohol." *Army* 22 (October 1972): 107–108.

Garland, Albert N. "Military Justice Before the Bar." *Army* 22 (January 1972): 27–29.

Garland, Albert N. "Motivate Me." *Army* 21 (December 1971): 43.

Gates, John M. "The Alleged Isolation of U.S. Army Officers in the Late-19th Century." *Parameters* 10 (1980): 32–45.

Gavin, James M. "The Airborne Armies of the Future." *Infantry Journal* 60 (January 1947): 21–25.

Gavin, James M. "Cavalry and I Don't Mean Horses." *Harper's* 208 (April 1954): 54–60.

Gavin, James M. "The Future of Airborne Operations." *Military Review* 27 (December 1947): 3–8.

Gavin, James M. "The Tactical Use of the Atomic Bomb." *Combat Forces Journal* 1 (November 1950): 9–11.

"Gavin Says Air Mechanization Will Win Wars of the Future." *Army and Navy Bulletin* 3 (5 April 1947): 3.

"General Chaffee's Views on War." *Army and Navy Journal* 47 (2 October 1909).

Glatthaar, Joseph G. "The Civil War: A New Definition of Victory." In *Between War and Peace: How America Ends its Wars*. Edited by Matthew Moten. New York: Free Press, 2011, 107–128.

Goldrich, Robert L. "The Art of Winning Friends on Campus." *Army* 21 (January 1971): 24–29.

Grandstaff, Mark R. "Making the Military American: Advertising, Reform, and the Demise of the Antistanding Army Tradition, 1945–1955." *Journal of Military History* 60 (April 1996): 299–332.

Grandstaff, Mark R. "Preserving the 'Habits and Usages of War': William T. Sherman, Professional Reform, and the U.S. Army Officer Corps, 1865–1881." *Journal of Military History* 62 (July 1998): 521–545.

Grissom, Adam. "The Future of Military Innovation Studies." *Journal of Strategic Studies* 29 (October 2006): 905–934.

Hallaren, Mary A. "The Women's Army Corps Becomes Permanent." *MR* 28 (March 1949): 8–13.

Hallock, Robert F. "Drill," *Combat Forces Journal* 2 (March 1952): 34.

Hamilton, Louis M. "The Training of the Non-Commissioned Officer." *Journal of the Military Service Institute of the United States* 35 (September–October 1904): 260–264.

Hampton, Celwyn E. "The Experiences of our Army Since the Outbreak of the War with Spain: What Practical Use has been Made of Them, and How May They be Further Utilized to Improve Its Fighting Efficiency." *Journal of the Military Service Institute of the United States* 36 (May–June 1905): 399–420.

Hamrick, Tom. "The Drill Sergeant Wore Skirts." *Army* 22 (September 1972): 38–42.

Hamrick, Tom. "Sophisticated Basic Trainees." *Army* 21 (September 1971): 39.

Hamrick, Tom. "Trying the Army on for Size." *Army* 22 (August 1972): 37–40.

Hanna, Matthew E. "Our Army a School." *Journal of the Military Service Institute of the United States* 41 (September–October 1907): 143–151.

Harbord, James G. "Theodore Roosevelt and the Army." *Review of Reviews* 69 (1924): 65–75.

Hauser, William J. "Professionalism and the Junior Officer Drain." *Army* 20 (July 1970): 17–22.

Heavey, John W. "Universal Military Training." *Infantry Journal* 17 (July 1920): 26–29.

Helmick, Eli A. "How May Public Opinion Concerning the Army and Navy Be So Educated as to Secure to the Soldier and Sailor in Uniform the Consideration Ordinarily Accorded to the Civilian." *Journal of the Military Service Institute of the United States* 42 (January–February 1908): 1–12.

Herring, George C. "Preparing *Not* to Fight the Last War: The Impact of Vietnam on the U.S. Military." In *After Vietnam: Legacies of a Lost War*. Edited by Charles E. Neu. Baltimore: Johns Hopkins University Press, 2000, 56–64.

Hill, J. G. "Peace-Time Morale." *Infantry Journal* 34 (April 1929): 402–405.

Hope, Offnere. "The Mechanical Specialist, Coast Artillery Corps." *Journal of the US Artillery* 34 (November–December 1910): 245–256.

Horner, Thomas J. "Killers, Fillers, and Fodder." *Parameters* 12 (September 1982): 27–34.

Howard, Michael. "The Use and Abuse of Military History." *Parameters* 11 (July 1981): 9–14.

Howze, Hamilton H. "The Mishandling of Noncoms." *Combat Forces Journal* 1 (February 1951): 37–38.

Hunt, I. L. "Public Opinion and the American Army." *Infantry Journal* 3 (January 1907): 64–88.

Hunter, Edward. "Our Military Judicial System," *Journal of the Military Service Institute of the United States* 32 (March–April 1903): 231–237.

Hutchinson, Robert W. "The Weight of History: Wehrmacht Officers, the U.S. Army Historical Division, and U.S. Military Doctrine, 1945–1956." *Journal of Military History* 78 (October 2014): 1321–1348.

Hyde, Arthur P. S. "The Training of the Non-Commissioned Officer." *Journal of the Military Service Institute of the United States* 35 (November–December 1904): 386–391.

Jablonsky, David. "Army Transformation: A Tale of Two Doctrines." *Parameters* 31 (Autumn 2001): 43–62.

JBS [pseud.]. "Beer in the Barracks Is Bad?" *Army* 21 (May 1971): 8–9.

Jenkins, Weston. "What Gave Birth to 'What Price Glory.'" *Infantry Journal* 30 (January 1927): 8–13.

Johnson, Hugh S. "The Lamb Rampant." *Everybody's Magazine* 18 (March 1908): 291–301.

Jones, Clifford. "The Personnel Outlook as Viewed from the Office of the Chief of Coast Artillery." *Coast Artillery Journal* 66 (January 1927): 30–43.

Jones, Paul. "Barrack-Room View of the 'Brass.'" *Saturday Evening Post* 218 (5 January 1946): 96.

Kelly, Hugh M. "The Heritage of Ham." *Munsey's Magazine* 31 (July 1908): 277–290.

Kelly, Hugh M. "Protecting the Uniform." *Infantry Journal* 4 (July 1907): 231–234.

Kelly, R. H. "Recruiting." *Infantry Journal* 11 (July–August 1914): 54–60.

Kerwin, Walter T. "Far-Flung Command Stays Combat Ready." *Army* 24 (October 1974): 34–38.

Kerwin, Walter T. "Youth's 'Why' Key Challenge in Today's Army." *Army* 20 (November 1970): 69–72.

Killebrew, Robert B. "Volunteer Army: How it Looks to a Company Commander." *Army* 21 (March 1971): 19–22.

Killebrew, Robert B. "Where the Squad Leader Makes a Difference." *Army* 24 (March 1974): 33–37.

King, Edward L. "Athletics for the Physical Betterment of the Enlisted Man of the Army." *Outing* 39 (January 1902): 432–436.

Knappen, Theodore M. "The Army as a School." *American Review of Reviews* 63 (June 1921): 627–635.

Koehler, Herman J. "Physical Training in the Army." *Infantry Journal* 1 (July 1904): 8–13.

"The Koehler Court-Martial." *Army and Navy Journal* 44 (30 March 1907).

Lacquement, Richard A. "The Casualty-Aversion Myth." *Naval War College Review* 57 (Winter 2004): 39–57.

Lacquement, Richard A. "Preaching After the Devil's Death: U.S. Post–Cold War Drawdown." In *Drawdown: the American Way of Postwar*, ed. James W. Warren (New York: New York University Press, 2016), 267–290.

Landon, Edwin. "The Needs of the Coast Artillery." *Journal of the United States Artillery (Coast Artillery Journal)* 25 (March–April 1906): 143–148.

Lawrence, E. A. "The Alcohol Problem and What the Army Is Doing About It." *Army* 26 (August 1976): 25.

Lee, Alton "The Army 'Mutiny' of 1946." *Journal of American History* 53 (December 1966): 555–571.

Lee, Wayne E. "Plattsburgh, 1814: Warring for Bargaining Chips." In *Between War and Peace: How America Ends its Wars.* Edited by Matthew Moten. New York: Free Press, 2011, 43–63.

Lewis, F. M. "Discipline—Its Importance to an Armed Force and the Best Means of Promoting It and Maintaining It in the United States Army." *Journal of the Military Service Institute of the United States* 28 (May 1901): 323–347.

Linn, Brian McAllister. "The Impact of the Philippine Wars (1898–1913) on the U.S. Army." In *Colonial Crucible: Empire in the Making of the Modern American State.* Edited by Alfred McCoy and Francis Scarano. Madison: University of Wisconsin Press, 2009, 460–472.

Linn, Brian McAllister. "Pruning the Deadwood: Samuel Huntington, Professionalism, and Self-Policing in the US Army Officer Corps." *Parameters* 51 (Autumn 2021): 91–100.

Linn, Brian McAllister. "The U.S. Army's Postwar Recoveries." *Parameters* (Autumn 2016): 13–22.

Lock-Pullan, Richard. "'An Inward Looking Time': The United States Army, 1973–1976." *Journal of Military History* 67 (April 2003): 483–511.

Loveland, Anne C. "Character Education in the U.S. Army, 1947–1977." *Journal of Military History* 64 (July 2000): 795–818.

Lovell, John P. "No Tunes of Glory: America's Military in the Aftermath of Vietnam." *Indiana Law Journal* 49 (Summer 1974): 698–717.

Lovell, John P. "Vietnam and the U.S. Army: Learning to Cope with Failure." In *Democracy, Strategy, and Vietnam: Implications for American Policymaking.* Edited by George K. Osborn, Asa A. Clark IV, Daniel J. Kaufman, and Douglas E. Lute. Lexington, MA: Lexington Books, 1985, 121–154.

Ludvigsen, Eric C. "Army Tightens Belt Against Inflation from Munitions to Maple Syrup." *Army* 24 (November 1974): 12–13.

Lukasik, Sebastian H. "Doughboys, the YMCA, and the Moral Economy of Sacrifice in the First World War." *Journal of Military History* 84 (July 2020): 774–797.

Macgregor, Douglas A. "Resurrecting Transformation for the Post-Industrial Era." *Defense Horizons* 2 (September 2001): 13.

Malone, Dandridge M. "The Prize." *Army* 23 (March 1973): 24–31.

Malone, Paul B. "The Army School of the Line." *Infantry Journal* 6 (January 1910): 511–532.

"Manila's Greatest Need." *Army and Navy Journal* 42 (12 August 1905).

Martin, Harold H. "Paratrooper in the Pentagon." *Saturday Evening Post* 227 (28 August 1954): 22–23, 81–83.

McColl, Alexander M. S. "On Restoring Discipline." *Army* 23 (July 1973): 3–4.

McKay, Karen. "Go Ahead—Exploit Us!" *Army* 22 (April 1972): 21–25.

McNeill, T. R. "An Up-to-Date System for Procuring Officers." *Army* 21 (June 1971): 32–33.

"Men of Quality." *CFJ* 1 (April 1951): 9–11.

Merrill, Dana T. "Desertions from the Army." *Infantry Journal* 3 (October 1906): 84–87.

"Middle East War—1973." *Military Review* 54 (February 1974): 48–49.

Miles, Sherman. "More Perfect Peace." *North American Review* 214 (November 1921): 577–587.

Millard, Bailey. "The Shame of our Army." *Cosmopolitan* 49 (September 1910): 411–420.

Moore, Harold G. "On Pay and Benefits, A Balanced Approach." *Army* 26 (October 1976): 100–102.

Moore, Roy. "Quality Manpower and the Modern Army." *Armor* 66 (July–August 1957): 22–23.

Morris, R. E. "Improving the Infantry Image Among Today's ROTC Cadets." *Army* 21 (March 1971): 56–57.

Moskin, J. Robert. "Our Military Manpower Scandal." *Look* 22 (18 March 1958): 27–33.

Moskos, Charles C., Jr. "Coping in Europe: Shorter Tours May be the Answer." *Army* 23 (November 1973): 13.

"Necessity for Construction at Fort Benning." *Infantry Journal* 27 (December 1925): 701–707.

Nenninger, Timothy K. "American Military Effectiveness in the First World War." In *Military Effectiveness*. Vol. 1, *The First World War*, edited by Allan R. Millett and Williamson Murray. Originally published 1988. Reprint, New York: Cambridge University Press, 2010, 116–156.

Nenninger, Timothy K. "Leavenworth and Its Critics: The U.S. Army Command and General Staff School, 1920–1940." *Journal of Military History* 58 (April 1994): 199–231.

Neumann, Brian F. "A Question of Authority: Reassessing the March-Pershing 'Feud' in the First World War." *Journal of Military History* 73 (October 2009): 1117–1142.

"The New Infantry Drill Regulations." *Infantry Journal* (November 1919): 375.

Newell, Clayton R. and Charles R. Shrader. "The U.S. Army's Transition to Peace, 1865–66." *Journal of Military History* 77 (July 2013): 8670–8694.

Nichols, Roger L. "Stephen H. Long." In *Soldiers West: Biographies from the Military Frontier*. Edited by Paul Andrew Hutton. Lincoln: University of Nebraska Press, 1987, 24–41.

Noble, Robert H. "Selection Versus Seniority." *Infantry Journal* 6 (July 1909): 63–77.

Norman, Lloyd. "Turbulence and Army Readiness." *Army* 21 (July 1971): 10–14.

O'Connell, Joseph J. "The Moral Preparation of the Soldier." *Journal of the Military Service Institute of the United States* 32 (January–February 1902): 115–121.

O'Donnell, James P. "The World's Newest Army." *Saturday Evening Post* 228 (1 October 1955): 36–37, 119–123.

"Only a Leader Can Command a Company." *Army* 21 (November 1971): 58–59.

"Our Army at Peace." *Army and Navy Journal* 41 (7 May 1904): 941.

Paone, Rocco M. "The Last Volunteer Army." *Military Review* 49 (December 1969): 9–17.

Parker, John H. "The Military Education of the Youth of this Country for a Period of at Least One Year as a Means of Developing the Military Spirit of this Country for National Defense." *Journal of the Military Service Institute of the United States* (March–April 1912): 153–172.

Patch, William A. "Professional Development of Today's NCO." *Army* 24 (November 1974): 15–20.

Pattulo, George. "Selling the Army to the People." *Saturday Evening Post* 193 (21 August 1920): 14–15.

"Personnel of the Army General Staff." *Army and Navy Journal* 41 (2 January 1904).

Pillsbury, Dennis C. "Why Not Dress Up the Soldier?" *Infantry Journal* 33 (July 1928): 74–75.

Pettit, James S. "How Far Does Democracy Affect the Organization and Discipline of Our Armies and How Can Its Influence Be Most Effectually Utilized." *Journal of the Military Service Institute of the United States* 38 (January–February 1906): 1–38.

Polsky, Andrew J., and Willian D. Adler. "The State in a Blue Uniform." *Polity* 40 (July 2008): 348–354.

Pope, James W. "Three States of Army Penology." *Journal of the Military Service Institute of the United States* 35 (July–August 1904): 37–42.

"The President's Warning." *Army and Navy Journal* 42 (15 July 1905).

Prosser, John R. "Reforming Military Justice." *Army* 23 (April 1973): 38–42.

"The Question of Army Morals." *Nation* 81 (October 1905): 333–334.

Reichmann, Carl. "In Pace Para Bellum." *Infantry Journal* 2 (January 1906): 3–19.

Reimer, Dennis R. "Leadership for the 21st Century: Empowerment, Environment, and the Golden Rule," *Military Review* 76 (January–February 1997): 47–51.

Rice, Grantland. "The Greatest Show on Earth." *Colliers* 76 (28 November 1925): 28, 173.

Ridgway, Matthew B. "The Indispensable Weapon." *Combat Forces Journal* 4 (January 1954): 9.

Rogers, Bernard W. "People the Key in the New Army." *Army* 23 (October 1973): 22–26.

"Rooseveltism in the Army." *Army and Navy Journal* 44 (3 November 1906).

Ruhl, Arthur Brown. "Army-and-Navy Game." *Outing* 49 (December 1906): 305–314.

Ryson, Harry. "Bellyful." *Combat Forces Journal* 2 (March 1952): 6.

Schwartz, William L. "Dealing with Drug, Alcohol Abuse: Good Vibes, Bad Vibes." *Army* 24 (May 1974): 29–34.

Second Relief [pseud.]. "The Deserter." *Army and Navy Journal* 42 (17 June 1905).

"Select Regular Appointments." *Army and Navy Bulletin* 3 (4 January 1947): 2.

Shanks, David C. "Administration and the Management of Men." *Infantry Journal* 13 (November–December 1916): 276–289.

Shortal, John F. "20th Century Demobilization Lessons." *MR* 78 (September–November 1998): 58–63.

Siler, J. F., et al. "Marijuana Smoking in Panama." *Military Surgeon* 73 (July–December 1933): 269–280.

Skelton, William B. "The Commanding General and the Problem of Command in the U.S. Army, 1821–1841." *Military Affairs* 34 (December 1970): 117–122.

Skelton, William B. "High Army Leadership in the Era of the War of 1812." *William and Mary Quarterly* 51 (April 1994): 253–274.

Smith, Lynn D. "A Question of Purpose." *Army* 23 (May 1973): 11–15.

Smith, Mark A. "The Politics of Military Professionalism: The Engineer Company and the Political Activities of the Antebellum U.S. Army Corps of Engineers." *Journal of Military History* 80 (April 2016): 355–387.

Spector, Ronald. "The Military Effectiveness of the US Armed Forces, 1919–39." In *Military Effectiveness*. Vol. 2, *The Interwar Period*, edited by Allan R. Millett and Williamson Murray. Originally published 1988. Reprint, New York: Cambridge University Press, 2010, 70–97.

Spector, Ronald. "The Vietnam War and the Army's Self Image." In *The Second Indochina War*. Edited by John Schlight. Washington, DC: Center of Military History, 1986, 169–186.

Stagg, J. C. A. "Freedom and Subordination: Disciplinary Problems in the U.S. Army in the War of 1812." *Journal of Military History* 78 (April 2014): 537–574.

Stagg, J. C. A. "United States Army Officers in the War of 1812: A Statistical and Behavioral Portrait." *Journal of Military History* 76 (October 2012): 1001–1034.

"The Standard of Living and Officers' Pay?" *Infantry Journal* 35 (August 1929): 162–169.

Starry, Donn A. "A Perspective on American Military Thought." *Military Review* 69 (July 1989): 2–11.

Stewart, M. B. "The Army as a Factor in the Upbuilding of Society." *Journal of the Military Service Institute of the United States* 36 (May–June 1905): 392.

Stilwell, Richard G. "Pro-Life Is Key in Korea." *Army* 24 (October 1974): 109–111.

Sydney [pseud.]. "Thoughts on the Organization of the Army." *Military and Naval Magazine of the United States* 2 (December 1833): 198.

"Text of Biennial Report of the Chief of Staff of the Army." *Army and Navy Journal* 83 (13 October 1945).

Thurman, Maxwell R. "Sustaining the All-Volunteer Force 1983–1992: The Second Decade." In *The All-Volunteer Force After a Decade: Retrospect and Prospect*. Edited by William Bowman, Roger Little, and G. Thomas Scilia. Washington, DC: Pergamon-Brassey's, 1986, 266–285.

"Times Are Perilous for 'Contractual Rights.'" *Army* 26 (January 1976): 6–8.

"Training the Eyes and Ears of the Army." *Popular Mechanics* 43 (1925): 418–423.

Traub, Captain Peter. "Esprit de Corps—How It May Be Strengthened and Preserved in Our Army Under the Present Organization and Method of Promotion." *Journal of the Military Service Institute of the United States* 34 (March–April 1904): 181–217.

Turner, Stephen D. "New Army Has No Room for Duds." *Army* 23 (September 1973): 43.

Ulbaker, Carl M. "Mess Management in the 29th Infantry." *Infantry Journal* 34 (April 1929): 344–346.

Upson, William Hazlett. "Good Old Army! Good Old War!" *Saturday Evening Post* 198. 5 June 1926, 7, 236–238.

Vargas, Mark A. "The Military Justice System and the Use of Illegal Punishments as Causes of Desertion in the U.S. Army, 1821–1835." *Journal of Military History* 55 (January 1991): 1–19.

Villard, Oswald Garrison. "Negro in the Regular Army." *Atlantic Monthly* 91 (April 1903): 721–729.

Villard, Oswald Garrison. "New Army of the United States." *Atlantic Monthly* 89 (April 1902): 437–451.

Wadleigh, Richard S. "Barracks Life Now a Little Brighter." *Army* 21 (January 1971): 6–8.

Wadleigh, Richard S. "The Now and VOLAR." *Army* 21 (June 1971): 5–6.

Wagner, Arthur S. "The Fort Riley Maneuvers." *Journal of the Military Service Institute of the United States* 32 (January–February 1903): 70–93,

Wagstaff, Jack K. "Army of the People." *Army* 22 (December 1972): 2.

Walker, Fred L., Jr. "Your Next War." *Infantry Journal* 60 (June 1947):10–14, 61 (July 1947): 32–36; (August 1947): 41–45.

Watson, Samuel J. "Continuity in Civil-Military Relations and Expertise: The U.S. Army during the Decade before the Civil War." *Journal of Military History* 75 (January 2011): 221–250.

Watson, Samuel J. "Knowledge, Interest, and the Limits of Military Professionalism: The Discourse on American Coast Defense, 1815–1860." *War in History* 5 (Fall 1998): 280–307.

Watson, Samuel J. "Military Learning and Adaptation Shaped by Social Context: The U.S. Army and Its 'Indian Wars,' 1790–1890." *Journal of Military History* 82 (April 2018): 371–412.

Watson, Samuel J. "Surprisingly Professional: Trajectories in Army Officer Corps Drawdowns, 1783–1848." In *Drawdown: The American Way of Postwar*. Edited by Jason W. Warren. New York: New York University Press, 2016, 73–106.

Weaver, R. A. "What Must We Do to Understand [a] New Soldier?" *Army* 21 (April 1971): 62.

Westmoreland, William C. "Straight Talk from the Chief." *Army* 21 (May 1971): 12–17.

"West Point Deaths Led." *Infantry Journal* 16 (October 1919): 254.

Wettemann, Robert P. "West Point, the Jacksonians, and the Army's Controversial Role in National Improvements." In *West Point: Two Centuries and Beyond*. Edited by Lance Betros. Abilene, TX: McWhiney Foundation Press, 2004, 144–166.

Weyand, Frederick C. "The Army in the Pacific is a Visible Presence for Peace." *Army* 23 (October 1973): 48.

"Who's in the Army Now?" *Fortune Magazine* (September 1935): 39–49, 126–144.

Willbanks, James H. "The Legacy of the Vietnam War for the U.S. Army." In *America and the Vietnam War: Re-examining the Culture and History of a Generation*. Edited by Andrew Weist, Mary Kathryn Barbier, and Glenn Robins. New York: Routledge, 2010, 271–280.

Willeford, Charles. "A Reflection on Retirement." *Combat Forces Journal* 3 (August 1952): 39–40.

Willey, Day Allen. "Spirit of Sport in the Army." *Harper's Weekly* 50 (4 August 1906): 1100–1101.

Wisser, John P. "The Coast Joint Manoeuvers—1902." *Journal of the Military Service Institute of the United States* 31 (November 1902): 837–879.

Wood, Leonard. "Why We Have No Army." *McClure's* 38 (April 1912): 677–683.

Woolnough James K., "Higher Priority to Be Given to Troop Morale and Welfare." *Army* 20 (November 1970): 37.

Wotherspoon, William W. "Training of the Efficient Soldier." *Annals of the American Academy of Political and Social Science* 26 (July 1905): 149–160.

"Y" to Editor. *Army and Navy Journal* 46 (9 January 1909).

US Army and US Government Publications

Adjutant General, US Army. *The Educational System of the United States Army: The Army as a National School.* Washington, DC: Adjutant General of the Army, 1920.

Anon. *Transforming the Army: TRADOC's First Thirty Years, 1973–2003.* Fort Monroe, VA: TRADOC, 2003.

Anon. *The U.S. Army in Multi-Domain Operations, 2028* (Fort Eustis, VA: TRADOC, 2020).

Assistant Chief of Staff for Military Intelligence. HQ, Hawaiian Division. *Digest of Information—The Hawaiian Department and the Territory of Hawaii.* Honolulu: Army Printing Office, 1930.

Bacevich, Andrew J. *The Pentomic Era: The U.S. Army Between Korea and Vietnam.* Washington, DC: National Defense University Press, 1986.

Baumann, Robert, Lawrence Yates, and Versalle F. Washington, *My Clan Against the World: US and Coalition Forces in Somalia, 1992–1994.* Fort Leavenworth, KS: Combat Studies Institute, 2004.

Ball, Harry P. *Of Responsible Command: A History of the U.S. Army War College.* Carlisle Barracks, PA: Alumni Association of the U.S. Army War College, 1983.

Bell, J. Franklin. "Reflections and Suggestions: An Address by General J. Franklin Bell." Fort Leavenworth, KS: N.p., 1906.

Bell, William Gardner. *Commanding Generals and Chiefs of Staff, 1775–2013.* Washington, DC: Center of Military History, 2013.

Bradley, Mark L. *The Army and Reconstruction, 1865–1877.* Washington, DC: Center of Military History, 2015.

Brown, John Sloan. *Kevlar Legions: The Transformation of the U.S. Army, 1989–2005.* Washington, DC: Center of Military History, 2011.

Carter, Donald A. *Forging the Shield: The U.S. Army in Europe, 1951–1962.* Washington, DC: Center of Military History, 2015.

Carter, Don[ald] A. *The U.S. Army Before Vietnam, 1953–1965.* Washington, DC: Center of Military History, 2015.

Chapman, Anne W. *The Army's Training Revolution, 1793–1990: An Overview.* Fort Monroe, VA: TRADOC, 1991.

Chapman, Anne W. *Mixed-Gender Basic Training: The U.S. Army's Experience, 1973–1985.* Fort Monroe, VA: TRADOC, 1991.

Clary, David A., and Joseph W. A. Whitehorne. *The Inspectors General of the United States Army, 1777–1903.* Washington, DC: CMH, 1987.

Converse, Eliot V., III. *History of Acquisition in the Department of Defense.* Vol. 1, *Rearming for the Cold War, 1945–1960.* Washington, DC: Historical Office, Office of the Secretary of Defense, 2012.

Coumbe, Arthur T. *Army Officer Retention: Historical Context.* Carlisle, PA: Strategic Studies Institute, 2010.

Coumbe, Arthur T. *A History of the U.S. Army Officer Corps, 1900–1990.* Carlisle, PA: Strategic Studies Institute, 2014.

Crane, Conrad C. *Avoiding Vietnam: The U.S. Army's Response to Defeat in Southeast Asia.* Carlisle, PA: Strategic Studies Institute, 2002.

Dabrowski, John R., ed. *An Oral History of General Gordon R. Sullivan.* Carlisle Barracks, PA: US Army War College, 2009.

Davis, Robert T., II. *The Challenge of Adaptation: The U.S. Army in the Aftermath of Conflict, 1953–2000.* Fort Leavenworth, KS: Combat Studies Institute, 2008.

Degen, Edmund J., and Mark J. Reardon, *Modern War in an Ancient Land: The United States,* 2 vols. Washington, DC: Center of Military History, 2021.

DePuy, William E. *Selected Papers of General William E. DePuy: First Commander, U.S. Army, Training and Doctrine Command.* Edited by Donald L. Gilmore and Carolyn D. Conway. Fort Leavenworth, KS: Combat Studies Institute, 1994.

Donnelly, William M. *Army Readiness Reporting Systems, 1945–2003.* Washington, DC: Center of Military History, 2018.

Doubler, Michael. *I Am the Guard: A History of the Army National Guard, 1636–2000.* Washington, DC: Department of the Army, 2001.

Doughty, Robert A. *The Evolution of U.S. Army Tactical Doctrine, 1946–1976.* Fort Leavenworth, KS: Combat Studies Institute, 1976.

East, Whitfield B. *A Historical Review and Analysis of Army Physical Readiness Training and Assessment.* Fort Leavenworth, KS: Combat Studies Institute, 2013.

Eltinge, LeRoy. *Psychology of War.* Fort Leavenworth: Army Service Schools Press, 1911.

Gavin, James M. *Airborne Warfare.* Washington, DC: Infantry Journal Press, 1947.

Griffith, Robert K. *The U.S. Army's Transition to an All-Volunteer Force, 1968–1974.* Washington, DC: Center of Military History, 1997.

[Haan, William G.]. "A Positive System of Coast Defense (Army)." In Joint Army and Navy Board, *Joint Army and Navy Action on Coast Defense.* Washington, DC: Government Publishing Office, 1920.

Hagood, Johnson. *Circular Relative to Pay of Officers and Enlisted Men of the Army.* Washington, DC: Government Publishing Office, 1907.

Herbert, Paul H. *Deciding What Has to Be Done: General William E. DePuy and the 1976 Edition of FM 100-5 Operations.* Fort Leavenworth, KS: Combat Studies Institute, 1988.

Hewes, James E. *From Root to McNamara: Army Organization and Administration, 1900–1963.* Washington, DC: Center of Military History, 1975.

Hunter, Fumiyo T. *Tenure Patterns of U.S. Commissioned Officers in the 1970s and 1980s.* Alexandria, VA: U.S. Army Research Institute of the Behavioral and Social Sciences, 1988.

Jones, Frank L. *A "Hollow Army" Reappraised: President Carter, Defense Budgets, and the Politics of Military Readiness.* Carlisle, PA: Strategic Studies Institute, 2012.

Keith, Jean E. and Howard K. Butler. *The US Army Combat Developments Experimentation Command: Origin and Formation.* Fort Belvoir, VA: US Army Combat Developments Experimentation Command, 1972.

Knapp. George E. *Buffalo Soldiers at Fort Leavenworth in the 1930s and early 1940s.* Fort Leavenworth: US Command and General Staff College, 1991.

Moenk, Jean R. *A History of Large-Scale Army Maneuvers in the United States, 1935–1964.* Fort Monroe, VA: HQ CONARC, 1969.

Moenk, Jean R. *Operation Steadfast Historical Summary: A History of the Reorganization of Continental Army Command (1972–1973).* Fort Monroe, VA: TRADOC, 1973.

Morden, Bettie J. *The Women's Army Corps, 1945–1978.* Washington, DC: Center of Military History, 1990.

Rayburn, Joel D., and Frank K. Sobchak, eds. *The U.S. Army in the Iraq War*. 2 vols. Carlisle, PA: US Army War College Press, 2019.

Reynolds, Alfred. *The Life of an Enlisted Soldier in the United States Army*. Washington, DC: Government Publishing Office, 1904.

Risch, Erna. *Quartermaster Support of he Army: A History of the Corps, 1775–1939*. Washington, D.C.: Center of Military History, 1989.

Romjue, John L. *The Army of Excellence: The Development of the 1980s Army*. Fort Monroe, VA: TRADOC, 1998.

Romjue, John L. *From Active Defense to AirLand Battle: The Development of Army Doctrine, 1973–1982*. Fort Monroe, VA: TRADOC, 1984.

Romjue, John L., Susan Canedy, and Anne W. Chapman. *Prepare the Army for War: A Historical Overview of Training and Doctrine Command*. Fort Monroe: TRADOC, 1993.

Scales, Robert H., Jr. *Certain Victory: The US Army in the Gulf War*. Washington, DC: Office of the Chief of Staff, 1993.

Sparrow, John C. *History of Personnel Demobilization in the United States Army*. Washington, DC: Department of the Army, 1952.

Steele, Matthew Forney. *American Campaigns*. 2 vols. Originally published 1909. Reprint, Washington, DC: US Infantry Association, 1922.

Stewart, Richard W., ed. *American Military History*. Vol. 1, *The United States Army and the Forging of a Nation, 1775–1917*. Washington, D.C.: Center of Military History, 2005.

Stewart, Richard W., ed. *American Military History*. Vol. 2, *The United States Army in a Global Era, 1917–2003*. Washington, DC: Center of Military History, 2005.

Sullivan, Gordon R. The Collected Works of the Thirty-Second Chief of Staff, United States Army, 1991–1995. Washington, DC: Department of the Army, 1996.

Upton, Emory. *The Military Policy of the United States*. Washington, DC: Government Publishing Office, 1904.

US Army Infantry School. *The Benning Plan for a Modern Volunteer Army*. 27 January 1971, DLFB.

US General Accounting Office. *The Army Can Improve Peacetime Use of Deployable Enlisted Personnel*. 7 September 1978.

US Infantry Association. *National Defense: A Compilation of Opinions*. Washington, DC: US Infantry Assoc., 1924.

Wass de Czege, Huba. *Commentary on "The US Army in Multi-Domain Operations in 2028."* Carlisle Barracks, PA: Strategic Studies Institute, 2020.

What the 1956 Soldier Thinks: A Digest of Attitude and Opinion Studies. Washington, DC: US Army Adjutant Generals Office, 1957.

Wilson, John B. *Maneuver and Firepower: The Evolution of Divisions and Separate Brigades*. Washington, DC: US Army Center of Military History, 1998.

US Army Unpublished Sources; Student Papers; RAND and GAO Reports

AEF Superior Board, *Report of the Superior Board on Organization and Tactics*. 27 April 1919, AHEC.

Alessi-Friedlander, R. Z. "Learning to Win When Fighting Outnumbered: Operational Risk in the U.S. Army, 1973–1982, and the Influence of the 1973 Arab-Israeli War." Master's thesis, CGSC, 2016, CARL.

Alger, James A. "Procurement and Distribution of Manpower." Lecture, AWC, 7 November 1955, AHEC.

Allen, William G. Van. "Revitalization of Senior Army Leadership." Student paper, AWC, 14 March 1955, AHEC.

Ames, T. L. "A Study of the Present Desertion Rates with Recommendations for Bringing About a Reduction of the Same." Student paper, AWC, 16 October 1926, AHEC.

Arrowsmith, C. D., et al. "Training for the Army of the United States." Student paper, AWC, 9 November 1926, AHEC.

Barratt, Tom. "The Officer Personnel Act of 1947." Student paper, AWC, 1 April 1953, AHEC.

Batts, John H., et al. "The Roles of Women in the Army and Their Impact on Military Operations and Organizations." Student paper, AWC, 23 May 1975, AHEC.

Bayliss, James E. "R.O.T.C. Units: Considered from the Viewpoint of the Procurement of Officers in the Event of General Mobilization, What Types of R.O.T.C. Units Should be Maintained?" Student paper, AWC, 28 February 1931, AHEC.

Beliak, Hilton R. "Personnel Turbulence and Time Utilization in an Infantry Division." Alexandria, VA: US Army Human Resources Research Organization, 1977, DTIC.

Blair, John D., Richard C. Thompson, and David Segal. *Race and Job Satisfaction in the U.S. Army*, December 1979. Alexandria, VA: US Army Research Institute for the Behavioral and Social Sciences, DTIC.

Bonner, Benjamin. "A Survey of USAREUR Entry Level Skills in the 11B Infantryman." Alexandria, VA: US Army Human Resources Research Organization, 1979, DTIC.

Brislawn, Mark G. "Allied Intervention in Russia." Student paper, CGSC, 1932, CARL.

Brooks, John B. "A Study of the Present Desertion Rates with Recommendations for Bringing About a Reduction of the Same." Student paper, AWC, 16 October 1926, AHEC.

Bryant, David T. "The 1969 Manual for Courts-Martial: A Guide for Commanders." Student paper, AWC, 3 December 1968, AHEC.

Burke, Joe E., et al. "The Future of Army ROTC." Student paper, AWC, 3 June 1974, AHEC.

Burwell, David W. "Morale as a Principle of War." Student paper, SAMS, 2000, CARL.

Calhoun, Mark T. "Complexity and Innovation: Army Transformation and the Reality of War." Student paper, SAMS, 2004, CARL.

Carroll, Robert M. "Army ROTC: The Future on the Campus." Student paper, AWC, 9 March 1970, AHEC.

Chaffee, Adna R., et al. "Enlisting, During Peace, Aliens Who Can Not Read, Write, or Speak English." Student paper, AWC, 24 December 1924, AHEC.

Churchill, J. M. "Shall the Enlistment Allowance Be Abolished in the Interest of Economy?" Student paper, AWC, 31 October 1925, AHEC.

Coles, Thomas F. "Brevet Promotions and the Hump." Student paper, AWC, 28 February 1969, AHEC.

Collins, James F. "Army Manpower." Lecture, AWC, 14 May 1958, AHEC.

Collins, J. Lawton. "The Role of the Army in Future Warfare." Lecture, US Air War College, 5 October 1948, box 43, J. Lawton Collins Papers, Dwight D. Eisenhower Presidential Library, Abilene, KS.

Conklin, A. S. "To Determine Whether or Not There Will Be in the Future a Surplus of Air Service Officers in the Higher Grades." Student paper, AWC, 24 December 1924, AHEC

Datel, William E. "Final Evaluation Report on Fort Ord Project VOLAR." 4 August 1972, Walter Reed Army Institute of Research, DTIC.

Drea, Ed. "Historical Perspectives on Reductions in Force." 1989, CMH Staff Study, CMH

Duffield, Mark F. "Into the Beehive: The Somali Habr Gidr Clan as an Adaptive Enemy." Student paper, SAMS, 1999, CARL.

Elliott, Ivan W. "The Officer Personnel Act of 1947." Student paper, AWC, 16 March 1953, AHEC

Farnsworth, C. S. "Object, Scope, and System of Training for the Infantry." Lecture, AWC, 26 April 1921, AHEC.

Frankenberger, Bertram. "Are Army Officers Too Conservative, as Sometimes Hinted in the Press?" Student paper, CGCS, 1930, CARL.

Funk, Steven L., et al. "Training Detractors in FORSCOM Divisions and How They are Handled." Alexandria, VA: US Army Research Institute, 1980, DTIC.

Gard, Robert G. "The Direction of Army Leadership in the 1970s." Lecture, CONARC Training to Lead Conference, May 14–18, 1973, DTIC.

Garrett, John. "Task Force Smith: The Lesson Never Learned." Student paper, SAMS, 2000, CARL.

Gilchrist, H. C. "The Responsibility of Senior Officers in Instructing Junior Officers in the Preparation of Their Future Career as an Officer of the Army." Student paper, CGCS, 1930, CARL.

Goins, Morris T. "Does the Perception of Casualties Affect Military Operations in the 1990's?" Student paper, SAMS, 1999, CARL.

Gray, George B. "ROTC: Military Training or University Military Science Education?" Student paper, AWC, 9 March 1970, AHEC.

Gruber, W. R. "The Army School System." Student paper, AWC, 4 May 1929, AHEC.

Grunert, George. "Desertion in the United States Army." Student paper, 1932, CGSC, CARL.

Hardenbergh, W. "The Capacity of the Regular Army at Its Present Strength to Train the Civilian Components." Student paper, AWC, 26 April 1929, AHEC.

Helmick, Eli A. "Leadership." Lecture, AWC, 17 May 1924, AHEC.

Helmick, Eli A. "The Relation of Psychology to Leadership." Lecture, AWC, 26 March 1925, AHEC.

Henning, Charles A. *Army Officer Shortages: Background and Issues for Congress.* Washington, DC: Congressional Research Service, July 2006.

Holbrook, Willard A. "Object, Scope, and System of Training for the Cavalry." Lecture, AWC, 4 May 1921, AHEC.

Hill, Glen A. "Control of Narcotic and Dangerous Drug Abuse Among Army Troops Stationed in the Continental United States." Student paper, AWC, 10 February 1970, AHEC.

Hitt, Parker. "A Brief History of the School of Musketry." http://1–22infantry.org /history3/musketry.htm.

Karcher, Timothy M. "Understanding the 'Victory Disease': From the Little Bighorn, to Mogadishu, to the Future." Student paper, SAMS, 2003, CARL.

Kimbrough, J. M. "Roles and Missions of the Armed Forces." Lecture, AWC, 19 November 1953, AHEC.

Kirkpatrick, Charles E. "Filling the Gaps: Reevaluating Officer Professional Education in the Inter-War Army, 1920–1940." Paper presented at the American Military Institute Conference, 1989.

Kirkpatrick, Charles E. "Orthodox Soldiers: Army Formal Schools Between the Two World Wars." Paper presented at the Society for History in the Federal Government, 1990.

Kirkwood, Robert G. "Present Desertion Rates in the Army." Student paper, AWC, 18 October 1926, AHEC.

Knight, H. E. "The Morale of the Regular Army." Student paper, AWC, 17 March 1928), AHEC.

Krebs James M. "New Directions for Army Alcohol and Drug Abuse Control." Student paper, AWC, 21 October 1975, AHEC.

Leon, Gustavo A. "Total Force Concept: Reality or Myth." Student paper, AWC, 21 November 1975, AHEC.

Loughry, H. K. "Present Desertion Rates." Student paper, AWC, 16 October 1926, AHEC.

Love, Joseph B. "Optimum Career Content of Selected Military Occupational Specialties." Student paper, AWC, 27 February 1969, AHEC.

Marrone, James V., et al., *Organizational and Cultural Causes of Army First-Term Attrition.* Santa Monica, CA: RAND, 2021.

Marshall, George C. "The Development of the General Staff." Lecture, AWC 19 September 1922, AHEC.

Matthew, Miriam, et al., *Organizational Characteristics Associated with the Risk of Sexual Harassment in the U.S. Army.* Santa Monica, CA: RAND, 2021.

McCaskey, Douglas. "Resignation of Second Lieutenants, Regular Army, Who Have Less Than Four Years of Commissioned Service." Student paper, AWC, 2 April 1928, AHEC.

McCord, Robert E. "The Challenge to Military Professionalism." Student paper, AWC, 9 March 1970, AHEC.

McElhenny, William S. "Problems Confronting the United States Army." Student paper, AWC, 19 March 1959, AHEC.

McMahan, Bernard S. "The Effect of the Uniform on Morale." Student paper, AWC, 15 October 1926, AHEC.

McRae, J. H. "The Personnel Division, G-1." Lecture, AWC, 27 February 1922, AHEC.

Mildren, Frank T. "US Army Vietnam for Period 22 June 1968 to 1 July 1970." 2 February 1970, DTIC.

Moran, William J. "Total Force Concept Requires Doers'—Not Advisors." Student paper, AWC, 5 March 1973, AHEC.

Mundy, Timothy S. "Casualty Aversion: Dispelling the Myth." Student paper, SAMS, December 31,1999, CARL.

Munroe, J. E. "Desirability of Use of Terms Master Sergeant and Technical Sergeant Replacing Old Name of Sergeant Major." Student paper, AWC, 30 October 1925, AHEC.

Parker, Ralph. "The Reserve Officers Training Corps: Its Problems and Development." Student paper, AWC, 30 March 1929, AHEC.

Paschal, Paul C. "Rotation of Officers of Combat Arms on Duty with Troops of Their Own Arm." Student paper, AWC, 11 March 1929, AHEC.

Pergerson, Bernard S., Jr. "Modern Volunteer Army: The 25th Infantry Division." Student paper, AWC, 29 May 1974, AHEC.

Peyer, Polly. "Hollow Force: Scare or Dare?" Research project, Industrial College of the Armed Forces, 1994, DTIC.

Pitney, Max L. "Retention of Junior Officers." Student paper, AWC, 19 March 1959, AHEC.

Porter, William R. "The Problem of Drug Abuse in the Army." Student paper, AWC, 31 January 1972, AHEC.

Powers, James H. "The Volunteer Soldier—A Self-Portrait." Student paper, AWC, 27 May 1980, AHEC.

Purdon, Frank L. "A Study to Cover Our Present System of Procurement, Treatment, Welfare, Separation, etc. of Enlisted Men with a View to Evolving a Better System Which Would Tend to Raise the Standard of Enlisted Personnel." Student paper, AWC, 17 February 1932, AHEC.

Rearick, Perry. "Force Protection and Mission Accomplishment in Bosnia and Herzegovina." Master's thesis, CGSC, 2001, CARL.

Rice, E. F., et al., "Morale in Armies." Student paper, AWC, 24 October 1928, AHEC.

Rich, Charles W. G. "Reserve Officer Career Program." Student paper, AWC, 1 April 1953, AHEC.

Riggs, Kerr T. "Officers' Efficiency Reports: How Can the Present System Be Improved?" Student paper, AWC, 15 January 1932, AHEC.

Screws, William P. "Civilian Components." Student paper, CGCS, 24 May 1929, AHEC.

Slaughter, H. H. "The Working Out of the National Defense Act of 1920." Student paper, AWC, 1 March 1931, AHEC.

Slocum, Michael J. "Maintaining the Edge: A Look At Army Officer Retention." Student paper, AWC, 2012, AHEC.

Smoak, John R. "Procurement of Personnel with Qualifications for Combat." Student paper, AWC, 26 March 1956, AHEC.

Staab, Lee A. "Transforming Army Leadership: The Key to Officer Retention." Student paper, AWC, 10 April 2001, AHEC.

Steele, Anneliese M. "Are the Relationships Between Junior and Senior Officers in the U.S. Army Officer Corps Dysfunctional?" Student paper, SAMS, 30 April 2001, CARL.

Stewart, Steven R., Chester I. Christie, and T. O. Jacobs. "Leadership Tasks Performed by U.S. Army Company Commanders in Europe." Alexandria, VA: US Army Research Institute for the Behavioral and Social Sciences, 1976.

Stuart, Archibald. "The Training of Noncommissioned Offers During Mobilization and War." 23 February 1951, Student paper, AWC, AHEC.

Summerall, Charles P. "Morale and Leadership." Lecture, AWC, 16 October 1930, AHEC.

Summers, Harry G. "The Astarita Report: A Military Strategy for the Multipolar World." Carlisle, PA: Strategic Studies Institute, 1981.

Tademy, Dudley L., James A. Musselman, and Donald L. Woodhouse. "Lieutenant Colonel and Colonel Command Declinations FY79." Student paper, AWC, May 1980, AHEC.

Tanzer, John B. "Analysis and Comparison of Williston Birkhimer Palmer, General, USA and James Hilliard Polk, General, USA." Student paper, AWC, 10 April 1973, AHEC.

Taylor, George E. "Motivation in the Grade of Colonel, US Army." Student paper, AWC, 19 November 1975, AHEC.

Taylor, James D. "Determination of Whether There Will Be a Surplus of Air Service Officers in the Higher Grades." Student paper, AWC, 24 December 1924, AHEC.

Tillson, J. C. F. "Efficiency Reports: How May the Present Report be Improved?" Student paper, AWC, 28 February 1931, AHEC.

Trybula, David C. "'Big Five' Lessons for Today and Tomorrow." Student paper, AWC, 2012, DTIC.

Vestal, Stanley C. "The Use in Battle of Allies, Auxiliaries, Colored Troops, and Troops Raised in Insular Possessions." Lecture, AWC, 30 April 1924, AHEC.

Westmoreland, William C. "Our Twentieth Century Army." Speech, Airborne Conference, 7 May 1957), box 1, William C. Westmoreland Papers, US Military Academy Library, West Point, NY.

Woodbury, E. N. "Morale: Improving the Standard of the Enlisted Many." Student paper, AWC, 28 February 1931, AHEC.

[Woodbury, Edward N.]. "A Study of Desertion." [1920], AHEC.

Yates, Louise G. "The Estimated Impact of SQT on USAREUR Infantry Units: Survey Results." Alexandria, VA: US Army Human Resources Research Organization, 1979, DTIC.

Young, R. N. "Responsibilities and Problems of the Army G-1." Lecture, AWC, 18 November 1953, AHEC.

Dissertations and Master's Theses

Allsep, Jr., Michael. "New Forms of Dominance: How a Corporate Lawyer Created the American Military Establishment." PhD diss., University of North Carolina at Chapel Hill, 2008.

Andrews, Richard A. "Years of Frustration: William T. Sherman, the Army, and Reform." PhD diss., Northwestern University, 1968.

Beugoms, Jean-Pierre. "The Logistics of the United States Army, 1812–1821." PhD diss., Temple University, 2018.

Carter, Don Alan. "From G.I. to Atomic Soldier: The Development of U.S. Tactical Doctrine, 1945–1956." PhD diss., Ohio State University, 1987.

Dillard, Walter Scott. "The United States Military Academy, 1865–1900: The Uncertain Years." PhD diss., University of Wisconsin, 1972.

Due, Jonathan Lee. "Seizing the Initiative: The Intellectual Renaissance That Changed U.S. Army Doctrine, 1970–1982." PhD diss., University of North Carolina at Chapel Hill, 2007.

Jussel, Paul C. "Intimidating the World: The United States Atomic Army, 1956–1960." PhD diss., Ohio State University, 2004.

Kendall, John Michael. "An Inflexible Response: United States Army Manpower Policies, 1945–1957." PhD diss., Duke University, 1982.

Koh, Thomas D. "Army Officer Retention: How to Retain the Best and Brightest." Master's thesis, Johns Hopkins University, 2018.

Lee, Robert M. "Flagging Vigilance: The Post-Vietnam 'Hollow Army.'" Master's thesis, Texas A&M University, 2001.

Markel, Matthew W. "The Organization Man at War: Promotions Policies and Military Leadership." PhD diss., Harvard University, 2000.

McKenna, Charles Douglas. "The Forgotten Reform: Field Maneuvers in the Development of the United States Army, 1900–1920." PhD diss., Duke University, 1981.

Melnyk, Les Andrii. "A True National Guard: The Development of the National Guard and its Influence on Defense Legislation, 1915–1933." PhD diss., City University of New York, 2004.

Nye, Roger H. "The United States Military Academy in an Era of Educational Reform." PhD diss., 1968, Columbia University.

O'Connell, Charles Francis, "The United States Army and the Origins of Modern Management, 1818–1860." PhD diss., Ohio State University, 1982.

Phillips, Dwight E., Jr. "Reengineering Institutional Culture and the American Way of War in the Post-Vietnam U.S. Army, 1968–1989." PhD diss., University of Chicago, 2014.

Raines, Edgar F., Jr. "Major General J. Franklin Bell and Military Reform: The Chief of Staff Years, 1906–1910." PhD diss., University of Wisconsin, 1976.

Sharp, Bert Marvin. "'Bring the Boys Home': Demobilization of the United States Armed Forces After World War II." PhD diss., Michigan State University, 1977.

Sinks, George W. "Reserve Policy for the Nuclear Age: The Development of Post-War American Reserve Policy, 1943–1955." PhD diss., Ohio State University, 1985.

Steinhauer, Dale Richard. "'Sogers': Enlisted Men in the U.S. Army, 1815–1860." PhD diss., University of North Carolina at Chapel Hill, 1992.

Stewart, Michael David. "Raising a Pragmatic Army: Officer Education at the U.S. Army Command and General Staff College, 1946–1986." PhD diss., University of Kansas, 2010.

Winfield, Lia Daphne. "Claiming Their Place: Women's Integration into the U.S. Army, 1970–1989." PhD diss., University of California Davis, 2013.

Zais, Barrie M. "The Struggle for a Twentieth Century Army: Investigation and Reform of the United States Army After the Spanish-American War, 1989–1903." PhD diss., Duke University, 1981).

Emails, Interviews, and Unpublished Private Manuscripts

Andrew J. Bacevich email, 2021.

John M. Collins, "The Care and Cleaning of NCOs: Policies and Practice, 1939–1969." Unpublished MS, courtesy of the author.

Roger Goodell interviews, 2020–2021.

Robert Griffith email, 2021.

Richard C. Hall questionnaire, 2019; interview, 2021.

Paul H. Herbert interviews, 2019–2022.

Edward G. Miller email, 31 May 2020.

Mark S. Pernell questionnaire, 2021.

E. Mike Perry questionnaire, 2019.

Gordon Rudd interview, 26 May 2021.

Robert A. Strong questionnaire, 2019.

Michael M. Toler questionnaire, 2020.

Richard G. Trefry interview, 2021.

Index